JACOB KLEIN

LECTURES
AND
ESSAYS

Edited by
Robert B. Williamson and
Elliott Zuckerman

ST. JOHN'S COLLEGE PRESS
Annapolis, Maryland

ACKNOWLEDGMENTS

"Phenomenology and the History of Science" and "The Idea of Liberal Education" are reprinted with the permission of the Harvard University Press. Copyright © 1940 and 1960 by the President and Fellows of Harvard College. "Aristotle, an Introduction" is chapter three of *Ancients and Moderns, Essays on the Tradition of Political Philosophy, in honor of Leo Strauss*, ed. Joseph Cropsey. Copyright © 1964 by Basic Books, Inc., publishers. Reprinted by permission of the publisher. "On the Nature of Nature" is reprinted with the permission of the *Independent Journal of Philosophy*. "On Dante's Mount of Purgation" is reprinted with the permission of the *Cesare Barbieri Courier* (Trinity College, Hartford). "On Liberal Education" is reprinted with permission from the May 1966 issue of *Liberal Education*, Vol. 52, No. 2, pp. 133–143. Copyright 1966 by the Association of American Colleges. "The Myth of Virgil's *Aeneid*" and "On Plato's *Philebus*" are reprinted with the permission of *Interpretation*. "A Note on Plato's *Parmenides*" is reprinted with the permission of Wilhelm Fink Verlag. "Plato's *Ion*" is reprinted with the permission of the *Claremont Journal of Public Affairs*.

ISBN 0–9603690–2–3

Contents

Biographical Note

Jacob Klein was born in 1899 in Libau, Russia. He studied at the Universities of Berlin and of Marburg, where he received his Ph.D. in 1922. In 1938 he came to the United States, and in the following year to St. John's College, Annapolis, where he taught in the New Program until his death in 1978. He was Dean of the College from 1949 until 1958.

He wrote three books: *A Commentary on Plato's Meno* (The University of North Carolina Press, 1965); *Greek Mathematical Thought and the Origin of Algebra* (The M. I. T. Press, 1968) — which is a translation (by Eva Brann) of "Die griechische Logistik und die Entstehung der Algebra" (1934 and 1936); and *Plato's Trilogy: Theaetetus, the Sophist, and the Statesman* (The University of Chicago Press, 1977).

During his Deanship, Klein delivered many annual lectures. He relied chiefly on terse notes, and as a consequence those lectures could not be included in this collection.

Preface

All but two of the pieces collected here were presented first as lectures. But Jacob Klein himself prepared most of them for publication, either for a periodical or a collection of essays or as a mimeograph to be circulated among interested students. There was a need to have them collected into a book. Our editorial changes have been kept at a minimum. The original text determined whether the references are cited parenthetically or as footnotes, and whether Greek words are transliterated.

We have chosen to present the pieces in the order of their composition. Klein would probably have deplored any attempt to arrange his writings under general topical headings. But the chronological order has a disadvantage. The first four pieces are among those that Klein himself did not prepare for publication. The first has been translated from the German, and the next three were written while he was still finding his way to that clear and unembellished English style for which his students and colleagues remember him. Had this collection been prepared during his lifetime, he undoubtedly would have insisted on extensive revisions of the earlier lectures. Yet as they stand here they can serve as helpful introductions to Parts One and Two of his demanding book on *Greek Mathematical Thought and the Origin of Algebra*, and the first, "The World of Physics and the 'Natural' World," summarizes a projected but never written Part Three of that work.

We have had help and advice on various matters from our colleagues and from former students of Klein. We wish to thank particularly Prof. David Lachterman, who translated the first essay from manuscript, and Mr. Leo Raditsa and the Reverend J. Winfree Smith, who filled out and put into final shape the lecture on Copernicus. Mrs. Klein helpfully gave us access to papers and manuscripts.

R. W. and E. Z.
Annapolis, August, 1985

1 ■ The World of Physics and the "Natural" World

I⊤ can scarcely be denied that at the present time physics and philosophy, two sciences of recognized durability, each handed down in a continuous tradition, are estranged from one another; they oppose one another more or less uncomprehendingly. By the nineteenth century a real and hence effective mutual understanding between philosophers and physicists concerning the methods, presuppositions, and the meaning of physical research had already become basically impossible; this remained true even when both parties, with great goodwill and great earnestness, tried to reach a clear understanding of these issues. When, in the second half of the last century, physicists themselves adopted certain basic philosophical positions, the Neo-Kantian or Machian, for instance, this scarcely affected their genuine scientific work. They did their work independently of any philosophical question; they conquered more and more territory and were not distracted from their course by difficulties

Delivered as a lecture to the *Physikalische Institut* of the University of Marburg on February 3, 1932. The first half, roughly, of the paper is in typescript, the second in manuscript with marginal additions, not always easily fitted into the text. The transcriber and translator, David R. Lachterman, has completed several elliptical references to texts.

appearing from time to time in the interpretation of the formal mathematical apparatus (as in the case of Maxwell's Theory) or in regard to the validity of ultimate physical principles (as in the case of the second law of thermodynamics).

In this respect the situation has now changed in an essential way. To be sure, mathematical physics, in conformity with the basic attitude it has never abandoned, is still content today with what can be established experimentally and can be given an exact mathematical formulation; it refuses to follow philosophy into the region of what is neither experimentally nor mathematically confirmable and hence is almost always controversial. Nonetheless, physics now sees itself faced by questions in its own fundamental work which have always been taken to fall within the domain of philosophy. In its own right physics raises questions about space and time, causality and substance, about the limits of possible knowledge and the epistemic sense of scientific statements and experimental results. Consequently, it now considers turning to "philosophy" as a reliable and valid court of appeal, if not for solutions to these questions, then at least for advice or for new points of view. The unsatisfactory relation between mathematical physics and philosophy has consequently become more acute than it usually was in the nineteenth century. The *particular* philosophical tendencies involved are a secondary matter. More importantly, it is clear that no agreement about the meaning of the most fundamental concepts which both physics and philosophy employ can be achieved, e.g., the meaning of the concepts "Space," "Time," "Causal Law," "Experience," "Intuition."

Sometimes it seems as if two languages were being spoken, languages that sound the same and yet are totally different. Physicists and philosophers assess this situation differently only insofar as the physicists are inclined — not always, certainly, but for the most part — to regard the language of philosophy as unscientific, while the philosophers — not always, to be sure, but frequently enough — suspect themselves of something like bad conscience in such debates, simply because they think they are incapable of getting to the bottom of the physical concepts amidst the formalistic thicket of differential equations, tensor calculus, or group-theory. This bad conscience is understandable. For, no matter how philosophy expresses itself philosophically, no matter what "standpoint" it might adopt, it cannot possibly pass by the problem of the *World*. And does not physics, most of all, have to do with the world around us? Don't the formulae of physics give an answer to the question of the "true world," however "truth" might here be understood? Even when philosophy believes it cannot accept the answer physics gives, even when it regards it as basically unsuccessful, it still has to reckon with it in some fashion, even if only to refute it. Above all philosophy must try to *understand* this answer. Even if philosophy concerns itself exclusively with things falling within that other hemisphere of science, the so-called "*Geisteswissenschaften*," it should never forget, even for an instant, that mathematical physics is at the foundation of our mental and spiritual life, that we see the world and *ourselves* in this world at first quite ingenuously as mathematical physics has taught us to see it, that the direction, the very manner of our questioning is fixed in advance by mathematical physics, and that even a critical attitude towards mathematical physics does not free us from its dominion. The idea of science intrinsic to mathematical physics determines the basic fact of our contemporary life, namely, our "scientific consciousness."

Mathematical physics and philosophy are nowadays split apart and at odds with one another; they depend on one another, even while time and again they are forced to acknowledge their mutual incomprehension. What is to be done in this situation? We must first of all try to find a common ground, a basis of shared questions, such that our questions are not in danger of missing their target from the start. Is there any common ground? Where should we try to find it? If we cannot glimpse it anywhere in the present, then we have to consider whether we can find it in the past.

Let us remember that there was an age that did not know this hard and fast division between philosophy and physics. Let us recall the title of Newton's work: *Philosophiae naturalis principia mathematica*. For Galileo the true philosophy coincides with the true science of the structure of this world. Likewise, Descartes' entire physics is contained in his *Principia philosophiae*. The *philosophia naturalis* of the seventeenth century is *scientia naturalis*, science pure and simple, the heir to the legacy of medieval and ancient science. The seventeenth century claimed that the foundations it gave to this *scientia* were identical with the foundations of *all* human knowing. Leibniz was the first to open a gap between physics and metaphysics, between the sciences of nature and of philosophy; however, Leibniz himself also exhibited their essential unity in an especially impressive way. In the middle of the eighteenth century, the paths of the new science of nature and the new philosophy parted, even though their common origin could never be forgotten. Furthermore, the contemporary tense division just noted between physics and philosophy has its roots in precisely this *history* of the two disciplines, a history which leads them from an original unit to an increasing mutual estrangement.

Accordingly, we must try to gain purchase on that common ground by going back to the initial situation, the situation of science in the seventeenth century; from this we might *possibly* gain a measure of enlightenment concerning present-day difficulties, even if we simply come to understand the *nature* of these difficulties better. We should not forget that all of the basic concepts of contemporary science were given their now-authoritative stamp in the seventeenth century. This holds especially true of the basic concepts of physics, at least of "classical" physics, to speak in the idiom of modern-day physics. However great the changes modern-day physics is about to make, or has already made in its foundations, no one will deny that it stands squarely on the shoulders of classical physics and, thus, of seventeenth-century physics.

Reflection on the historical foundations of physics is not an utterly wayward and irrelevant beginning, since physics itself, even in its most recent phase, has been forced again and again to look back to the past in order to recognize the limited character of many of its basic concepts. Thus, the designation "classical physics," used to refer to the physics of the seventeenth, eighteenth, and nineteenth centuries, arises from the debate between quantum mechanics and relativity theory and the basic concepts of Galilean and Newtonian mechanics. In their own day, the debates between the mechanistic and the energistic conceptions within physics led to the historical investigations of Mach and Duhem. What we have to do, in my judgment, is make this turn to historical origins even more radical. Not only is this demanded by the issue itself, it is most intimately connected with the basic presuppositions of our knowledge of the world.

II

Let us begin by picturing the general situation of science in the seventeenth century: A *new* science, desirous above all of being a science of Nature and moreover a "natural" science *opposed an already extant science.* The conceptual edifice of this new science was built up in continuous debate with the traditional and dominant science of the *Scholastics.* The new concepts were worked out and fortified in *combat* with the concepts of the old science. As has been emphasized time and again, the founders of this new science, men like Galileo, Stevin, Kepler, Descartes, were moved by an original impulse quite alien to the erudite science of the Scholastics. Their scientific interests were inspired by problems of practical mechanics and practical optics, by problems of architecture, machine construction, painting, and the newly-discovered art of optical instruments. An open and unprejudiced eye for the things of this world took the place of sterile book learning.[1] However, it is no less true that the conceptual interpretation of these new insights was linked in every case with the old, traditional concepts. The claim to communicate true science, true knowledge, necessarily took its bearings from the firmly-established edifice of traditional science. At all events, such a claim presupposes the fact of "science"; it also presupposes the most general foundations of the theoretical attitude which the Greeks displayed and bequeathed to later centuries. The battle between the new and the old science was fought on the ground and in the name of the *one, uniquely true* science. One or the other had to triumph; they could not subsist side by side. This explains the great bitterness of the battle which lived on in the memory of succeeding generations, a bitterness immediately evident even today in the difficulty we have

---

1. Leo Olschki has forcefully emphasized this point in his important work *Geschichte der neusprachlichen wissenschaftlichen Literatur,* I-III (Heidelberg 1919–1927).

when we try to distance ourselves from the interpretation the victors gave both of the battle and of the enemy they vanquished.

What especially characterizes this battle is not only the *common* goal marked out by those most general presuppositions, viz., the one, unique science, but, over and above this, a definite uniformity of the weapons with which the battle was fought. However different their viewpoints, however antithetical the contents designated by their concepts might be, the antagonists are very largely in accord as to the way in which these contents are to be interpreted, the way in which the concepts *intend* what is meant by them whenever they are employed, in short, the conceptual framework or intentionality [*Begrifflichkeit*] in which their antithetical opinions are expressed. This accord has all too often been overlooked. The only issue is: Which of them handled these weapons more suitably, which of them filled in the conceptuality common to both with contents genuinely in harmony with it? No doubt, the outcome gives the victory to the *new* science. When it mocks at the physics of the Scholastics, the physics of "substantial forms," the new science is striking primarily at the unquestioning attitude of the old science, the Scholasticism of the sixteenth and seventeenth centuries, an attitude which made this old science unable to detect the tension between the *contents* of its concepts and the *use* it made of these. Such an unquestioning understanding of oneself always exhibits a failure to comprehend one's own presuppositions and thus a failure really to grasp what one pretends to know. This is the danger to which science is always exposed; this is the danger to which Scholastic science in the sixteenth and seventeenth centuries succumbed as no other science had done before.

To penetrate to the foundations of the new science and, in this way, to the foundations of mathematical physics, we have to keep this general situation of science in the seventeenth century constantly in mind. It determines in the most basic way the horizon of this new science, as well as its methods, its general structure. It determines, above all, the intentionality of its concepts as such.

There is a long-standing controversy over how the experiential bases of physics fit together with its specific conceptuality. The very possibility of distinguishing "experimental" from "theoretical physics," a distinction which surely rests on nothing more than a didactic, or technical, division of labor, illustrates the problem. The reciprocity of experiment and theory, of observation and hypothesis, the relation of universal constants to the mathematical formalism — all of these issues point again and again to the two antithetical tendencies pervading modern physical science and giving it its characteristic stamp. This controversy, familiar to us from the nineteenth century, fundamentally concerns the preeminence of one or the other of these two tendencies. Nowadays, depending on the side one takes, one speaks of Empiricism or Apriorism; physicists themselves customarily side with the so-called empiricists and confuse apriorism with a kind of capriciously speculative philosophy. The good name of Kant has been made to bear the burden of furnishing ever-new fuel for this controversy. I am not going to take sides in this controversy. The controversy itself first grows from the soil of the new science and must be clarified by turning back to its origins in the seventeenth century. What is primarily at stake is an understanding of the *particular* intentionality, the *particular* character of the concepts with whose aid the mathematical physics which arose in the seventeenth century erected the new and immense theoretical structure of human experience over the next two centuries.

This intentionality is that of contemporary Scholasticism. The Scholastics believed that by using it they were faithfully administering the legacy of knowledge handed down to them by tradition. They believed that they were reproducing ancient doctrine, especially ancient cosmology, in exactly the same way as it was understood and taught by the Greeks, that is, by Aristotle. They identified their own concepts with those of the ancients. The new science, moreover, followed them in this matter. It, too, interpreted ancient cosmology along the lines of contemporary scholastic science. It was, however, certainly not content with this. Rather, it called upon the things themselves in order to rebuke the untenable doctrines of this Scholastic science, with its seemingly unquestioning certitude. In doing so, it exposed the incongruity between Scholastic intentionality and the contents the traditional concepts were intended to refer to. Furthermore, it went back to the sources of Greek science, neglected by Scholastic science; these sources, too, were interpreted in terms of the intentionality it shared with Scholastic science. And this interpretation of the legacy of ancient teachings, involving a characteristic modification of every ancient concept, is the basis of the whole concept-formation of the new science.

As a result, the special character of these new concepts can be brought to light in one of two ways. First, we can contrast the Scholastic science of the sixteenth and seventeenth centuries with genuine Aristotelianism. If we do so, a direct path leads from the lengthy and little-read compendia of Cremonini,[2] Francesco Piccolomini,[3] Buonamico,[4] Zabarella,[5] Toletus,[6] Benedictus Pereirus,[7] Alessandro Piccolomini,[8] etc., and, above all, of Suarez, as well as from the humanistically-influenced interpretation of Aristotle (e.g., in Faber Stapulensis and Petrus Ramus), back to the Nominalism of the fourteenth century. As Duhem has shown, initiatives leading to the modern science of Nature are present everywhere in fourteenth-century Nominalism. Secondly, we can confront Aristotle himself as well as the other sources of Greek science, most importantly Plato, Democritus, Euclid, Archimedes, Apollonius, Pappus, and Diophantus, with the interpretation given them by Galileo, Kepler, Descartes, Fermat, Vieta, et al. In what follows I want to discuss only this second path, selecting just a few characteristic examples. Nonetheless, before I begin I must make a more general remark.

Since the pioneering works of Hultsch and Tannery on the history of ancient mathematics, the relation between ancient and modern mathematics has increasingly become the focus of historical investigation as well as the theme of reflection in the philosophy of history. Two general lines of interpretation can be distinguished here. One—the prevailing view—sees in the history of science a continuous forward progress interrupted, at most, by periods of stagnation. On this view, forward pro-

---

2. *Disputatio de coelo,* 1613.
3. *Librorum ad scientiam de natura attinentium pars prima,* 1596.
4. *De motu,* 1591.
5. *De rebus naturalibus libri XXX,* 1589.
6. *Commentaria una cum quaestionibus in octo libros Aristotelis de physica ausculta-tione,* 1574.
7. *De communibus omnium rerum naturalium principiis et affectionibus,* 1562.
8. *De certitudine mathematicarum,* 1547.

gress takes place with "logical necessity,"[9] accordingly, writing the history of a mathematical theorem or of a physical principle basically means analyzing its logic.[10] The usual presentations, especially of the history of mathematics, picture a rectilinear course; all of its accidents and irregularities disappear behind the logical straightness of the whole path.

The second interpretation emphasizes that the different stages along this path are incomparable. For example, it sees in Greek mathematics a science totally distinct from modern mathematics. It denies that a continuous development from the one to the other took place at all. *Both* interpretations, however, start from the present-day condition of science. The first measures ancient by the standard of modern science and pursues the individual threads leading back from the valid theorems of contemporary science to the anticipatory steps taken towards them in antiquity. Time and again it sees contemporary science in ancient science; it seeks in ancient science only the seeds of now-mature fruits. The second interpretation strives to bring into relief, not what is common, but what divides ancient and modern science. It, too, however, interprets the otherness of ancient mathematics, for example, in terms of the results of contemporary science. Consequently, it recognizes only a counter-image of itself in ancient science, a counter-image which still stands on its own conceptual level.

Both interpretations fail to do justice to the true state of the case. There can be no doubt that the science of the seventeenth century represents a direct continuation of ancient science. On the other hand, neither can we deny their differences, differences not only in maturity, but, *above all,* in their basic initiatives, in their whole disposition (*habitus*). The difficulty is precisely to avoid interpreting their differences and their affinity one-sidedly in terms of the new science. The new science itself did exactly that, in order to prove that its own procedure was the

9. Compare, e.g., Léon Brunschvicq, *Les étapes de la philosophie mathématique*, Paris 1912, 105.
10. See Pierre Duhem, *La théorie physique, son objet et sa structure*, Paris 1906, 444 [English translation, *The Aim and Structure of Physical Theory*, trans. P. P. Wiener, Princeton 1954.]

only correct one. The contemporary tendency to substitute admiration or tolerance of ancient cosmology for condemnation contributes little to our understanding of that cosmology. The issues at stake cannot be divorced from the specific conceptual framework within which they are interpreted. Conversely, these issues cannot even be seen within a conceptual framework unsuited to them; at best, they can only be imperfectly described. The best example comes from modern physics itself: the discussion of modern physical theories is ensnared in great difficulties when physicists and non-physicists alike try to ignore the mathematical apparatus of physics and present the results of research in a "commonsense" manner!

We need to approach ancient science on a basis appropriate to it, a basis provided by that science itself. Only on this basis can we measure the transformation ancient science underwent in the seventeenth century — a transformation unique and unparalleled in the history of man! Our modern "scientific consciousness" first arose as a result of this transformation. This modern consciousness is to be understood not simply as a linear continuation of ancient ἐπιστήμη, but as the result of a fundamental conceptual shift which took place in the modern era, a shift we can nowadays scarcely grasp.

I want to try to grasp the nature of this conceptual shift more precisely, that is, to determine more precisely the character of the new concepts in contrast with the old.

III

The unambiguous and explicit preference for quantitative over qualitative determinations in the new science sets it distinctively apart from the old. There cannot be any difference of opinion on this point. How often have those lines from Galileo's *Il Saggiatore* (1623) been cited, that philosophy is written in mathematical language in the great open book of the Universe! To be able to read it one has first to understand this language, one has to know the script, the letters in which it is written. These letters are "triangles, circles, and other geometrical Figures"; without their aid we cannot understand even a single word of that language.[11] In the second chapter of Kepler's *Mysterium cosmographicum* this idea finds its most pointed formulation:

> God wanted quantity to make its appearance in reality before anything else, so that the relation between the curved and the straight might exist (*Quantitatem Deus . . . ante omnia existere voluit, ut esset curvi ad rectum comparatio*). Hence, He first selected the curved and the straight in order to spread a reflection of the splendor of the divine creator over the world (*ad adumbrandam in mundo divinitatem Conditoris*); for this purpose the 'quantities' were necessary, namely, figure (*figura*), number (*numerus*) and extension (*amplitudo* or *extensio*). For this reason He created the *body* which embraces all these determinations.[12]

These words point immediately back to Nicholas of Cusa, whom Kepler explicitly mentions, and anticipate Descartes' later theory. However, they are also directly connected with the whole Platonic-Pythagorean and Neo-Platonic tradition and, above all, with Plato's own *Timaeus*. This tradition had always remained alive. For example, in Roger Bacon's *Opus Maius* (1266-68) we can find statements such as these: "Mathematics is the gateway and key to all other sciences." "Anyone who does not know it cannot understand either the other sciences or the things of this world" (*Qui ignorat eam, non potest scire caeteras scientias nec res huius mundi*). "Logic, too, depends on mathematics. Nothing of great significance in the other sciences can be understood without mathematics" (*Nihil in eis potest sciri magnificum sine mathematica*).[13] What distinguishes Kepler's and Galileo's words from such statements in the earlier Platonic tradition? There clearly must be a distinction here, one that shows itself in the quite different influence, that is, the entirely different role played by mathematics in ancient and modern science. Is the distinc-

---

11. Galileo Galilei, *Opere*, Edizione nazionale, 6, 232.
12. Kepler, *Opera*, ed. Frisch, I, 122 f.
13. Pars IV, Dist. 1, Cap. I & II.

tion merely that Kepler and Galileo spoke from a firsthand, living experience of things, while the earlier authors were attached only to traditional texts? Or did the two traditions understand something different by "quantity," by "mathematical science"?

To answer this question, I have chosen examples relevant to the foundation of analytical geometry and algebra. Both analytical geometry and algebra stand in the closest relation to one another from the outset, although algebra asserted its primacy within this relation. Both belong to the foundations of mathematical physics. Vieta took the decisive step in the realm of algebra, basing himself both indirectly and immediately on Diophantus. Fermat and Descartes, who, as is well known, count as the founders of analytical geometry, rely directly on Diophantus and Apollonius, as well as on Pappus. In both cases, then, we can confront the old and the new concepts by paying attention to the way Diophantus and Apollonius were received and construed. In both cases, what is at issue is nothing less than the creation of a formal mathematical language, without which mathematical physics is inconceivable. I shall begin by considering Apollonius' relation to Fermat and Descartes.

IV

A. Two works by Apollonius particularly captured the interest of sixteenth- and seventeenth-century mathematicians: (1) the first four books of his *Treatise on Conic Sections*, available in the original Greek since the fifteenth century and since 1566 in the first usable Latin translation made by Fredericus Commandinus; (2) his "Plane Loci" in two books. Only fragments of the latter are preserved in the *Mathematical Collection* of Pappus, the Latin translation of which — also by Commandinus — appeared in 1588. These works — along with those of Diophantus, Archimedes, and Euclid — are among the basic books of seventeenth-century mathematical science. Fermat, for example, undertook to reconstruct the "Plane Loci" on the basis of the fragments in Pappus and in the light of the *Conic Sections*. In an introduction added later, the *Isagoge ad locos planos et solidos*, and an appendix, Fermat sketched the basic features of analytical geometry. Among other things, he shows that every equation of the first and second degree in two unknowns can be coordinated with a plane geometrical locus, that is, a straight line or a curve, if one represents the two unknowns as (ortho-gonal) coordinates, as we would say today. Among the infinitely many possible curves of this kind are the circle, the parabola, the ellipse, and the hyperbola, that is, the conic sections Apollonius treats in his major work. Independently of Fermat, Descartes, by solving a locus-problem posed by Pappus which goes back to Apollonius, arrived at the definitive conception of this procedure now familiar to us from analytical geometry. In doing so, Descartes took up again a line of thought that had occupied him in his youth. Nonetheless, since the studies of Moritz Cantor, Fermat has rightly been considered the genuine founder of analytical geometry, since his *Isagoge* had certainly already been written when Descartes' *Géométrie* appeared (1637). Strikingly, neither Fermat nor Descartes unleashed one of those struggles over priority so common in the seventeenth century. Fermat made Descartes acquainted with his own works in analytical geometry after the *Géométrie* had appeared; nonetheless, neither of them placed any value on claiming prior-ity for himself. This is all the more astonishing since they did embroil the entire Republic of Letters in the most unpleasant disputes over much flimsier points, as Gaston Milhaud has em-phasized.[14] The only explanation must be that neither Descartes nor Fermat believed he had advanced beyond Apollonius on any essential points. What we take to be the enormous achievement of Descartes and Fermat they themselves believed they had learned in essence from Apollonius or Pappus. Fermat finds fault with Apollonius only because he did not present matters "generally enough" (*non satis generaliter*).[15] He says very cautiously that his general procedure for constructing geometrical loci "was *perhaps* not known to Apollonius" (*ab Apollonio fortasse ignorabatur*).[16] And Descartes is quite con-vinced that the Ancients — he expressly names Pappus along with Diophantus — deliberately erased the traces of their true knowledge out of a kind of perverted cunning (*perniciosa*

---

14. *Descartes savant*, Paris 1921, 124–148.
15. *Oeuvres de Fermat* (ed. Tannery and Henry), I, 91.
16. *Oeuvres de Fermat*, 99.

quadam astutia) and divulged to us, not their own art, but only a few of their results.[17] I want to examine this matter more closely.

When Apollonius considers a conic section, e.g., the ellipse in Book I, Theorem 13 of the *Treatise on Conic Sections*,[18] he begins by passing a plane through the axis of a cone and then lets the cone be intersected by another plane in such a way that the desired figure, an ellipse in this case, emerges on the surface of the cone; the line of intersection of these two planes forms the diameter of the ellipse (see Fig. 1).

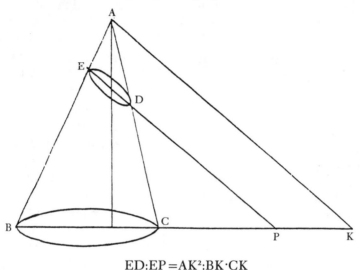

$$ED:EP = AK^2:BK \cdot CK$$

Figure 1

An auxiliary line is drawn from the vertex A which meets the plane of the base of the cone at point K; AK is parallel to the diameter ED. From an arbitrary point F on the ellipse a straight line FM is drawn to the diameter in a determinate manner, namely, in such a way that the chord FF¹ is bisected by point M. Consequently, FF¹ becomes — as we say today — a conjugate chord to the diameter ED. (Compare Fig. 2.)

17. *Regulae ad directionem ingenii*, Rule IV, *Oeuvres*, ed. Adam & Tannery, X, 376.
18. *Opera*, ed. Heiberg, I, 48 ff.

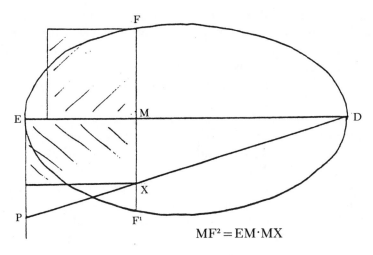

$$MF^2 = EM \cdot MX$$

Figure 2

It is then *proved* that the square on FM equals the rectangle made up of EM and a segment MX (in modern notation: $FM^2 = EM \bullet MX$), where the segment MX is defined as follows: on a perpendicular line dropped to E the segment EP is drawn, which stands in the same ratio to the diameter ED as the rectangle $\overline{BK,\ CK}$ to the square on AK (in modern notation: $EP:ED = BK \bullet CK:AK^2$). (Compare Fig. 1.) The straight line EP corresponds to what today we call the parameter of the ellipse and in Apollonius is called ὀρθία, because it is perpendicular to the diameter and hence is "straight." If, now, a perpendicular to ED is drawn at M, and P is connected with D, then the segment PD cuts the perpendicular from M at point X, which determines segment MX. The segments EM and FM thus stand in a ratio that can be exactly determined geometrically and this holds true of any point F on the ellipse. In other words, this ratio is characteristic of the entire ellipse and, consequently, of *any* ellipse as such. Apollonius calls the segments EM and FM, respectively, ἡ ἀποτεμνομένη (the line "cut off" by the diameter of the chord) and ἡ τεταγμένως κατηγμένη (ἐπὶ τὴν διάμετρον) the line "drawn down" to the diameter in a determinate way (that is, not in an arbitrary, but in an "ordered" way) — in Latin translation, *abscissa* and *ordinatim applicata*, or for short, *or-*

dinata.[19] Apollonius uses these segments, the "abscissa" and the "ordinate," in every individual case, in order to define the general properties, the basic "planimetric properties," characteristic of different conic sections.

What distinguishes these segments from our "co-ordinates" employed for the first time by Fermat and Descartes? First of all, the axes to which they are referred, viz., in the present instance, the diameter ED and the tangent to the conic at E, "do not constitute a system of lines on their own, but like other auxiliary geometrical lines make their appearance only in connection with the conic section; they are brought into existence by the theorem to be proved in each instance."[20] This procedure, which for the Greeks themselves belonged to "Analysis," has been called "geometrical algebra." This expression, first used by Zeuthen[21] and now widely current, is quite felicitous insofar as it hints at both the affinity as well as the difference between the Greek and the modern procedure. The term, however, does not indicate that the procedure can only be carried out on *different* conceptual levels in these two different cases. In each case Apollonius has in view the *particular* ellipse, which is cut out on the surface of a *particular* cone by two *particular* intersecting lines. The representation in the drawing gives a true *"image" [Abbild]* of *this* cone, *these* intersecting lines and *this* ellipse. There are infinitely many possible cones, sections, and ellipses. The procedure specified is applicable to all of them — its generality consists in this — but to this *generality of procedure* there does *not* correspond the generality of the object. There is no "general object" for the drawing to represent in a merely symbolic way [*symbolisch*]. There are infinitely many possible, more or less good, images of the one ellipse represented here. And there are, in turn infinitely many such ellipses which can be exhibited or "imaged." The characteristic of the μαθηματικά, mathematical

---

19. See also Apollonius, ed. Heiberg, I, 6, Def. 4. (The term "abscissa" was first used in the eighteenth century; cf. Tropfke, *Geschichte der Elementar-Mathematik* [2nd ed., Leipzig 1921–24], VI, 116 f.)

20. Moritz Cantor, *Vorlesungen über Geschichte der Mathematik* (3rd. ed., Leipzig 1907), I, 337.

21. Zeuthen [The author may have had in mind H. G. Zeuthen, *Geschichte der Mathematik in Altertum und Mittelalter* (Copenhagen 1896), ch. IV: "Die geometrische Algebra," 44–53. Translator's Note.]

objects in the Greek sense, is precisely that they can be grasped by the senses only in images, while they themselves, in their unalterable constitution, are accessible only to the discursive intellect; however, there are infinitely many of these objects.[22] What the phrase "there are" is supposed to mean here, how the mode of being of mathematical objects is to be understood, is one of the great disputes in Greek philosophy. No one disputes, however, that mathematical science as such has to do with these "pure" figures or formations [*Gebilde*] whose nature is accessible to the intellect alone. The lines drawn in any particular diagram and their ratios belong to this "pure" ellipse which is exhibited by them. To be sure, in the case of every individual ellipse — thanks to the generality of the procedure — such "abscissas" and "ordinates" can always be singled out, but each time line-segments belonging to the particular ellipse in question are intended. This is not due to the imperfection of Greek mathematics, its defective means of presentation, or its inadequate capacity for generalization, but is rather entailed by the specific intentionality of Greek science. Its concepts in each instance intend the individual objects themselves; they are — to speak in Scholastic language — *intentiones primae* ["first intentions"] — that is, concepts which refer immediately to individual objects. This is in harmony with the means of presentation which Greek science employs. The lines drawn in the figure exhibit the object, they "image" it. Consequently, the mode of presentation of Greek mathematics — with a single exception which we shall come to later — is never merely representative [*stellvertretend*], never symbolic, but is always the presentation of an image [*abbildlich*], and in this way first-intentional. For this reason, the designation "geometrical algebra," which perhaps takes its bearings too much from the exceptional case we shall discuss later, does not really do justice to the facts of the case.

In contrast to analysis in our own sense, Greek analysis does not merely have a different style of presentation, but embodies a fundamentally different relation between the style of presentation and *what is presented*. What, in fact, do the lines which Descartes and Fermat employ as abscissas and ordinates signify?

----

22. See Plato, *Republic* VI, 510 D-E and Aristotle, *Metaphysics*, A 6, 987b15 ff.

What do the curves which they draw mean? In the second part of his *Discourse on Method,* Descartes gives us exhaustive information on this point.[23] In these curves he intends to exhibit only relations or proportions (*nihil aliud quam relationes sive proportiones*)[24] and to do so in the greatest possible generality (*et quidem maxime generaliter sumptas*).[25] The exhibition of these relations in line-segments is only the *simplest and clearest illustration* for the senses and the imagination, so long as it is a matter of a *single* relation. In order to survey many such relations together and to be able to keep them conveniently in memory, they have to be simultaneously *represented* [*representiert*] by appropriate signs of ciphers, namely, by letters. Illustration by lines and representation by letters are thus merely two modes of the very same symbolic style of presentation. Lines and letters both are here simply the most suitable *bearers* of the *general* relations and proportions being considered; they are merely "*les sujets qui serviraient a m'en rendre la connaissance plus aisée.*"[26] The ellipse inscribed within coordinate-axes (as we employ them today, using the method worked out by Descartes and Fermat) (Fig. 3) is thus no longer an image of the "pure" ellipse. The coordinate-axes drawn are no longer images of a pair of straight lines applicable to the "pure" ellipse, but merely symbolize the generally possible use of such a pair. The abscissa and the ordinate of a point when actually *drawn* no longer exhibit particular line-segments in the manner of images, but "illustrate" the *general procedure* of Apollonius; in other words they stand immediately only for the general concepts of "abscissa" and "ordinate" resulting from that procedure and not for the line-segments directly intended by these concepts in each individual instance. Accordingly, the modern *concepts* of "abscissa" and "ordinate" are *intentiones secundae* ["second intentions"], concepts which refer directly to other concepts, to *intentiones primae,* and only indirectly to objects. In the language of mathematics this means: They are concepts of the

23. *Oeuvres de Descartes,* ed. Adam & Tannery, VI, 19–20.
24. *Oeuvres de Descartes,* 551 (Latin text).
25. *Oeuvres de Descartes.*
26. *Oeuvres de Descartes,* 20.

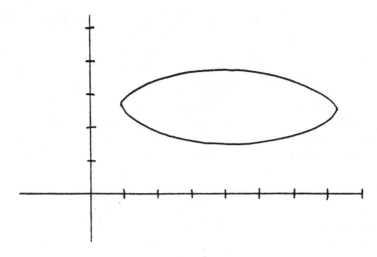

Figure 3

"Variable n." For this reason the abscissa and ordinate axes can be detached from the realm of objects. All the curves investigated with their help are from now on nothing but symbolic exhibitions of various possible relations, or of the different "functional" relations, between two (or more) variables.

All this, however, is only one side of the matter (the side emphasized principally by the Neo-Kantians and viewed by them as the only essential aspect). It is no less essential that these *symbolic* curves were *understood* as the images of the curves exhibited by the Ancients. For example, the ellipse inscribed within coordinate-axes was regarded as the very same ellipse treated by Apollonius. Precisely this assumption led Fermat and Descartes to believe that they were not proceeding any differently than Apollonius had. Although, in fact, there has been a shift in conceptual levels, Fermat thinks that he has simply interpreted many of Apollonius' theorems more generally (*generalius*),[27] that his procedure merely opened up a "general path" to the construction of geometrical loci (*generalis ad locos via*)[28] in exactly the sense in which Apollonius says that Book One of his *Conic*

---

27. *Oeuvres de Fermat*, 93.
28. *Oeuvres de Fermat*.

Sections treats things more generally or universally (καθόλου μᾶλλον)[29] than his predecessors had done. (And not even this is certain for Fermat, if we reflect on his word *fortasse* ["perhaps"].) What Fermat and Descartes call "generalization" is in reality a complex conceptual process ascending from *intentio prima* to *intentio secunda* while, *at the same time*, identifying these. Only in this way can we understand what Descartes means when he characterizes his analytical procedure as a unification of the geometrical analysis of the Ancients with algebra. This unification is brought about through a symbolic interpretation and exhibition of geometrical forms, on the one hand, and of arithmetical ratios, on the other. Both kinds of "quantities" are viewed together with regard to their common, "general" quantitative character and exhibited in this generality. Consequently, the modern analytical procedure has to do immediately only with "general quantities." However, these "general quantities," on the whole, can only be sensibly exhibited because their generality at the same time is understood as variability, that is, because these magnitudes are thought of from the start as "alterable." (And, indeed, this holds true as much of the magnitudes posited as "constant" as it does of genuine variables.) The "being" of "general magnitudes" consists here only in their peculiar ability to take on all, or all admissible, values one after the other. This is exactly what gives all of them the capacity to replace *particular line-segments* or *particular numerical values*. Their symbolic exhibition corresponds to what Kant understands by a *schema*. Kant says:

> This representation of a universal procedure of imagination in providing an image for a concept [i.e., assigning to a first intention the image belonging to it], I entitle the schema of this concept.[30]

The schema can be directly transformed into an image [*Abbild*], if the segments and ratios of segments, of which it consists, assume numerically determinate lengths and values. The

---

29. Ed. Heiberg, I, 4.
30. *Critique of Pure Reason*, B 179.

possibility of identifying *prima* and *secunda intentio* is, therefore, based on this, that the schema is ordinarily understood as a schema already transformed into an image. Schematic imageability [*Abbildlichkeit*]is thus the element which allows us to illustrate the generalization of *Arithmetic* into Algebra, or, in other words, to "unite" geometry and algebra.

Only in this way can we come to understand that Descartes' concept of *extensio* identifies the extendedness of extension with extension itself. Our present-day concept of space can be traced directly back to this. Present-day Mathematics and Physics designate as "Euclidean Space" the domain of symbolic exhibition by means of line-segments, a domain which is defined by a coordinate system, a relational system [*Bezugssystem*], as we say nowadays. "Euclidean Space" is by no means the domain of the figures and structures studied by Euclid and the rest of Greek mathematics. It is rather only the symbolic illustration of the *general character of the extendedness* of those structures. Once this symbolic domain is identified with corporeal extension itself, it enters into Newtonian physics as "absolute space." At the present time it is being criticized by Relativity Theory, which has been steered by the question of "Invariance" into trying to break through these symbolic bounds, while continuing to use this very symbolism.

B. The founding of analytical geometry by Descartes and Fermat is also conditioned by the immediately preceding development of algebra and the language of algebraic formulae. Vieta, as I have said, provided the decisive impetus here. I want to consider now, as a further example of this conceptual shift, Vieta's relation to traditional algebra.

The science of algebra, in the form in which Vieta encountered it in the sixteenth century, namely, in the form of a doctrine of equations, was received in the West from the thirteenth century on as an Arabic science. This Arabic science was, in all probability, nourished essentially by *two* ancient sources. We can identify one of these straightaway, viz., the *Arithmetic* of Diophantus; the other can only be indirectly inferred. (Tannery believed that he could recognize it in a lost work by a contemporary of Diophantus, sc., Anatolius.) In any case, Diophan-

tus is by far the most important source, as the very name
"Algebra" indicates: the word "Algebra" (a "*nomen barbaricum*",
as Descartes says) is in Arabic nothing more than the first half
of a formulaic expression for the basic rule for solving equations that Diophantus sets out at the beginning of Book I of his
Arithmetica.[31]

The doctrine of equations had made great progress in the
West, before people began, in the second half of the sixteenth
century, to take up Diophantus' work itself. Modern algebra and
modern formalism grew out of Vieta's direct occupation with
Diophantus; later writers merely elaborated and refined his
work. Here, then, in Vieta's reception of Diophantus, we encounter one of those nodal-points of development, a point where
the new science arose from the confrontation of two distinct conceptual planes.

The surviving six books of Diophantus' *Arithmetic*[32] teach
how to solve problems of reckoning which today are familiar
to us as determinate and indeterminate equations of the 1st and
2nd degree. Diophantus, in giving these solutions, uses, in addition to other signs, a series of abbreviations for the unknowns
and their powers. In *every* case it is only a matter of a simple
abbreviation; this is above all the case with the sign for the
unknown, which is nothing other than an abbreviation of the
word ἀριθμός. Heath has conclusively explained this point.
Diophantus' "epochal invention" (to use Hultsch's phrase)[33] consists in his having introduced this sign into the logistical procedure of solution, that is, he *reckons* or calculates with the
unknown. Apart from the unknown or unknowns and their
powers he admits only formations that correspond to rational
numbers, i.e., to integers and fractions. In modern terminology,
only numerical coefficients appear. What does an equation look

31. [The full Arabic phrase is "al-jabr wa'l-muqabalah." For a contemporary discus-
    sion of the meanings of "jabr" and "muqabalah" see G. A. Saliba, "The Meaning
    of al-jabr wa'l-muqabalah," *Centaurus* 17 (1972), 189–204. Translator's Note.]
32. The "lost" books of Diophantus' *Arithmetica* have now been discovered in an Arabic
    translation. See Jacques Sessiano, "Books IV to VII of Diophantus' 'Arithmetica',"
    in *The Arabic Translation Attributed to Qustā Ibn Lūgā* (New York *et alibi*, 1982:
    Sources in the History of Mathematics and Physical Sciences, Vol. 3).
33. F. Hultsch, Article: "Diophant," in: *Pauly-Wissowa Realenzyklopädie*, Paragraph 9.

like in Diophantus? Let us look at a very simple example which
I shall write in its simplest form:

$$\mathcal{S}^{\text{οἱ}}\overline{\beta}\mathring{M}\overline{\gamma} \; \text{ἴσοι εἰσὶν } \mathring{M}\text{σι } \zeta$$

That is, ἀριθμοὶ δύο μονάδες τρεῖς ἴσος εἰσὶν μονάσι ἑπτά. Or,
in English, "Two numbers [ἀριθμοί] and three units are equal
to seven units." The sign $\mathcal{S}$ is a ligature for ἀριθμός; the sign $\mathring{M}$
is an abbreviation for μονάς or μονάδες (the plural is also writ-
ten $\mathring{M}^{ες}$). The corresponding equation in Vieta, which for the
sake of simplicity I shall write in modern form, since this does
not basically deviate from his, is: $2x + 3 = 7$. Is this merely a
technically more convenient form of writing? Do the two equations say entirely the same thing, if we disregard the mode of
writing? To answer this question we have to look a little more
closely at the Greek manner of writing. (It is of no importance
here whether Diophantus wrote in exactly this way; the extant
manuscripts reproduce what is essential.) What is particularly
surprising is the addition of the sign for μονάδες. Scholars have
tried to explain this as intended to discriminate with sufficient
clarity the numerical signs which specify the number [*Anzahl*]
of ἀριθμοί, i.e., the number of the unknowns (thus, in our case,
the sign $\overline{\beta}$), from the signs for the purely numerical magnitudes
(in our case the sign $\overline{\gamma}$). If the sign $\mathring{M}$ did not stand between
$\overline{\beta}$ and $\overline{\gamma}$, then the expression could be read: 2 ἀριθμοί and 3
ἀριθμοί together make 7. Regardless of the fact that in a great
many instances confusion is not possible at all, this interpretation fails to recognize the fundamental importance of the monad,
or the monads, for Greek arithmetic. Hence, it also misjudges
the Greek concept of ἀριθμοί, the Greek "number"-concept in
general. Ἀριθμός does not mean "*Zahl*," [number in general]
but "*Anzahl*," viz., a definite number of definite things: πᾶς
ἀριθμός τινός ἐστι ("Every number is a number of
something").[34] In daily life we frequently have to do with

---

34. Alexander of Aphrodisias, *In Aristotelis Metaphysica Commentaria*, ed. M. Hayduck,
85.5–6. See also Aristotle, *Physics* IV 4, 224a2 ff.

numbers of visible and tangible objects, each of which is in each case just *one*. However, the very possibility of counting, where we utter the same words again and again, viz., "two," "three," "four," etc., while referring to different things at different times, points to objects of a quite different sort, namely, to incorporeal, "pure," ones, to "pure" monads. The Greek science of arithmetic is occupied with *these* monads. For this reason the well-known definition of τὸ ἀριθμός in Euclid runs as follows: τὸ ἐκ μονάδων συγκείμενον πλῆθος (Euclid 7, Def. 2), "a multitude composed of monads, of unities." What it means that there *are* such monads, the question of the mode of being of these pure monads, is the great issue in Greek philosophy, as I have already mentioned. Indeed, the case of the monad is one of the ultimate issues which divide Plato from Aristotle. It is *not* a matter of controversy, however, that only these pure monads *as such* can be the object of scientific arithmetic. According as one interprets the mode of being of these pure monads, there can or cannot exist a scientific doctrine of reckoning, a logistic, alongside arithmetic, the doctrine of pure numbers and pure numerical relations. Diophantine arithmetic is in this sense a *scientific logistic* and stands to arithmetic in much the way the metrics of Heron of Alexandria stand to theoretical geometry.[35] It focuses upon the field of pure monads. Every single number which it treats is a number of such monads. Its mode of writing is accommodated to this fact. Even the unknown, the ἀριθμός which has to be reckoned, is a definite number of monads, although still unknown at first and "indeterminate" in this sense alone. All the signs used by this logistic refer immediately to the enumerated objects in question here.

How does the *new* science interpret this situation? In his work "*In artem analyticen Isagoge*" published in 1591 Vieta introduces the fundamental distinction between a "*logistica numerosa*" and a "*logistica speciosa*." The former is a doctrine of numerical equations; the second replaces numerical values with general "symbols," as Vieta himself says, that is, with letters. (We can, in this context, disregard the fact that Vieta, in

---

35. Compare Heron, *Metrica* (ed. Schöne), I, 6 ff.

accordance with his "Law of Homogeneity," has these symbols apparently refer to geometrical formations.) *Logistica speciosa* gives Vieta the capacity not only of *writing* an expression such as $ax+b=c$ (in a much more detailed form, with which we are not concerned here) — initiatives in this direction can be found prior to Vieta — but also of calculating with this expression. With this step, he becomes the first creator of the *algebraic formula*.

How are we to understand this step from $2x$ to ax, from the numerical coefficient (the term "coefficient" stems from Vieta himself) to the literal coefficient? Could Diophantus have taken basically the same step? The answer to this depends directly on how we interpret the numerical sign "2." For Vieta the replacement of "2" by "a" is possible because the concept of "two" no longer refers, as it did for Diophantus, directly to an object, viz., to two pure monads, but in itself already has a "more general" character. "Two" no longer means in Vieta "two definite things," but the general *concept* of twoness in general. In other words, in Vieta the concept of two has the character of an *intentio secunda*. It no longer means or intends a determinate number of things, but the general number-character of this one number, while the symbol "a" represents the general numerical character of each and every number. In this sense the sign "a" represents "more" than the sign "2." The symbolic relation between the sign and what it designates is, however, the *same* in both cases. The replacement of "2" by "a" is in fact only "logically required" here. However, in this case as well, this "2" is identified with the sign employed by Diophantus — and *this* is the decisive thing. The concept of twoness is at the same time understood as referring to two entities. (Modern *set theory* first tries to separate these two constituents, to clarify what "at the same time" means.) In any case, Vieta, as the result of this identification, understands Diophantus' logistic as a *logistica numerosa* which "logically" presupposes the "more general" *logistica speciosa*. Thus, Vieta says in paragraph 14 of his *Isagoge* that Diophantus practiced the art of solving equations most cleverly. He continues: "*Eam vero tanquam per numeros, non etiam per species, quibus tamen usus est, institutam exhibuit*" ("However, he exhibited it [this art] as if it were based on numbers and not also on *species* [that is, the literal-signs,] although he nonetheless made use of these species").[36] Diophantus kept silent about the latter, in Vieta's opinion, only so as to make his acuity and his skill shine more brightly, since the numerical solution-procedure is indeed much more difficult than the convenient literal-reckoning. The relation between Fermat and Apollonius finds its exact counterpart here: Vieta sees in literal-reckoning only a more convenient, because more general, path to the solution of the problems posed. He can do this because he interprets the numbers with which Diophantus dealt from a higher conceptual level, because, in other words, he identifies the *concept* of number with the number itself; in short, he understands *Anzahl* [counting-number] as *Zahl* [number in general]. Our contemporary concept of number [*Zahlbegriff*] has its roots in this interpretation of the ancient ἀριθμός.

We can now understand how important it is that Bachet, who in 1621 (hence, after Vieta) published the first usable edition and Latin translation of Diophantus, abandons the current rendering of the sign for the μονάς. "Who," he says, "does not immediately think of six units when he hears the number 6 named?" ("*Ecquis enim cum audit numerum sex non statim cogitat sex unitates?*") "Why is it also necessary to say 'six units,' when it is enough to say 'six'?" ("*Quid ergo necesse est sex unitates dicere, cum sufficiat dicere, sex?*")[37] This discrepancy — felt to be self-evident — between *cogitare* (thinking) and *dicere* (saying and also writing) expresses the general shift in the meaning of the concept from *intentio prima* to *intentio secunda*, together with their simultaneous identification. Consequently, there is no longer anything to prevent Vieta's *logistica speciosa* from becoming a part of geometrical analysis; this is exactly what Fermat and Descartes explicitly did. The unification of these two disciplines is basically complete in Vieta's *ars analytica*. Modern analysis is, therefore, not a direct combination of ancient geometrical analysis with the ancient theory of equations, but the unification of both on the basis of a transformed

---

36. [Vieta's *Isagoge* has been translated by J. Winfree Smith as an appendix to Jacob Klein, *Greek Mathematical Thought and the Origin of Algebra* (Cambridge, Mass., 1968). The passage cited occurs on page 345. Translator's Note.]

37. 1621 edition, 4.

intentionality. The same shift in meaning can be established in a whole series of concepts. For instance, the mathematical term δύναμις, "power" in ancient mathematics, means only the *square* of a magnitude, while we speak as well of the third, the fourth power, etc. We do not encounter this relation in the mathematical domain alone. It also holds between the modern concept of "method" and the Greek term μέθοδος, between our "theory" and Greek θεωρία. In two cases, those of *substance* and *causality*, this shift in meaning was of the greatest importance for the construction of the new science. I cannot discuss these now. I want simply to remark that the relation here is more complicated, inasmuch as these concepts — like all concepts belonging to πρώτη φιλοσοφία, the ancient ontological fundamental-science — themselves already have the character of *intentiones secundae*; this is why the new science considered itself the sole legitimate heir of ancient philosophy, why, in other words, mathematical physics can in a certain sense replace ancient ontology for us. I want now, by way of conclusion, to turn to the exception I mentioned earlier and thereby compare one of the bases of ancient cosmology with the fundaments of the modern study of nature.

C. I said that what is peculiar to the conceptual intention of ancient science — and especially of Greek mathematics — is that its concepts refer *immediately* to definite objects. This obviously does not hold true of the fifth book of Euclid's *Elements* which goes back to Plato's friend Eudoxus. This book contains the so-called *general theory of proportions*, that is, it treats ratios and proportions of μεγέθη, magnitudes in general. Accordingly, it does not treat the ratios of particular magnitudes, geometrical forms for instance, or numbers or bodily masses or time-segments, but ratios "in themselves," the wholly undetermined bearers of which are *symbolized* [*symbolisch. . .versinnbildlicht*] by straight lines. The fifth book of Euclid, in fact, contains a "geometrical algebra." The exceptional character of this branch of Greek mathematics brings it into immediate proximity to Greek ontology. It is not surprising, therefore, that it had an exemplary, although diverse, significance for both Plato and Aristotle.

This καθόλου πραγματεία,[38] this *scientia generalis* or *universalis*, took on an even *greater* importance for the new science, if that is possible. A direct path leads from the fifth book of Euclid and the late Platonic dialogues, through the preface of Proclus' *Commentary on Book One of Euclid*, and the Latin translation of that work by Barozzi in 1560, to Kepler's astronomical researches, to Descartes' and Wallis' *mathesis universalis*, to Leibniz's universal characteristic, and *finally* to modern symbolic logics, on the one hand, and, on the other, to Galileo's mechanical investigations and to the conception of natural laws in general. (The latter connection has not been sufficiently emphasized up to now.) The close relation between the general theory of proportions and the new science is established from the start by their kindred conceptual basis.

What is important, however, is the very different ways in which ancient cosmology and seventeenth-century physics made use of the concept of proportion. I want to try to define this difference by using the example of seventeenth-century interpretations of Plato's *Timaeus*. In that dialogue, the mathematician, the "Pythagorean" Timaeus, gives a genetic presentation of the construction of the world. (In this context, and only in this, can we disregard the fact that this presentation does not claim to be a valid ἐπιστήμη, a true science, but claims only to give an εἰκὼς μῦθος, an image approximating the truth as closely as possible.)[39] A chaotic state of the world-matter precedes the origin of the world: Fire, Air, Water, and Earth are in disharmonious and disordered motion, they pass freely into one another, they are at first nothing but πλημμελῶς καὶ ἀτάκτως κινούμενα.[40] The divine demiurge brings them from this condition of dis-order into the condition of order, of τάξις: εἰς τάξιν . . . ἤγαγεν ἐκ τῆς ἀταξίας.[41] How does he bring about this condition of order? By producing a self-maintaining equilibrium among the world-materials, so that their restless passage into

---

38. See, for Aristotle, *Metaphysics* Δ 1, 1026a23–27; K 4, 1061b17 ff; M 2, 1077a9–12; M 3, 1077b17–20; *Posterior Analytics* A 5, 74a17–25; A 24, 85a38–b1. Compare also Marinus on Apollonius [i.e. the mention of a now-lost "General Treatise" (καθόλου πραγματεία) in *Euclidis Opera*, ed. Heiberg-Menge, VI, 234. Translator's Note.]
39. *Timaeus* 29D
40. *Timaeus* 30A
41. *Timaeus* 30A

one another yields to well-balanced rest, turns into ἡσυχία. Ἀναλογία, proportion, is best suited for this purpose, in the first place, because it knits together a firm connection, a firm bond, a δεσμός,[42] among the world-materials, a bond which proves to be unbreakable throughout almost all internal changes in these materials, that is, throughout the overwhelming majority of possible permutations of the elements within this proportion; secondly, because the proportion is a bond which, among all possible bonds, is itself most of all bound to what it binds together, that is, it binds itself most intimately with what is bound together so as to form a unitary whole: αὐτόν τε καὶ τὰ ξυνδούμενα ὅτι μάλιστα ἓν ποιῇ.[43] Proportion has both of these features by virtue of its incorporeality. Thus, its incorporeality, by virtue of which it institutes wholeness and brings about order, makes it akin to what we call "soul," ψυχή. Indeed, it is difficult to say whether the *Timaeus* allows us to draw any distinction at all between ψυχή and ἀναλογία. All of the world-materials together from now on form a structured whole, because their quantity, the size of their respective bulk (cf. ἀριθμῶν ὄγκων— 31c), remains in a fixed ratio throughout all changes or at least comes very close to this fixed ratio: as Fire is to Air, so Air to Water, and as Air is to Water, so Water to Earth. Just as a single, living, "besouled" organism maintains itself as a whole throughout the constant changes of its bodily materials, so, too, the entire visible world maintains itself, thanks to this proportion among its materials, as this one, perfect whole (ἓν ὅλον τέλεον).[44] And that means: as this *living* whole. It is only through this proportion that a "world" arises at all, that is, an ordered condition of the world-materials, which we call a cosmos. Κόσμος thus means a self-maintaining condition of τάξις (order). This condition is the basis of life, life that maintains itself, produces itself time and again. For life alone creates itself *ad infinitum*. Hence the world, precisely as an ordered world, is a self-sufficing animal, a ζῷον αὔταρκες.[45] Its own being, as well as the being of its parts, is φύσις, that is, "natural"

---

42. *Timaeus* 31C
43. *Timaeus* 31C
44. *Timaeus* 33A-B
45. *Timaeus* 33D; 37D

being. The natural being of every entity existing "by nature"
is determined by the fact that it continues to produce itself anew,
renews itself again and again as what it already is within the
texture of the world-order. Thereby it helps this world-order,
this τάξις, to be continuously maintained. The being of every
natural thing, therefore, is determined by the world-order as
such, the τάξις of the world, the ψυχὴ τοῦ κόσμου [soul of the
world] and, finally, by the ἀναλογία. Τάξις is thus the basic
concept of ancient cosmology, not only Plato's, but also Aristotle's, in the version transmitted to the Christian centuries.[46]
But τάξις, order, essentially means in every case a definite order,
an ordering according to a definite point of view, in conformity with which each individual thing is assigned its place, its
location, its τόπος. Order always means well-ordering. For this
reason ancient cosmology, as topology, is not possible without
the question of this ultimate ordering point of view, without
the question of ἀγαθόν, the Good. And ancient cosmology
reaches its fulfillment in the doctrine of the different τόποι
[places]. This doctrine also investigates the ratios and proportions in which the celestial bodies appear arranged in their
spheres.

How did the new science receive this ancient doctrine of
τάξις and ἀναλογία, of *ordo* and *proportio*? In his *Dialogue on
the Two Chief World Systems*, Galileo takes his bearings continuously from the two basic books of traditional cosmology, Aristotle's *De caelo* and Plato's *Timaeus*; in battling against Aristotle
he relies again and again on Plato. The entire construction of
Galileo's dialogue is in a certain sense determined by the construction of the *Timaeus*. Like the *Timaeus*, Galileo, too, bases
all further cosmological explanations on the thesis that the world
has an *order*. Its parts are coordinated in the most perfect manner ("*con sommo e perfettissimo ordine tra di loro disposte*").
In this way the best distribution ("*l'ottima distribuzione e col-
locazione*") of the heavenly bodies, the stars and the planets,
arises. However, what is important here is how Galileo

---

46. See Aristotle, *Metaphysics* M 3, 1078a36–b6 and compare the title of Ptolemy's work:
ἡ σύνταξις (sc. τῶν ἑ πλανωμένων, The Ordering-Together of the Five Planets).
For this title, see *Pauly-Wissowa*, s.v. "Astronomie."

understands the Platonic principle that the divine demiurge
brought the world-material from disorder to order. He thinks
that Plato meant the following: each of the different planets
has a different orbital velocity within the present order of the
world. In order to reach these velocities, they must, from the
instant of their creation, have passed through all the grades of
lesser velocity. The creator let them fall close to the mid-point
of the world in rectilinear motion, so that the uniform accelera-
tion peculiar to falling-motion (free fall) could bring them
gradually to their present velocity, at the moment when they
reached the place assigned to them. Only then did He set them
rotating, so that they proceeded from the non-uniform rectilinear
motion to the henceforth uniform circular motion in which they
persist until today. Non-uniform rectilinear motion along the
vertical corresponds, for Galileo, to the state of disorder, ἀταξία,
of which Plato speaks, while uniform circular motion, that is,
motion along the horizontal line (for "horizontal" originally
means the direction of the circle of the horizon) corresponds to
the present state of order. With this interpretation, Galileo intends above all to defend the Platonic principle against Aristotle's
criticisms in *De caelo*.[47]

It is not crucial here that Galileo's interpretation finds no
support in Plato's text. What is significant is the direction in
which he looks for the distinction between order and disorder:
not in the ratio or absence of ratio among the quantities of the
basic materials, not in the correlative positions of the celestial
bodies (although these do appear, in accordance with the construction of the *Timaeus*, as the genuine theme of his inquiry),
but in the differences in the states of motion as such. The bodies
themselves are not subject to comparison (*comparatio*, as Cicero
in his translation of the *Timaeus* says for *proportion* as well),
only a mode of being of these bodies, namely, their motion. The
application of proportion in Galileo's mechanical works is also
consonant with this. The connection with the Greeks' general
theory of proportions is immediate here, thanks to the direct
reception of Euclid and Archimedes, as well as indirectly, by

---

47. Γ 2, 300b16 ff.

way of a qualitative doctrine of geometrical ratios stemming
from the fourteenth-century Nominalist school.[48] What we today call Galileo's laws of free-fall are intended by Galileo himself
as Eudoxian-Euclidean proportions. In the *Discorsi* (Third day,
Second Book, Theorem II, Proportio II) a proportion is derived
with Euclidean means which we today would write as:

$$S_1 : S_2 = T_1{}^2 : T_2{}^2 .$$

Both types of magnitude (S and T) are symbolized by straight
lines, in accordance with Book Five of Euclid. The decisive difference from the cosmological proportion in the *Timaeus* is that
time becomes one of the elements of the proportion. What I
have said about Galileo also holds true of Kepler, whose lifework,
in his own opinion, consists in the restoration of the Platonic
doctrine of order and proportion. The relation between the
squares of the periods of the planets and the cubes of the great
axes of their orbits, familiar to us as Kepler's Third Law, is once
again conceived as a Euclidean proportion, of the form

$$t_1{}^2 : t_2{}^2 = r_1{}^3 : r_2{}^3 ,$$

or, as it has to be written to conform with Kepler's own wording in Book One of the *Harmonice mundi*:

$$t_1 : t_2 = (r_1 : r_2)^{3/2} .$$

Taken together with the other two proportions which we today
call Kepler's First and Second Laws, it determines the cosmic
order in which we live. In these Galilean and Keplerian proportions the concept of law, of the *lex naturae*, becomes visible
for the first time (although neither Galileo nor Kepler uses this
word as a technical term; it is first given a fixed sense by
Descartes).

The relation of the new to the old intentionality here becomes
immediately comprehensible. For Greek cosmology, ἀναλογία

---

48. Compare P. Duhem. [The author most probably had in mind *Études sur Léonard
de Vinci* (Paris 1905–1913). Translator's Note.]

is the expression of τάξις, of order; for the new science, it is a "law." Accordingly, the new science interprets τάξις, *ordo*, as law, and construes the order of the world as the lawfulness of the world. The shift in the meaning of the concept of *ordo* has its concrete basis here in the possibility of transferring proportion from the ratios among the quantities of the relevant elementary-bodies, or from the ratios of their correlative positions, to the state of motion of these bodies. This shift, however, eliminates the order of the elementary-bodies, their τάξις, in the sense of well-ordering. For the lawfulness of their motion, the regular sequence of their states of motion, can be constructed only on the basis of their complete equality in rank, their lack of ordering in the strict sense, that is, their complete indifference to the *place* they occupy. The new science now understands just this lawfulness in the *course* of motion, in the *temporal* sequence of states of motion, as the order of the world. The order of things moves up one story higher, so to speak, when the temporal dimension is added. At the same time, however, the disorder of the elementary-bodies, on which the lawfulness of the world is based, is now understood as "order." Let us hear Descartes: In chapter 46 of the Third Part of his *Principia* he sets out the basic assumptions of his physics. In the next chapter Descartes refers to his earlier attempt to derive the present state of the world by assuming an original chaos. He says: "Even if, perhaps, this very same order of things, which we encounter now (*idem ille ordo qui iam est in rebus*) can be derived from chaos with the help of laws of nature (*ex chao per leges naturae deduci potest*), something I once undertook to show [sc. in *Le Monde*], nonetheless I now assume that all the elementary parts of matter were originally completely equivalent to one another both in their magnitude and their motion . . . because chaotic confusion (*confusio*) seems to be less fitting to the highest perfection of God, the creator of things, than proportion or order (*proportio vel ordo*) and also can be less distinctly known by us, and because no proportion and no order is simpler and more accessible to knowledge than the one which consists in universal equality." It was only later, through the work of Boltzmann and then of Planck, that this "hypothesis of elementary disorder," as it was called, was made explicit in statistical terms. Its importance for physics is clear from the fact that Planck called the essence of the Second Law of Thermodynamics the "Principle of Elementary Disorder."[49]

The world of mathematical physics built upon this presupposition, the world of natural processes occurring in accordance with law, determines the concept of nature in the new science generally. "Nature" means for it a system of laws, means—to speak with Kant—"the conformity to law of appearances in space and time." All the concepts in this formula (as I have tried to show for "space" and "law") can only be understood by contrast with the corresponding concepts of ancient science. Above all, the concept of conformity to law signifies a modification of the ancient concept of τάξις; τάξις is now understood as *lex*, that is, as order over time. The ascent from *prima intentio* to *secunda intentio* is initiated here by the insertion of the time-dimension.[50]

How, then, does the new science, on the basis of *its* intentionality, interpret ancient cosmology? How does it interpret the "natural" world of the Ancients, the world of τάξις? It interprets it as the qualitative world in contrast to the "true" world, in contrast to the quantitative world. It understands the "naturalness" of this qualitative world in terms of the "naturalness" of the "true," "lawful" world. Eddington, in the introduction to his recent book, speaks in a characteristic way of these two worlds: "There are duplicates of every object about me—two tables, two chairs, two pens." The one table, the commonplace table, has extension, color, it does not fall apart under me, I can use it for writing. The other table is the "scientific" table. "It consists," Eddington says, "mostly of emptiness. Sparsely scattered in that emptiness are numerous electrical charges rushing about with great speed."[51]

Translated by David R. Lachterman

---

49. Max Planck, *Die Einheit des physikalischen Weltbildes*, Leipzig 1909.
50. M. Planck, *Das Weltbild der Physik* (Leipzig 1931, 2d. ed.).
51. Sir Arthur Eddington, *The Nature of the Physical World*, New York 1929, ix-x.

2 ■ On a Sixteenth-Century Algebraist

The short historical survey I am going to make may interest you on account of its relation to the foundations of modern mathematics. Although the development of human thought is continuous, it can be fairly said that the foundations of modern mathematics were laid by two men: François Viète (or Vieta) and Simon Stevin. I will deal with the latter only.

In the first place I must admit that the title of this paper is misleading, since Stevin died in 1620 and belongs, therefore, also to the seventeenth century. But his main work, entitled *Arithmetic*, appeared in 1585. The time at my disposal is very short. So I can talk only about the first pages of this work, which contain in my opinion propositions fundamental to the modern understanding of mathematics—especially Algebra.

But let me first say a few words about the life of Stevin. He was born in 1548, five years after the publication of the great book of Copernicus. He was of Flemish stock and lived in a part of Europe, namely the Netherlands, which after their declaration of independence in 1581 became a center of learning and education and actually the first European country having religious tolerance. Like many men of his time, Stevin was ac-

Lecture given on December 10, 1938, to the Mathematical Association of America at the University of Maryland, College Park.

tive in very different practical and theoretical fields. It is characteristic of his way of thinking never to separate theory and practice. He was an engineer who constructed dams, bridges, marine fortifications; furthermore, he was Quartermaster General of the Dutch army, General Comptroller of the finances; he thought out improvements in the methods of bookkeeping; he was an astronomer, a geographer, a linguist; his main interest, however, lay in the mechanical arts, especially statics, and in mathematics, especially Algebra; he made the discovery of the principle of the parallelogram of forces and is best known for that; and he was the most advanced algebraist of his time. He was very much aware of the peculiarity and novelty of his intellectual preoccupations. His own interpretation of his work — and this is important — is characteristic of the way in which modern science thinks about itself. He was captivated by the idea of an "age of wisdom" which had existed before the Greeks and which he and his contemporaries were going to renew. The sixteenth century as a whole strove for a renewal, a rebirth, a restoration of almost lost or forgotten wisdoms. Stevin is peculiar in that he goes back beyond the Greeks. He gives a "definition" of the "age of wisdom" thus:

> We call age of wisdom that age wherein men have had
> an admirable knowledge of the sciences, and this age
> we recognize infallibly by certain marks, although we
> do not know who those people were or where they
> lived or at what time.

At any rate, he calls the entire period from the Greeks to the fifteenth century the "age of barbarism". And he thinks that the leading personalities of that age of wisdom which precedes the age of barbarism were, for example, Zeus, Hermes, Apollo and other Greek gods, as well as Abraham, Isaac, Moses and other people in the Old Testament. For him all these personages were actually scientists whom the age of barbarism misrepresented as gods or shepherds.

In order to restore the "age of wisdom," he proposes a general plan of scientific research — the first of this kind, I presume — containing four articles: 1) As many observations as possible should be made, especially in Astronomy, Alchemy (that is to say, Chemistry) and Medicine, by a great many people living in different regions of the earth and belonging to different nations. 2) The results thus obtained should be expounded methodically, according to the mathematical method used by Euclid. The order followed by Euclid is to Stevin's mind the "natural order" which that Greek author had gotten somehow from the "age of wisdom." 3) It is possible to carry out so many observations by so many people only if these people use their own language and not the scholarly Latin, the command of which is possessed by but a few people. Even the Greeks used their own language and not a special learned or artificial one. 4) It might, however, be very convenient to use the Flemish idiom, because of the abundance of monosyllabic words in that language. For science requires terms, and terms are often very complex words; the composition of words is easily done, if the words are monosyllabic. Hence the usefulness of the Flemish idiom, which is much richer in monosyllables than French or Latin or Greek, as Stevin tries to demonstrate statistically. As a matter of fact, Stevin taught mathematics only in Flemish and wrote most of his works in this language, although he knew Latin and himself translated some of his works into French. His official title at the University of Leyden was "Professor of Dutch Mathematics." (Flemish and Dutch were identical at that time.) It is noteworthy that Descartes, who probably was his disciple in 1618–1619, writes in a letter of January, 1619, that at that time he is mostly concerned with the study of the Flemish language (*sermo Belgicus*, as he calls it in Latin). We shall see why the influence of Stevin on Descartes is so decisive.

Stevin himself considered the question of a right language highly important and was rather pessimistic about the possibility of renewing the age of wisdom, merely on account of the unfortunate fact that the Flemish language was used on this earth by a comparatively small number of people. But on a different level he found the proper, and at the same time universal, language in the symbolism of Arithmetic and Algebra. And that is the topic which we shall now approach. What reason did he have for going back beyond the Greeks and for formulating the hypothesis of an "age of wisdom"— an hypothesis accepted by many of his contemporaries, and by Grotius among others? Mainly this: the Greeks had no notion of the Zero. The entire "age of barbarism" is characterized by this ignorance, whereas the "age of wisdom" is distinguished by the knowledge of the Zero and the Arabic numeral system.

The Arabic numeral system had been brought into Europe in the twelfth century and had been in constant use since then. But it was Stevin who first recognized the tremendous importance of this innovation. Of course, the Greeks also were able to reckon and to solve problems, which we today call arithmetical and which they called logistical. But calculation and also the solution of numerical equations did not belong for them to Science in the proper sense of the term. Stevin ascribes that fact to a fundamental confusion on their part with respect to their use of this sign: ".". According to Stevin the point "." was the sign for 0 in the "age of wisdom." The Greeks, however, misinterpreted this Zero-sign as the sign for the Unit. Hence a great many fundamental errors — for example: the definition of number, the definition of the principle of number, the distinction between Geometry and Arithmetic, the misunderstanding of the nature of Algebra.

According to the Greeks, the definition of number is "multitude of units," a definition universally accepted until the seventeenth century. The principle of number is the Unit, in the sense that you cannot count without distinguishing the single units of a number, whatever the number or the units in question might be: apples or horses or stars or pure mathematical units. The Unit or the One is, therefore, not a number itself. The main consequence of this understanding of the Unit and the Number is the sharp distinction between the numbers, as consisting of separated, discrete units, and the continuous magnitudes, as lines, planes or solids — that is to say, the sharp distinction between Arithmetic and Geometry. Furthermore, numbers in the precise sense of the word (in Greek — ἀριθμοί) are only integers. Fractions are understood as parts of the unit occurring in the calculation. Fractions are not numbers. Scientifically they can be dealt with as ratios, more exactly as ratios between integers. "Negative" and "irrational" numbers are not conceivable at all. During the fifteenth and sixteenth centuries irrational numbers, although actually used by calculators and algebraists, are called "absurd" or "inexplicable" or "deaf" numbers. As late as 1560 a French mathematician, Peletier, admits readily that we cannot avoid making use of such "inexplicable" numbers, especially in measuring continuous magnitudes, but goes on to say that their relation to true or "absolute" numbers (as he calls them) is similar to that of beasts to men.

According to Stevin, all this is the consequence of the wrong definition of the principle of number. Says he: "O unhappy hour wherein was first uttered this definition of the principle of number! O cause of the difficulty and obscurity of things which in Nature are so easy and clear!" To him, "in Nature" the true principle of number is the Zero, which he calls the "arithmetical point," in analogy to the principle of the line, namely the "geometrical point." That is even more than an analogy. To understand the full extent of Stevin's radicalism in mathematics, we have to consider for one moment the Arabic system of numeration in itself.

The Arabic numeral system has two main features: 1) it is a decimal system, and 2) it is a system of positional numeration. The composition of signs in 333 is of the kind that the sign 3 in the middle means thirty and the sign 3 on the left means three hundred, merely on account of their respective positions. The decimal numeration as such is common to many peoples. The positional numeration as such was already used by the Babylonians, or more exactly Sumerians, but on the basis of the sexagesimal system. The Arabic system is unique in that it combines both, the decimal and the positional numeration. Stevin was the first to draw the final consequences out of these characters of the numeral system of the Arabs, whom he was inclined to consider as the true heirs of the unknown peoples of the "age of wisdom." To begin with, he identified the ciphers, the signs meaning the various numbers, with the numbers themselves. Thus he was able to argue as follows. We can see that the Zero and not the Unit is the principle of Number and that the Zero is the equivalent of a geometrical point by comparing directly the succession of ciphers with the extension of a line. A line is not extended through the addition of one or many

points (Figure 1). Nor is a number increased by addition of one
or many Zeros. But even if we think of a quasi-extension of a
line through the addition of a point thus (Figure 2):

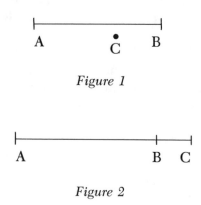

Figure 1

Figure 2

we can conceive a quasi-increase of a number through the addition of a Zero, thus: 0.6, 0.60. This argument involves the use
of decimal fractions. I shall return to this point in a moment.
But the argument shows clearly that Stevin could not conceive
of a difference between the nature of a continuous magnitude
and the nature of a discrete number. The unit and any fraction
of the unit are parts of a number, and consequently numbers
themselves, just as a fraction of a line is part of that line, and
consequently a line itself. The Zero, however, is not a part of
a number, but a principle of number, just as the point is not
part of a magnitude, but a principle of magnitude. Therefore,
number and magnitude are not to be distinguished through
discreteness and continuity. He says: "As to a continuum of water
there corresponds a continuum of humidity, so to a continuous
magnitude there corresponds a continuous number. Again, as
the continuum of humidity of all the water undergoes the same
division and separation as the water, so the continuous number
undergoes the same division and separation as the magnitude."
In other words: for Stevin there is not only an analogy between
the Zero and the point or between number and magnitude, but
perfect correspondence. In this respect his influence on Descartes
cannot be overestimated. In fact, Stevin thus contributed more

than anybody else to Descartes' discovery of Analytical Geometry. Descartes — and this applies more or less also to Fermat — interpreted Apollonius, as it were, through the eyes of Stevin.

A further consequence of Stevin's understanding of the Arabic positional numeration was the recognition of irrational quantities as true numbers. It has been only since Stevin that we could speak of rational as well as of irrational numbers. Stevin also understood an expression like this: $4x^2 - \sqrt{5}x + 3$ as one number, which he called a number representing an "algebraic multinomial." He was also the first to understand subtraction as the addition of negative numbers.

I mentioned the use of decimal fractions by Stevin. Actually, he was not the first to use them, but he was the first to understand them as basically connected with the general system of numbers. The "tenfold progression"— as he says — of the decimal numeration can be continued infinitely not only to increase the numbers, but also to diminish them in the same way. Thus we can get rid of all fractions in the ordinary sense of the word. Whenever we deal with numbers, we have to put them in certain columns, as for example.

$$
\begin{array}{ccccc}
⓪ & ① & ② & ③ & ④ \\
6 & 3 & 0 & 4 & \\
5 \quad 4 & 0 & 1 & & \\
0 & 2 & 0 & 7 & 8 \\
\end{array}
$$

We would write the first number of this series, namely 6.304, in the following way:

$$6(1/10)^0,\ 3(1/10)^1,\ 0(1/10)^2,\ 4(1/10)^3$$

The ciphers within the circles are really decimal exponents. "He had understood that any decimal fraction was identical to an integer but for a decimal coefficient," as George Sarton put it. Thus he became the real discoverer of the decimal fractions as we use them today. Moreover, not only did he suggest the universal use of the decimal fractions, but he suggested also the application of the decimal system to all kinds of calculation and measurement. He demanded that all measures and weights be expressed in decimal units, a demand which was to be fulfilled in France during the French Revolution and which was later followed by practically all the world, except for England and the United States. Strangely enough, Stevin linked his symbolism of the decimal system with that of his Algebra. He writes what we express today as the unknown quantities x, x^2, x^3, x^4 . . . as follows: ①,②,③,④. . ., whereas ⓪ means not — as we may think — the unit, but any known number.

I cannot speak about his Algebra any further, because my time is up. But I should like to emphasize that Stevin's idea of an "age of wisdom"— that is to say, a golden age of science or, more exactly, an algebraic age of science — is still leading the modern conception of Science in general. The only difference between the idea of Stevin and the modern outlook is that we place that golden age not in the past but in the future. It is a question, whether we are right.

3 ■ The Concept of Number in Greek Mathematics and Philosophy

The subject of my paper is the concept of number in Greek mathematics and Greek philosophy. This subject is of some importance, if we consider the role of mathematics not only in Greek philosophy but also in modern science. Indeed it is doubtful whether philosophy exists today, but certainly the existence of mathematical physics is not doubtful. All our life and thoughts are molded by it. In fact, mathematical physics, this immense construction of our mind, is one of the most important things, if not *the* most important, of our modern world. Now the medium of mathematical physics, or rather its very nerve, is symbolic mathematics. Physics, as we know it today, is not conceivable without symbolic mathematics. We are used to this kind of symbolic expression to the extent that we have no difficulty in handling symbols and are not even aware of the fact that we are dealing with symbols. A school of thought which calls itself Logistic is trying to interpret this fact in its own way. I think, however, they do not understand it, because the existence of symbols appears to them to be self-evident. But symbols are in themselves a great problem. They didn't exist for the Greeks, at least not in the same way they exist for us. The great

A paper delivered before the Philosophy Club of the University of Virginia, March 6, 1939.

mathematical tradition of the Greeks is Geometry. It began probably in the sixth century B.C. with people who were later called by the Greeks by the collective name, Pythagoreans. These people were "mathematicians" in a quite different sense from the one we have today. Μάθημα is something that can be learned and understood, and once learned is *known*. The idea of "knowledge" (ἐπιστήμη) is intimately connected with that concept of μάθημα. Thus "mathematics" is the model for all Greek philosophy and science. And this is especially true for Plato — and Aristotle as well. The main steps are: Theodorus (420 B.C.), Theaetetus (400 B.C.), Archytas (390 B.C.), Eudoxus (370 B.C.), Euclid (300 B.C.), Archimedes (250 B.C.), Apollonius (220 B.C.). We should also mention a later compiler, Pappus (300 B.C.). There is also another, non-geometrical tradition more directly connected with the Pythagoreans represented by Nicomachus and Theon of Smyrna (120 A.D.), and Domninos (fifth century A.D.). Finally there are Diophantus (60 A.D.) and Proclus (fifth century A.D.), one of the commentators of Euclid. I should like to mention in passing that modern mathematics, as it arises in the sixteenth century, is the result of a rediscovery and reinterpretation of Apollonius, Diophantus, Pappus, and Proclus.

We are not going to deal with that great mathematical tradition. Our task will be to describe the Greek concept of number and the problems which arise in connection with that concept. We must start with the "Pythagoreans." Modern books on the history of philosophy and mathematics usually state that the main contention of the Pythagoreans was: the essences of things are numbers. This statement in itself is without sense. The meaning of "essence" is very complicated. It is a mediaeval term which translates an Aristotelian term. The words "things" and "numbers" are both ambiguous. It would be safer to render the Pythagorean contention in the following way: everything that we see or hear can be counted. This is a remarkable, but unfortunately false, statement. But even its falsity is of the utmost importance, for the discovery of the falsity of that statement means nothing less than the discovery of incommensurables.

What were the things counted by the Pythagoreans and what does the very process of counting mean? The answer to the first question is: all things which are perceivable by our senses, especially all visible things. As to the process of counting *it always comes to a rest* when we pronounce a word like "five," "twelve," "hundred," etc. Each of those words signifies a "number" (in Greek: an ἀριθμός). Thus, ἀριθμός means *a definite number of definite things*. And this meaning of the word ἀριθμός doesn't change throughout all stages of Greek mathematics and philosophy. It is also the meaning of the word "*numerus*" until the sixteenth century.

This concept of number involves two problems, two fundamental problems of Greek mathematics and philosophy. (1) What is the character of things in so far as they are counted? In what sense are they "units" submitted to numeration? (2) In what sense is the number of those things or "units" in itself a unity? Is the number expressed by *one* word a unity at all?

The Pythagoreans were not very much concerned with the first question. Their chief concern was the second problem. How is it possible that *many* things should be comprehended as *one*? We say five chairs, seven people, ten cows. In every case the number (five . . . , seven . . . , ten . . . , etc.) signifies many things (one and another one and another one, and so on), but at the same time we comprehend by means of the number those many things as forming *one* set, *one* group, of things. The science of numbers, "Arithmetic," as it was elaborated by the Pythagoreans, tries to give a solution of that problem. As far as it is concerned with all visible things, the Pythagorean "Arithmetic" is not merely a "mathematical" discipline (in our sense of this word) but also and mainly a science of the visible universe, a *cosmology*, i.e., the science of the unity and the order of this universe.

The books of Nicomachus, Theon, and Domninos, although late, have preserved the main features of Pythagorean Arithmetic. They give a classification of numbers, a classification which we partly find also in the so-called arithmetical books of Euclid (VII, VIII, IX). The first distinction is that of odd and even numbers. "ODD" and "EVEN" can be also found in the Pythagorean list of contraries as recorded by Aristotle. And it is worth while mentioning that these terms, "ODD" and "EVEN," are listed in a peculiar way. The list of contraries has two columns: on the one side the terms represent things of a positive nature, and on the other, things of a negative nature. Thus GOOD is opposed to EVIL, LIGHT to DARKNESS,

RIGHT to LEFT, ONE to MANY, MALE to FEMALE, etc. According to the colloquial usage of the words ODD and EVEN, ODD had to be placed among the "BAD" things. For περισσός means in Greek, exactly as in English, something which is rather queer, more exactly, something superfluous. But the Pythagoreans reversed that order. What appears to be superfluous in an odd number is nothing less than a One. We can separate four dogs into two dogs and two dogs, i.e., into two equal parts. But we can't do the same thing with five dogs: ONE dog remains (unless I cut one into two parts and kill him). Since ONE is on the side of the "good" things, ODD must therefore also be placed on that side—a remarkable shift from the "popular" understanding.

Further distinctions are EVEN-EVEN, EVEN-ODD, ODD-EVEN. Today we would express those words by means of the following "formulas":

$$2^n, \ 2(2n+1), \ 2^n+1(2n+1).$$

Furthermore there are distinctions—and these are even more important—of the following kind: triangular numbers, square numbers, pentagonal numbers, etc. The Pythagoreans represented those numbers in this way:

In modern expressions:

$$\frac{n(n+1)}{2}, \ n^2, \ \text{etc.}$$

All these numbers can be obtained by adding a "gnomon" to the first One, which is later called the "limiting quantity" (περαίνουσα ποσότης). A "gnomon" is a configuration of dots (or of lines) which added to a figure of dots (or lines) produces a *similar* figure. (*Our method* for obtaining all those numbers consists in substituting for n and m in the respective formulas the series of numbers beginning with one.)

There are many other distinctions of numbers in Pythagorean Arithmetic, for example, prime (or linear) numbers, perfect, deficient, superabundant numbers, etc. We are not going to deal with all of them. We must rather ask, What is the reason for this classification? What is the purpose of this Pythagorean science of numbers? I have already said it tries to give a solution to the problem of the unity of any number. Every class of numbers is called by the Pythagoreans an εἶδος, a Form of numbers. ODD, EVEN, EVEN-ODD, Triangle, Square, etc., are Forms (or Species), each of them being something which is one in itself and therefore makes the unity of any number possible. Six is "one," or rather any six things can be conceived as *one* group, namely, "six," because the Form "triangle," which is one in itself, causes these six things to be one. All numbers under a certain Form belong to that Form exactly as all trees belong to the species "Tree." The different species of numbers are their "natural" order, whereas what we call the natural series of numbers, the actual order of numeration, doesn't appear to be "natural" at all. The universe as a whole is arranged according to those species of numbers. Every visible thing belongs somehow to a group of things and therefore to a certain numerical species. In that sense the "nature" of every visible thing is "Number," or rather a definite Form of numbers.

This cosmological Arithmetic can be expanded further, if we take into consideration all possible *relations* between the species of numbers and the numbers themselves. Thus we can relate all audible things — and furthermore all things that are neither visible nor audible but are conveyed to us by means of words, i.e., through audible sounds — to *ratios*, proportions, and their various forms and properties. The science of ratios (and proportions) is called Logistic (from λόγος). It is the basis of all our calculations, since calculating things is nothing else but bringing the respective numbers of things in relation to each other.

The Pythagorean Arithmetic (and Logistic), especially the figures of numbers, are probably the origin of the whole system of Greek mathematics in its later "geometrical" form. It seems as if the Pythagoreans attributed special importance to the smallest number of each species. They called them πυθμένες, "root" numbers, because every other number of the same species grows as it were out of those "roots" by means of the "gnomons." The πυθμένες might have been all included within the Ten, i.e., the famous Pythagorean tetractys. (One of the last remainders of the Pythagorean science and terminology lies in the fact that we call (n^2) "n *square*," and (n^3) "n *cube*.")

The Pythagorean solution of the problem of the unity of a number is the εἶδος. The unity is due to something that is itself one. This one is the "Form." It makes a unity out of a multitude. This solution is certainly one of the sources of the Platonic philosophy. Plato himself speaks of the "astonishing" proposition that One is Many and Many are One as a gift of the gods to mankind (*Philebus* 140, 160). But Plato goes much further in dealing with that problem. To begin with, he turns to the first question which arises in connection with the concept of number as a definite number of definite things. We may count six stars or six oxen or any six small or huge things. Obviously then "six" is not necessarily related to stars, oxen, or any other things. What is this "Six" in itself? More exactly: of what things is this "Six" six, since "Six" is necessarily six definite things? These things are neither stars nor oxen nor any other things. The very possibility of counting a number of stars or oxen or any other things presupposes the existence of "pure" numbers, i.e., the existence of numbers of "pure" units, which are not perceivable by our senses, but are conceivable only by our intelligence. There exists an unlimited field of such units, all equal to each other. Their being consists in nothing but being one. Insofar as they are nothing but one, they are indivisible. This unlimited field of "pure" units is the true subject matter of the *science* of Arithmetic. The whole Pythagorean system of the forms of numbers must be understood as related to those pure units. (It is possible that this was already the point of view of Archytas.)

The conception of pure, indivisible and merely intelligible units has an important bearing on the science of Logistic, i.e., the science of ratios as the basis of any calculation. To be sure, Logistic as the science of ratios remains intact, and is still interpreted as the science of audible things — harmonics (music).

But a doctrine of relations between pure, indivisible units having existence in themselves can no longer form the "theoretical" basis of our "practical" calculations. For, in our calculations, we continually make use of fractions, in other words, we divide the units which we compute. The relations between pure, indivisible units don't allow a computation of those units involving the use of fractions. The art of calculation — *our* Arithmetic — is, therefore, relegated to the rank of a merely practical art, the subject of which is sensible things. This remains true within the entire Platonic, Neo-Platonic, and Neo-Pythagorean tradition. Their term Logistic becomes ambiguous, meaning either the pure doctrine of ratios and harmonics or — to a much greater extent — the practical art of computation.

The new point of view from which Plato approaches the problem of numbers leads him to a further step in answering the second question connected with the concepts of numbers. The question is: How can many pure units form *one* number. The answer to this question given by the ("purified") Pythagorean Arithmetic is not entirely satisfactory. The unifying Pythagorean "Forms" are partly alien to the numbers themselves. The "Forms" don't explain the real differences between numbers under the same Form. According to Plato, Arithmetic cannot be sufficiently explained by itself, which is true also for the whole system of mathematics in the restricted sense of the word. The true "principles" of the unity of any number can only be found in *Ideas of Numbers*. And those ideas of numbers may solve at the same time, as we shall see, the great Platonic problem of "participation." Let me state the problem in Plato's own terms. In the *Phaedo*, Socrates wonders how *one* thing brought to another *one* thing produces *two* things. Neither of the things is two. Is the "two" something apart from the single things, so to speak, outside of them? Where is the "two"? (We must not forget that our symbol "2" doesn't mean anything in itself.) In the *Greater Hippias* Socrates asks the sophist Hippias whether he thinks that something which is common to two things may belong to neither of them. Hippias contemptuously rejects this suggestion. He argues this way: If we, Socrates and Hippias, are *both* just or healthy or wounded, and so on, then Socrates is just, healthy, wounded, and Hippias is just, healthy,

and wounded, and so on. Hippias charges [Socrates with not
looking at "the whole of things . . . but you take apart the
beautiful and each of the things that are, and you pick at it in
your talk until it is cut down to size," as] Socrates' present question shows. Hippias doesn't see that this reproach is applicable
to himself rather than to Socrates. Socrates answers: What you
say is true but still we *both* are two, whereas you and I are *each*
one and not two. This "formula": each — one, but both — two
(ἓν ἑκάτερον, ἀμφότερα δὲ δύο), occurs rather often in Plato.
In the *Sophist*, the stranger who is a *dialectician*, a follower of
Parmenides, discusses with the young *mathematician* Theaetetus
the question of Being and Non-being. The stranger, as he con-
fesses, could never find an answer to this question, nor can
Theaetetus, as the discussion shows. The stranger suggests that
neither of them attack the problem alone (239c: σὲ μὲν καὶ ἐμὲ
χαίρειν ἐῶμεν) but that they should try *together* to solve it.
Finally they get to the discussion of *Rest, Change*, and *Being*
(στάσις, κίνησις, ὄν): Being is said to be Rest *and* Change, and
nothing but that. Assuming that this is the case, are we in the
presence of two, or of three, ideas? Rest "is," Change "is,"— is
then Being one of them or neither of them? Or is Being
something "outside" of them? All these possibilities must be rejected. Plato doesn't give a solution of this problem "with complete clearness" in the dialogue. But it is obvious that the solution lies in the fact that Being is Rest and Change "together"
(ἅμα), that the ideas of Rest and Change constitute *together*,
and only together, the idea of Being. In other words, Rest is not
Being as Socrates is not "two," and Change is not Being as Hippias is not "two." But Rest and Change together are Being as
Socrates and Hippias are "two." In both cases we have a similar
structure: Rest and Change are bound *together* as the idea of
Being; and the very fact that neither of them is Being, although
they are Being *in common*, leads to the assumption that the relation between these three ideas or rather between the "genus"
Being and its "species" Rest and Change might be an
"arithmetical" one. The difference between the number "two"
and the "number" "Being" is this: the units of the number "two"
are equal to each other and, moreover, equal to any other
arithmetical unit, so that the number "two" can be added to

any other number; but the "units" of the "number" Being are not equal to each other (they are contraries: Rest—Change) and can't be "added" to any other "number" of this kind. The structure of the "number" Being should be called *arithmological* rather than arithmetical. (The term "Arithmology" was originated in the sixteenth century.) It is a "number" in a more peculiar sense than arithmetical numbers; its structure is—if we try to understand Plato's meaning—the paradigm of the structure of any arithmetical number and not conversely. The "number" Being is the idea of "two," is the idea, "TWO." The idea Being is an ἀριθμὸς εἰδητικός, the arithmetical number "two" is an ἀριθμὸς μαθηματικός or μοναδικός, and finally any two things of our sensible world constitute an ἀριθμὸς αἰσθητός.

Thus the solution of the problem of the unity of any number lies in the conception of corresponding ideas of numbers. It seems—according to the testimony of Aristotle—that Plato thought only of the first nine "numbers" of this kind, the first being the ideal "TWO," which is identical with the idea BEING. ONE, i.e., the "absolute" One, which is unique and not one unit among other units, is not a "number" at all. (One in the arithmetical order is not a number either; the first arithmetical number is "two." This is valid for all Greek Arithmetic, simply because an ἀριθμός is a "number of things" and "one" thing is not a number of things.) *The* ONE is beyond the arithmological structure, beyond any structure at all, beyond Being (ἐπέκεινα τῆς οὐσίας: Republic 509b)—it is the Idea of Good.

The arithmetical numbers have unity because they are images of the "ideal Numbers." In that sense Aristotle is perfectly right in his contention (*Metaph.* A6, 987 b 10-13) that Plato only changed the Pythagorean term μίμησις into μέθεξις. The "ideal numbers" of Plato are analogous to the "root-numbers" of the Pythagoreans. What the Pythagoreans did with respect to the sensible world, Plato tries to do with respect to the "true," i.e., "ideal" world.

The arithmological structure of the ideas allows also a solution of the Platonic problem of "participation." The real problem of participation is the problem of the community among ideas (κοινωνία τῶν εἰδῶν). This community can be conceived as an arithmological one. Each genus is the arithmological community of its species: each species is one, and on the other hand its participation in the genus doesn't affect the unity of the genus, since this unity consists in nothing but the community, the belonging together, of all its species.

Finally we have to say a few words about the attitude of Aristotle towards the problem of numbers. His objection against the Platonic solution is a double one. First, he denies the independent existence of the pure arithmetical units. The subject matter of Arithmetic is indeed the field of arithmetical units. Their "purity," however, doesn't consist in their independent existence but in their "neutrality" with respect to all sensible things. This "neutrality" is the result of abstraction (ἀφαίρεσις). In counting things we deprive those things of all qualities except their property of being-one. In counting — and computing — things we "abstract" this character of being-one from those things. This Aristotelian doctrine of abstraction, a doctrine of tremendous importance for the history of human thought, is not a "psychological" theory. It is rather an attempt — and a very radical one — to determine the peculiar character of the being of mathematical objects and furthermore of all possible objects of *knowledge*. According to this point of view a science of computation involving the use of fractions is perfectly possible: the arithmetical units are "indivisible" as far as every counting presupposes a field of real units, but we can always change the units, abstracting them not from the whole things but from parts of them.

Secondly, Aristotle denies — and this again is a very radical contention — that there is any unity in a number of things. A number of things signifies *many* things and isn't itself one at all. The community of the units of a number doesn't mean the unity of that number. The only possible "unity" of a number is the unity of the unit which is subjected to the process of counting. The unity of six apples is "apple."

However questionable the Platonic position with respect to numbers might be, it seems as if Aristotle didn't see the real problem of numbers. This problem still awaits a solution.

4 ■ Modern Rationalism

L adies and Gentlemen: I am sorry that I must read this lecture instead of speaking without any notes, but I don't
speak English very well. However, this has one advantage, that
it will make me speak without any ambiguity: a person who
is familiar with the language is, as a matter of human nature,
often inclined to be eloquent and therefore often vague. Since
I am dealing with a difficult and diffuse subject, the utmost
clarity and precision is necessary in words and expressions. First
of all, I must state my premises so that we will find a common
ground. I am going to speak about the relationship between Rationalism and Capitalism. I am not an economist, so I can't consider the question from the point of view of economics. Since
my field is the History of Science and what people generally
call Philosophy, naturally I approach the subject from this angle.
But I should say here that the delimitation of different sciences,
however necessary it seems to be, is somewhat dangerous. We
are accustomed to filing the truth in a certain number of
drawers, such as Religion, Politics, Economics, Science, Art.
These subdivisions of the truth are apt to depend not on the

The time and place at which this lecture was delivered are not known. Presumably
Klein delivered it at some time in 1938–1940 as a guest speaker in a class on Rationalism
and Capitalism.

nature of truth itself but on the number of drawers we have, so that we may easily miss the essential features of the subject, which may take on entirely alien features. It is a danger that we must always bear in mind.

Since the fourteenth century, man has undergone a profound change in his way of thinking, in his attitude towards the world, in his general behavior. This development was almost accomplished by the seventeenth century, when modern man, in the sense in which we use the expression now, became apparent. There is, as you know, the Marxist concept of the leap to freedom, a concept applied to the future, to something that has never occurred before. When you look at the change in man completed in the seventeenth century, you can't help saying that that change was also really a jump — perhaps to freedom, perhaps to slavery. This jump was concurrent with the rise of what we term capitalism. At the same time began the rationalization of all human life. When this term rationalization is used, as I think it is used in this class, it is applied to the following extraordinary phenomenon: we live in an entirely ordered world. Every day we get our mail at the same time, except of course when the postman is late; the subway runs regularly, although occasionally there may be an accident; all kinds of timetables, statistics, measures govern our lives, although not always precisely. Our whole life is modeled on certain patterns.

I intend now to study this kind of rationalization more carefully, leaving aside all facts that are at the root of our economic system. Whatever explanation you may give for the development of the world since 1600, either by invoking divine providence or by relying on the Marxist interpretations of history or by trusting to liberal economic theory, you can't deny that this development is primarily dependent upon a certain frame of mind, on a certain way of thinking. It is in this connection that we generally speak of rationalism. I shall try to explain what rationalism does not mean, what it can mean, and what it ought to mean.

First, we must disregard the meaning of the word "rationalism" as being opposed to the word "irrationalism." The literal sense of the word "irrational" is "nonsense," and it is really a pity that this word nowadays should (and does) mean anything else. I think it is not useless to remind you of the fact that the emphatic use of the words "irrational" and "irrationalism" has come into being only since the work of Henri Bergson, which as a whole is of tremendous importance for the understanding of the mentality of present-day Europe. I do not overestimate the influence of scientific or philosophic books on people in general, but it seems to me that each important book of this kind is only an expression of a certain unconscious public senti- ment, which after a certain passage of time — generally thirty years — is awakened to consciousness by those books which it has inspired. From this time on, this opinion is expressed without doubt or hesitation, however inconsistent it may be.

Rationalism, as the opposite of irrationalism, is considered at the present time, especially in Europe, as something inferior, as something lacking in vitality. It is supposed to apply to things which are dead, whereas the irrational power of man, especially of artists, reaches heights and depths which are not accessible to the mere intelligence. As if there were anything in this world of more value and more power than the intelligence of man.

I think we can completely set aside this use of "rationalism" as opposed to "irrationalism" as being quite meaningless. As a matter of fact, the use of this word implies a more positive significance than mere opposition to irrationalism. This significance is attached to the early and most fundamental stage of modern thought. In this stage rationalism became opposed to empiricism; or more exactly, a certain school of thought, beginning with John Locke, created, through contradiction of a certain point in the work of Descartes, an opposition between empiricism and rationalism. In order to understand this opposi- tion and, by implication, the meaning of rationalism, we must consider for a moment the general aspects of the philosophy of Descartes.

The thinking of Descartes resulted in the conception of two kinds of being which was likewise one of the most important premises from which he started: the *res cogitans*, the thinking substance, and the *res extensa*, the extended substance. The "thinking substance" meant for Descartes what has always been and is still called intelligence, mind, soul or consciousness, in a broader sense, the inner world, while the "extended substance" constitutes the external world. There is no connection whatever between them, except for one particular part of the human body, namely the pineal gland, where they mysteriously meet through the agency of a third substance, God. The question immediately arises how the external world can be known through the intelligence, how the thinking substance and the extended substance can get into touch with each other, since they are totally alien to each other. Even our simplest acts become incomprehensible. If, for example, I wish to pick up my pencil, my arm must make the proper movement. But how can a wish belonging exclusively to the "thinking substance" initiate such a movement as belongs purely to the "extended substance"? Furthermore, how can any object in the external world be received in the mind and become a matter of knowledge? In the attempt to answer these questions (the so-called psycho-physical problems) a philosophical discipline arises known as the theory of knowledge.

Descartes' attempt to solve this problem by plotting the meeting of the two substances in the pineal gland was obviously unsatisfactory. However, no matter what the procedure might be by which we attain to knowledge, one condition according to Descartes is indispensible: that the thinking substance have within it such qualities as correspond to similar qualities of the external world. Using ancient terminology, he calls the qualities of the mind *ideae innatae*, innate ideas, which guarantee the possibility of a perfect knowledge of the external world. They are (apart from the idea of God) number, magnitude, figure, space, time, and movement.

I have emphasized this doctrine of Descartes, namely that of the *ideae innatae*, because it was precisely this alone to which Locke and the entire school of empiricists objected. Locke and his followers contend that there are no such *ideae innatae* but that all the knowledge of the external world is the result of experience by means of the senses. Ever since that time this divergence between the two schools of thought has existed, one, the rationalistic school, proclaiming the sufficiency and power of intelligence for complete understanding of the world, and the other, the empiricist school, denying the sufficiency and power of intelligence and relying rather on the capacity of our senses. For the latter, therefore, the theory of knowledge is the subject matter of psychology. From this follows one definition of rationalism. It is that the essential reality of the external world is accessible to pure intelligence and to pure intelligence alone.

However, don't overlook [the fact] that the fundamental distinction of Descartes' between thinking substance and extended substance, the external and inner worlds, is universally accepted by the empiricists as well as by the rationalists; furthermore, that the essential premises of the empiricist psychology as well as of all contemporary physiology have been established by Descartes himself in his book, *Les passions de l'âme*. Above all, the difference between the two doctrines as regards the *ideae innatae* becomes totally unimportant in comparison with the agreements implied by the acceptance by both schools of the truths of mathematical physics, the main principles of which were again also first established by Descartes. Rationalists and empiricists, differ as they may on the question of how we acquire knowledge, must be in full agreement on the methods of thinking involved in the principles of mathematical physics. Mathematical physics is the most important part of our entire civilization and actual life. This is true not only in respect to the technics so inseparable from our modern life, and not only because it determines our own understanding of the world, but also because the principles of mathematical physics are basic to our whole way of thinking and behavior. We are therefore led to a new and more exact definition of rationalism. In a broader sense rationalism is that approach to an understanding of human behavior, history and the world around us implied by the premises of mathematical physics.

Now what are these premises of mathematical physics and therefore of all our thinking? The answer to this will give us a deeper insight into the character of rationalism as I think we must understand it. First of all, the science of nature as initiated by Descartes (and parenthetically this would apply also to Galileo) presupposes the distinction between thought and the external world as totally disconnected entities. All efforts to bridge the two and the claim that intelligence is sufficient to grasp the external world (as in mathematical physics) must not make us overlook the fundamental fact that this dichotomy involves a profound distrust of the reality of the world. The mere fact that we question the possibility of receiving the outside world and the manner in which it may be received, that is, the very existence of the theory of knowledge, indicates the deep cleavage between mind and the outside world. The fact of supreme importance is that we consider our mind as a mind shut up within its own cell, that we consider our soul as a soul isolated and without any possible contact with the outside world. Hence the paradox that the mind which is taken to be all sufficient for understanding the world is preconceived as being entirely dissociated and alienated from the world. This is a strange kind of rationalism indeed! Still stranger when we compare it with the thinking of the ancients.

There, though there is a clear distinction between mind and world, there is no separation between them, but rather mind is very emphatically the receiving of the world and nothing but that. As the Greeks put it, we receive the world in our mind by means of the λόγος. Λόγος comes from λέγειν, which means "to speak." By speaking we do not mean merely the pronunciation of a conglomeration of words, but the telling of something to someone. The literal and correct Latin translation of λόγος is *ratio*, which implies that speaking about a thing is understanding it, although the understanding may not be perfectly clear. The task of philosophy, according to the Greeks, is to make the speaking which is common to everyone perfectly clear.

We could rightly call the ancient thought rationalistic in the sense that for the ancients world and mind are inseparable from each other, that the nature of the world consists in being comprehensible. This is not just another philosophical theory but the very premise of their whole thought. *Modern* thought issues not from the understanding of man through speech but from the idea of a universal science, the *mathesis universalis*. Curiously enough, the idea of such a science is the result of an interpretation of certain passages in the commentary to Euclid's *Elements* by Proclus. Proclus refers in these passages to a general mathematical science which does not apply to numbers or figures or anything else but to relationships and proportions between such mathematical objects in general. Apart from a few axioms and postulates, he has in mind the fifth book of Euclid's *Elements*, the so-called general doctrine of proportions, the real author of which is, as we know, Eudoxus. The man who translated this book of Proclus into Latin in 1560, Barocius,

added to his translation a number of marginal notes. He marked
these passages with the words "Divine Science" (*Divina Scientia*).

On the other hand, the general doctrine of proportions was
combined with the *arithmetics* of Diophantus, which contained
the solution of equations of the first and second degree. Thus,
the general doctrine of proportions became identical with the
general theory of equations and was interpreted as the *mathesis
universalis*, the universal science. Since algebra, a doctrine
familiar to the Arabs and known in western Europe since the
thirteenth century, was similar to the doctrine of Diophantus,
algebra was also identified with that same universal science. I
hope you will forgive me for recording all these details, but they
seem indispensible for our purposes. As a matter of fact, the
idea of the universal science in the form of algebra becomes the
dominant idea of the sixteenth and seventeenth centuries and
develops ultimately into the system of our mathematical physics.
Therefore we can try to determine the main premises of our
physics and consequently of what we have already defined as
rationalism by investigating the structure of the *mathesis
universalis*.

The first point is this: algebra as the universal science is
characterized as an art. This means that the universal science
itself is interpreted as an art. What do we understand by this
statement?

For the Greeks, as well as for the medieval tradition, science
is the systematic representation of the truth. The "universal
science" of the seventeenth century is conceived not as a representation of the truth but as the art of *finding* the truth. Descartes,
as well as Vieta and Stevin, the founders of modern mathematics,
reject entirely the idea that mathematics consists of representing and *proving* a certain number of true theorems. Descartes
speaks contemptuously of such sterile truths (*steriles veritates*).
The purpose of these mathematicians is to find the way in which
all possible truth can be found. Algebra, the so-called "great
art" (*ars magna*) is the "art of finding" (*ars inveniendi*). More
exactly, the "universal science," in the form of the "art" of algebra,
is nothing else but the finding of the way of finding the truth.
Therefore, science as an art becomes primarily a method. Our
modern idea of science is inseparably linked with the idea of
a methodical procedure, according to certain rules. It is

noteworthy that the idea of procedure as a goal in itself was totally excluded from Greek science. In modern science there are no definite borders between pure science on the one hand and the so-called applied sciences and technics on the other. Modern science, as a whole, is not only applicable to certain procedures, the result of which is technics, but is in itself technical. Despite its heritage of the idea of ancient science, modern science is not so much the understanding of nature as the art of mastering nature. The rationalism of modern science consists mainly in the rationalization of methods, and it results in that extraordinary organization of our whole life, which we mentioned earlier.

By what means does modern science attain its goal? At this point I can't avoid disturbing you with some rather unusual observations. I must speak about the nature of concepts. Concepts are supposed to be a very familiar institution, but I can assure you that it is by no means easy to determine their true character.

Generally speaking, there are two kinds of concepts, those which apply to objects and those which apply to concepts themselves. If I say, "This is a *dog*," or "This is *red*," the words "dog" and "red" are concepts, used here to indicate individual objects. But if I say, "Red is an *attribute*," or "Idealism is a *theory*," the words "attribute" and "theory" are concepts applied not to individual objects but to concepts, "red" in the one case and "idealism" in the other. Since Albertus Magnus, scholars have called the first class of concepts *"intentiones primae"* or literally "first concepts," and the second class has been called *"intentiones secundae."* The ancient sciences dealt chiefly with concepts of the first class, while philosophy, or, more exactly, the main philosophical doctrine, was chiefly concerned with concepts of the second class. This distinction has nothing to do with abstraction. Every concept is, as such, abstract. That is, the concept is drawn, is abstracted, from individual objects, is general in itself, and has its own reality only in the mind. Abstraction, an Aristotelian term, means a process of our thought by which, for instance, the concept of "dog" is drawn from individual dogs as something common to all of them, or, the concept of a mathematical triangle is drawn from objects of triangular shape. Unfortunately, this word is applied today to the description of all kinds of concepts and has even come to have a derogatory connotation. I fear that some of you may be tempted to apply this magic word to my own statements.

Now, what kind of concepts are used by the "universal science"? How can we describe the nature of symbols as they are used in algebra? In answering these questions we are approaching the second and major point which characterizes the idea of the *"mathesis universalis."* We are all familiar today with the kind of symbolic notation used in algebra. We write, without any difficulty, such formulae as $(a+b)^2 = a^2 + 2ab + b^2$, or, $ax^2 - bx + c = 0$. However, a considerable effort was necessary to produce such a symbolic "language." This effort, made by the end of the sixteenth century, is usually interpreted as the last step in a long line of development, a step necessitated by the progress of algebraic knowledge and procedure. This may be true, but we ought not to forget that Greek mathematics, despite its extraordinarily high level, could not conceive such a step. Actually the step to the symbolic notation of algebra and, therefore, to the conception of mathematical physics involves an entirely new way of thinking, presupposes an entirely new manner of handling concepts. The symbolic language of algebra, that is, the language proper to mathematical physics, is not a purely technical or instrumental matter. It is a common mistake to believe that we can translate the theorems of mathematical physics into ordinary language, as if the mathematical apparatus used by the physicists were only a tool employed in expressing their theorems more easily. The mathematical method of our physics is inseparable from the very nature of this science. It represents, moreover, the most important character of our general frame of mind, which we have referred to as rationalism. Take the following examples:

(1) five horses and six horses make eleven horses,
(2) five unknown quantities and the number six equal the number sixteen,
(3) $ax + b = c.$

The transition from the first to the second can properly be described as the transition from concrete numbers to abstract numbers, since the arithmetical number *six* is abstracted from any possible group of six objects. However, the transition from the second, which is an equation we can find in the textbook of Diophantus, to the third, which is an algebraic equation as used by the *mathesis universalis*, cannot be simply described as a greater degree of abstraction. If the step from the numerical coefficient, "five," to the symbolic coefficient, "*a*," can be understood at all as an abstraction, it is an abstraction of a peculiar kind. We will try now to explain this peculiar kind of abstraction or, rather, generalization.

Numbers—I mean "whole numbers"—belong to the first class of concepts. If I say, "There are four chairs here," I indicate *first* that there are certain objects here, namely chairs, and secondly that there are just so many of them. If I say, "There is a certain number of chairs in this room," I also indicate first that there are chairs here and secondly that there are many of them without stating precisely how many. This is the natural use of numbers, and the Greeks recognized only such a use. For the Greeks, number (ἀριθμός) meant precisely a definite number of definite things, for instance, four chairs, ten dogs, fifty people. Arithmetical numbers, that is, numbers used as objects of a science called arithmetics, are for them precisely of the same kind. The number four, as an object of arithmetics, means a definite agglomeration of neutral units, also called "pure" units. "Four" doesn't mean the figure 4 but this :: . This simple fact is very important because we are spoiled by the use of the Arabic numeral system. Any arithmetical number is abstracted from the corresponding multitude of concrete things. For this reason the Greeks could not conceive of such a thing as an indefinite number "*a*," because to them, by its very nature, a number meant a "definite number of definite things." Therefore, their classic definition of a number was "a multitude of units," as in the seventh book of Euclid, or a "definite multitude," as Eudoxus put it.

Now, if we have an expression such as *a* + *2ab* + *c*, what does "*a*" mean? "*a*" can mean, of course, any possible number of the kind the Greeks dealt with. "*a*" can be 4, or 6, or 150, or any possible one, but "*a*" *is not* 4, or 6, or 150, or any other one. Thus, "*a*" doesn't mean certain objects, namely units, the multitude of which it indicates, but rather the *concept* of the number as a multitude of units. So, at first glance, "*a*" belongs to the concepts of the second class, to the class of concepts which are applied not to individual objects but to concepts themselves. This, however, is only the first step. Actually, we deal with "*a*" and with all such algebraic numbers in exactly the same way as arithmetics deals with ordinary numbers. In other words, in algebra we use concepts of the second class as though they were concepts of the first class. We identify, in the process of algebraic thinking, concepts of the first class with concepts of the second class. What we call a symbol is nothing else but a concept of the second class interpreted as a concept of the first class. Therefore, we can now state that the "peculiar kind of abstraction" used in algebra is a *symbolic* abstraction. This is the peculiar kind of generalization involved in the idea of "universal science" which has developed into our science of nature, or mathematical physics.

This description of the two main features of the "*mathesis universalis*," namely its character as an art and its functioning by means of symbolic abstraction, may appear very far from our subject. Remember, however, that the idea of the "*mathesis universalis*" determines that whole orientation of our lives which we call "rationalism." Our rationalism is a symbolic one. It is the true result of the Cartesian distinction between "mind" and "external world." It is the true expression of the paradox of which we have spoken, that the mind, which is supposed to be sufficient to understand the world, is preconceived as a mind alienated from this same world. We approach the world not directly but by means of concepts which are abstractions of abstractions and which at the same time we interpret as being in direct contact with the world.

These features of the *mathesis universalis*, which appear most forcefully in our Science of Nature and dominate our entire manner of thinking, can, I trust, be traced in the social and economic fields in which we live. Along the lines of our society, every one of us must "do his job" according to certain rules imposed on us by ever-working machineries. The production and consumption of goods have acquired a sort of "automatic" character. No one can escape the fatality which is the result of this automation. Our life, then, even our most intimate life, is completely conditioned by social and economic necessities which are alien to ourselves and which we nevertheless accept as the true expression of ourselves. Our work, our pleasures, even our love and our hatred are dominated by these all-pervading forces which are beyond our control.

Thus, our own life does not belong to us. We appear to be in the most direct contact with the world around us, but in reality the vast machinery of our society permits us to perceive the world only through generally accepted views. The directness of our contact with the world is of the same symbolic character as the concepts we use to understand it. We can comprehend how our whole social and economic system, which we term Capitalism, and which is, in its origins, closely connected to the modern idea of knowledge and science, has acquired such symbolic unreality.

There may be many ways to overcome this symbolic unreality. One of these ways is to understand how ancient science approached the world.

5 ■ Phenomenology and the History of Science

I

"**P**hilosophy . . ., by its very essence, is the science of true
beginnings, of origins, the ῥιζώματα πάντων. And the
method of a science concerned with the roots of things, the
method of a radical science, must itself be radical, and this in
every respect."[1] It may be said, not inappropriately, that Husserl,
throughout his life, directed his thought to the problems of
origin. His earlier writings formulated the approach to the "true
beginnings"; he worked all his life discovering, rediscovering,
and elucidating these beginnings and the approach to them and
finally he adumbrated the aims which should control research
in the history of science. It is the purpose of this paper to show
the essential connection, as Husserl understood it, between these
aims and the "true beginnings."

In attacking "psychologism," Husserl was in fact facing the
problem of "history." Any "naturalistic" psychological explanation of human knowledge will inevitably be the history of human

---

1. "Philosophie als strenge Wissenschaft," *Logos*, i, 340.

First published in *Philosophical Essays in Memory of Edmund Husserl*, ed. Marvin
Farber (Cambridge: Harvard University Press, 1940).

development with all its contingencies. For in such an account any "idea" is deduced from earlier experiences out of which that idea "originated."[2] In this view, the explanation of an idea becomes a kind of historical legend, a piece of anthropology. The *Logical Investigations* showed irrefutably that logical, mathematical, and scientific propositions could never be fundamentally and necessarily determined by this sort of explanation.

In order to understand the ultimate validity of logical and mathematical propositions, it is necessary, according to Husserl, to liberate first the problems of origin from an interpretation of mind which confuses mind with nature. "A thing is what it is, and remains in its identity forever: nature is eternal." Nature "appears": it is experienced as something that appears to us through the senses, never "absolutely," rather in different aspects, in different "adumbrations." But the object of mind "appears as itself, through itself," is in itself a "phenomenon," appears as an "absolute" and at the same time "as passing in an absolute flow, appears right now and already fading away, sinking back continuously into what is the past, and this in a way which can be perceived in an immediate intuition." Therefore, whereas a natural thing can be investigated and analyzed by repetition of an experience which is intrinsically the same in so far as the object is the same, a mental object can be re-examined only by reflection, by "retention," in memory, i.e., by a specific change ("modification") in the "manner of givenness." In other words, a natural object, although "temporal," remains constant with respect to our investigation: the object of mind is immersed in "eternal" time, "a time which cannot be measured by any chronometer."[3]

Naturalistic psychology ignores the distinction between the time of mind and the time of nature. As a result, mind itself and all its objects become natural objects, and all problems of origin become problems of origin within natural time. If we liberate these problems from this naturalistic distortion, they become "phenomenological" problems in Husserl's sense of the term.

---

2. *Ibid.*, p. 307.
3. *Ibid.*, pp. 312 f. Cf. *Ideen*, pp. 76 ff.

A typical "phenomenological problem" consists in finding the "invariables" within the absolute flow (the "internal temporality") of the mind, in determining the "invariants" which remain unchanged by reason of an essential necessity. This can be accomplished by means of a continuous and arbitrary "variation" of a given "example," a variation that takes place in the "freedom of pure phantasy." "Through such a free and continuously modified variation the necessarily unchangeable, the invariant, comes to the fore, something that is unshakably the same in all the otherness and renewed otherness, the universal and common essence"— the *"eidos,"* the *"a priori* form" which corresponds to the example and all its possible variations.[4] But this is only the first step—first in the actual development of Husserl's thought, and first in any phenomenological analysis. The reflection upon this kind of analysis, its implications and its significance leads to a deeper understanding of the nature of a "phenomenological problem." Far from being complete in itself, the finding and facing an "essence" requires a further investigation into its intrinsic "possibility." Whatever we discover as having a definite significance— an essence, its "inflections," its essential characteristics, the compresent "halo," and so forth—has also a "backward reference" to a more original "significant formation." Each "significant formation" *(Sinngebilde)* has its own essential "history of significance" *(Sinnesgeschichte)*, which describes the "genesis" of that mental product. It is the "history" of the "formation" (or "constitution") of that mental product.[5] This curious kind of "history" is a peculiarity of the mind, whose manner of being is nothing but "work" *(Leistung)*, a constructive work, tending to the formation of "units of significance"— an "intentionality at work." All the intended or "intentional" units are thus constructed or "constituted" units, and we can address inquiry to the perfected units as to their "intentional genesis." The discovery of the "intentionality at work" makes us understand the essential and objective possibility of each single significant phenomenon, whether it refers to true being or to mere appearance.[6] Its be-

---

4. *Logik*, pp. 218 f. Cf. p. 26.
5. *Ibid.*, pp. 184 f.
6. *Ibid.*, p. 226.

ing constructed (or constituted) makes up its "subjectivity." And the last step of the phenomenological analysis is the grasping of the problem of "constitution" in its universality, which in turn leads to a new understanding of phenomenology as the fundamental doctrine of "transcendental subjectivity," the ultimate goal of all possible knowledge, the *sapientia universalis.*[7] Through it is revealed the "constitutive work" of consciousness that determines the "ontic sense" of the world, "consciousness" being understood not as a given "thing" among all other things of the given world, not as the actual thinking of human (or human-like) beings, but as the "intentionality at work" that constitutes any possible thing as a "significant unit," including the significant unit "world" itself. It is an immense and unavoidable task to reveal this working life in its totality, to make everything that "is" intelligible, ultimately out of its constitutive origins.[8] It is this immense task that Husserl sets to his "transcendental phenomenology."

However vague this general outline of Husserl's philosophy might be, it shows, I think, that from the very outset the problem of history has a definite, if not the most important, place in Husserl's mind. The intervention of Dilthey[9] gave a special accentuation to that problem. The essay "Philosophy as a Rigorous Science," which we mentioned at the beginning of this paper, is partly devoted to the praise as well as to the criticism of Dilthey and his history of human thought.[10] It is quite obvious, however, that Husserl in criticizing the attitude of historicism puts it on the same level with psychologism. In fact, the former is but an extension and amplification of the latter. Now, Husserl's radical criticism of psychologism implies anything but a simple opposition between never-changing "abstract" principles and ever-changing "empirical" things. The fact that Husserl's phenomenological descriptions in the *Logical Investigations* were immediately interpreted as psychological descriptions (of a more subtle nature — as was readily conceded — than those which

---

7. *Ibid.*, p. 4. Cf. Descartes, *Regulae ad directionem ingenii*, Reg. I.
8. *Logik*, p. 216.
9. Cf. the correspondence between Husserl and Dilthey published by G. Misch, *Lebensphilosophie und Phänomenologie* (Leipzig and Berlin, 1930).
10. Cf. especially the note on p. 326.

usually are laid down in psychological textbooks) shows not merely that a great many readers of Husserl were not able to understand his thought, but that there is a definite affinity between psychological and phenomenological research. Husserl himself always pointed out that Hume was the first to see the problem of a transcendental phenomenology, although he misunderstood its true character and therefore failed entirely to solve it. The psychology of mental phenomena must not necessarily differ from their phenomenological analysis as far as the actual description, the wording, is concerned.[11] The real difference can only be found in the fundamentally different attitude of the thinker toward his objects: on the one hand, the psychologist considers them in a "mundane apperception," taking them as existing elements or parts or qualities of the existing world; on the other hand, the phenomenologist deprives these same objects of their "index of existence," performs the "phenomenological reduction" (the "bracketing") and faces them as "pure" phenomena. Thus, the psychological and phenomenological description of logical operations may be identical, although their real significance differs profoundly. More exactly, we have to distinguish between psychological phenomenology and transcendental phenomenology. The first considers the mind as a "natural" object; the second, the mind as the "transcendental subjectivity." In doing so, however, transcendental phenomenology, as the universal theory of "constitution," is primarily concerned with the problems of origin, the problem of true beginnings. It is worth noting that Husserl, in the passage quoted above, uses as an image the (Empedoclean) term ῥιζώματα πάντων, "roots" of all things, rather than the traditional ἀρχή. A "root" is something out of which things grow until they reach their perfect shape. The ἀρχή of a thing—at least in the traditional "classical" sense of the term—is more directly related to that perfect shape, and somehow indirectly to the actual beginning of the growth. The "radical" aspect of phenomenology is more important to Husserl than its perfection. This is the attitude of a true historian. But it is obvious

---

11. Cf. especially *Logik*, p. 224.

that the phenomenological approach to the true beginnings requires a quite special kind of history. Its name is "intentional
history."

II

In order to clarify Husserl's notion of "intentional history,"
it may be useful to look at the development and the general
background of Husserl's philosophy from a different angle.
Husserl's earliest philosophic problem was the "logic" of symbolic mathematics.[12] The paramount importance of this problem
can be easily grasped, if we think of the role that symbolic
mathematics has played in the development of modern science
since the end of the sixteenth century. Husserl's logical researches
amount in fact to a reproduction and precise understanding of
the "formalization" which took place in mathematics (and
philosophy) ever since Vieta and Descartes paved the way for
modern science. Husserl himself is, of course, well aware of that
historical development. He realizes that the discovery of a formal symbolism by Vieta[13] in his establishment of algebra (*ars
analytice, logistice speciosa*) is at the basis of modern
mathematics as well as modern science. He ascribes to Leibniz
the conception of a universal and symbolic science (*mathesis
universalis, ars combinatoria*) which is prior to any "material"
mathematical discipline and any "material" logic.[14] He does not
seem to appreciate, in this connection, the importance of Stevin's
algebraic work and, strangely enough, the Cartesian idea of a
mathesis universalis, based at least partly upon Stevin and
leading directly to the corresponding, if modified, Leibnizian
concept.[15] He recognizes the close connection between
mathematical "idealization" and the idea of an "exact" nature,
first conceived in the physics of Galileo. He stresses the fundamental importance of the Cartesian *cogito*, the correct

---

12. *Philosophie der Arithmetik* (1891). Cf. *Logik*, p. 76.
13. *Logik*, p. 70.
14. *Ibid.*, pp. 70 f. Cf. *Log. Unt.*, I. pp. 219 ff.
15. See Section IV, herein.

understanding of which leads, in his opinion, to his own "transcendental phenomenology." In all that he is the great interpreter of modern thought — he reveals its hidden implications and presuppositions, he follows and judges its essential tendencies. The contingent sequence of mathematical, scientific, or philosophical theories does not concern him: he is not a historian of accidents. But in descending to the "roots of things" he cannot help meeting "history" as one of the basic tendencies of the modern period.

We should not overlook the fact that the development of modern science is closely followed by the development of "historical consciousness." The "new science" of nature has its complement in the *scienza nuova* of history (Vico).[16] Modern history is neither a chronicle of events nor an edifying or moralizing or glorifying report of memorable deeds in the past, but the discovery and the description of man as a specifically historic being, subject to a "development" which transcends any individual life or even the life of peoples or nations. Modern history is not only — as ancient history is — an interpretation and dramatic exposition of "facts," but also an interpretation of the historic "movement" as such. It is, in this respect, the twin brother of mathematical physics. They are both the dominant powers governing our actual life, setting out the horizon of our thinking and determining the scope of our practice. The historicism of recent decades is but an extreme consequence of that general historic trend. We have already characterized historicism as an extension and amplification of psychologism. On the other hand, psychologism, as developed by the English empiricists of the seventeenth and eighteenth centuries, is, in fact, the first attempt to combine the new mathematical and physical sciences (in either their Cartesian or Newtonian aspects) with a "historical" outlook: Locke and Hume try to set forth the "natural history" (Hume) of our concepts upon which our science, our morals, and our beliefs are founded. This holds for the empirical schools of the nineteenth century as well. It is par-

---

16. For the role of history in the seventeenth-century, v. L. Strauss, *The Political Philosophy of Hobbes, Its Base and Its Genesis* (Oxford, 1936), especially chapter vi.

ticularly true of John Stuart Mill, who found, as he writes, a "considerable approximation" to what he wanted[17] in William Whewell's *History of the Inductive Sciences*.[18] The history of science appears as a kind of prolegomenon to the system of logic, which in turn is considered mainly as an exposition of the methodical and conceptual foundations of science. It is not merely an accident that both J. S. Mill and Spencer wrote autobiographies (not to forget the short autobiography of Hume), nor that Hume is the author of *The History of England*. As to the prolific historical study in all fields of human activity, which makes up most of the scholarly work during the nineteenth century, it is intended, as it were, to fill the gap between the ever more "formalized" scientific approach to the surrounding world and our daily life, entangled, as it is, in a maze of immediate "practical" problems, difficulties, ambitions, and passions. History, in the usual sense of the term, is not a matter-of-course attitude. The origin of history is in itself a nonhistorical problem. Whatever historical research might be required to solve it, it leads ultimately to a kind of inquiry which is beyond the scope of a historian, whose purpose is to give the "story" of a given "fact." It may, indeed, lead back to the problem of inquiry, the problem of ἱστορία as such,[19] that is, to the very problem underlying Husserl's concept of an "intentional history."

To inquire into an object means, according to Husserl, first to "bracket" its "objectivity" and then to seek for its "constitutive origins," to reproduce its "intentional genesis." Any object, as a "significant" or "intentional" unit, contains the "sedimented history" of its "constitution."[20] That "history," of course, did not take place within "natural time." Yet it can be understood as a "history" because the intentional genesis belongs to the "life of consciousness," and consciousness itself is primarily constituted as an "absolute stream" determined by the "internal temporality." "Internal temporality" is thus the universal eidetic "form" of

---

17. See his *Autobiography*, ed. J. J. Coss (New York, 1924), p. 145.
18. Cf. the title of his later book: *Philosophy of the Inductive Sciences, Founded upon their History*.
19. Cf. Plato, *Phaedo*, 96a ff.
20. *Logik*, p. 217.

the intentional genesis.[21] In any inner experience of an intentional object, that object is given originally in the mode of immediate "presence"; this immediate "presentation" is followed, of necessity, by a "retention" of the object, in which the object appears in the mode of "just-having-been-experienced"; through all the successive modes of retentional consciousness — that is to say, through a continuous "modification"— the object is constituted as persisting, as one and the same (identical, "invariant") object. But just as there is a "limit" which the continuous modification of the retentional consciousness approaches and beyond which the "prominence" of the object flows away into the general substratum of consciousness,[22] there is the "past history" of the original "presentation" of the object, which is the proper domain of transcendental phenomenology. It is here that the "evidence" experienced in the immediate presentation assumes the character of a transcendental problem of constitution. It is here that the intrinsic "possibility" of the identity of an object is revealed out of its categorial constituents, that the "intentional genesis" leads back to the "constitutive origins," that the "sedimented history" is reactivated into the "intentional history." Moreover, such a transcendental inquiry into an object may reveal the essential necessity of its being subjected to a history in the usual sense of the term. In other words, it may reveal the essential necessity of a historical development within natural time.

This is the case if the object in question is in itself an "ideal formation" like all mathematical and scientific objects. Any science, in the precise sense of the term, has of necessity its own history. It is founded upon the "intentional history" of its ideal objects. The greatest examples to which Husserl himself referred are Euclidean geometry and Galileo's physics.[23] They are explicitly dealt with in two papers worked out in 1935 and 1936[24] and conceived as parts of a comprehensive work on

---

21. *Ibid.*, p. 279.
22. *Ibid.*, p. 280.
23. *Ibid.*, pp. 215, 257.
24. "Die Krisis der europäischen Wissenschaften und die transcendentale Phänomenologie, Eine Einleitung in die phänomenologische Philosophie," *Philosophia*, vol. I, 1936; "Die Frage nach dem Ursprung der Geometrie als intentional-historisches Problem," published by E. Fink in *Revue internationale de Philosophie*, i, 2.

phenomenological philosophy to which Husserl devoted his last years.[25] The problem which Husserl faced in those papers is precisely the relation between intentional history and actual history. Here again he takes up a task that psychologism could not solve with its own premises but had attacked in its own way. In doing so, Husserl actually confronted the two greatest powers of modern life, mathematical physics and history, and pushed through to their common "root."

III

The article about the "Origin of Geometry" is but a fragment the importance of which lies in the fact that the concepts of history and of tradition, especially that of the tradition of science, are subjected therein to a careful, if incomplete, analysis. An application of this analysis is given in the "Crisis of the European Sciences and Transcendental Phenomenology." We shall begin with the "Origin of Geometry," and try to connect its main problem with Husserl's more fundamental "transcendental" considerations.

We have already seen that any significant formation is constituted as an "invariant" within the absolute stream of consciousness. As an invariant, as identically the same, it seems to transcend any possible time. Its "eternity," however, is but a mode of "eternal" time: its identity is an intentional product of the transcendental subjectivity which is "at work" through all the categorical determinations that constitute a significant unit. This nexus of significance between the "subjectivity at work" and its intentional products (*Leistungsgebilde*) is thus the real problem of historicity taken in its universal and transcendental meaning. That is to say, the problem of historicity is ultimately the problem of philosophy itself.[26] The "intentionality at work" implies historicity (as "the historical *a priori*") which makes intelligible not only the eternity or supertemporality of the ideal significant formations but the possibility of actual history within

---

25. Cf. the introduction by E. Fink, *loc. cit.*, p. 203.
26. *Loc. cit.*, p. 219.

natural time as well,[27] at least of the historical development and tradition of a science. The "discovery" of geometry, for instance, as a historical event, is dependent upon a world of "things," understood and dealt with according to their "thingness." But thingness as a significant unit bears essential features, quite independently of any scientific approach to them. "Things" have "bodies," have color, weight, hardness or softness, are smooth or rough, have a shape and a size, can be measured, can be in motion or at rest, and so on. These are not merely so-called "empirical data," but characterize the intuitable "essence" of a "thing" as such. Some of those essential features are apt, by an intrinsic necessity of their own, to be made prominent, for instance their shape or their measurability. This prominence is utilized for "practical" purposes, and the practical handling of things may lead to a more or less satisfactory technique. Here again there is the essential possibility of discovering "in" them a set of somehow privileged "shapes" or "figures" which can be more perfectly measured and brought into relation to each other. The actualization of that possibility rests upon the actual handling of such "material"; and finally the "discovery" of geometry as a "science"— however great the change of attitude, the shifting from practical to theoretical purposes might be — is still dependent upon familiarity with that perfected technique.

The actual way leading to the discovery of geometry may have been entirely different from this one, to which Husserl alludes.[28] It is quite possible, even probable, that geometry as a science came into being as a result of arithmetical and musical preoccupations. But even so, that discovery presupposes a characteristically articulated world, presupposes the acquaintance with a definitely shaped and featured "material," presupposes, in short, the experience of "things."

But the discovery of the science of geometry presupposes *also*, on the part of the "first geometer," an "anticipation" *(Vorhabe)* of what comes into being through his "accomplishment" *(gelingende Ausführung)*.[29] These notions of "anticipation" and

---

27. *Ibid.*, p. 225.
28. Cf. pp. 223 f.
29. P. 208.

"accomplishment" are most important for the understanding of Husserl's thought. They provide us with the link between "intentional history" and actual history. They account for the "evidence" of all the "significant formations" belonging to a science such as geometry. For "accomplishment or what is anticipated means evidence to the active subject: herein the product shows itself originally as itself."[30] But since the product, in the case of geometry, is an ideal product, "anticipation" and the corresponding "accomplishment," as "acts" of the subject (the "first geometer"), are founded upon the "work" of transcendental subjectivity: the ideal formations of geometry are products of the "intentionality at work." "Anticipation" and "accomplishment" *translate* into terms of "reality" what actually takes place within the realm of "transcendental subjectivity." On the other hand — and this is the important point — the constitution of those ideal "intentional units" presupposes, of necessity, the whole complex of experiences leading to the situation in which geometry as a science is capable of being "anticipated" *and* "intended."[31] In other words, *"science, especially geometry, as a subjective intentional product, had to have some definite historical beginning,"*[32] i.e., a beginning within the course of actual history. At this definite moment the "original foundation" *(Urstiftung)* of geometry occurred.

Needless to say, this analysis does not refer to any known or even knowable historical event. It only shows the essential connection between geometry as a supertemporal product of the mind and its "creation" in actual history. At this starting-point geometry is not yet capable of being handed on: it has not yet attained the stage of "ideal objectivity," as a condition of its becoming the common property of many individuals. At least three steps are required in order to reach this stage. To begin with, the original evidence, experienced during the first actual production, passes over into a "retentional" consciousness and finally fades away into forgetfulness. But it does not disappear completely: it can be awakened, and the "active" remembrance of the original production of any ideal significant formation car-

30. P. 209.
31. Cf. *Logik*, p. 278.
32. "Geometrie," *loc. cit.*, p. 208.

ries with it the evident experience of the sameness of that formation, carries furthermore the insight into its unlimited reproducibility. This experience does not, however, transcend the personal sphere of the subject. The second necessary — and decisive — step is the embodiment of that experience in words, which makes it communicable to other subjects: these others are thereby enabled to reproduce the same evident experience out of their own mental activity. The "ideal significant unit" acquires its peculiar manner of existence only through speech and in speech. A last step remains to be taken in order to secure the *lasting* existence of the "ideal objects," to establish their perfect "objectivity." It is the translation of the spoken word into the written word. At this stage the real history of a science may begin. It is, of necessity, not only the history of "progress," of the accumulation of knowledge, but also a history of failure. The means which secure the objectivity of a science at the same time endanger its original integrity. No science, in its actual progress, can escape the "seduction" emanating from the spoken and written word. For the signifying function of a word has, by its very nature, the tendency to lose its revealing character. The more we become accustomed to words, the less we perceive their original and precise "significance": a kind of superficial and "passive" understanding is the necessary result of the increasing familiarity with spoken and written words. The original mental activity, the production of significance, embodied in sounds and signs, is not reproduced in the course of actual communication. Yet it is there, in every word, somehow "forgotten" but still at the bottom of our speaking and our understanding, however vague the meaning conveyed by our speech might be. The original "evidence" has faded away but has not disappeared completely. It need not be "awakened" even; it actually underlies our mutual understanding in a "sedimented" form. "Sedimentation is always somehow forgetfulness."[33] And this kind of forgetfulness accompanies, of necessity, the development and growth of a science.

To be sure, the original evidence can be "reactivated," and actually is at definite times, in order to restore the full

---

33. P. 212.

significance of all the previous steps leading to a given stage within the development of a science. This interlacement of original production and "sedimentation" of significance constitutes the true character of history.[34] From that point of view there is only *one* legitimate form of history: the history of human thought. And the main problem of any historical research is precisely the disentanglement of all these strata of "sedimentation," with the ultimate goal of reactivating the "original foundations," i.e., of descending to the true beginnings, to the "roots," of any science and, consequently, of all prescientific conceptions of mankind as well.[35] Moreover, a history of this kind is the only legitimate form of epistemology. The generally accepted opposition between epistemology and history, between epistemological and historical origin, is untrue. More exactly, the problem of history cannot be restricted to the finding out of "facts" and of their connection.[36] They embrace all stages of the "intentional history." History, in this understanding, cannot be separated from philosophy.

Reactivation of the "sedimented history" may become the most imperative need in a given situation. The "sedimentation of significance" can reach such a degree that a particular science, and science in general, appear almost devoid of "significance." This has been becoming increasingly the state of affairs in recent centuries and is the case now.[37] Husserl deals explicitly with this unique situation in his "Crisis of the European Sciences." We shall confine our considerations of this matter to the special problem of mathematical symbolism as the main instrument *and* the real basis of mathematical physics.

IV

Husserl's philosophy, as it appears in its latest phase, is an admirable attempt to restore the integrity of knowledge, of ἐπιστήμη, threatened by the all-pervading tendency of "sedimentation." His analysis of the meaning of "tradition" and "historical

34. P. 220.
35. Pp. 212, 218 f.
36. Pp. 220 f.
37. P. 217.

development" is directly motivated by this purpose. The increase of "sedimentation" follows closely the establishment of the new science of nature, as conceived by Galileo and Descartes. Or rather, the new science itself, with all its amazing accomplishments and far-reaching potentialities, is basically the product of an accumulated sedimentation, the reactivation of which is usually not conceived as a possible or even desirable task. As Husserl puts it: "Galileo, the discoverer . . . of physics and of the corresponding kind of nature, is both a revealing and a concealing genius."[38] In analyzing the foundations of Galileo's physics, Husserl does not intend to give a detailed historical account. Galileo's name is, in this connection, somewhat of a collective noun, covering a vast and complex historical situation.[39] On the other hand, this analysis is intended to shed light on the origin of modern consciousness in its universal aspect.[40] The problem of the origin of mathematical physics is the crucial problem of modern history and modern thought.

We shall not follow Husserl's pattern here, but try to give a general outline of that actual historical development, referring, in due course, to Husserl's corresponding statements. It should be emphasized that Husserl's "intentional-historical" analysis of the origin of mathematical physics, although not based upon actual historical research, is on the whole an amazing piece of historical "empathy."

The establishment of modern physics is founded upon a radical reinterpretation of ancient mathematics,[41] handed on through the centuries and acquiring a new dignity in the middle of the sixteenth century. The *Elements* of Euclid are subjected to careful studies, are commented upon and continuously re-edited and reprinted. The "Euclidean spirit" spreads rapidly. Archimedes and Apollonius, newly rediscovered, are studied but are understood by relatively few. On the other hand, the discovery of manuscripts of Diophantus helps to transform the Arabic art of algebra — a dark art, comparable to alchemy — into a science accepted as a supplement to the traditional

---

38. "Krisis," p. 128.
39. Cf. p. 133.
40. P. 132.
41. Cf. p. 95.

quadrivium of the mathematical disciplines. The publication
and translation of Proclus' commentary on the first book of
Euclid allows a fusion of the traditional theory of ratios and
proportions with the "algebraic" *art* of equations. The importance of this book by Proclus cannot be overestimated. The
algebra (leading back, at least partly, to a Greek tradition
represented by Diophantus and Anatolius) and especially the
Arithmetic of Diophantus are understood as an immediate
application of the theory of ratios and proportions. Moreover,
the (Eudoxean) "general" theory of proportions, as laid down
in the fifth book of Euclid, seems to indicate that the "vulgar"
algebra as well as the *Arithmetic* of Diophantus is but a rem-
nant of a more general theory of equations, of a *true* and more
general algebra. It is Vieta who works out the logical and
mathematical consequences of this insight and becomes thus the
"inventor" of modern mathematics. Let us consider briefly the
way in which he proceeds.

The method of Diophantus consists in setting up an indeterminate equation which is immediately converted into a determinate one by the arbitrary assumption of a numerical value.
This equation has a purely numerical character: apart from the
unknown quantity, the "given" quantities as well as the coefficients of the unknown are definite numbers. Having solved an
equation by methods which are often very ingenious, Diophantus
refers in not a few cases to the easily performed checking of the
result in these terms: καὶ ἡ ἀπόδειξις φανερά (and the
demonstration [the "proof"] is obvious). Now, a "demonstration"
in Greek mathematics means the "synthesis" which is the reverse
of the preceding "analysis." Therefore Vieta calls the Diophantean solution an "analytical" process, referring himself to the
traditional definition of analysis as the "way from the unknown
taken as a known, through the consequences, down to something
which is known."[42] This Greek definition applies, however, to
the geometrical analysis, which in its procedure does not make
use of any definite magnitudes, comparable to the definite
numerical values of a Diophantean equation. Assuming that the
"general" method behind the "Diophantean analysis" must be

---

42. Pappus, ed. Hultsch, II 634. Cf. the scholium to Euclid xiii, prop. 1-5.

applicable to the numerical *as well as to the geometrical procedure*, Vieta postulates a reckoning (*logistice*, λογιστική) using not number but merely "species" (taking over the Diophantean term "species," εἶδος, applied by Diophantus to the various powers of the unknown). Thus he opposes a "restored" and "pure" algebra, the *logistice speciosa*, to the commonly used Diophantean *logistice numerosa*.[43] At the same time, this pure algebra represents, in his mind, the general theory of proportions. Described by Proclus as the "highest" mathematical discipline, the general theory of proportions in the form of Vieta's pure algebra becomes from now on the fundamental discipline not only of mathematics but of the system of human knowledge in general.[44] The translator of Proclus into Latin, Barocius, in order to designate this highest mathematical discipline, uses the term *mathesis universalis*, referring to it on the margin as *scientia divina*. It is from this source that Descartes,[45] and the entire seventeenth century, have derived the term and the conception of a "universal science" which includes all possible sciences of man.

This universal science bears from the outset a *symbolic* character.[46] In creating his *ars analytice*, Vieta introduced for the first time, fully conscious of what he was doing, the notion of a mathematical *symbol* and the rules governing symbolic operations: he was the creator of the mathematical *formula*.[47] In doing this, he preserved, however, the original "ideal" concept of number, developed by the Greeks out of the immediate experience of "things" and their prescientific articulation. In Vieta's notion of "species" the original understanding of number is retained, as it is, of course, in the *Arithmetic* of Diophantus. But his immediate successors, Ghetaldi, Harriot, Oughtred, and Wallis (partly under the influence of Stevin and, as far as Wallis is concerned, of Descartes' *Geometry*), have already lost the original intuition. The technique of operating with symbols replaces the science of numbers.[48] Descartes, for his part, aiming at the all-comprehensive *mathesis universalis*, and follow-

43. Cf. "Krisis," p. 97.
44. Cf. pp. 120 ff.
45. Cf. *Regulae*, Reg. iv.
46. Cf. "Krisis," pp. 119, 123.
47. Cf. pp. 115 f., 118, 123.
48. Cf. p. 123.

ing the algebraic doctrine of Stevin, transforms the traditional understanding of Euclidean geometry into a symbolic one, which transformation is at the basis of his analytic geometry.[49] His mathematical significance lies in the fact that he subjects the traditional geometry to the same kind of symbolic "formalization" to which Vieta subjected the Diophantean arithmetic.

This establishment of a fundamental analytical discipline, planned in advance by Vieta as well as by Descartes for the sake of founding a "true" astronomy and a "true" physics, inaugurates the development of a symbolic science of nature, commonly known as mathematical physics.[50] As to Galileo, he has not yet at his disposal the powerful instrument of symbolic formulae. His physics is conceived as an application of Euclid's (and Archimedes') geometry,[51] especially of the Euclidean theory of proportions. But he is already under the spell of that general symbolic tendency: he anticipates mathematical physics in his concept of an "exact" nature as a great book written in mathematical characters. The implications of this concept of an "exact" nature are unfolded in this work and in the work of the following generations. But the "sedimented significance" upon which this work and the concept of an exact nature itself rest, have hardly been "stirred up," or even touched, ever since Galileo, Kepler, and Descartes laid the foundations of mathematical physics.[52] The "intentional history," as suggested by Husserl, may accomplish this task: it may "reactivate" the "sedimented" "evidences," may bring to light the forgotten origins of our science. A history of science which fails to tackle this task does not live up to its own purpose, however valuable and indispensable it otherwise might be.

The problem of the origin of modern science thus presents a threefold aspect. There is first the "anticipation" of an exact nature, implying the possibility of reducing *all* appearances to geometrical entities. Not only the "prominent" features men-

---

49. The analytic geometry itself is, as an algebraic geometry, a "formalization" of the methods used by Apollonius. This holds for the analytic geometry of Fermat as well. Both, however, considered the analytic geometry as an expansion, a "generalization," of the procedure of Apollonius, not as a "new" discovery.
50. Cf. "Krisis," p. 97.
51. Cf. pp. 98 ff., 102 ff., 113.
52. Cf. p. 117.

tioned above (i.e., some of the so-called primary qualities), with their essentially geometrical characteristics, but also the so-called secondary qualities, such as color, sound, odor, warmth (i.e., the "specific" sensory qualities)[53] as well as change and motion, are understood to be convertible either into geometrical magnitudes or at least into something that can be treated geometrically, having definite ratios and proportions. This kind of approach to all possible qualities of things can be traced back to the nominalistic school of the fourteenth century, especially to Nicolaus Oresmus (Nicole Oresme), whose work *De uniformitate et difformitate intensionum*[54] has profoundly influenced all following thinkers up to Galileo, Beeckman, and Descartes.[55] The "sedimentation" involved in this "Euclidean" approach to the world consists in the matter-of-course attitude toward geometrical evidence.[56] Accordingly, our *first* task is the intentional-historical reactivation of the origin of geometry.

In trying to fulfill the anticipated conversion of *all* "natural" appearances into geometrical entities, in trying to geometrize nature, the physicist faces immediately the problem of finding the adequate means for such an undertaking. This problem is solved through what can be called the method of *symbolic abstraction*, which is quite different from the ancient ἀφαίρεσις. It is the method used consciously by Vieta in his establishment of a "general" algebra and by Descartes in his early attempt to set up the *mathesis universalis*.[57] It amounts to a symbolic understanding of magnitudes *and* numbers, the result of which is an algebraic interpretation of geometry. The roots of this development can be found in the adoption of the Arabic system of numeration which leads to a kind of indirect understanding of numbers and ultimately to the substitution of the ideal numerical entities, as intended in all Greek arithmetic, by their symbolic expressions. That is to say, a "sedimented" understand-

53. Cf. pp. 104, 108.
54. The same work is also known under the significant titles: "De figuracione potentiarum et mensurarum difformitatum," and "De configuracionibus qualitatum."
55. Cf. P. Duhem, *Études sur Léonard de Vinci*, vol. iii (1913); and also the correspondence between Beeckman and Descartes in *Oeuvres de Descartes* (ed. Adam Tannery), vol. x, and Descartes' *Regulae*, Reg. xii.
56. Cf. "Krisis," p. 111.
57. Cf. Descartes, *Regulae*, Reg. xiv.

ing of numbers is superposed upon the first stratum of
"sedimented" geometrical "evidences." This complicated network
of sedimented significances underlies the "arithmetical"
understanding of geometry.[58] The second task involved in the
reactivation of the origin of mathematical physics is, therefore,
a reactivation of the process of symbolic abstraction and, by implication, the rediscovery of the original arithmetical evidences.

Upon those combined "sediments" reposes finally our actual
interpretation of the world, as expressed not only in our science
but also in our daily life.[59] In fact, the "scientific" attitude
permeates all our thoughts and habits, no matter how
uninformed or misinformed about scientific topics we may be.
We take for granted that there is a "true world" as revealed
through the combined efforts of the scientists, whatever doubts
the scientists themselves may have on the subject. This idea of
a true, mathematically shaped world behind the "sensible"
world, as a complex of mere appearances, determines also the
scope of modern philosophy. We take the appearances of things
as a kind of disguise concealing their true mathematical nature.
But we have "forgotten" that this nature, "anticipated" by the
founders of modern science, was to be *constructed*[60] by means
of ingenious methods, that the original *hypothesis* of an "exact"
nature had to prove true, without ever being able to lose its
character as a hypothesis.[61] The "anticipation" of an exact nature
is the anticipation of its history. Its history is the development
of the method of symbolic abstraction. It takes the form of an
art, consisting in the continuously perfected technique of
operating with symbols.[62] The "exact" nature is not something
that is concealed behind the appearances, but rather a symbolic
disguise concealing the original "evidence" and the original
experience of things.[63] Hence a *third* task arising from the
attempt to reactivate the "sedimented history" of the "exact"
nature: it is the rediscovery of the prescientific world and its
true origins.[64]

---

58. Cf. "Krisis," p. 119.
59. Cf. p. 124.
60. Cf. p. 107.
61. Cf. pp. 113, 114, 115, 116 f.
62. Cf. pp. 115, 121.
63. Cf. p. 126.
64. Cf. pp. 124 ff., 132.

6 ■ The Copernican Revolution

This an historical lecture. And that means that it will hardly be convincing and the best it can do is to raise in you some questions and to make you try to answer these questions and perhaps to read some books. And in this sense, it may be useful; otherwise, it is not.

Copernicus' book, *On the Revolutions of the Celestial Spheres*, appeared in 1543. That was the year he died. He had no way of supervising the publishing. When the book first appeared, and even in later editions, the text was full of misprints. Hardly a number is correct. Now the main significance of the book is, as you know, that it tells that the earth, our earth, is one of the planets moving around the sun and, in addition, rotates daily on its own axis. Furthermore, as you all know, I am sure, there is a third motion, and we'll talk about that a little later. This theory — let me use this modern word — this theory was in itself nothing new, and Copernicus insisted on its not be-

---

For many years Jacob Klein gave a yearly talk on Copernicus. He spoke from notes without a written text. The following text is pieced together from transcriptions and tapes of three of these talks. Leo Raditsa, when editing the text for the *St. John's Review*, made minor changes throughout and bracketed them only in instances where they were important enough to need notice. In several instances he omitted sentences, for the most part, asides to the audience. Winfree Smith edited the first section (until the asterisks). For the sake of clarity he slightly expanded the sections accompanying the three diagrams.

ing new. A number of people in antiquity and later on, especially in the fourteenth and fifteenth centuries, had envisioned the possibility of a daily rotation of the earth, in antiquity Heracleides of Pontus, in the fourteenth century Nicolaus Oresmus and in the fifteenth century Nicolaus of Cusa. But, above all, Aristarchus of Samos, around 275 B.C., had a heliocentric system. We know that from Archimedes. Also there were more or less legendary Pythagoreans who thought of the revolution of the earth in an orbit around the center of the universe. And all the consequences or, rather, the necessary assumptions connected with this theory were certainly known in antiquity. The Copernican astronomical theory is in itself no revolution. It gained its revolutionary character through the interpretation it was subject to and through the immediate, far-reaching conclusions drawn from it and, I hasten to add, latent in it. By the way, you know the title of the book is *On the Revolutions of the Celestial Spheres*, and our word "revolution" [as used in reference to certain historical events] is indirectly related to this title.

Now the Ptolemaic theory and all classical ancient theories, like those of Eudoxus and Hipparchus, are based on a mathematical-physical postulate, which can be formulated as follows: All motions of celestial bodies must be deducible from, or reducible to, regular, that is, uniform motions on circles.

You probably know that in the seventeenth century a law was formulated by Newton and others, which is called the law of inertia. You know about it, I think, because you heard about it in school. This law of inertia says that a body, if nothing troubles it, continues in its motion uniformly in a straight line. When I was about 16 or 17, I thought that was perfectly self-evident. Well, it is far from being self-evident. It is not even true. One of the great difficulties in this law is the notion of a straight line. You will all remember the fourth definition of the first book of Euclid where the straight line is defined and that the definition is not quite clear.

Now the postulate I just enunciated, that the motion of celestial bodies must be deducible from or reducible to uniform motions in circles, can be called the classical law of inertia. That's how bodies behave. That's what this postulate says. It is implied in this postulate that the motion in the circle is uniform about the center of the circle. The tradition attributes this postulate, and the attribution may or may not be true, to Plato. A late commentator on Aristotle, Simplicius, quotes other commentators such as Sosigenes and Eudemus to the effect that Plato posed a certain problem out of which classical astronomy arose:

> What are the uniform and orderly movements, the assumption of which permits to save the appearances in the movements of the planets?

The phrase "save the appearances" seems very simple. It isn't so very simple. To be cautious, it is pretty certain that Simplicius understood that in an Aristotelian way. That means that, given a certain phenomenon that is not quite understandable, you have to make certain assumptions so that from these assumptions you can make the phenomenon understandable, intelligible, rational. By doing that you save the phenomenon as phenomenon. That is, if a certain planet makes strange motions in the heavens which are observed as strange and you don't quite understand what they mean, then if you introduce certain assumptions or, as the classical term is, certain hypotheses, then these hypotheses will make you understand what goes on in the motion of the body and will save the appearances. It is not certain that Plato ever formulated this problem the way it is reported, i.e., whether he meant it the way Simplicius and the entire tradition, and certainly Ptolemy, meant it.

So what we have is that the fundamental hypotheses are necessary. These are made in Ptolemy. They include, for instance, circles called deferent circles because the centers of other circles called epicycles are traveling on them, the motions of planets on the epicycles and of the epicycles' centers on the deferents being uniform. Furthermore, I am sure you remember, Ptolemy proves the total equivalence of the epicyclic and eccentric hypotheses, the eccentric hypothesis being that something moves on a circle the center of which is not the earth's center. Now this is one way in which Ptolemy deviates from the fundamental postulate. He assumes the equant. You all remember the equant, right? He assumes that a body can move on a circle while its motion is uniform about a point that is not the center of the circle. That is not what the classical postulate demands. Ptolemy is quite aware of all the difficulties his view presents. He apologizes for them. In Book IX of the *Almagest*, Chapter 2, he says:

> We are compelled by the very subject we are dealing with to use devices that go against reason, as for instance, when for the sake of convenience we carry out demonstrations on simple circles described by the movement of the planets in their spheres and supposed to lie in the plane of the ecliptic. We are also compelled to lay down some fundamental hypotheses, starting not directly from an appearance, but conceiving them after a continuous series of trial and adjustment. (This seems to refer to finding the center of the equant.) We are, moreover, compelled to assume for all the planets not one and the same kind of motion and, as to their circles, not one and the same kind of inclinations. We agree to do all that because we know that the use of those devices does not lead to any appreciable difference in the results and, consequently, does not impair in any way the solution of our problems; and also because we know that the hypotheses arrived at in a way that cannot be strictly demonstrated, once they are found to agree with the appearances, could not have been arrived at without some methodical thinking, though it is hard to describe how they are got hold of, which is not surprising since universally the fundamental principles have either no cause at all or one that by its nature can hardly be grasped; and also because we know that as far as the hypotheses of circular motion are concerned their diversity cannot be considered strange or unreasonable, since the appearances of the planets themselves are found to be different for every planet; provided that we save in qualifying in all cases the regular motion in circles and give a demonstrative account of each of the appearances according to a higher and more universal similitude in all the hypotheses.

Now let's turn to Copernicus and remind ourselves of what Copernicus does. First of all, Copernicus is much more Ptolemaic than Ptolemy. That happens very often in the history of human thought. He rejects the equant. There can be no equant. Then, in addition to the rotation of the earth and its revolution about the sun, he assigns to the earth a third motion. For he supposes that without this third motion the axis of the earth would not during a single revolution about the sun point to the same place in the sky, whereas in fact it always points to a place very near the "pole" star. The picture we would get would be like this (Figure 1). Why does Copernicus suppose that? Because he still thinks of a moving epicycle. He thinks of the equator of the earth as an epicycle with aphelion F and perihelion G. So he has to introduce a third motion, namely, such a motion of the axis that in a wonderful way describes a double cone in a little less time than it takes for the earth to complete its revolution about the sun in relation to the fixed stars.[1] Just by making the time a little less, Copernicus accounts for the great phenomenon of the precession of the equinoxes.

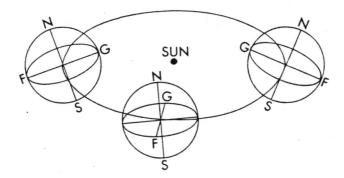

Figure 1

---

1. For the double cone see figure XXV in *Ptolemy and Copernicus, Theory of the Planets* (St. John's Press).

Now let us compare the way Copernicus explains the motion of an outer planet, for example, Mars, with Ptolemy's explanation. Figure 2 exhibits this very well. What this figure shows is the superimposition of the Copernican view on the Ptolemaic view. For Ptolemy the earth is at E. The center of the deferent is D and the center of the equant is Q. Then there is an epicycle with center M_1 that moves around the deferent. This Ptolemaic figure takes care of both the so-called heliacal anomaly and the zodiacal anomaly. But there is that villain, the center of the equant, the point Q. It is only in reference to Q that the motion of M_1 on the deferent is regular. Now, if we take Copernicus' view, then, first of all, we replace the earth at E with S, the sun; and the earth moves, right?, the earth moves. It moves in the circle E_1 E_2 S_1 S_2. In the Ptolemaic diagram M_1, the center of the epicycle, is the mean planet, while

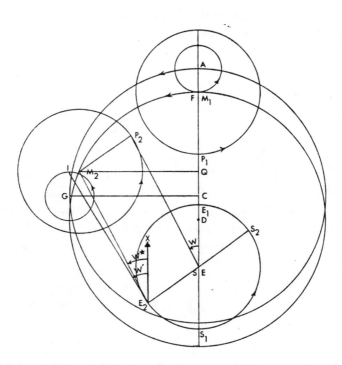

Figure 2

the planet itself is moving on the epicycle. Now Copernicus chooses as center for his deferent circle not D, and *certainly not* Q, but a point halfway between Q and D. That's point C. This is the center of Copernicus' deferent, which is a deferent because it bears an epicycle, the little circle with center A in the figure. This little circle is much smaller than it appears in the figure — this diagram doesn't reproduce the relative sizes of things but is really only the pattern in which the circles and their motions may be conceived. On this little epicycle the planet really moves. Now Copernicus might have substituted the planet for the Ptolemaic mean planet, the center of the Ptolemaic epicycle. Then he would have had a single circle for the planet's motion with center D, and if we take the positions E, P_1, and M_1 as Ptolemaic starting positions for earth, planet, and mean planet and S, E_1, and M_1 as Copernican starting positions for sun, earth, and planet, then with the Ptolemaic planet and mean planet, after a certain time, at P_2 and M_2 and with W as the angle of observed motion we would have the Copernican earth and planet at E_2 and M_2 with W^* as the angle of observed motion. It is easily proved, as you must have done, that $W^* = W$. But then the planet would have its motion uniform about the equant point Q, a thing intolerable for Copernicus. Copernicus, therefore, introduces the little epicycle with center at A.

Now, once more we assume the same Ptolemaic and Copernican starting positions. Only we suppose that Copernicus' position for the planet is on the little epicycle on which the planet is moving in a clockwise direction and with the same uniform angular velocity about A with which the center of that epicycle is moving on its deferent circle about the center C. Now, as you remember, the planet will not describe the circle which the mean planet describes in Ptolemy. For instance, the point I on the left does not coincide with the point M_2. Moreover, the diagram here has two angles, W^* and W'. W^*, which equals W, is the angle of vision, or observed motion, in Ptolemy and W' is the angle of vision in Copernicus. These two are not quite the same, so that, if Ptolemy's angle agrees with the observations, Copernicus' does not. But the difference between the angles is very, very small, much smaller than the diagram shows, so small that it couldn't really be drawn in a diagram [or detected with any instruments that Ptolemy or Copernicus had]. Now, therefore, the planet does not describe, strictly speaking, a circle, but something which is very close to a circle, very close. [The dotted curve FGL in the diagram on page 742 of *On the Revolutions of the Celestial Spheres* (Chicago, 1952).] And there is an eccentric deferent circle and an epicycle. Everything is totally Ptolemaic.

Now I have to say two things here. This diagram presupposes something very important which you all know; namely, it presupposes that the sphere of the fixed stars is at an immense distance from the system of the planets. Let's say that the earth is at E_1 in Copernicus and we on the earth look at the sky at a certain hour of night, perhaps in the direction of E_1, F. We see certain stars. Then the earth moves, let us say to the position E_2. So it changes position. We again look at the sky and locate one of the stars we saw before. It is exactly where it was before in relation to the other stars. No parallax. Why? Why? Let's formulate it this way. The stars are so far away, so terribly far away, that it doesn't make any difference where our earth on this ridiculous little orbit is. No matter where E_2 is, the distance between E_2X and E_1F, though it may be millions of miles, is as nothing compared with how far away the stars are. That's one thing.

The second thing has to do with Ptolemy's observations. You know that Ptolemy possesses the first of many kinds of observations. Certainly he himself made some observations; and these are on the whole very precise. The word "precise" is a very difficult word, by the way. They *are* very precise. And the margin of error is about ten minutes, ten minutes of arc.[2] Ptolemy and those people whom he quotes could make measurements that were that close and, by the way, they had very simple instruments. But they had great patience. They could do this good measuring because the sky over the Mediterranean is clear and wonderful. But Copernicus sat somewhere in East Prussia and

---

2. It used to be thought that this was the Ptolemaic margin of error. But it is now generally agreed among those who have really studied the question that this is not so. Ptolemy must have made some observations with the instruments he describes; but, since it is known that some of what he reports as observations are not genuine observations, it is hard to tell which are genuine and which are not. One, therefore, cannot say anything with certainty in comparing Ptolemy and Copernicus as observers. J.W.S.

Poland where the sky is awful. Copernicus never could measure and observe anything well. And all the observations he made are certainly not within the Ptolemaic margin of error. And then Copernicus has the conviction that all observations preserved through the centuries from Hipparchus and Ptolemy on to his days were good. And, therefore, they must all be accounted for. And, therefore, incredible hypotheses must be made. And he accounts for all his observations, be they right or wrong. That doesn't matter. They must be accounted for. In his way Copernicus is an incredibly great artist.

Now, the thing is that when finally Copernicus decides that the Ptolemaic account is not right, he publishes this book, *On the Revolutions of the Celestial Spheres*; by the way, he worked on it for years and years and years, and there were pupils of his that helped him to work and one of the most important ones is a man whose name I am sure you have heard. His Latin name is Rheticus, his real name George Joachim, and before Copernicus published his book Rheticus published a first report *(Narratio Prima)* on it from which we learn many things. Now, for example, this is what Rheticus says about what Copernicus is doing:

> My teacher was especially influenced by the realization that the chief cause of all the uncertainty in astronomy was that the masters of this science — no offense is intended to the divine Ptolemy, the father of astronomy — fashioned their theories and devices for correcting the motions of the heavenly bodies with too little regard for the rule which requires that the order and motions of the heavenly spheres agree in an absolute system.[3]

And Copernicus himself says:

> Former astronomers have not been able to discover or to infer the thing which is chief of all, that is, the

---

3. From the *Narratio Prima* translated by Edward Rosen in *Three Copernican Treatises*, New York 1939, 138.

form of the world and the certain congruity, or symmetry, of its parts. But they are in exactly the same
fix as someone taking from different places hands, feet,
or head, and the other limbs, very fine of themselves,
but not formed with reference to one body and having no correspondence with one another. So that such
parts make up a monster and not a man.[4]

That is, he means that if you take together all the statements
Ptolemy makes in the *Almagest* and, by the way, the tradition
on which it was made, then you do not get an orderly world,
a cosmos, but some monstrous construction.

There is a book which is called *The Hypotheses of the
Planets*. This book is attributed to Ptolemy. It is probably written by him, though some doubt is allowed. This book is to some
extent an attempt to make the world, to see the world, as one
body. But, while I am saying that, I must call to your attention
that this is not necessarily the intention of this book. One can
say only this much, that it tries to give a view of the solid body
of heavenly motion; I mean, of the heavenly motion in three
dimensions. Whether one can really connect the different
planetary motions which are given by Ptolemy, namely, those
of the Moon, Mercury, Venus, the Sun, Mars, Jupiter, and
Saturn, to make one big body with spheres that fit into each
other with solid rings or drums where the epicycles are located,
is a big question. It would certainly be a very difficult undertaking. Now that's what Rheticus criticizes, and he means that
in Copernicus it is not this way.

In Copernicus we have one work; there is unity and congruity and simplicity. For instance, as Rheticus says, all irregularities in the motion of the earth and, by the way, there
are quite a few (some that are truly irregularities and others
based on faulty observations), all irregularities are determined
by the motion on one tiny little circle. How many of you know
this? Please raise your hands. How many know? That all irregularities in the motion of the earth on its orbit are due to

---

4. From Copernicus' Preface to *On the Revolutions of the Celestial Spheres*.

the motion of a certain point on a tiny little circle. I know you know it because Mr. Winfree Smith told me that. Aha, we'll see, we'll see. Look at the diagram (Figure 3).

According to Copernicus, the earth has three regular motions, the daily rotation, the annual revolution, and the motion of the axis that makes the double cone. Of these the third motion is affected by two irregularities which can be thought of as librations of the poles, and the second, the annual revolution, is affected also by two, a change in eccentricity and a motion of the line of apsides, the line that joins aphelion and perihelion. Now look at the diagram (Figure 3). If you understand the earth as moving counterclockwise, eastward, on the circle that has G as center and make G revolve clockwise on a little circle, with center C, that does not enclose the sun, which is at D, then the eccentricity will change from maximum when G is at E to minimum when G is at F, and so on. This change constitutes, according to Rheticus, the wheel of fortune. Have you never heard of that? Surely you have heard of the wheel of fortune. That is the wheel of fortune. It determines all ir-

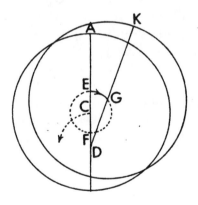

Figure 3

regularities,[5] including the motion of the apsides which it produces as the whole wheel with its center C moves regularly with
the signs, eastward, 24 seconds annually. Now let me read what
Rheticus has to say about the wheel of fortune. I am sure some
of you have heard it. But it is good to hear it again. "I shall
add a prediction." It is Rheticus who says that.

> We see that all kingdoms have had their beginnings
> when the center of the eccentric was at some special
> point on that small circle. Thus, when the eccentricity
> of the sun was at its maximum, the Roman govern-
> ment became a monarchy; as the eccentricity
> decreased Rome too declined, as though aging, and
> then fell. When the eccentricity reached the bound-
> ary and quadrant of mean value, the Mohammedan
> faith was established; another great empire came into
> being and increased very rapidly, like the change in
> the eccentricity. A hundred years hence, when the
> eccentricity will be at its minimum (by the way, this
> is written in 1540), this empire (the Mohammedan em-
> pire, the Turks) will complete its period. In our time
> it is at its pinnacle from which equally swiftly, God
> willing, it will fall with a mighty crash. (Now it is
> true that a hundred and forty years later the Turks
> were chased out of Europe.) We look forward to the
> coming of our Lord Jesus Christ when the center of
> the eccentric reaches the other boundary of mean
> value, for it was in that position at the creation of the
> world. This calculation does not differ much (not
> much, but somewhat) from the saying of Elijah, who

---

5. There is no obvious link between the irregular change in eccentricity and the irregular librations, which are crosswise to one another, of the poles of the earth.
Of these librations (which, of course, have to be reduced to regular circular motions) one gives the change in the rate of the precession of the equinoxes and the
other the change in the angle of obliquity of the ecliptic (the angle between the
plane of the earth's equator and the plane of its orbit around the sun). Copernicus
supposes (without giving sufficient reason) that the period for one complete cycle
in the change of eccentricity (i.e., one complete motion of point G in circle EGF
in figure 3) is 3434 years, the same period that he assigns (without reason) to the
change in the obliquity of the ecliptic (*Narratio Prima*, 121) and which he claims
(also without reason) is double the period of the change of rate of precession. That
is what is meant by saying that "all irregularities are determined by the motion of
one tiny little circle." J.W.S.

prophesied under divine inspiration that the world
would endure only six thousand years, during which
time nearly two revolutions are completed. Thus it
appears that this small circle is in very truth the Wheel
of Fortune, by whose turning the kingdoms of the
world have their beginnings and their vicissitudes. For
in this manner are the most significant changes in the
entire history of the world revealed, as though
inscribed upon the circle.[6]

Why did I read that to you? I read it to you to show you that
what goes on in this book, *On the Revolutions of the Celestial
Spheres,* is more than astronomy. It implies certain things which
regard the whole world and which concern us men here on our
earth. That is how Rheticus understood it from the very beginning. And that's how I think we all should always understand
anything that's presented to us as a theory.

Now let me continue with the report. The tendency to what
is unity and simplicity is especially clear in the fact that the one
orbit of the earth, and I will have to repeat it later, replaces
five Ptolemaic circles, namely, three epicycles in the outer planets
and two deferent circles in the inner planets. And this again
is determined ultimately by the little circle, the small circle, the
wheel of fortune.

*   *   *   *   *

What now does the Copernican system accomplish, simply
and strictly, in terms of a mathematical description of the
universe? It does unify the universe by means of the great circle
of the orbit of the earth. It does give a greater unity to the whole
thing because there are [in Ptolemy's conception] these whirling epicycles with their tremendous radii from which certain
inconveniences arise, namely, if you take Venus' epicycle, which
is much larger in that it is actually three quarters of the radius
of the deferent circle, and if you note Venus at the perigee and
Venus at the apogee, then it's clear that Venus ought to appear,
I think, something like sixteen times larger sometimes than at
other times — which it never does. That's the case of the moon,

---

6. *Narratio Prima,* 121–122.

too, but not very important there, because Ptolemy could have changed that also.

Then if I were to trace the path of the planet in Ptolemy, I would get an incredibly involved curve. I have a book in which anyone interested can see the path of Mars, for instance, in a period of approximately twenty years. It is a very beautiful curve with incredible loops and so on, but terribly complicated. If you trace the path of the Copernican planet, as you will remember, you will get in each case what he calls almost a circle, a quasi circle, so that although the planet itself does not move in a circle its motion is simply the result of certain circular motions. There is a certain unification and, in virtue of this, a greater simplicity.

Let us not forget that this greater simplicity is brought about at the expense of a fantastic complication with incredibly many irregularities. Also the sun, although being the center of the universe, has nothing to do with the whole thing. Each planet has its own center around which it moves and each center is at a different distance from the mean sun. And then the mean sun is at a certain distance from the big sun — and the big sun simply is and shines and does nothing else.

The question that is very much in my mind is this: Why should anyone have accepted the Copernican hypothesis? And that is a terribly difficult question to answer because the physical arguments advanced by Ptolemy are simply not negligible. Any kind of proof and any kind of evidence for the plausibility of the Copernican system was not available for hundreds of years afterward. Further, certain great and really important discoveries that were made following the publication of this book and which culminate in the discoveries of Galileo when he first looked at the sky through a telescope at no point could justify the acceptance of Copernican astronomy.

Now I must talk about these discoveries because they are essential to what I want to say. First, in the years between 1543, when the book appeared, and 1572, and then later in 1604, there were two incredible appearances in the heavens. Now such things occur often, not daily, but often. (You read about them in newspapers and magazines, although you don't pay too much attention to them.) These are called the appearances of a *nova*. Now a *nova* is a new star and that means that at a certain spot in the heavens where there was no star (not even through a telescope) suddenly a star appears — an unbelievable star, brighter than all the others. And it burns brightly for years and then declines and, after a certain time, disappears. This happened especially in 1572 and 1604.

Now of course these stars had appeared before, too, and people, since at that time they looked at the sky more carefully because there was not so much electric light from cities, being aware of the sky as sometimes we aren't, noticed this. The understanding of these phenomena was that they occurred within our own atmosphere — within, in Ptolemaic or Aristotelian terms, the sublunar sphere. Beyond this nothing could change. For if it could, such an appearance as a bright new star would indicate an incredible change up there in the divine intelligence. That could not be.

Now, when these phenomena occurred in the sixteenth century, Tycho Brahe, one of the greatest observers of all times, began immediately to calculate the possible distance away of these new bodies. He found that they could not be so close to the earth as people imagined, and his observations were impeccable.

You know there are certain difficulties the moon presents to all of us, including Ptolemy, since you can never observe it accurately because of the parallax. The position of the moon differs because of the position of the observer on earth. Now if a thing appears within the sublunar sphere, then the parallax would be very bothersome. But Brahe established by extensive travel and observation that these new bodies involved no parallax. Therefore, these bright objects could not be closer than the moon. He wrote a book about that; by the way, quite a few people did. It was a tremendous thing to find that there are changes beyond the moon.

The next thing is that a comet appeared. Now these, too, appear very often and these, too, had been understood to belong to the sublunar sphere. And Brahe again, by computations of a very ingenious kind, proved that this comet traversed the outer regions of the world. Moreover, if one observed it carefully, it was clear that it had to traverse other spheres — the spheres of Saturn, Jupiter and Mars, which at that time were supposed rigid, transparent but rigid. Let me mention that there is nothing particularly dumb or archaic about that because, even until 1905, the ether, in which all the electromagnetic motions were supposed to take place, was considered to be a rigid body — mathematically necessarily so. But certainly comets could not pierce this rigidity and, if they did, obviously these spheres could not exist. Therefore, Tycho Brahe did one very important thing, quite apart from Copernicus, in his computations and his observations. Due to his work — mostly the work of observation, by the way — he did away with the notion that celestial bodies move on spheres or by means of spheres, which made it more imperative to find out how they did move.

Now Tycho Brahe, as you know, never agreed with Copernicus. On the contrary, he thought Copernicus was dead wrong. Copernicus said that this transition could only take place if the stars are very far away. And Brahe proceeded to compute how far away they must be if they were not to show parallax. By the way, I can't guarantee the figures I write — they are only approximately correct, but the order of magnitude is right.

In the ancient view, the distance from the center of the universe, namely, the earth, to the sphere of the fixed stars was approximately 20,000 radii of the earth. Now Brahe computed that, in order for the stars not to show parallax in the motion of the earth on its orbit, the stars had to be 60,000,000 earth radii away, that is, 3,000 times farther away as a minimum requirement.

Then he argued: Look what happens. Here is the sun, according to Copernicus, at the center. Then there are, in this succession, Mercury, Venus, the earth, Mars, Jupiter and Saturn, and then the stars are very far away. That means that between the region of Saturn and the fixed stars, especially since there is no rigid sphere anymore, there is nothing. Nothing. Could God have done that? Such a waste of space. And, furthermore, which is much, much worse, if the stars are that far away and I can still see them, twinkling at this immense distance, think how big they must be. One must be bigger than the solar system — certainly bigger than the great circle. How can one imagine such a thing?

These are the two arguments of Brahe which, by the way, were absolutely reasonable. You, of course, are accustomed to this sort of thing — tremendous galaxies and so on.

How do you know, by the way?

These things are very difficult to understand and Brahe had a perfect right to put this difficulty before everyone. I suspect that Copernicus had asked himself the same question because, obviously, he was as intelligent as Brahe. I suspect that this has something to do with that strange and immensely interesting little remark which he makes in the first chapter of the first book. He says that it is possible that this world of ours, including the sphere of the fixed stars which are far away, is simply a big hole in an infinite solid universe. He simply envisages this possibility. The best example is Swiss cheese.

There might even be more holes. One of the holes is ours and there we sit and enjoy life. Now the question is (by the way, there are many questions): Why did Copernicus envisage this possibility? There is one thing about it which might have something to do with Brahe's objection. If there is this big hole extending to the sphere of the fixed stars set in the infinite solidity, then it is not quite impossible that there are many huge, fiery objects at the edge of this solid, which is also perhaps a kind of solid fire. And Brahe's objection was, since there was no solidity anymore beneath and beyond the moon, that there was an incredible expanse that could not be justified. Nevertheless, he said that Copernicus might be right.

Within Ptolemy's account of the planetary motions, we could adopt the hypothesis of the moving eccentric circle for the outer planets and the hypothesis of the epicycle for the inner planets. In that case we have the centers of the eccentric circles and the centers of the epicycles all moving with the speed of the mean sun. Then, why not identify those centers with the sun itself?[7] And so Brahe had this simple and wonderful system in which all the planets move around the sun, and the sun and moon move around the earth. Now I maintain that all appearances and phenomena from 1543 for centuries after are completely justified and made intelligible by Brahe's theory. This includes Venus, by the way, which does not appear sixteen times bigger at some times than at others. Even all the things that Galileo saw fit completely into Brahe's pattern.

---

7. Winfree Smith wrote the sentences up to this point in this paragraph to substitute for a murky passage in the transcription.

And now I must tell you what Galileo saw. In 1610 when he looked at the sky by means of a telescope — one of the most exciting moments in the history of man — he saw, first of all, that the moon's surface is like that of the earth. That is strange, although we are very used to it. (One of the craters here is now called Copernicus, but that doesn't mean much.) Secondly, he saw that the light of the stars was conspicuously different from that of the planets; thirdly, that the Milky Way is a conglomeration of stars. He saw the four moons of Jupiter and that Saturn had a strange shape which he called three-cornered. Not until a little later did it become clear that this last was not three-cornered, but a ring. After a while he saw that Venus had phases like the moon. And then finally he saw the spots on the sun, which everyone had seen before but never interpreted as belonging to the sun. They also were supposed to have belonged to the sublunar sphere. [These things do not necessarily support Copernicus' view.]

You must understand what the incredible excitement was when people looked through this rude kind of telescope and saw that. Nevertheless, simply looking through a fantastic new machine didn't vitiate anything. What went on in that machine had to be evolved into a theory. People were deeply impressed by these new phenomena, but every single one could be explained by Brahe's theory.

And now this is the important thing. Many people of the time *did* accept Brahe's theory. That is, in 1610 and after, many respectable professors of astronomy in all the universities of Europe accepted Brahe's theory. And it was the right thing to do: it was reasonable, accounted for all these appearances, and it preserved the theories and savings of the other phenomena as they were done by Ptolemy. Don't forget that Brahe's theory is, again, merely a transition.

And, yet, there were some people who said no. There were some people who said that Copernicus was right, and only Copernicus — that the earth does move and there is nothing hypothetical about it. There was no physical evidence for accepting the Copernican theory until the nineteenth century. Instruments that could show the distances of the stars and the parallax came much later, in 1837. The rotation of the earth can be shown by a certain experiment which was first performed in 1851. It had been tried before but never was conclusive.

The question is: What made some people — not too many, don't forget — claim that Copernicus was right? I spent some time in counting the number of people who accepted this theory. I cannot guarantee the accuracy of this because, if I kept searching and kept reading books and I don't know what, I would come to a greater number. I know of 25 people certainly who, in the course of 70 years, accepted the Copernican theory. I don't think that this number can be increased to more than 40 with any amount of research. So 40 people accepted that. And the interesting thing is *how* they accepted it. They accepted it as if everything depended on it, as if this were the only thing, as if the life of mankind would be different after acceptance of this. Men of the greatest importance — certainly Galileo and Kepler — accepted it. Giordano Bruno accepted it. And what I want to ask is — why?

I shall read part of the Preface to *On the Revolutions of the Celestial Spheres*, which, as you all know, was written not by Copernicus but by his pupil, Osiander, who feared certain things:

> Then, in turning to the causes of these motions or the hypotheses about them, he must conceive of a device, since he cannot in any way attain to the true causes. He must conceive of and devise such hypotheses as, being assumed, would enable the motions to be calculated correctly from the principles of geometry, for the future as well as the past. (This is what is done in Ptolemy all the time.) The present author (Copernicus) has performed these duties excellently. For these hypotheses need not be true nor even probable; if they provide a calculus consistent with the observations, that alone is sufficient. Perhaps there is some person so ignorant of geometry and optics that he regards the epicycle of Venus as probable and thinks that this is the reason why Venus sometimes follows or precedes the sun by 40° or even more. Is there anyone who is not aware that from this assumption it follows that

the diameter of the planet at perigee must appear
more than four times, and the body of the planet more
than sixteen times, as great as in the apogee — a result
contradicted by the experience of every age? In this
study there are other no less important absurdities
which I will not state here. It is quite clear that the
causes of the apparent, unequal motions are simply
unknown to this art. And if any causes are devised by
the imagination, as indeed very many are, they are
not put forward as if they were *true*, but merely to
provide a correct basis for calculations. When, from
time to time, different hypotheses are offered to explain one and the same motion (as, for instance, eccentricity and an epicycle), the astronomer will accept above all others the one which is easiest to grasp.
The philosopher will perhaps seek the semblance of
the truth. But neither of them will understand or state
any such thing as certain unless it has been divinely
revealed to him. Let us, therefore, permit these new
hypotheses to become known together with the ancient hypotheses, which are no more probable. Let
us do so especially because the new hypotheses are admirable and also simple, and bring with them a huge
treasure of skillful observations. So far as hypotheses
are concerned, let no one expect anything certain from
astronomy, which cannot furnish anything of the kind,
lest he accept as the truth ideas conceived for another
purpose, and depart from the study a greater fool than
when he entered. Farewell.[8]

I say: Why wasn't that accepted? Why, on the contrary,
should a certain man, 80 years later, say of this very good
Osiander that he is "an ignorant and arrogant ass, who pretends
to help Copernicus, but who only permits people like himself
to pick lettuce and vegetables in that book"?
Let me say that the usual understanding is that Osiander
wrote the preface in order to protect Copernicus from persecu-

---

8. From Osiander's address to the reader at the beginning of *On the Revolutions of
the Celestial Spheres*. The translation is Klein's.

tion by the Church. This seems to me a terribly simple and, I would say, not quite true statement. It is true that, from the very beginning, everybody was a little apprehensive about what the ecclesiastical authorities would say. By the way, it was not only the Catholic ones; it was also the ones in Wittenberg, especially the Protestants and Lutherans.

And immediately after publication of the book, a whole literature sprang into being (Rheticus among the first of these writers) to prove that this astronomical theorizing did not in any way contradict scripture. This literature persisted, literally, for a hundred years. Everyone participated in writing some kind of book or pamphlet or letter to show that what is stated in the scripture is not contradicted in any way by what is stated in Copernicus, that the scripture talks a certain language which is not scientific language, and that it is silly to assume that divine revelation has to be of an astronomical nature. This is perfectly true by the way and I, personally, don't think that this is the essential point in the struggle.

Further, I do not think that Osiander simply meant to protect Copernicus from the persecution of the Church. I rather think that he was, in this preface at least, quite seriously of the opinion that truth about these matters can only be revealed divinely and that we men must be satisfied with certain mathematical devices, according to the lights that God has given us. Also, it is not the job of astronomy to state the truth. I do not state this as true, but it is quite possible that Osiander felt this strongly.

And let me also say that, later on, when Galileo, who is *the* great Copernican, was indeed convicted by the Church in Rome, the charge wasn't for entertaining such hypotheses. He was convicted for stating these hypotheses as truth, and the only truth. There is no other reason.

The Church did not forbid men to try to show that the appearances in the heavens could be saved and made intelligible by the Copernican assumptions. The Church forbade men to state this as *the* truth; as a matter of fact, there was something right about that.

Why are the Church and Protestant authorities so concerned about this — concerned not immediately after 1543, by the way, but about 60 years later? This is not simple. This is very dark

at this point. Do not forget that the vulgar kind of arguments
for the salvation of the soul and such cannot be advanced, for
they simply don't hold water. It is too easy to show that Copernicus doesn't contradict scripture. It is easy to show that what
the Church teaches is affected not at all by heliocentric or other
systems. On the one hand, there is a kind of black obdurance
on the part of the ecclesiastical authorities and, on the other,
a kind of wonderful insight on the part of the "scientists." It
doesn't seem to me that this is simply the case. I think that it
can be shown that this is not true.

People insisted that the Copernican system was truth without
sufficient evidence, and the ecclesiastical authorities combated
this opinion without ever stating why. Now this is a very interesting thing, because it is in this that the Copernican revolution truly consists. The question is then: What are the reasons?
And I will give you four — four very different reasons which do
not at all, by the way, go together. I wish they would go together,
but they don't. I would even say that they contradict each
other — at least in part.

The first one is simple. I must repeat the question: Why did
people so fanatically claim that something was true, although
there was no real evidence? And, on the other hand, why did
the Church and other authorities oppose this, although it wasn't
clear why it was so terribly important that they should do so?
Now I am concerned with 25 or 40 people. Historically, and
now I must speak historically, this is the time when nothing
pleases more than that which is not accepted. Such times are
called revolutionary. This is the time when the authorities of
Aristotle and all the ancients, of Thomas, of the Pope, of kings,
become shaky. It suddenly seems wonderful to come up and say:
That which I learned from Ptolemy is all nonsense; it should
be just the other way around. And sometimes this is one of the
strongest ways to convince people. I give you a diabolic device:
in seminar, sometimes, try this. Don't pick simply a little point,
but say about the whole: That's all wrong — it's JUST THE
OTHER WAY AROUND. Shortly, everyone will agree with you,
maybe. Now this general kind of opposition is one of the reasons
that one can advance. It pervades the times and there is
something very attractive about that. Let me hasten to add that
it's a rather poor reason, not unimportant, but poor.

And in this case it *is* important — the universe is stated to be just the other way around. In Ptolemy the earth is in the middle and the sun revolves around it at a certain distance. And now Copernicus and all of his immediate and later followers say that the sun is in the middle and the earth is where the sun was. Simply a reversal. And you must not forget that this is not simply stated as a geometrical transposition and astronomical theory, but as the truth. . . .

Now [there] is something which I will call the Protagorean fascination. I refer to the man called Protagoras, whom you have met in Platonic dialogues, among other places. Now we know from tradition that Protagoras has a famous sentence which is called, in the sixty-four dollar phrase, the *homo mensura* proposition, and you have all heard about that. "Man is the measure of all things, of those that are that they are and of those that are not that they are not." Now Copernicus in the dedication to the Pope says, and I quote:

> I finally discovered through long and intensive study that if the movements of the other wandering stars were referred to the circle of movement of the earth, and if the movements were computed in accordance with the revolution of each star, not only would the phenomena they present follow from that but also the order in magnitudes of all the planets and of their orbits, and it would bind the Heavens together so closely that nothing could be transposed in any part of them without disrupting the remaining parts in the universe as a whole.

Then in the beginning of the fifth book he says, "The mobility of the earth binds together the order and magnitude of the planets' orbital circles in a wonderful harmony and sure symmetry." Rheticus, again in that first report says, I quote:

> These phenomena, the apparent motions of the planets, besides being ascribed to the planets, can be explained, as my teacher shows, by irregular motion of the globe of the earth, that is, by having the sun occupy the center of the universe while the earth

revolves, instead of the sun, on the eccentric circle
which it has pleased him to name the great circle. Indeed, there is something divine in the circumstance
that a sure understanding of celestial phenomena must
depend upon the regular and uniform motions of the
terrestial globe alone.

By the way, the expression "great circle" (the Latin is *orbis
magnus*) is used until the late seventeenth century, even Locke
uses it. About the six moving spheres of the other planets,
Rheticus says, "their common measure is the great circle which
carries the earth, just as the radius of the earth is the common
measure of the circles of the moon, the distance of the sun from
the moon, et cetera." And, by the way, he has something to say
about the expression "great circle." He says, "if emperors have
received the surname 'Great' on account of successful exploits
in war, of conquest, of peoples, surely this circle deserves to have
that august name applied to it. For almost alone it makes us
share in the laws of the celestial state, corrects all the errors of
the motions and restores to its rank this most beautiful part of
philosophy."

The orbit of the earth, then, is the great unifying factor in
the spectacle of the wandering stars. Moreover, the daily motion of the earth, its rotation around its own axis, accounts for
the daily motion of all the other stars. The higher and more
universal similitude in all the hypotheses of the planets becomes
an *identity* in Copernicus. We see the earth's motion in its orbit
projected into the heavens in the guise of the irregular motion
of the planets, especially their apparent retrogradations. The
irregular motion of the planets is the result of their own regular
motion plus *our* regular motion. The appearance of irregularity
is due to the different rates of speed of the planets and of the
earth. Our own motion, more precisely, the difference between
our motion and the other planets, projected outside of us, is visible in the heavens. We see it, as it were, in a mirror, as an image. I quote Copernicus: "When a ship floats over a tranquil
sea, all the things outside seem to the voyagers to be moving
in a movement which is the image of their own. And they think,
on the contrary, that they themselves or the things with them

are at rest." *We* determine *by our motion* the appearances in the heavens. Once we understand that, we also understand that, to quote Rheticus, "the order and the motions of the heavenly spheres agree in a most absolute system." The Protagorean proposition receives an absolute twist: applying the right measure, namely, our own motion, to things outside our orbit, we grasp their true and absolute order. The measure becomes an absolute measure.

Kepler's astronomy, as well as his physics, is under the spell of what I have been calling the Protagorean fascination. The earth is to him "the home of the contemplative creature," that's a quotation, "of the measuring creature," and occupies a position in the universe most suitable for measuring purposes. The orbit of the earth is the yardstick of the universe. Far from detracting from the dignity of man, which some people say the Copernican theory does, the new function of the earth gives man an unprecedented dignity and priority. . . .

Any cosmology is a science of the order in which and through which everything exists. This cosmology, as any cosmology, has certain metaphysical and theological implications. Now, for the first time in a long period, the sun has recovered its former position of dignity, which we observe in Plato, in the neo-Platonic tradition, and in a certain cult called the Mithras cult.

The Mithras cult is the cult of the sun-god. In the early centuries A.D. it was as popular as Christianity. At certain points in the history of Christianity it is very difficult to distinguish the part that Jesus plays from that of Mithras, the sun-god. This, by the way, is not my opinion — it is part of a long tradition that stems from the Orphic and other ancient mysteries. Macrobius, a pagan writer of early Christian times, says:

> It is not a vain supposition to believe that almost all gods, to wit, the celestial ones, refer to the sun. A divine reason supports this belief. The sun is the ruler of the universe.

Behind this is that tradition I mentioned before, which goes back unbroken to the early Greeks. You can find such statements everywhere — the sun is the ruler of the universe, the king of the universe, the father of the universe, the self-born father of the universe. Proclus, whom you know as one of the great commentators of Plato and Aristotle, wrote a hymn to the sun. And I will quote a bit of it from the translation by Thomas Taylor:

> Hear Golden Titan, King of Mental Fire, Ruler of Light — to Thee Supreme belongs the splendid key of life's prolific font. And from on high, Thou pourest harmonic streams in rich abundance into . . . [the] world. Hear, for, high raised about the ethereal plains and in the world's bright middle orb, Thou reignest. While all things by thy sovereign power are filled with mind exciting providential care. . . .

Now this tradition, and there are many more examples of the kind, was perfectly well known to Copernicus and his followers. Copernicus himself mentions in the tenth chapter of the first book that the sun is the lamp of a very beautiful temple, lantern of the world, mind of the world, mentor of the world. He quotes Hermes Trismegistus (a fantastic man who is quoted by everyone in a broad neo-Pythagorean and gnostic literature, and no one knows who he is) as having called the sun the visible God. Copernicus also, as you remember, quotes Sophocles: "The sun is that which sees everything." Now, he translated Sophocles from Greek into Latin and he knew him very well. And in Sophocles you can find many things of this sort; for instance, in Oedipus, he says:

> Sun, God of all gods, the father of everything . . .
> everyone worships the whirling disk of the sun. . . .

Rheticus, when he comes to speak of the sun in the *Narratio Prima*, says:

> The sun was called by the ancients leader, governor of nature, and king. But whether it carries on this administration as God rules the entire universe, a rule excellently described by Aristotle in *De mundo*, or whether, traversing the entire heavens so often and resting nowhere, it acts as God's administrator in nature, seems not yet altogether explained and settled.

Now let me repeat this thing of Rheticus in order to be perfectly clear. There are two ways in which the ancients seemed to see the sun, either as God ruling the universe or as the administrator of nature empowered by God. Which of the assumptions is preferable, he leaves to be determined by the geometers and philosophers who are mathematically equipped, for without mathematics this cannot be solved. In the trial and decisions of such controversies a verdict must be reached, not in accordance with plausible opinions, but with mathematical laws. The former manner of rule, that is, that God rules the universe, has been set aside, and the latter accepted, that the sun does not rule as God rules, but as an administrator empowered by God. He goes on:

> My teacher (that's Copernicus) is convinced, however, that the rejected method of the sun's rule in the realm of nature must be revived, but in such a way that the received and accepted method retains its place. For he is aware that, in human affairs, the emperor need not himself hurry from city to city in order to perform the duty imposed on him by God; and that the heart does not move to the head or feet or other parts of the body to sustain the living creature, but fulfills its function through other organs designed by God for that purpose.

He's saying, then, that if the sun moves around in the heavens a controversy might arise, since the ancients spoke of the sun as the ruler of the universe. Does it mean that the sun is God? Or does it mean that God entrusted to a divine messenger the subsidiary role of a minister who goes around the universe to see that everything is in order. That controversy has been adopted, but his teacher now says that that is all changed now because the others move around but the sun stays fixed — right in the center.

Now it seems to me (this belongs to the 30 % opinion in this lecture) that this had something to do with the fanaticism with which the Copernican theory was adopted, in the sense that a suppressed ancient theology of the sun rose to the surface. This then would be what the ecclesiastical authorities were afraid of really, because this would mean a real revival of pagan understanding. And Rheticus seems to me, in what I have quoted, to state that quite clearly.

It was certainly, you understand, not a very popular movement. It was confined to a small group of people who had an esoteric cult, who nowadays would be called *intelligentsia* — a strange word from Russia. That is a thing which has happened, and which will happen, often. It is a thing which has many possibilities if once you understand the full implications of it. I don't think you can ignore this when you look in the middle of the sixteenth century and see the whole world in a great excitement over the very foundations and meanings of religion. So I think we can call this one of the reasons why Copernicus was put forward by certain people. . . .

Now we have a curious document. And that is a book called *The City of the Sun* by Campanella. [Campanella was one of the people who championed Copernicus.] He was born in 1568 and died in 1639. He lived mostly in jail, mainly for political reasons — the attempt to overthrow the kingdom of Naples to establish a republic, and so on. He wrote a defense of Galileo in 1616, the year of his condemnation, and began writing *The City of the Sun* in 1602. It was first published in Italian in 1614, then translated into Latin and published in 1623. The book is conceived after the model of Plato's *Republic*. It is written in direct opposition to *The City of God*. And throughout the book there is a constant transposing, and upsidedowndom.

Somewhere in the book, speaking of the people in that city, he says, "they praise Ptolemy, admire Copernicus, but place Aristarchus and Philolaus before him." In fact, the cosmological basis of the book seems to be not Copernicus but Tycho Brahe. But it is not difficult to see its Copernican roots. Let me quote:

> They (the people in the city) say it is very doubtful whether the world is made from nothing, or from the ruins of other worlds, or from chaos, but they certainly think that it was made, and did not exist from eternity. Therefore, they disregard Aristotle, whom they consider a logician and not a philosopher. From analogies with other writers they can draw many arguments against the eternity of the world. The sun and the stars

they regard, so to speak, as the living representatives and signs of God, as the temples and holy living altars, and they honor but do not worship them. Beyond all other things they venerate the sun, but they consider no created thing worthy the adoration of worship. This they give to God alone, and they serve Him that they may not come into the power of a tyrant and fall into misery by undergoing punishment inflicted on them by creatures of revenge. They contemplate and know God in the image of the sun and they call it the sign of God, His face and living image, from which light, heat, life and the making of all things good and bad proceed. Therefore, they have built an altar like to the sun in shape, and the priests praise God in the sun and in the stars, as it were, His altars, and in the heaven, as it were, His temple; and they pray to good angels who are, so to speak, the intercessors living in the stars. For God long since has sent signs of the beauty in heaven and of His glory in the sun. (They reject Ptolemy's and Copernicus' eccentrics and epicycles.) They say there is but one heaven. And the planets move and rise by themselves when they approach the sun or are in conjunction with it.

Campanella seems to have been the first champion of what became known later as the natural religion. All positive religions, including Christianity, were considered by him merely political and social institutions. He saw himself as entrusted with a great mission to establish before the end of the world the religion, the laws, and the perfect republic of the golden age. In 1632 he writes to Galileo as follows: "I venture to say that if we could spend one year together in a country house great things would be accomplished. These novelties of ancient truth, the new worlds, new stars, new systems, new nations, are the beginning of a new era. May he who guides the universe make haste. As for us, let us help him on our small globe. Amen." He considered Columbus the greatest of heroes: "Spain found the new world so that all nations could be gathered under one law." *The City of the Sun* is the blueprint of the new order, of the one law, under which mankind was to live in the approaching golden and last age. The high priest personifying the new law was called Sol, which is the Latin word for sun, in the edition of 1623. And Campanella also uses the astronomical symbol ☉ for the sun to designate him. The main helpers of the priest are Pon, the abbreviation for *potentia*, power; Sin, abbreviation for *sapientia* or *scientia*, wisdom, knowledge; and Mor for *amor*, love: the natural trinity — and this is under the direct influence of Giordano Bruno.

The sun for Campanella is not God. It is an image or a symbol of divinity. God itself is the universal reason. To worship God is to follow reason, that is, to free oneself from all institutional chains, to be a "free thinker." In the letter to Galileo I just mentioned, Campanella refers to the personage who in Galileo's dialogues represents unbiased reason, as a "free mind." And, by the way, Kepler calls Copernicus that too. But Rheticus had already chosen as a model for the first report (*Narratio Prima*) this sentence of Albinus, which was attributed to Alcinous, and he quotes the sentence again in his book. And the sentence is: "Free in mind must he be who desires to have understanding." That's what Copernicans saw in Copernicus. And that's why there has been a Copernican revolution. . . . .

[There is finally] the question of the immensity of the universe, which seemed to be foremost in the minds of certain people, notably a man named Giordano Bruno. It is the idea of immensity that fascinates Bruno. Copernicus himself, as you have seen, hesitates to attribute infinity to the world. He says that "the heavens are immense and present the aspect of an infinite magnitude." Bruno blames Copernicus because he does not say whether the universe is finite or infinite. "If the first principle is the creator of the world," Bruno says, "he is an infinite one and the creator of an infinite effect. As the active power of God is infinite, so is the subject worked upon by it. . . . If he intended body and dimensions, he intended them to be infinite. . . . The intelligible species of body is infinite." The intelligible species of body is space.

Why is this so important? The finiteness of the world is a main point for the ancients and for the medievals. The Aristotelian philosophy stands or falls with the finiteness of the world. For Aristotle, there is nothing outside, not even nothing. There is a clear understanding of what πέρας means. This seems to be in contradiction with the infinite power of God. The understanding of God as an infinite being begins in the sixteenth century. One of the assumptions of our mathematical science is the infinity of God. We have forgotten that the Copernican revolution is a revolution.

May I repeat again that everything that I said cannot be convincing, can only raise certain questions and lead you to consider certain problems and read certain books. It is now ten to ten. I am perfectly willing to sit here and answer questions.

7 ■ The Problem of Freedom

I have been assigned as subject for this lecture *Men, Machines, and Slaves*. This is the first lecture in a series of lectures on the general theme "Human Freedom." I hope you will grant me the freedom not to speak of machines tonight. I shall speak of Freedom and Slavery, deeply conscious of the vastness of this theme and its immense complexity. The lecture will probably degenerate into a sermon. Grant me the freedom not to apologize for that.

The theme of Freedom has immediate political connotations. And this is as it should be. For Freedom — let me state this at the very outset — is essentially and foremost a political and social problem. It is not surprising, therefore, that right now, for example, in international politics and in the wrangling on domestic issues a great deal of talking is devoted to "Freedom." We hear accusations, protestations, claims and counterclaims on this subject. But let us not forget that all these claims and counterclaims are merely echoes of more universal conflicts. Since I am in the fortunate — or unfortunate — position of delivering the *first* lecture on the Subject of Freedom, I propose to discuss this sub-

Lecture delivered at the Aspen Institute for Humanistic Studies, 1952. First published in *The College*, Vol. XXI, No. 4 (December, 1969).

ject in its *universality*. I am not trying to brush aside the very concrete and burning questions that confront all of us today. I am trying to win the right perspective in which to see them.

When am I free? When nothing *compels* me to act in a certain manner, when nothing *compels* me to do certain things, when nothing *compels* me to think in a certain way. That is to say, we cannot consider Freedom without considering its opposite: Compulsion. Note please: all the symbolism about Freedom is about its opposite. In any account of Freedom the great symbols are chains and fetters. There is no universal and immediately transparent symbol of Freedom as such. The torch of the Statue of Liberty, the Phrygian cap, the gesture of open and uplifted arms — these all symbolize freedom at best indirectly, by way of some historic or sentimental connotations. But *chains* — that's different. They mean directly, always and under all circumstances, compulsion. Why is this so? I think, because, in the most concrete way, we are never free. We are inescapably bound to the necessities of life, we cannot escape death; we depend intrinsically on everything around us, in the present as well as in the past. We are chained by Necessity with a capital N. We are at best Prometheus-like.

In what sense then is it still possible to say that we can be free of compulsion? Let me answer tentatively: We can be free — or unfree — 1) as thinking beings, 2) as beings having a will, 3) as beings living with other beings, i.e., as social and political beings.

In what sense are we free or unfree as thinking beings? We are always immersed in our daily routine, our eyes are closed to many aspects of things, we cannot detach ourselves from our immediate tasks, worries and fears. We do not think about the world we live in, it has been thought through for us by others. *We* do not think, *others* think for us: customs, current opinions, lawgivers behind some screen, determine what we think and how we think. Moreover, passions obscure any clear vision. They are as much the masters as customs and current opinions are. The world rules tyrannically over our thinking. We are its slaves. This is, in fact, the great theme of ancient philosophy, which has never been abandoned completely in the vicissitudes of the succeeding ages. Here is the classical picture: we are prisoners in a cave; we are chained to our passions and prejudices; we listen to echoes; our speaking is babbling; if we think at all, it is in a shadowy way and about nothing but shadows. To free ourselves from the rule and the chains of the cave, we have to be led out of the cave into sunlight — an arduous task. We become free in our thinking by detaching ourselves from the familiar, the self-evident, by turning away from the easy pillows of our waking sleep. This can only be done by educating ourselves. The very idea of education is the consequence of our striving for freedom in our thinking. This idea conceived in antiquity has ever since dominated the western world. It has suffered modifications, has been made subservient to ends of a very different nature, has even been perverted completely, and yet it is still a decisive factor in our lives. At worst, we pay lip service to it. As long as lip service is felt to be necessary, the idea is still a force.

But once this freedom of our thinking is secured, a grave difficulty seems to arise: Must we not think in the right way, that is, avoid error? Must not our thinking, in which the truth of things is supposed to be revealed to us, be guided by *truth*? Is not our thinking under the authority and rule of truth? To accept its authority, one might say, is to accept a new tyrant. That is what has bothered the "free thinkers," the "free minds" of all ages. It does not seem enough to shake off the chains of the cave. No other authority can be tolerated, if we want to be really free. Free means then — free to err; or free to withhold judgement. There is no freedom in thinking but at the fork of truth and error. At any other point we are not really free in our thinking, so the argument goes. And yet the authority of truth has to be accepted. It hardly matters how we understand "truth"; compliance with some criteria of right thinking seems unavoidable. May we conclude then — that freedom in thinking is the freedom to accept this authority of truth? But this again seems to depend on an act of will. Is then this freedom based on another one? Let us examine the next point.

In what sense are we free, or unfree, as being having a will? We seldom follow our will. We yield to external impulses, we follow trends, we consider ourselves, even while acting, victims of circumstance. Necessity, the origin of which is not to be found in ourselves, seems to dictate our actions. Not merely whims guide us, not merely spontaneous and irresistible desires, but also the trepidation of our hearts, the generosity of our feelings or the cowardice of our flesh — but not the will. The will is not the undisputed master. To make the will free, i.e., to make our own will the very origin of our action or inaction, of our thinking and not thinking, amounts to winning mastery over all necessities, amounts to finding in ourselves something that nothing and nobody can challenge or suppress. This is the great teaching of the Stoics. I am free when I follow nothing but my own will. It is within my power to do so. My bodily existence can be crushed but not my free will. I might *appear* a slave but I *am not* a slave. I enjoy sovereign independence. It is within my power not to be touched by feelings of misfortune, by anger, envy or jealousy. It is within my power, my sovereign power, to be like God.

Needless to say, the freedom of the will is also one of the great themes of the Judaeo-Christian tradition. There is, of course, a profound and unbridgeable difference in the understanding of the very nature of the will in the Stoic and the Christian traditions. But what is common to both traditions (and I may add to the Epicurean also) is precisely the emphasis on the freedom of the *will*. According to the Christian tradition, the will is the only freedom that man has. Man has been created in the image of God, and the similitude is confined to the will. Man himself decides what he wills.

But here again a new sense of unfreedom emerges. This freedom of the will — for Stoics and Christians alike, in spite of their profound and unbridgeable difference — is related to the divine will. Our will is free, paradoxically enough, when it wills *what it ought to will* — in conformity with what is right and good according to the divine decree. We are free to accept or to reject the Good, but this freedom itself is mad, or corrupt, or guided by Satan, *if* we reject it. The authority of the Good determines whether the will is really free or unfree. The will is thus bound by golden chains, but golden chains are still chains. May we conclude then that freedom of the will is the freedom to accept the authority of the Good? This would be the freedom that makes us *moral* beings. And this would still be the case, if the Good loses its divine connection, and becomes the expression or summary of a "code of ethics," as we are fond of saying. And are we not then enslaved again?

Let us turn to the third point. In what sense are we free or unfree as social and political beings? There is an everlasting experience of mankind — and this is oppression. It has many guises and disguises: the rule of a despot, the reign of an "ideology," the discrimination against groups of people, the "insolence of office," the bullying of a master sergeant. All these and many more are the forms of Tyranny. The paradigm of all tyrannical relationships is the relation of Master and Slave. It is perennial. Perennial also is the rebellion against it.

The relation of Master and Slave is one of the *three* possible relationships between men, in which or by means of which things that are wanted by men can be accomplished. The other two are Friendship and Contract. I may do things or be prevented from doing them out of friendship. I may do things or be prevented from doing them by agreement, by contract. All three, Master-Slave, Friendship, and Contract, are society-building and state-building relationships. If what we do and what we do not do depend on the arbitrary decree of one man or a group of men who have the power of life and death over us, we are slaves under tyrannical rule. The political wisdom of all ages has tried to establish forms of political life which would eliminate, to some extent at least, such arbitrariness of political rule and would make perpetual rebellions unnecessary. It has tried, in other words, to secure a minimum of freedom. For to be free as beings living with other beings means to be free from arbitrary, i.e., tyrannical rule. How can this state of affairs be brought about? How can things be done or left undone if we are *not ordered* to do or not to do them? *Either* in virtue of a commonness of purpose based on friendship. *Or* by contract. The first possibility, that of friendship, although often enough actualized on a small scale, does not seem to be operative on a larger one. It still remains the dream of anarchists, for example. The second one, that of contract, is more powerful. Social freedom, that is, freedom from arbitrary rule, can be achieved, if the acceptance of social ties is based on agreements among the persons involved. But an agreement among people needs something that will make it valid, that will set a penalty if a breach occurs. It needs a higher sanction. And this is the sanction of the Law, the sanctity of the Law. To escape arbitrary rule means to accept the rule of the Law. This insight is as old as mankind, as old as Tyranny and Slavery.

But here again the question arises: Is not the Law a new kind of tyrant? Cannot laws rule as tyrannically over us as despots do? Was not even slavery a lawful institution?—that is, construed as the result of a contract or as the application of the laws of war? Is there a way to make the law or the laws, be they written or unwritten, the safeguard of freedom without any tyrannical ambiguity? This is the real political problem of all ages. It has been actually solved in modern times, in the seventeenth and eighteenth centuries. And this solution is *one* of the great achievements of the modern age, rivalling the only other one: the conception of a mathematical science of Nature. In what does this solution consist?

The danger of laws becoming tyrannical has its root in the fact that laws can be *imposed* upon people, be they bad or even good laws. In other words, the *lawgiving* is the problem. To avoid the danger, the lawgiving itself has to proceed in terms of a contract. The very notion of a contract has to be generalized. Two men entering a contract do so out of their own free will, and the procedure of contracting is prescribed and protected by the Law. Roman Law had set the precedent. The political philosophy of the seventeenth and eighteenth centuries generalized the contractual procedure in applying it to the Law itself. The law itself has to be understood in terms of a contract in which the two partners happen to be one and the same. The people as a whole makes a contract with itself to observe certain rules. By this very act *Law is generated*. It cannot henceforth be understood as imposed upon men—it is self-imposed. I obey the law because I participated in the lawgiving, I gave it to myself. In recognizing the authority of the Law I remain free because it is my own authority that I recognize. This primordial political act of lawgiving, in constituting the social and political body, establishes once and for all political freedom. Nothing compels me in this act but myself. The political body, the state and all its manifestations, are a free creation of man. The state and its laws, far from endangering the social freedom of man, is the very embodiment of this freedom. Such is the grandiose conception of the thinkers of the seventeenth and eighteenth centuries. The primordial act of lawgiving is perpetuated in all succeeding lawgiving operations.

It is important to understand that what this theory of lawgiving is primarily interested in, is not the giving of good laws but the securing of the *lawfulness* of the law itself. The emphasis is altogether on the procedure by means of which laws come into being, the procedure of self-imposition. The emphasis is on the way in which a law is being enacted, the way in which its constitutionality can be tested and secured in terms of the primordial lawgiving act, and on the machinery of representative government. The content of the law, its goodness or badness in terms of human welfare, in terms of the common good, is not the ultimate concern. Here in the United States this fact is somewhat obscured by the maintenance of the spirit as well as of the letter of the Anglo-Saxon common law. But at the very root of the modern understanding of political life is the desire to be free from arbitrary, tyrannical rule. That is the idea of Freedom.

Let me pause here for a moment. There is something admirable in this solution of our problem. Freedom appears as a free creation of men. Oppression and Tyranny appear crushed forever. The indignation of man facing the perennial phenomenon of enslavement seems to have had its way. The lawfulness of the law is not only the safeguard of freedom but also of justice. There is something not only admirable in this solution, but also something deeply fascinating. And to this fascination let us now turn our attention.

The fascination exerted on human minds by the problem of freedom and especially by this solution of the problem accounts, I think, for the fact that the problem of the content of the laws has been seriously neglected. The content of the laws was supposed to emerge as a result of the fights between the contending interests of men. The lawfulness of the lawgiving once secured, the laws themselves had to come out by way of trial and error, by way of compromise among those contending interests. The idea of a political art, of Politics, based on practical wisdom seemed to transform itself into the idea of tactical maneuvering for votes, for parliamentary advantage, for bargaining positions. Witness the strange modification in the meaning of the term "politics."

But what is perhaps more important is the influence that the political solution of the problem of political freedom has had on our understanding of our freedom as thinking beings and as beings having a will.

Let me retrace my steps. When I spoke of these two freedoms, I constantly used, and had to use, terms derived from the political domain. I spoke of the authority of the truth and the rule of truth, of tyranny and slavery in the relation of the Good to the will, of truth to thinking. Freedom in our thinking, I had to conclude, was freedom to accept the authority of truth. Freedom of the will — the freedom to accept the authority of the Good. I could not help using these terms because our terminology, our thinking itself, is deeply influenced by considerations derived from our experience as political beings. This is nothing new or exceptional, of course. The problem of Freedom is, as I said in the beginning, a predominantly political one. More generally, almost the entire body of traditional philosophical terminology is derived from the language of political life, and especially from the language of the courts. This shows the general preponderance of political interest in all our thinking. It was primarily the questioning of political patterns and habits which gave rise to an inquiry into the nature of things, gave impulse to philosophical questioning, led to the idea of a contemplative life. Classical philosophy arose out of the preoccupation with political problems and tried to give guidance to political thought. Its dependence on politics is of a genealogical, not a logical, nature. Kings always needed wise counsellors, and the wise counsellors could not live without the kingly purse, but the wisdom of those counsellors was quite independent of the kings and their purses. It was meant to guide them and not to be guided by them. The fascination with the problem of freedom and the solution I have spoken of seems to have changed this relation of wisdom to political action profoundly. Moreover it changed our understanding of our freedom as moral and as thinking beings.

As far as our *free will* is concerned, the political solution showed the way to a re-interpretation of the relation of the will to the Good. The Law, to safeguard our political freedom, was understood as self-imposed. Why cannot that which the will *ought* to will be also determined by the will itself? If the Good is not given to the will from the outside, as it were, but set by the will itself, man as a willing being, as a moral being, can dispense with those golden chains, can be completely free, completely autonomous. This is possible, if the willing itself is identified with the self-imposition of what ought to be willed, if the character of the categorical demand is identified with the very freedom of the will. This is Immanuel Kant's solution, the influence of which on all of us is greater than many seem to realize. And there can be no doubt here that Kant transposed deliberately and consciously the political solution of the problem of freedom, especially in the form given to it by Rousseau, into the moral sphere. There can be no doubt that here the fascination with the problem of freedom has done its work. The lack of content in Kant's understanding of the Good is apparent. But far beyond the Kantian teaching goes the understanding of the will as setting its own goals and determining as good whatever it wills. It does not make much difference whether the will is understood as the will of an individual or as the collective will of a people or a culture. This teaching is current in the schools the world over, in the form of historical sociology or sociological history or history of cultures. Here again the fascination of freedom is at work. This teaching makes us morally free indeed, but rather empty.

As far as our freedom as *thinking* beings is concerned, it seemed to be endangered by the compelling nature of Truth. But what if truth itself is of our own making? Could not truth be the product of our thinking? a "construction of our mind"? Could not the fullness of our thinking be identical with truthfulness? This possibility has not merely been envisaged. You will have no difficulty in recognizing the prevailing philosophical opinion of today.

I said these consequences of the fascination exerted by the problem of freedom are more important than the impoverishment of our political life. In fact, it is these consequences that contribute the most to it. How can the art of politics flourish, if it is not guided by political wisdom? But the availability of this wisdom depends, in turn, on our ways of thinking and our ways of willing. The three freedoms I spoke of in the beginning cannot be neatly separated from each other. That is what makes the problem of Freedom so immensely complex.

Let me raise a strong objection to what I am saying. The art of politics, as I understand it, namely guided by political wisdom, has never existed. There were some writers who propounded it and some pupils and apprentices in this art who failed miserably. It might be proper to recall the saying of that old Swedish chancellor to the effect that one can hardly imagine with how little wisdom this world is actually governed. Will that not always be the case? Should we not be satisfied with the practice of political freedom that we have inherited and defend it as best we can?

But the point is that what we have inherited is indeed our own creation of freedom, a most precious thing which it is in our power to preserve or to lose. The state of affairs we live in is itself a product of art, a manifestation of freedom and perhaps one of the greatest manifestations of that freedom. We have gone far beyond the realm of natural life lived by our ancestors. Once again, it seems to me, we should examine our assumptions, try to discover at what point our thinking and willing enter the mechanism and automatism of our political practices or are subjugated by them. Once again, we have to face the immense task of education which such an exploration entails. Once again, we have to picture ourselves in a cave, perhaps a deeper and vaster one than our forefathers ever imagined. The freedom we enjoy has perhaps created more chains and chains of a novel nature that hold us down. Once again we have to try to disentangle ourselves. We might fail in this enterprise, of course. But in failing we would still be exerting our freedom.

8 ■ History and the
Liberal Arts

F riends and enemies of the St. John's Program, visitors to
the college and many of its alumni often raise the question: Why is History neglected in the St. John's curriculum? They
point to the obvious contrast between the chronological order
in which the "Great Books" are read and the remarkable lack
of historical awareness displayed by the students. The time has
come, I think, to deal with this question extensively. I propose
to do that in this lecture. Let us reflect on the role and
significance of History in a liberal arts curriculum.

The first, rather simple, statement that can be made is this:
Man, having the ability to understand and being inquisitive by
nature, wants to explore everything that he sees about him —
the various plants and animals, the stars and the clouds and the
winds, the surface of the earth, the rivers and the forests and
the stones and the deserts. Whether this preoccupation stems
from his immediate and urgent need, whether his inquisitive
attitude is merely an extension of his concern to provide the
necessities of life for himself, whether it is the manifestation
of his very nature or simply idle curiosity, need not be discussed

---

Lecture first delivered at St. John's College, Annapolis, June 5, 1953.

at this point. Whatever the origins of this desire, man wants to find out, to figure out, to know. In this sense, then, man may be said to be inquisitive not only about what surrounds him, at the present time, but also about the future: he wants to know what is going to happen to him as well as to everything else around him. And finally he wants to know what happened in the past. Out of this latter desire, we may somewhat naively say, grows History, i.e., the exploration of the past, the finding of the past, the description of what has happened in the recent as well as in the most remote past. Curiously enough, as you know, the Greek word *historia* means originally exploration of any kind. Gradually, it came to mean, even to the Greeks, the exploration of the past and the description or narration of past events.

Thus we have History, i.e., historical books: Herodotus, Thucydides, chronicles of all kinds, histories of Europe, America, India, of Guatemala, of the city of Annapolis, of the Universal Postal Union, of St. John's College, of the Imperial Palace in Peking. Such histories may be more or less correct. Descriptions of events must be checked as to their accuracy with the help of all the evidence available: books, old records, letters, inscriptions, etc. Special skills in exploring and checking the evidence must be developed. Historical science and the methodology of historical science become a branch of knowledge; history can be taught and learned. Departments of History and archives are established. Historical journals come into being, dedicated to the improvement and enlargement of historical knowledge. All this circumscribes what may be called the domain of History. Is this, then, what History is?

You sense immediately: this is not quite it, this is not a sufficient description of History and what History means.

First of all, there is a special emphasis in the pursuit of History which is lacking in other branches of learning. Take the science of geology, for example. However important and interesting its investigations and findings might be, this science does not make *universal* claims, it restricts itself to a definite domain. There is no such thing as a "geological approach" to any given problem. And yet there always seems to be an "historical approach" to almost any kind of problem in almost any field.

Secondly, it is not quite correct to state that history is the description and narration of past events. Not everything that is past is "historic." That one of us here went to Washington or to San Francisco last week or some time ago does not necessarily belong to any history. It might, though. From a certain point of view, with regard to an event we judge a significant one, we can — retrospectively — recognize the importance of events which led to that significant one. Nobody, indeed, ever assumed that all events and happenings are equally important and significant and could become recorded in history books. Even Tolstoi, who formulated the idea of such an all-comprehensive history, based on integration procedures in the face of infinite series of minute events, of historical infinitesimals, as it were, did that merely to reduce history thus understood to absurdity. All written and traditional history is based on a principle of *selection*. This means that we must have — and in fact do have — some yardstick to measure the significance and importance of events, whatever history we may be writing.

It is not too difficult to discern these yardsticks in Herodotus or Tacitus or Gibbon, for example; more difficult perhaps, but not impossible, to discover them in Thucydides. We can even venture to say that in general the yardstick is provided either (a) by the consideration of the present state of affairs, the salient features of which want to be traced back to their origins, in a sort of *genealogical* procedure, or (b) by the desire to derive a lesson for the future either from mistakes and failures or from exemplary actions in the past, which desire leads to what has been called, since Polybius, *pragmatic* history. Sometimes both kinds of yardstick are combined.

I say that both — the universality of the tendency to subject any theme to an historical investigation and the selecting of events or facts to be dealt with historically — help us to win a better understanding of this human enterprise called History. This enterprise does not seem to be grounded in an inherent property of events or facts that permits us to arrange them in a sequence, an historical sequence, but seems rather to depend on a certain way of looking at things which stamps them into an historical pattern. One might be tempted to apply Kantian terminology to this phenomenon — and people have actually done so —: there might be something of an historical *a priori*, a form of our thinking that inescapably leads us to see things in an historical perspective. Let us consider this for a moment. Let us beware though lest we indulge in an empty, if easy, construction.

As far as pragmatic history is concerned, the selection is based on our sense of moral virtues or our understanding of practical maxims of conduct. *Hybris* versus Moderation, Tyranny versus Freedom, false hopes and foolish fears versus prudence — these are presented and pointed out to us in the unfolding drama of historical successes or catastrophes. Here, then, the historical scene is merely the enlargement of our daily life, providing us with great examples in large script. History in this sense is founded on completely "unhistorical" points of view. That is why this kind of history writing does not constitute a specific domain like Physics or even Poetry. Note that Aristotle, the great systematizer of human knowledge, in the face of such history — the only one he knew — did not treat it as a *pragmateia*, a discipline in its own right. The same Aristotle who investigated, defined, elaborated on every conceivable art and science — grammar, logic, physics, botany, zoology, astronomy, theology, psychology, politics, ethics, rhetoric, poetry — did not elaborate on history, although he so often prefaces his investigations with a review of positions and opinions held in the past. I conclude: there is no historical *a priori* in pragmatic history.

The same holds true of the genealogical type of history, although not in the same way. The very notion of genealogy comprises notions of origin, source, development, more generally, the notion of a temporal order. But these notions are not strictly historical ones. They also determine our understanding of biological phenomena, or more generally, of phenomena of change. They are not constitutive categories of historical experience. They are operative in any myth, they help to picture the growth and the decay of institutions, the expansion of dominion and power; but the emphasis is on the nature of those institutions and the overwhelming character of that power. The bases of this type of history, exemplified in Polybius and the Roman historians, are still unhistorical, mostly legal and political.

But when we turn to that universal tendency to view things historically, to use the historical approach in almost any field, the picture changes. It seems, indeed, as if here the form of History shapes the material under consideration so as to make anything we look at assume historical clothing, as if the very basis of our looking at things were — we hear it so often — History itself. When, a moment ago, I denied that this was the case in pragmatic and genealogical history, I implicitly assumed, by way of contrast, the possibility of such a view. The question, then, is whether this historical way of looking at things is itself a necessary form of our understanding. One way of answering this question would be to apply the following test: Can we approach and solve *this* problem historically?

The pragmatic and genealogical types of history are the only ones known in antiquity and the understanding of the nature of history corresponds to them. But a new understanding of history begins with the advent of Christianity. Let us consider briefly in what it consists. I shall use two outstanding examples: Augustine and Dante.

Augustine, in the *City of God* (XV–XVIII), gives a World History based on a fundamental distinction. Mankind consists of two parts: there are those who live according to Man, i.e., in sin, and those who live according to God; there are two communities, the city of men and the city of God. The latter is in the making and after the Second Advent will become the everlasting kingdom of God. The earthly city will then be destroyed and its inhabitants will join Satan. As long as this world exists, both cities are intertwined. Augustine distinguishes six ages: 1) from Adam to the Deluge; 2) from Noah to Abraham; 3) from Abraham to David (the "prophetic age"); 4) from David to the Babylonian captivity; 5) from the Babylonian captivity to Jesus Christ; 6) from Jesus Christ to the end of this world. This universal history is conceived mainly in terms of the Biblical account; but the great oriental kingdoms, as well as Greece and the Roman Empire, have their place allocated in the general flow. This is not a "Philosophy of History"; it is rather History itself, i.e., the description of succeeding ages according to God's providential ordering of all events. The important thing for us to note is that historical succession itself, the fact of History, the fact that men's lives weave the History of the World, is not an accidental property of those lives but their very essence. Our and our fathers' years have flowed through God's eternal Today, says Augustine in the *Confessions*: "from this everpresent divine 'To-day' the past generations of men received the measure and the mould of such being as they had; and still others shall flow away, and so receive the mould of their degree of being." History, then, reflects the essential temporality of man, but reflects no less the eternal timeless pattern of his being. In following up the chain of historical events we do not select significant links. We follow God's providential plan. *Our* historical perspective is *our* view of an eternal order, just as the flow is our way of incomplete existence. For us "to exist" is identical with "to exist historically." But that, again, means that our existence spreads out in time the timeless pattern of God's wisdom. This is neither pragmatic nor genealogical history. It is, one might say, symbolic history. History presents the symbols that unfold in succession the eternal relations between creation, fall, redemption, and salvation.

Let us turn to Dante. Here, again, we see a World History conceived in terms of God's timeless providential pattern. History is the sinister chronicle of man's fall pursued through all generations of men. The Greek and Roman worlds occupy a far more important place in this chronicle than in that of Augustine. The horrors of Thebes more than those of Babylon indicate the complete abnegation of God's grace. It is not the contrast between the City of Men and the City of God which determines Dante's general view of historical events, but rather the contrast and intertwining of God's spiritual and God's secular order, of Church and Empire. The secular order, stemming from God, reflects but is not identical with the spiritual order. Troy and its destruction are symbols of man's pride and man's fall. "And it happened at one period of time," Dante writes in the *Convivio*, "that when David was born, Rome was born, that is to say, Aeneas then came from Troy to Italy. . . . Evident enough, therefore, is the divine election of the Roman Empire by the birth of the Holy City (i.e., Rome), which was contemporaneous with the root of the race from which Mary sprang." The history of the world is here a kind of symbolic duplication of the spiritual history of man. It is by this very nature, as in Augustine, two-dimensional. Or, to put it in different words, the horizon of this kind of history, or better, of this kind of historian, is not historical. In this respect this kind of history is akin to the pragmatic and genealogical kinds. Here, again, it is worth noting: the primary liberal disciplines listed by Dante in the *Convivio* and linked to the ten heavens of the world (the spheres of the Moon, Mercury, Venus, Sun, Mars, Jupiter, Saturn, the sphere of the fixed stars, the *primum mobile* and the Empyrean Heaven) are Grammar, Logic, Rhetoric, Arithmetic, Geometry, Music, Astronomy, Physics and Metaphysics, Ethics, Theology. History is not one of them.

When Machiavelli and Hobbes dethrone classical philosophy and revert to pragmatic history as the best teacher man can have in planning and conducting his life, they still cling to a two-dimensional history to build their own political philosophy.

But now the scene changes: Vico's New Science marks a new beginning. Like Machiavelli and Hobbes he defies all preceding philosophy. He bases his work on the fundamental (Leibnizian) distinction: the *true* and the *certain*. What is true is common and therefore abstract. What is certain is the particular, the individual, the concrete. "*Certum* and *commune* are opposed to each other." The philosophers pursue what is common. They lack certainty. Only history (which includes philology) deals with the certain. The most certain for us is that which we ourselves have made, the *facta*, the facts. "The world of civil society has certainly been made by man; its principles are therefore to be found within the modifications of our own human mind. Whoever reflects on this cannot but marvel that the philosophers should have bent all their energies to the study of the world of nature, which, since God made it, He alone knows; and that they should have neglected the study of the world of nations or civil world, which, since man had made it, men could hope to know."

Vico sets out to fulfill this hope. This is the scope of his New Science. It is historical by definition. The historian looking at man-made worlds can understand their innermost core. He will thus attain a more certain truth than the philosophers ever could; he will discover "the common nature of nations" or the "ideal eternal history" of nations established by divine providence. The New Science will thus be "a rational civil theology of divine providence." "Since divine providence has omnipotence as minister, it develops its orders by means as easy as the natural customs of men." This also means that this science is a "history of human ideas"(not a philosophical reflection on ideas). There are recurrent cycles in the history of nations that always comprise three stages: the divine, the heroic, and the human. The proper field of the historian is the customs of men, their institutions, their laws, their writings, their poetry. In understanding them he understands truth that is certain — truthful certainty — precisely what the philosophers are unable to accomplish.

At first sight it seems as if history in Vico's understanding preserved its two-dimensionality, since the objects of his findings are the "universal and eternal orders established by providence." But these orders do not exist outside of time. Divine providence is not the providential plan of salvation anymore. Vico's history is bent on finding the laws governing the human world in contradistinction to the laws governing the world of nature. Historical reality with its recurrent stretches is one-dimensional. On the other hand, the historian alone is now the true philosopher. The methods of interpretation and of philology he has to use constitute a *new organon* comprising axioms, definitions and specific rules of inference. In other words: Vico's work competes with the work of Natural History, with the work of Mathematical Physics.

We have here a rather amazing historical fact before us. Let us remember. Towards the end of the sixteenth century a reinterpretation and reconsideration of the traditional, "classical," mathematical sciences lead to the establishment of Algebra, a hitherto obscure and "vulgar" discipline neglected by all recognized institutions of learning, as the eighth Liberal Art. Its progress coincides with the development of a new symbolic discipline, understood as Universal Mathematics, a new and most powerful instrument of human knowledge which is meant to replace the traditional Aristotelian Organon. The science of nature becomes mathematical physics, begins to dominate all human understanding and gradually transforms the conditions of human life on this earth. The only force opposing this development is History with its claim to universality, first attributed to it by Vico and maintained with increased vigor up to this moment. It is significant, I think, that Vico's idea of an "ideal eternal history" is a derivative of the idea of a Universal Mathematics, a shadow, as it were, that the latter casts. As Universal Mathematics is to all specific mathematical disciplines so is the "ideal eternal history" to all specific histories of nations. But this parallelism between Universal Mathematics and Universal History is to be understood in the light of the distinction between that which is "abstractly true" and that which is "concretely certain." The new science of Mathematical Physics leaves the natural experience of nature far behind: all that is concrete vanishes behind a screen of mathematical symbols. Any teleology loses its meaning. The new science of History tries to restore the dignity of the concrete, fills the gap between the abstract symbolic understanding of nature and the immediate human experience of the world around us. It cannot dispense with the notions of means and ends. It is the distinction between the true and the certain which underlies the familiar and superficial distinction between Science and the Humanities. The latter are conceived as inseparable from History, can only be approached in historical perspective, come actually to life only in the medium of History. Since Vico, the idea of an eternal pattern of history, a vestige of the original Christian understanding, although occasionally forcefully advanced, has been generally abandoned. The emphasis is on the development of what has been called the *historical sense*.

Three consequences follow.

First, the fascination with the "otherness" of the past: the discovery or reconstruction of cultures and civilizations "different" from ours, each with a different "sense of values" ascertainable in customs, institutions, works of art, architecture, literature, philosophy, religion. This very notion of an autonomous "culture," underlying the various manifestations of human activity can arise only within an historical horizon. Truth itself becomes a function of "culture," the existence of which appears a certain fact; "relativity of values" becomes inevitably the concomitant of the historical perspective.

Secondly, the sense of participating in the relentless historical flow makes observable *trends* the guide of our actions. The acceptance of events and doctrines that are supposed to follow the "historical trend" is one of the most potent causes for the predicament in which European nations have found themselves in recent decades. The impact of Marxism which goes under the name of historical materialism and the reaction to it derive their strength from the historical sense projected into the future. The

Gallup Poll is one of the most recent and most ridiculous examples of this preoccupation with trends.

Thirdly, a man understands himself completely as an historical being. "Historicity" becomes his very nature, but not in the sense that it reflects some timeless pattern. His Self disintegrates into a series of socially, and that means historically, conditioned reflexes. Historicity does not mean Tradition. To see ourselves as historical beings means to break the invisible traditional ties in which we live. At best, tradition then becomes a romantic notion, at worst, an academic phantom.

If we consider the disciplines taught in our schools, it is easy to see that all natural sciences are patterned on the model of mathematical physics. The idea of a universal mathematics as the new organon of all science, however, dies away. On the other hand, all the disciplines within the realm of the humanities have become historical to the very core. The study of literature, philosophy, religion, music and the fine arts, for example, is almost exclusively the study of the history of literature, the history of philosophy, the history of religions, the history of music, the history of art. Fields of study of a more practical applicability as, for example, languages, political science and economics, retain a certain automony. The theoretical dignity they may have, however, is safeguarded only by historical considerations or, for that matter, by methods borrowed from mathematical physics.

It seems, then, that Mathematical Physics and History divide between themselves, in a fairly exhaustive way, the rule over the entire domain of human knowledge. Does this permit us to consider them as the two necessary ways and forms of our understanding? If this be so, Mathematical Physics and History would come close to being the two Liberal Arts of the modern age. Any liberal arts curriculum ought then to concentrate on these two great bodies of learning in keeping with the trend of events and in preparing students to follow it further.

At this point, we can pause and reflect on the results we have reached.

As to Mathematical Physics, the task before us is clearly not the tracing of its historic development. We have rather to understand the methods and the nature of the concepts that have made this development possible. We have to understand the specific use made of mathematical symbols, the relation of a mathematical deduction to a verifying experiment, the relations between observations, hypothesis, theory and truth. That is indeed what we are trying to do in our Mathematics Tutorials and in the Laboratory. And if we do not do that fully and in the most satisfactory manner, we have to improve our ways. The danger we are running in this case is the very same that has threatened the integrity of scientific understanding since the seventeenth century and which has barely begun to be warded off in recent developments: the danger to confuse the symbolic means of our understanding with reality itself.

If we turn to History, we have first to remember the question which gave rise to the preceding historical account. The question was: Is the historical way of looking at things a necessary form of our understanding? The answer—in the perspective of History—is in the negative: The universal historical approach is itself a product of, and presumably nothing but a phase in, an historical development, which cannot claim any absolute validity, no matter how "natural" and familiar it seems to us at the present moment. We have to recognize, moreover, the possibility of a dangerous confusion similar to the one I just mentioned with regard to Mathematical Physics. The results of historical investigations based on specific historical concepts and methods of interpretation ought not to be confused with the real picture of a real past. Not to see that, means to surround us with a pseudo-historical horizon of almost mythical quality so as to make us talk glibly of "Greek culture," "medieval times," "Renaissance," the "Seventeenth Century," the "Age of Enlightenment," etc. Such pseudo-mythical notions are usually in the minds of people who recommend that we take into account the proper "historical background" whenever we read and discuss a book. The assumption behind this recommendation is a rather naive one, to wit, that in the effort we make to understand a book or a series of books we could fall back on an objective and certain datum, the general culture in which the ideas expressed or propounded in those books are rooted and from which they derive their strength and intelligibility. We ought to see instead that the commonly accepted picture of an historical period is largely due to an interpretation of the content of books and other documents which presupposes in the first place the ability to deal with grammatical patterns, to discern rhetorical devices, to grasp ideas in all their implications. In point of fact, the main task of any historian is of necessity the interpretation of whatever data he may collect. The art of interpretation and all the other arts which minister to it depend on the understanding of the function of signs, of the complexity of symbolic expressions, and of the cogency of logical relations.

To understand a text is not a simple matter. To arouse and to cultivate this understanding is one of the primary tasks of our Language Tutorials. More than anything else, more, certainly, than the historical sense fed so often on sheer ignorance, an improvement of our interpretative skills could help foster genuine historical research and writing. We may ultimately get to see that the problem of History is itself not an historical problem.

It follows, then, that in pursuing these goals we should ignore history's claim to universality, ignore History itself, if you please, in order to devote our full attention to the development of all the arts of understanding and all imaginative devices man can call his own. It takes courage to pursue a rather narrow and steep path hardly visible from the highways of contemporary learning. But let us remember the inscription on the old seal of the College: No path is impassable to courage. The reward may be high.

9 ■ The Problem and the Art of Writing

The subject of this lecture is, as announced, The Problem and the Art of Writing. And that is what I am going to talk about. My real theme, however, the theme that prompts me to deliver this lecture, is — Reading. For what we do here, are supposed to do here, most of the time, is — reading. I submit — and I hope you will not mind my saying this — that, on the whole, we do not read too well. There are obviously many reasons for this failure, varying from individual to individual, from circumstance to circumstance. It would be quite a task to try to account for all of them. But there is one reason — one among so many — which is sometimes conspicuously noticeable. Reading means first of all to face a written text. And it seems to me that we do not sufficiently reflect on what this fact entails, on what writing itself implies or presupposes, and on what it, of necessity, precludes. To talk about Reading leads thus unavoidably to the subject of Writing. Hence this lecture. And it is, alas, equally unavoidable for me to become quite pedantic and boring. I shall have to give examples, cite chapter and verse, and even write references on the board. I am going so far as to invite you — at least those of you who are interested — to copy those references

Lecture first delivered at St. John's College, Annapolis, October 30, 1959.

so that you could check them — and me — after the discussion period.

In reflecting about writing it is impossible to disregard the spoken word. How could we, indeed? For human speech, this marvel, this greatest marvel perhaps under the sun, is right there, behind or beneath or above the written word. It is difficult (although not impossible) to conceive that there could have been writing without human speech existing in this world. I mean, writing seems to follow speaking. Writing and speaking exhibit, at any rate, common aspects as well as aspects in which they differ. Let me discuss those similarities and differences at some length.

The differences are not so clear as one might suppose at first. Speaking, we might say, appears, of necessity, as an audible sequence of sounds, a sequence in time; actual human speech is never available as a whole, while anything written is visibly there at once, in a book or on a piece of paper or a chunk of stone. While reading, even silent reading, takes time, as does the *act* of writing, a written text, which takes up some space, is present all at once in all its parts. But what about a tape-recorded speech or conversation? Is not the whole right there, on the marked tape? Are not written records of the proceedings, say, in a law court complete in such a way as to project the temporal sequence of all the speaking that goes on into a more or less limited space in which the entire sequence is duplicated — and thus preserved — at once? Such projections, duplications, and preservations of live speech by means of manual skills or mechanico-electrical or electronic devices amount to canning processes. The result is indeed canned speech that can be released again into its proper medium by vocal or mechanical or electrical means. The written word, however, is not at all canned speech. The primary cause for the existence of the written word is not the desire to duplicate and to preserve the sound of the spoken word, but the desire to preserve its meaning so that it could be conveyed to others over and over again. Writing tends, therefore, to a shortening of the spoken word, a shortening that manifests itself in a variety of ways. Let us consider this phenomenon in some detail.

First of all, *any* writing is shorthand writing. Any writing will do violence to the sound of the spoken word for, although it cannot help reproducing words, its primary purpose is to convey the meaning of those words. The various methods of writing show that clearly. Chinese characters, as you all know, although they can be read, are drawn not to be read but to be understood without recourse to the medium of sounds. They are appropriately called ideograms. Egyptian hieroglyphs, at least the oldest ones, convey their meaning directly, even though out of them evolved a syllabic and alphabetic script, something that happened to Chinese characters, too. But even alphabetic writing, i.e., writing reproducing the sounds of words with the help of some thirty letters and combinations of letters, can often be read only if the meaning is grasped first. This is particularly true in the case of the English writing. We would not know how to pronounce, for instance, the assemblage of the three letters *B O W* or *R O W* without the context that gives this assemblage one of its several meanings. The reason for this ambiguity is that the number of letters is not sufficient to indicate the various sounds we are producing while speaking. Although in many cases, as in the examples given, it might be easy to remedy the situation by changing the spelling, it does not seem possible to reproduce in writing the sound of all spoken words with complete faithfulness. And that would probably still be true if we adopted a phonetic system of signs, as the linguists do, unless we multiplied the number of those signs immeasurably. It is rather remarkable that the inadequacy of our sign systems does not really bother us.

It is true that something very similar can be said of spoken words (in any language) inasmuch as the same sound may convey different meanings depending on the context, as for example the sounds "spell," "lie" (lye), "die" (dye), or the sound of inflections in nouns and verbs. In cases like those, writing might help to distinguish the meanings, but does not always do that. The relation of written signs to the sounds of words seems, on the whole, more ambiguous than the relation of those sounds to their meanings.

Now, what seems to me significant is that the shortcomings of our character or letter systems appear to reflect the tendency inherent in all writing to shorten the flow of spoken words for the purpose of clarifying and, above all, of preserving their meaning. This shortening is done by reducing the number of the spoken words, by condensing them, as it were, and this in turn is done by selecting and arranging them in a proper way. That's where the problem of writing begins to emerge.

Such shortening and condensing cannot be attempted, let alone achieved, unless the *whole* of what is to be written is in some way present to the writer — I mean the whole as a whole, not necessarily all its details. In shortening and condensing the spoken word, writing extends the devices by which words and sentences are conjoined in live speech. The device of shading the meaning of words by inflections or prepositional and adverbial linkages and, above all, the device of combining not only words but whole sentences by means of conjunctions and variations of verbal forms — the sum total of all such devices constitutes what we call the arts and disciplines of Grammar and Syntax. These terms refer to disciplines which are the result of some reflection on the manner of our speaking. It is not without interest to observe that such reflection bore fruit, in other words, that those disciplines took shape, in confrontation with the written word, as the very word "grammar" indicates. But writing itself transforms those grammatical and syntactical devices by applying them on a much larger scale to the *whole* of a written work. The term "syntax" (σύνταξις), in particular, acquires a much more comprehensive meaning. The word means "co-ordering," "putting things together in a certain order," "composing." Anticipating the whole of what is to be written down, the writer has to fit the parts of that whole into a proper order. We have a direct pointing to this procedure in the title of Ptolemy's book that we study here: it is called *Mathematical Composition* (σύνταξις μαθηματική) —"mathematical" in contrast to a possible non-mathematical composition relating to celestial phenomena. But the same term could be applied to *all* written works. The anticipated whole imposes upon the writer the task of com-posing its parts with the graduated emphasis due to each of them. And just as the devices of such a composition are extensions of syntactical devices (in the restricted sense of the term "syntax"), the devices involved in varying emphases, the devices of articulation, appear to be extensions of grammatical shadings observable even in simple sentences of live speech.

The shortening and condensing of spoken words in writing demand, then, modifications and extensions of grammatical and syntactical devices. In writing, the devices of Articulation and Composition add a new dimension above and beyond the one governed by grammatical and syntactical rules. It is in these new devices that the problem of writing resides. That problem can be formulated as follows: How can the anticipated whole be made to unfold itself so as to become an actual whole, that is, in Aristotle's immortal phrase, to become something that has a beginning, a middle, and an end?

Right at this point, we see that the term "writing" may be somewhat misleading if it is understood to suggest that the act of writing must be done with some kind of instrument on some visible material. A speech in a political assembly, in an election campaign or on some other public occasion (a lecture, for example) may well be delivered without any written text, even any written notes; the speaker could, of course, have prepared his speech beforehand in writing, but he need not have done so; he must, however, have prepared it somehow by thinking about what he is going to say and about how he is going to say it; he must thus have anticipated the whole of his speech and have committed this whole to his memory, again not necessarily in all its details, but in such a way that its composition and its main articulations are present to his mind. A speaker of this kind is a writer, too. His rhetorical problem is not different from the problem the writer faces. The speaker's memory is covered, as it were, with the "imprints" of the whole. On the other hand, a letter, a hastily scribbled note, can, on occasion, be something like canned speech, if that letter or note reproduces faithfully what would have been said without writing.

The distinction, then, between the spoken word and the written word reduces itself to the distinction between saying something spontaneously and saying something in the light of an anticipated whole. Yet, this does not seem sufficient. It could become more meaningful if we looked at the *effect* speaking or writing may have or may not have on the listener or reader.

We all remember a phrase that Homer uses so often when

describing human speech, the phrase "winged words" (ἔπεα πτερόεντα). Whence this image? The phrase seems to occur for the most part when a personage, a god or a man, addresses another single personage, a god or a man. Very rarely does it occur when someone speaks to a group or a crowd of people. Minstrels in Homer are never said to utter or to sing "winged words." It may be worth noting that four times, in the last books of the *Odyssey*, and only there, speech is said to have stayed "wingless" (ἄπτερος ἔπλετο μῦθος) in somebody's throat upon somebody else's uttering a command, as if to indicate that no answer was needed. Words are not called "winged" to indicate their soaring or lofty quality. The image seems rather to imply that words, after escaping the "fence (or barrier) of the teeth" (ἕρκος ὀδόντων), as Homer puts it, are guided swiftly — and therefore surely — to their destination, the ears and the soul and the understanding of the addressee. Words, especially spontaneous words, can indeed be spoken in such a way as to "sink in," as *we* say. But this possibility grows more uncertain with the growing indefiniteness of the addressee. It is more difficult to reach a crowd of men than a single man. Exertions of a special kind are then required. In writing, the indefiniteness of the addressee becomes almost complete. Live speech is spontaneous, not confined within the boundaries of an anticipated whole, and more often than not endowed with wings. Written speech — visibly put down or invisibly committed to memory — is prepared, composed, and articulated as a whole, and may yet lack wings. The problem of writing, then, is: how to give wings to written words so that they may reach their destination, the soul and the understanding of men.

To solve this problem, that is, to know how to compose and to articulate words so as to give them wings, is to possess the art of writing. However artful the composition, some of us, of course, will not be touched by the wings. There are no safeguards against it.

Now there are, *in the main*, two ways in which this problem can be solved.

One is: to say *explicitly all* that is *necessary* for the meaning of the written text to be grasped, that is, not to omit any link in the chain which binds our understanding, and not to say anything which could disrupt that chain. This kind of composition is conspicuously present in mathematical works, in Euclid, Apollonius, good calculus textbooks, and so forth; it is prevalent in any writing meant to convey to us an understanding of the ways of nature, of nature's structure, of the interlocking of natural phenomena; its traces may be found elsewhere, too, especially in legal writing. The articulation of such works tends to follow up the joints of logical sequences. In fact, it is the reflection on what is implied in this kind of composition that leads to the conception and establishment of a very special art and discipline. This discipline has as its subject that element in human speech, that element of the λόγος, which gives it the character of reasoned discourse. It concerns itself with the pure structures of the λόγος and bears therefore the name of Logic. Subsequent reflection may make us doubt whether words derived from actual speaking can serve as vehicles of logical inferences. This doubt, in turn, leads to more refined versions of the discipline of logic, leads to what is called today Symbolic Logic. Any writing termed mathematical or scientific is under the spell of the idea of a strictly logical demonstrative discipline that proceeds from accepted premises through a chain of inescapable inferences to irrefutable conclusions. Seldom, if ever, does a composition embody this idea in its purity. The degrees to which this idea is being approximated form a wide range. What interests us here is the character of the wings proper to compositions of this kind. This character is the *necessity* inherent in our *thinking*.

The other way in which the problem of writing can be solved is quite different. Here the most important and decisive is *not* said explicitly at all. Compositions of this kind tend to articulate the whole in such a way as to make us wonder why the parts are arranged as they are. We are compelled to raise questions about the link that holds them together. And it is *our* answer that will either illuminate the whole or plunge us into further darkness out of which we shall be groping anew for some light. Writings of this kind taunt us. The character of the wings proper to them is the taunting presence of a hidden answer, yet of an answer within our reach. In what follows I shall try to give examples of this second way of writing. I shall take them from

Homer and Plato. But before embarking upon this dangerous enterprise I have to add a not unimportant remark to what I just said.

I said that in the main there are two ways of solving the problem of writing and I have tried to indicate what they are. I said "in the main" because there are — as always — border cases and fringe phenomena in writing that may loom large before our eyes and glow in a peculiar light. Among the oldest cases of writing are written laws, for example. There are also monuments, themselves something like imprints on the collective memory of mankind, but imprints made visible, and there are inscriptions on them glorifying the deeds of some great man or of some great ruler or of an infamous one. There are epitaphs. There are short poems expressing a mood or a whim, aphorisms, sayings and proverbs. I omit mentioning other examples. (There are too many of them.) We tend to cherish such border cases and fringe phenomena and to devote special attention to them. But I should venture to say that they find their place on the map of writing in terms of co-ordinates derived from the two main stems of writing I was talking about.

And now, let me turn to the first example of the second of these main stems.

Consider the *Iliad*. Among the great many events that follow each other in the story and the description of which constitutes the whole of the poem, there are certain ones of decisive importance, which are quite familiar to us: (I) the quarrel between Agamemnon and Achilles which leads to Achilles' withdrawing from the fight; (II) the victorious advance of the Trojans; (III) the intervention and death of Patroclus; (IV) the reappearance of Achilles on the field of battle; (V) the death of Hector; (VI) the funeral of Patroclus; (VII) the surrender of Hector's body to Priam. All these decisive events could be put in a diagram as follows:

Disregarding the more or less superficial division into books or songs and even allowing for all kinds of tampering with, and dislocations of, the original text, there is no denying that the decisive events are crowded into the last third of the whole. Between (I) and (II) events of great significance certainly do occur, as for example the death and the wounding of many and important warriors, the Diomedian terror, the wounding of two gods, the encounter of Diomedes and Glaucus, the peaceful scenes in Troy, the unsuccessful embassy to Achilles, inconclusive duels among men and delightfully treacherous actions on the part of the gods — all of which contribute in varying degrees to the unfolding plot. In the main, however, all the time the battle is swaying back and forth until finally the Trojans reach the ships of the Achaeans. During all that time Achilles sits in his tent, sulking, and only occasionally watching the fight. The pivotal event, the death of Patroclus, which changes, which reverses everything, occurs very late in the poem (in the 16th book). It is as if the poem took an exceedingly long breath to reach that point and afterwards rushed with breathtaking speed to its end. This is the more remarkable since the entire period of time the poem encompasses is one of 49 days and Patroclus' death occurs on the 26th day, that is, very nearly in the middle of that period.

Why is the composition articulated in such an unbalanced way? we wonder. Let us see.

There are two events — among many others — which I have not mentioned at all. Yet it is these two events that seem to be the two foci from which all light dispersed throughout the poem stems.

The first takes place when Thetis, Achilles' mother, is visiting Zeus to ask for his help on behalf of her son, reminding Zeus of the help he once received from her. She wants Zeus to turn the scales of the war, to let the Trojans have the upper hand until finally, in the hour of the Achaeans' greatest peril, Achilles — and only Achilles — could save *them* from certain defeat, lead them to victory and thus regain *his* honor, which he allegedly lost through Agamemnon's action. It is then said (I, 511–12): "But Zeus, the cloud-gatherer, said nothing at all to her and sat in silence for a long while (δήν)." An awful silence! Thetis repeats her plea. At last, Zeus consents and nods, a sign of an irrevocable decision. Olympus shakes. Thetis departs, apparently satisfied that she has accomplished her mission. Has she?

The second event occurs after Patroclus' death (XVIII, 165–229), while the battle for Patroclus' body rages before the ships between Hector and the Aiantes and while Thetis is on her way to get new arms for her son from Hephaestus. Hera sends Iris to Achilles, without Zeus and the other gods knowing anything about this mission, to urge Achilles to intervene in the struggle for Patroclus' body. Since Achilles has no arms at this juncture, he is asked by Iris to do nothing but to show himself to the Trojans, to frighten them by his mere appearance. Achilles, "dear to Zeus" (203), obeys and does *more* than what Hera through Iris asked him to do. Pallas Athene, who is nearby, does her share: she casts the tasselled aegis around his shoulders and she sets a crown in the guise of a golden cloud about his head and from it issues a blazing flame. Thus he appears — alone, separated from the other Achaeans — in the sight of the foe, a flaming torch. But not only does he appear — he shouts, three times, a terrible shout, clearly heard, and "from afar Pallas Athene uttered her voice" (217–18). Unspeakable confusion and terror seize the Trojans. Patroclus' body is saved.

What kind of shout is this? Is it one of triumph? Of threat? Is it an ordinary war cry, raised to a very high pitch? It is certainly not like the bellowing of the wounded Ares (V, 859, 863). Two verbs are used to describe that shout, one of a rather neutral tint and, at the decisive moment, another, ἰάχω (288), which has a range of meanings. One of these meanings is "crying out in grief." Shortly before (29) the same verb was used in precisely this meaning to describe the lament of the maidens at the news of Patroclus' death. It will be repeated shortly afterwards (XIX, 41) to describe Achilles' shouting when he rouses the Achaeans to battle. Why does Achilles shout now, not urged to do so by Iris? Certainly, to frighten the Trojans, to make them desist from Patroclus' body. But can this shouting fail to express the unspeakable pain that fills his heart and had just brought his mother to him from the depth of the sea? Here indeed is a terrible sight to behold: a man raised to his highest glory by Pallas Athene, wearing the aegis, crowned by flames, radiant, truly god-like — and this same man crushed by grief, miserable in his awareness of having himself brought the immensity of this grief upon himself. The apotheosis of Achilles is the seal on his doom. And it is his voice, his brazen voice (XVIII, 222), his terrible shouting, which brings terror to the foe, that expresses his misery and his doom. Pallas Athene's voice seems but a weak echo of that of Achilles or even completely drowned out by the latter's intensity.

But are not these two events related?

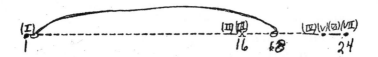

Does not Achilles' shouting sonorously echo Zeus' silence? Can we not guess now why Zeus remained silent for a long while? Surely, he had to take account of the susceptibilities of his wife, as any husband would do — and in his marital relations Zeus is no exception; but is it only Hera that he was silently thinking about? Must he not have been concerned about the whimsical nature of Achilles' plight and Thetis' plea? And, on the other hand, how could he have refused to satisfy Thetis, in whose debt he was? Is it not right then and there that Zeus decided, in wisdom and sadness, irrevocably too, to accede to Thetis' demand, to give honor and glory to Achilles, but to do so in a manner which neither Thetis nor Achilles suspected? The long stretch of the poem which corresponds to Achilles' inactivity fills Zeus' silence. While the tide of the battle is being reversed, Patroclus' approaching death is announced twice (VIII, 476; XV, 64–67); the steps which lead to it are carefully pointed out (XI, 604, 700–804, especially 792–3). Achilles will get what he wants, but at the price of the greatest loss he could suffer — the loss of his beloved friend, his other self (XVIII, 81–2). In the hour of his triumph he will be the most miserable of men. The ways of Zeus are as wise as they are crooked. Zeus does not know about Iris' mission. But do the strong-headed and light-minded goddesses, Hera and Pallas Athene, know what is going on? They don't, nor does Achilles' mother (XVIII, 74–5). While Pallas Athene transfigures Achilles into a god, Achilles is mortified. *He* has grasped Zeus' intent. He says himself (XVIII, 328): "Not all the thoughts of men does Zeus fulfill," as Homer has said before (XVI, 250–2), commenting on Achilles' prayer (before the slaying of Patroclus): "One thing the father granted him, the other he denied." Zeus denied him the safe return of Patroclus. He denied it for Achilles' true glory's sake. For, as Zeus confides to Poseidon, mortal men are his concern even in their perishing (XX, 21). That's what neither Hera nor Pallas Athene understands. Hera does not understand the biting irony of Zeus' remark to her (XVIII, 357–9): "Well, then, *you* have accomplished this, *you* have aroused Achilles fleet of foot. Verily, the flowing-haired Achaeans must be *your* children."

Achilles' suffering at the moment of his triumph is Achilles' own. It cannot be matched by anything on Olympus. It is as much the prerogative of a mortal as it is the attribute of a hero. Homer is the teacher no less of Aeschylus than he is of Plato.

This, then, is one example of the way in which a piece of writing taunts us to understand what is being said not in so many words, but through the articulation and composition of the whole. The answer I have given may not be the right one or may not suffice. It is up to you to find a better one. I shall put the references in the order of my reading on the board.

Let us turn to the second example, Plato's *Phaedrus*. This example has the virture of being not only an example of writing, but also a piece of writing the main theme of which is *writing* itself.

The two people who do the talking in this dialogue are Socrates and Phaedrus. Phaedrus is a young man who loves passionately everything connected with words. He is a φιλόλογος and so is Socrates. The conversation is between two lovers of words and takes place, on a summer day, outside the walls of Athens, near a cool brook, under the shade of a tree in which cicadas make a continuous and — I suppose — sometimes deafening noise.

The dialogue is divided as follows: there is an introductory part which I shall omit, although it is highly significant. (I have a very bad conscience about this omission.) Then there are two clearly distinguishable parts as follows:

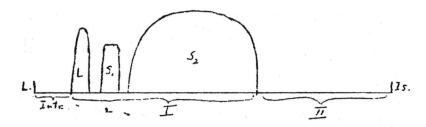

The whole dialogue is framed, as it were, by two figures. One is Lysias, a famous speech-writer, who, at the very beginning of the dialogue, appears on the scene in the most suitable mask, to wit, as the scroll in Phaedrus' left hand. (The scroll contains a speech written by Lysias.) Lysias remains present in that guise (although presumably not always in Phaedrus' left hand) throughout the entire dialogue. The other figure is Isocrates, another famous speech-writer, who is conjured up by Phaedrus and given stature and dignity by Socrates at the very end of the dialogue. One emerges as a past master of bad writing and the other full of promise of becoming a writer of superior standing. Between these two extremes Phaedrus is confronted with the problem of Speaking and Writing—and so are we.

In the first part, three speeches are being heard, the one written by Lysias and read by Phaedrus, the other two spoken by Socrates, who keeps attributing their authorship variously to somebody he cannot remember, or to the local deities, the Nymphs and Pan, or to the poet Stesichorus, or to the cicadas, or to Phaedrus. The two speeches spoken by Socrates are, at any rate, painstakingly elaborate and, if they are not to be taken strictly as written speeches, can hardly be conceived as improvised unless, indeed, "inspired," that is, *dictated* by divine or superior powers.

Lysias' speech is the plea of a man to a young boy, in which it is contended that it is better to favor a non-lover than a lover. Phaedrus considers it a wonderful speech, "charming," as he would say to-day. Socrates finds plenty of faults in it and proceeds to deliver a better speech on the same theme, except that this speech blames the lover and stops short at the point when it is supposed to begin praising the non-lover. Phaedrus does not succeed in making Socrates finish that speech. It remains truncated. Instead, Socrates, by way of recantation—because he has offended Love — delivers another speech in praise of Love. This — most eloquent — speech occupies the middle part of the dialogue and is spoken by Socrates while the sun goes through its highest course.

There is a definite change in the tenor of the dialogue after the speeches are done with, and this changed tenor persists throughout the second part. The conspicuous difference in the tenor of the two parts poses the problem of the dialogue's composition.

Socrates and Phaedrus begin to speak — quietly and soberly — about the spoken and the written word and continue doing so until the very end of the dialogue. Phaedrus agrees with Socrates that the real problem concerning writing is to distinguish good writing from bad writing and is ready to embark on a discussion of this subject. It is here (258 e–259 d) that Socrates calls Phaedrus' attention to the cicadas over their heads. He tells a story about their origin: they were once human beings, even before there were Muses; now, in their present form, they are supposed to report to the Muses, so says Socrates, who among men honors whom among the Muses; they are watching, says Socrates, him and Phaedrus now, at noontime, and if they see both talking to each other and not asleep — like sheep and most men — they might be pleased and report accordingly. The question arises: Why does Socrates tell this marvellous and fantastic story of the cicadas' origin and nature at this moment? It seems to be done to underscore that, from now on, Phaedrus and Socrates, instead of exchanging elaborate speeches, that is, written or dictated words, will, in leisurely and sober fashion, *converse* about speech-making and speech-writing and thus restore to the spoken word its proper and unchallengeable function. The trouble is that Socrates' tale interrupts this sober conversation. And let us not forget that this sober conversation is embodied in a *written* text.

In what follows, we are witnessing that the previous speeches are being criticized and analysed. The beginning of Lysias' speech is subjected to a special scrutiny. And in the course of it this beginning of Lysias' speech is made to repeat itself, twice (262 e; 263 e–264 a), word for word. We hear Socrates interpreting freely the speeches he himself made, assuming the role of their "father," so freely indeed that they appear somewhat changed: the doubtful is omitted, the wording is modified, additions are made (264 e ff.) It is Socrates' way of supporting and defending the truth they might contain. We observe Socrates and Phaedrus bearing down on various books which claim to teach the art of speaking. Phaedrus, the "lover of the Muses," is not altogether satisfied with this kind of conversation which he describes as "somewhat bare" (262 c).

At the crucial point, when the discussion seems to revert to the problem of good and bad writing (274 b), it is again interrupted by Socrates. He suddenly asks: "Do you know in what way you would best please divinity in the matter of words, either in making speeches or talking about them?" Phaedrus replies: "I certainly do not. Do you?" Socrates: "A tale, no more, I can tell from hearsay, a tale that has come down from our forefathers; as to the knowledge of the truth, it is theirs alone." And Socrates casually adds: "But should *we ourselves* find this truth, would any human fancy or opinion (δόξασμα) about it still be of any concern to us?" To which Phaedrus replies: "A ridiculous question!" Urged by Phaedrus to report what he heard, Socrates proceeds to tell the tale of Theuth and Thamus, legendary Egyptian personages, a tale in which Theuth is reported to have invented letters — and thereby writing — and to have presented this invention to the god-king Thamus. I shall read now what Thamus, according to Socrates, says (274 e-275 b): "Most artful Theuth, one man has the ability to beget artful things, another the ability to judge of their usefulness or harmfulness to their users; and now you, who are the father of letters, have been led by your affection to ascribe to them a power the opposite of that which they possess. For this invention will produce forgetfulness in the minds of those who learn to use it, because they will neglect their memory, inasmuch as their trust in writing will make them recollect by means of external marks which are no part of themselves and will not make them recollect from within through their own effort. You have thus discovered an aid not to memory but to reminding. And you give to those who learn not truth but merely the appearance of wisdom: they will become acquainted with many things without proper teaching and will seem to know, while remaining for the most part ignorant and hard to get along with since, instead of getting wise, they will merely have acquired the reputation of being wise."

We should not forget that this is a tale and that we have been warned by Socrates: hearsay is no substitute for our own discovery of the truth. Again, we should not forget that this tale presents itself to us as a written text which, according to the very content of the tale, cannot be relied upon without proper teaching. Neither should we forget that the discussion of the problem of good and bad writing has, once more, been successfully interrupted.

What follows in the written text is a description of writing that makes it appear a playful thing, undertaken for "amusement's sake" (276 b-d). One cannot expect written words to be serious. For, as Socrates says (275 d), "you would think that they [the written words] speak as if they had understanding, but should you, from a desire to learn, ask them anything about what they say, they do nothing but repeat always one and the same thing." They cannot, therefore, defend themselves against misunderstanding and abuse. Furthermore, they cannot and do not discriminate among those to whom they speak. Any author who holds that there could be much solidity and clarity in his written work, whatever its subject, deserves to be blamed for that, regardless of whether there is anyone to voice the blame or not (277 d-e; 275 c).

What, then, about the distinction between good and bad writing that Socrates and Phaedrus set out to discuss? *Nothing* is *said* about it. The answer to that question has been — of necessity, it seems — playfully withheld. Still, whatever has been said about the problem of writing has been *enacted* in the dialogue. The repetitiousness of the written word, its inability to defend itself, the superiority of the spoken word in spontaneous conversation which interprets with understanding what was written down — all that has been *enacted* by Socrates and Phaedrus in the dialogue. Must we not continue the conversation to solve the problem of good writing, to find the answer which was not *stated* in the dialogue? And does not precisely the *Phaedrus*, as it is written, offer an example of how good writing can be done?

I have a few concluding remarks.

Is Plato right in attributing superiority to the spoken word, to any conversation in which winged words can be exchanged spontaneously? There is a point at which this superiority seems to disappear altogether.

A most remarkable similarity obtains between *words*, spoken words of live speech, and *money*, money, that is, available in coins and bills. Both are precious, both circulate freely, coins and bills from hand to hand, words from mouth to mouth. The fixtures on coins and bills are gradually erased, effaced, rubbed off, just as the meanings of words seem to become fuzzy, blurred and empty with the passage of time. There is even counterfeiting in language as there is in money. Human speech, that greatest marvel perhaps under the sun, can and does indeed deteriorate to an extent which renders it obnoxious and totally wingless.

It is at this point that the written word may come to its rescue. As we so aptly say, words can be "coined." This happens both ways: words can be coined in support of clichés, fostering and increasing the ever-present tendency to diminish the vigor and meaning of speech; but words can also be coined afresh.

In a letter to a friend, Vergil, a writer, says that he gives birth to verses in the manner and according to the rite of bears (*parere se versus modo atque ritu ursino*), that is to say, that he handles his verses the way the mother bear handles her newly born cub: assiduously and persistently she licks it into its proper shape. Such assiduous work, performed on the written word and undertaken to assure the right articulation of a composed whole, can — and does — restore and preserve the integrity of human speech. It is thus that the written word repays its eternal debt to the spoken word.

10 ■ The Idea of Liberal Education

The volume of noise made about education all over the country for many years now has, in recent months, increased to such a crescendo that no man with a sane mind should try to add a note to it. Yet this is what I am doing. There is, of course, always some justification for talking about education: the desire to clarify the problem itself and to outline certain principles of education that ought to underline all possible practical applications. The problem of education, and certainly of liberal education, has nothing to do with satellites, rocketry, the organization or disorganization of the Pentagon, or the Soviet Union. And yet it is not by chance, as we shall see, that these topics creep into all that educational talk. Nor can it be spoken about in the jargon of educational psychology that takes for granted a great many things and ignores even more. I shall use simple terms at the risk of being trite and saying things that everyone seems to know anyhow. All I want is to remind you of things that you do know.

First published in *The Goals of Higher Education*, ed. W. D. Weatherford, Jr. (Cambridge, Mass.: Harvard University Press, 1960).

I

Every one of us (that is, every human being on this earth, without exception) is in some way educated. By this I mean that everyone assimilates from his early childhood sets of customs, beliefs, opinions of all kinds, ways of behavior, and even ways of feeling and reacting. Without this elemental kind of education we could not become members of our families, of clans, and of all the smaller or larger communities to which we belong. To be a human being means to be educated in this elemental way, to be educated in the elements of human life. Ours is a double growth, double nourishment, double ripening. Our maturity as human beings does not necessarily coincide with our maturity as living organisms, whereas no such discrepancy seems to exist in the case of our incomprehensible cousins, the animals. The nourishment that leads to our human maturity is provided for us by our parents, our friends, by the innumerable relations, associations, and hierarchies that bind us to the life of our communities; most of the time we are rather passive recipients of this kind of feeding, the lowest and yet perhaps most important level of what I have called elemental education. Most of the time we are not even aware of it.

We are much more aware of another level of elemental education, the one that takes place through what is loosely called "experience." When we invoke experience, we mean mainly the disappointments, difficulties, troubles, obstacles, sufferings, and catastrophes that we have encountered, succumbed to or overcome, and keep anticipating. We become wise (not all of us, to be sure) through such adverse experiences. An elemental generalization takes place, variously called ritual, or tradition, or "ways of doing things," or "the wisdom of the ages."

And at this point a new medium of education comes to the fore, the medium of deliberate reflection and of systematic procedure. In this medium the troubles and obstacles are lifted, by a process of conscious formalization, to a new level, the theoretical level. They become problems. How to solve them has to be learned: formal disciplines are required to bring a problem into focus; that is, to disentangle the kernel from the shell, to proceed methodically, to aid our memory, to make visible what is obscure. This cannot be done without effort and, just as experience is basically painful, formal learning is intrinsically difficult. What I am now describing is the way of formal education that grows out of our elemental education and remains rooted in it. We can dispense with it only at the expense of our winning clarity and greater skills and greater ease to cope with the necessities of life.

Have I now given a complete story of education? Obviously not. I spoke of lifting the troubles and obstacles encountered in experience to a new level that I call theoretical, and I introduced the notion of formal disciplines that have to be mastered before theoretical problems can be solved. But how does this lifting take place? How is elemental education transformed into formal education? Did I not skip something crucial at this point? I did. I neglected to mention the level of that lifting and transforming operation: our questioning. I have, therefore, to retrace my steps and to digress quite a bit in order to consider the phenomenon of questioning at some length.

II

There are many ways of questioning and as many, of course, of answering. Most of our questions are concerned with actions and the means to carry them out. Not only questions like these: "How do you do that?" or "How does one proceed to achieve this end?" but also ones like these: "Have you a pencil?" or "Where is Swarthmore Avenue?" For these latter questions mean that I need a pencil to write something down and that I have to go to that street for some definite purpose. Most questions are indeed of a practical nature; that is, they refer to our doing and acting. Another class of question is formed by queries of a gossipy nature, stemming from our passions — for example, from malice, grudge, vanity, or envy. I suspect that this class of questions is numerically as large as the first one, if not larger. And closely related to the gossipy class there exists a class of questions rooted in what may be called "idle curiosity." It is worthwhile to reflect for a moment upon the nature of idle curiosity, a curiosity, that is, not guided by any malevolent or benevolent feelings. All gossip has an element of curiosity in it, of wonderment, and that means some quest, however infinitesimal,

however distorted, for knowledge. If we were to adopt the
metaphor "body of knowledge," we might perhaps say, using a
famous phrase from recent political and military history, that
gossip constitutes the soft underbelly of knowledge. Gossip is
the small tribute that our passionate and appetitive life pays — in
very, very small coins — to intellectual life. And it may even reach
a nobler part of the body of knowledge, if channeled in a proper
direction. This brings us to still another class of questions, where
idle curiosity is replaced by a kind of passionate or, if you please,
serious curiosity. Questions raised out of idle curiosity are, strictly
speaking, none of our business. But when we raise them because
we attach very definite importance to the answers — that is, when
we make it our business to know the answers — we deal with
questions of a different nature. In a trial, where crucial facts
have to be established, or in our travels, confronting unfamiliar
customs, we ask questions in order to win certainty about things,
situations, people and their character, and so forth. Such queries
could be properly called exploratory questions. In raising them
we want to know, either in order to base a judgement on the
knowledge obtained or just simply in order to know. It must
be granted that it is not always easy to draw the line between
idle curiosity and this nobler kind of curiosity. And I should add,
of course, that there are other kinds of questions that do not
quite fall into the classes I have mentioned — for example, polite
questions, affectionate questions, rhetorical questions — that we
need not consider now.

Whatever the difference between these kinds of questions,
the practical ones, the gossipy ones, the exploratory ones, and
all the others, they all have something in common. They all
originate within the horizon of our daily lives, a horizon that
includes the familiar and the surprising, routine and novelty,
that which has precedents and that which has not. The usual
and the unusual are labels put on things and events within the
frame of our common and conflicting experience. The unexpected is still woven out of the texture of the expected. And it
is this frame of the fundamentally familiar that actually allows
us to formulate our questions. That is: they can be put into
words. Our questioning is guided by language itself, which is
oriented toward the world around us as we know it, including

those parts or elements or factors that in some way remain hidden to us. There are usually some dark corners behind or beneath pieces of furniture in a room full of light. The world has many such dark corners. Questions of the kind I have mentioned are like flashlights, the beam of which we direct towards those dark corners. This beam is our language. And it is not too difficult to see that the articulations of language correspond to the ways in which we raise questions and try to answer them. Aristotle, in his analysis of language, has shown how the various modes of being which determine the structure of what we call a world, our world, our not too hospitable home, are prefigured in the various forms of our questioning. The names of his categories are, for the most part, interrogatives.

Let me now consider another aspect of our questioning. In raising a question we expect an answer. A question, by its very nature, wants to be satisfied. Or, in other words, questions as such are possible (including the so-called impossible ones) only on the assumption that there is something which we do not know but which can be known. And this something is expected to appear in any answer. A question is indeed a state of mind (the state of mind of us as questioning beings) in which we want to know what we do not know. The phenomenon of questioning points to the possibility, at least, of knowledge. The answer that we get is, for the most part, an opinion. We live, for the most part, in holding and meeting opinions. But the important thing about opinions is precisely that they cannot avoid putting on the cloak of knowledge. The possibility of our having opinions rests on the possibility, at least, of our having truth. In our thoughtful moments — and there are not too many — we try to see whether our opinions, our answers to questions, are true or not.

Questioning, then, presupposes as unquestionable that there is something not known: the unknown. And it does that, it seems to me, in two fundamentally different ways. The unknown is understood either as something not yet known or as something once known but forgotten. Whatever the relation between time and the substance or state of knowledge, the temporal character of questioning compels us to envisage the way to knowledge in this double temporal perspective. The way to knowledge can be understood either as the pursuit of the not yet known (as discovery of the not yet known) or as the pursuit of the once known (as recovery of the once known). Prophecy and divining are the primordial forms of the first kind of pursuit, myth-making the primordial form of the second kind. Derivative forms (by this term I do not mean to imply any censure) are what we call science and history. Science is forever on the way to discover the not yet known; history is forever recovering the once known. Both embody the type of questioning that I have called the exploratory kind in its purest form. But both also depend on a quite different kind of questioning that I have, with some trepidation, to consider now.

I have said before that within the confines of our horizon there is the expected as well as the unexpected, the old and the new, the known and the unknown, the familiar and the unfamiliar. We do, however, experience a kind of question which, as it were, tends to smash the bounds that limit us. We do occasionally stop altogether and face the familiar as if for the first time — anything: a person, a street, the sky, a fly. The overwhelming impression on such occasions is the strangeness of the thing we contemplate. This state of mind requires detachment, and I am not at all certain to what extent we can contrive its presence. We suddenly do not feel at home in this world of ours. We take a deep look at things, at people, at words, with eyes blind to the familiar. We re-flect. Plato has a word for it: *metastrophē* or *periagogē*, a turnabout, a conversion. We detach ourselves from all that is familiar to us; we change the direction of our inquiry; we do not explore the unknown any more; on the contrary, we convert the known into an unknown. We wonder. And we burst out with that inexorable question: Why is that so? To be sure, we have raised the question "why" before. I can certainly ask: Why did it snow yesterday and does not snow today? Why did Mr. X say this or that to Mr. Y? But this "why" I am talking about now is of a different kind. It does not lead to any discovery or recovery. It calls myself in question with all my questioning. It compels me to detach myself from myself, to transcend the limits of my horizon; that is, it educates me. It gives me the freedom to go to the roots of all my questioning. I can begin to understand that even our gossiping may ultimately rest on the transcendent power of this "why"; that even the children's "why," repeated endlessly to the disgust of their mothers and fathers, may ultimately derive from the human possibility of a total conversion.

III

It is time to revert to the point that prompted me to digress into a consideration of the phenomenon of questioning. The question was: How does elemental education transform itself into formal education? I can try to answer that now.

Elemental education that comes to us through experience, and mostly through adverse experiences, congeals into many kinds of habitual opinions and traditional beliefs. But human questioning never stops. In particular, there is the tendency to go to the roots of our experience, to explore the not yet known or the once known but forgotten. On the other hand, we are bound, at some point at least, to reflect, in wonderment and detachment, not only on all that offers itself to our exploration, on all the visible, the audible, and the intelligible about us, but also on our doing this questioning and exploring, on the means and tools that we use in this enterprise, on ourselves as questioning and exploring beings. This metastrophic reflection, in conjunction with our exploratory questioning, leads us to the establishment of those formal disciplines that I mentioned before. The phenomenon of language, for example (it is only an example, but a significant one), presents itself to us in all its strangeness. We reflect about it, about our speaking to each other. And in exploring this phenomenon this is what we see: we understand each other in speaking and, no doubt, we also misunderstand each other, the latter perhaps more easily than the former. But it is not difficult for us to see that all misunderstanding is based on some understanding. In our speaking, in our language, we convey to each other thoughts that we want to be understood, and we achieve this purpose in spite of all the failings that we may experience. This means that we know how to speak, even if our speech is imperfect. We know how to link words with each other, how to arrange a sequence of such assemblages of words, how to emphasize or de-emphasize some of them, how to make sense, how to tell what we mean, and how to conceal what we mean. Not only do we know how to speak—that is, to speak imperfectly—we also know about this very imperfection. This knowledge, if formalized and formulated, becomes the discipline of grammar. It is of little use in our actual speaking, and yet, upon reflection, we cannot fail to see how utterly dependent on grammatical forms we are in our actual speaking. A similar reflection upon speech leads us to the formal discipline of logic. And I should like, at the risk of being tiresome, to add another example derived from a continuing reflection upon our speech. The act of speaking presupposes the distinguishing of one word from another and the relating of one word to another. It presupposes, that is, counting. For counting is distinguishing and at the same time relating one thing to another. At all times, therefore, speaking and the thinking involved in it have been understood as a sort of computing. This does not mean that in speaking we have an explicit knowledge of numbers. But reflecting and pursuing our exploratory questioning, we arrive at the formal discipline of arithmetic; that is, the science of numbers and their relations on which all our computing is based.

There is no limit to the further exploration of those formal disciplines. They get enlarged and refined, branch off into other disciplines, combine and support each other, and finally encompass whatever might be knowable in our world; they become all the scientific and historical disciplines taught and learned around the globe. Their acquisition is called *formal education.* And I can repeat now with somewhat greater clarity what I said earlier: formal education grows out of elemental education but remains rooted in it. The formal disciplines come into being as the result of our human ability to detach ourselves from our familiar and conflicting experiences, to turn about, to ask the radical question "why" and to persist in it, pursuing at the same time the exploratory questioning within the horizon in which we live. That is why the theoretical level thus reached always remains a two-sided one: the formal disciplines and sciences can also be applied disciplines and sciences; theoretical problems have or can have direct relation to our doing and making, to our practical life. It is only when we dedicate ourselves to the radical, metastrophic questioning, when we free ourselves from the ever-present concern that the burden of life imposes upon us, that formal education becomes *liberal education*, that the formal disciplines become liberal disciplines or liberal arts. Obviously, this is a precarious and even perilous kind of business. But I do not know of anything worthwhile that is not precarious and perilous.

IV

The idea of liberal education was conceived by the Greeks. For them it meant an education proper to the free and noble men in contradistinction to slaves and other people engaged in any kind of menial work. To be a free man meant to be a man enjoying leisure — that is, precisely, a man not under any necessity or compulsion to do servile work. But to have leisure in turn meant primarily dealing with affairs of the state, pursuing political ends, and also pursuing knowledge and wisdom. The Greek word for leisure, *scholē*, is significantly the root of the word "school" in Latin as well as in all our vernacular languages. Leisure meant schooling; that is, the opportunity to learn. The history of education is the history of the meaning of the term "school." Let me quote from Aristotle's *Politics* (VIII,3): "Nature herself, as has often been said, requires that we should be able not only to work well, but to use leisure well; for, as I must repeat once and again, the first principle of all action [that is, the end for the sake of which any action is undertaken] is leisure . . . and therefore the question must be asked in good earnest, What ought we to do when at leisure? Clearly we ought not to be amusing ourselves, for then amusement would be the end of life." And Aristotle goes on: "It is clear, then, that there are branches of learning and education which we must study with a view to the enjoyment of leisure, and these are to be valued for their own sake." To study for the enjoyment of leisure and in leisure means to be engaged in liberal education. It is an arduous task. This kind of education does not look for some goal or good beyond itself. It is in itself its own end. Long before Aristotle and long after him, even under totally different social conditions, this statement defined liberal learning and liberal education. What this understanding of liberal education assumes is that man's most proper and specific character is his desire to know. Only in pursuing this goal is man really man and really free. To acquire the various means that enable man to persist in this pursuit is to cultivate the arts of freedom.

The idea of liberal education, then, whether you accept or reject it, is not definable in terms of some peculiar subject matter. Some applied sciences may well fall outside its scope. But, by and large, any formal discipline may form its vehicle and basis. It is not the subject matter that determines the character of studies as liberal studies. It is rather the way in which a formal discipline, a subject matter, is taken up that is decisive: whenever it is being studied for its own sake, whenever the metastrophic way of questioning is upheld, whenever genuine wonderment is present, liberal education is taking place.

Foremost among the formal liberal disciplines are, of course, the mathematical disciplines, the physical sciences, the science of life, the sciences of language — grammar, rhetoric, and logic — and also the great works of literature, those incomparable mirrors of man. But it is a rather fantastic idea to equate liberal studies with the so-called humanities; as if mathematical and scientific disciplines were less human than historical or poetic or philosophical studies. And do we not know that philosophy itself can be studied in the most illiberal way?

V

Liberal education is a precarious and even perilous kind of business. Let me show you the great obstacles that stand in its way. These obstacles are not external impediments, nor do they stem from nonrational sources in man. On the contrary, these obstacles are rooted in what is specifically human in man, and it is not possible not to meet them.

1. The first obstacle is the learning situation itself. What is the ideal learning situation? It is the more or less continuous contact between a student and his teacher, who is another student, more advanced in many ways, but still learning, himself. This situation usually does not prevail; in fact, it is extremely rare. Since time immemorial, institutions of learning, especially higher learning, have been established, called "schools"— and

the ambiguity of the term becomes immediately apparent. Institutionalization means ordering of activities into certain patterns; in the case of learning activities, into classes, schedules, courses, curriculums, examinations, degrees, and all the venerable and sometimes ridiculous paraphernalia of academic life. The point is that such institutionalization cannot be avoided: both the gregarious and the rational character of man compel him to impose upon himself laws and regulations. Moreover, the discipline of learning itself seems to require an orderly and planned procedure. And yet we all know how this schedule routine can interfere with the spontaneity of questioning and of learning and the occurrence of genuine wonderment. A student may even never become aware that there is the possibility of spontaneous learning which depends merely on himself and on nobody and nothing else. Once the institutional character of learning tends to prevail, the goal of liberal education may be completely lost sight of, whatever other goals may be successfully reached. And I repeat, this obstacle is not extraneous to learning. It is prefigured in the methodical and systematic character of exploratory questioning. It has to be faced over and over again.

2. The second obstacle to liberal education is our condition as heirs of intellectual traditions. Here again, it is man's own rational nature that brings this obstacle about. Animals do not pass on their skills to their progeny in such a way that those skills can accumulate and grow. Man, and only man, does precisely that. His skills and knowledges are many-storied edifices. Each generation adds something to what has been previously built and preserved. We are proud of this fact and call it progress. And, indeed, such progress does exist in definite areas. But this very fact confronts us with the ever-present danger of sedimentation, fossilization, or petrification of our knowledge. We are fond of pointing to the European universities of the fifteenth and sixteenth centuries which exhibit those petrifying tendencies rather clearly and are prone to exalt the fresh wind of the Renaissance and Humanism that blew all the accumulated dust away. But it behooves us to look at our own institutions of higher learning and to discern these same tendencies among us. We are not immune. This danger is inherent in all learning and all

scholarship, and liberal education can never ignore it.

3. But the most serious obstacle is the relation of liberal education to the political community, the state. The Greeks, you remember, saw in leisure, in schooling, the source of a twofold activity: the pursuit of learning and of political ends. Greek thought, in fact, circles continuously about these two highest poles of human life. The relation of man to his citizenship, to the obligations that flow from his being a citizen, a member of a political community — this relation is one of the great and standing themes of all classical philosophy. Man conceived as a political animal and man conceived as a being desirous to know are not necessarily identical. What complicates matters is the immediate and compelling interest that any state takes in the education of its children and youth. Plato's *Republic* is devoted to this theme. Aristotle says *(Politics,* V, 9): "Of all things I have mentioned, that which most contributes to the permanence of constitutions is the adaptation of education to the form of government," and (in VIII, 1): "No one will doubt that the legislator should direct his attention above all to the education of youth, or that the neglect of education does harm to states. The citizen should be moulded to suit the form of government under which he lives." And let us listen to champions of political doctrines differing sharply from the conservative and aristocratic views of Aristotle. We all know how decisive Jefferson considered education to be for the preservation of the republican form of government. In a letter to John Adams (October 28, 1813), for example, he speaks of a bill he had prepared but which was not adopted by the Virginia legislature: "It was a bill for the more general diffusion of learning. This proposed to divide every county into wards of five or six miles square, like your townships; to establish in each ward a free school for reading, writing, and common arithmetic; to provide for the annual selection of the best subjects from these schools, who might receive, at the public expense, a higher degree of education at a district school; and from these district schools to select a certain number of the most promising subjects, to be completed at an university, where all the useful sciences should be taught. Worth and genius would thus have been sought out from every condition of life and completely prepared by education for defeating the competition of

wealth and birth for public trusts." This educational scheme is
conceived as a means to an end, a political end. And Horace
Mann, in the middle of the nineteenth century, has this to say:
"The establishment of a republican government without well-
appointed and efficient means for the universal education of
the people is the most rash and foolhardy experiment ever tried
by man." How often is the phrase "education for citizenship"
used in our schools today! I need not mention the present-day
pressure for a change in the educational system of the country
to be undertaken for the sake of political ends. The demands
of the political community to which we belong are indeed
inexorable. It is important to understand, however, that the idea
of liberal education cannot be easily reconciled with those
demands. It is important to see that there is a definite tension
between the exigencies of political life and the self-sustained goal
of liberal education. This tension is very great. Consider that
ultimately the existence of a state (any state) involves the question of life and death for any of its members. But consider also
that no less is at stake for a commitment to leisure in the true
understanding of this word. I can hardly think of a better
illustration of that tension than the story of Archimedes' death,
which I shall recount by way of conclusion.

There are many versions of that story. It seems, at any rate,
that Archimedes took an active and even decisive part in the
defense of Syracuse, his home town, when it was besieged by
the enemy, and he contrived, by means of ingenious machinery,
to repel the attacker. He was fulfulling his civic duty. His end
came when a Roman soldier stepped close to the place where
he was drawing his figures on the sand. This is how Plutarch
relates one of the versions: "A Roman soldier, running upon him
with a drawn sword, offered to kill him . . . . Archimedes, looking back, earnestly besought him to hold his hand a little while,
that he might not leave what he was then at work upon
inconclusive and imperfect; but the soldier, nothing moved by
his entreaty, instantly killed him." The figures on the sand and
the problem they represented were for Archimedes a question
of life and death; or should we perhaps say a question of more
than life and death? Whether this story be true or not, it makes
us see the precarious position that is the lot of any genuine

searching and questioning; it makes us see the ultimate incommensurability between this kind of searching and questioning, the basis of all liberal learning, and the implacable conditions of our existence. But what would the world be like if that searching and questioning were not possible at all?

11 ■ Aristotle, an Introduction

Many, many years ago, I attended a series of lectures on Aristotle's philosophy. The lecturer began his exposition as follows: "As regards Aristotle himself, as regards the circumstances and the course of his life, suffice it to say: Aristotle was born, spent his life in philosophizing, and died." This beginning seemed to me then most appropriate, for Aristotle means to us, indeed, nothing but what we know of him, or fancy we know of him, as a man engaged in that extravagant enterprise which, since Pythagoras (according to the tradition), has borne the name of "Philosophy." There is a difficulty, though. Whenever we try to understand what Aristotle is saying, we stumble on something that we simply cannot ignore, and that is that his words bring up the words of another man who was his teacher and bore the name of Plato. There is no alternative; we have to face that peculiar circumstance in Aristotle's life.

It is pretty certain that, at the age of seventeen or eighteen, Aristotle joined the community founded by Plato outside the walls of Athens and called (from its geographical location) the Academy. He stayed there until Plato died, that is, for about

Enlarged version of a lecture first delivered at St. John's College, Annapolis, April 20, 1962. First published in *Ancients and Moderns, Essays on the Tradition of Political Philosophy in Honor of Leo Strauss*, ed. Joseph Cropsey (New York: Basic Books, 1964).

twenty years (367–347). In the following twelve years he taught
for a while in Asia Minor and was invited to tutor a young
Macedonian prince who later became known as Alexander the
Great. In 335 he returned to Athens and established, again outside the walls of the city, a spot of leisure, that is of study, called
the Lyceum. Not being a citizen of Athens, he could not own
this place. He merely taught there. About a year before he died,
it pleased the city of Athens to accuse him of impiety, that is,
of undermining the city's life. Aristotle decided to leave Attica
rather than stand trial. He is supposed to have said on that occasion that he did not want the Athenians to commit a crime
against Philosophy for the second time.

TABLE (*with approximate dates*)

Born in Stagira (Chalcidice)	Academy	Abroad	Lyceum	Death
384	367–347	347–335	335–323	322
	20	12	12	

Now, if we look at what is known as "The Works of Aristotle," we cannot help being amazed by both their bulk and their
diversity. These works have come down to us in nearly the same
condition in which they were edited by Andronicus of Rhodes
in the first century B.C. We know that this edition did not contain a series of other works attributed to Aristotle and not
available today (except for the book entitled *The Athenian Constitution*, the text of which was found in 1880). Above all, that
edition did not contain — and was not supposed to contain — a
series of genuine works of Aristotle — dialogues, epistles, and
compositions in verse, already published and well-known in antiquity. We possess only a few fragments of them. As to the body
of Aristotelian works available to us, it consists, beyond any
doubt, of some of the material directly related to the lecturing
and studying that went on at the Lyceum and presumably also
at other places where Aristotle taught. Parts of that material
are lectures or treatises composed with great care, but other parts
are more or less loosely conjoined treatments of topical themes,
notes, and perhaps mere abstracts from, or comments on, more
original compositions. There are, on the one hand, different and

sometimes irreconcilable versions of one and the same theme, and, on the other hand, identical passages recurring in different contexts.

It seems not unimportant to note that all these writings, the extant ones as well as the lost ones, can hardly have been produced in the twelve years of the Lyceum period, in which short time, incidentally, Alexander succeeded in conquering a world. The writings concerning the classification, the physiology, and the anatomy of animals alone must have required many, many years of study and observation on the part of quite a few people. It is even doubtful whether the tremendous effort to which the extant Aristotelian writings — as well as the titles of the lost ones — testify can be thought of as confined within the limits of the 24-year period between 347 and 323. It seems more reasonable to conceive of that effort as having begun in the Academy period, long before Plato's death. We have, indeed, some evidence to the effect. It is undeniable, furthermore, that Aristotle and those who assisted him in his work utilized studies made before Plato's days. But it is still true that everything we read in that collection of Aristotelian writings bears an unmistakable stamp: the language and the peculiar terms in which it is written. Whatever the degree of incoherence or coherence in the body of Aristotelian writings, their language has always the same characteristic mold. And, what is more, the shadow of Plato is always perceivable in them.

As is well known, classical scholarship in the last 150 years has concentrated on the task of finding the correct chronological sequence of the Platonic dialogues. This task has been brought to a more or less successful end. Let us not forget, however, that it is one thing to establish the chronological order of the dialogues and quite another to understand what they are about, what they represent, what they say and do not say, and why they do so. To interpret the chronology of the dialogues as mirroring the development of Plato's own thinking — even under the assumption that such a development did actually occur — is a sign of considerable naïveté or of no less considerable rashness. Recently the attempt has been made to construct the development of Aristotle's thinking and to distinguish a "Platonic period" in Aristotle's life from a post-Platonic, and finally an anti-Platonic phase. Granted that Aristotle's thinking must have had a history, granted that what we call his philosophy did not spring out of him as Pallas Athena did out of Zeus' forehead, the evidence presented by his work, fragments and all, is far from sufficient for establishing and delineating with any degree of accuracy such stages of his thought.

Two things, however, are overwhelmingly clear: (1) the basic postulates of Aristotle's thinking are to be found in what we conceive to be Platonic — and Socratic — philosophizing, and (2) there is an unshakable unwillingness on Aristotle's part to follow Plato's lead in certain crucial respects. It is safe to say, I think, that Aristotle's relation to Plato is a supreme example of the true pupil-teacher relationship: the pupil's unswerving loyalty to his teacher manifests itself in the pupil's commitment to Truth, even if that commitment makes the pupil reject the teacher's teaching. Let us hear Aristotle himself on that subject.[1] About to begin an investigation into what is meant when people talk about "The Good," Aristotle remarks that such an investigation is "distasteful" to him because it involves "men dear to him" (φίλοι ἄνδρες) who introduced the doctrine of "ideas" (τὰ εἴδη), that is — to use the Latin term — the doctrine of "species," or — to use the equivalent English term — the doctrine of "looks." These men are Plato and his followers. Aristotle goes on to say: "But — for those pursuing philosophy, at least — it would seem that it is probably better and, to safeguard the truth, even necessary to go against the grain; for, both one's friends *and* the truth being dear to one, it is right and proper to give greater honor to truth." The companions in the Academy called themselves "friends" (φίλοι). In an elegy, a fragment of which has been preserved, Aristotle speaks of an altar dedicated to "holy Friendship" and unmistakably refers to Plato (without naming him) as a "man whom bad men have no right even to praise."[2] Let us, then, keep in mind this exemplary relation of Aristotle, the pupil, to Plato, the teacher, in trying to understand Aristotle's own way.

Without making any attempt to encompass in a brief statement the whole of Aristotle's philosophy, I shall simply point

---

1. *Nicomachean Ethics* A 6. 1096 a 11 ff.
2. Fr. 623, 1583 a 12. Cf. Werner Jaeger, *Aristotle* (Oxford, 1961), pp. 106 ff.

to, or rather hint at, some of the fundamental features of this vast edifice. Let me begin with a somewhat simplified table of Aristotle's main themes, as indicated by the following terms:

φύσις *(nature)*	ζωή *(life)*			
ψυχή *(soul)*	νοῦς *(—)*	ἄνθρωπος	τέχνη	λόγος
τάξις *(order)*	κόσμος *(world)*	*(man)*	*(art)*	*(———)*

None of these terms is specifically "Aristotelian." They are Greek words commonly used in a somewhat confused and ambiguous way. In Aristotle they acquire to a large degree an uncommon and unambiguous significance. Let us look at them.

Unavoidably, we have to begin with λόγος. The principal and inextinguishable meaning of this word is speech. We mean by speech — everybody means by it — a sequence of sounds uttered by somebody in such a way as to be understandable to others. The verb "to understand" refers primarily, if not uniquely, to speech. Hearing somebody speak, we may say, "I understand what you are saying." We may, in fact, misunderstand, but even misunderstanding involves understanding. But *what* do we understand in hearing somebody speak? Not the sounds in themselves, the audible and articulated, low and high-pitched noises issuing from somebody's mouth (or some machine, for that matter). We *hear* these noises. But hearing is not understanding. That is why we do not understand speech in a foreign tongue. In a manner which, itself, is hardly or not at all understandable, the sounds carry with them — or embody or represent — something else, precisely that which *makes* us understand, whenever we understand. This source and target of our understanding consists of units to which single words correspond, as well as of combinations of those units to which whole sequences of words correspond. The speaker and the hearer share — or, at least, intend to share — the understanding of those units and of those combinations of units. The speaker transposes what he means into sounding words, and the hearer who understands reverses that process in reaching back to the intended meaning. The intended meaning is what the Greeks call τὸ νοητόν; its single units are the νοητά (νοητόν being a verbal adjective of νοεῖν). Speech and understanding are inseparable. Λόγος means inseparably both speech and that which can be and is being understood *in* speech. It is in *man* and through *man* (ἄνθρωπος) that λόγος manifests itself conspicuously, so much so that Aristotle is able to say: "Man is a living being possessing speech," and that means possessing the ability to *understand* the spoken word (ζῷον λόγον ἔχον).

But what does speech "bespeak"? The answer is: everything man is familiar with — the sky and the earth, the rivers and the sea, the living beings around him, on land, in water, in the air, the things he himself builds and produces, as well as the tools and appurtenances that his arts and skills require to produce those things, and furthermore, the knowledge that guides his arts and skills, not only to satisfy his most elementary needs, but also to establish customs and institutions in which his life flows from generation to generation, in misery or happiness, in friendship or enmity, in praise or blame, and to which customs and institutions he is attached beyond his most pressing wants. That is what his speech and his understanding are *mostly* about.

But speech and the understanding that goes into it and can be got out of it are not just "about" something. To be sure, we can choose a theme and talk about it, circumscribe it, beat about the bush. But what we say, however circuitously or confusedly or loosely, is said in words and sentences, each of which conveys immediate meaning. The λόγος cannot help moving in the medium of the immediately understandable. To be sure, words and sentences can be involuntarily or deliberately ambiguous. But they can be that only because they carry with them several distinct meanings which, separately, are clearly understood. To be sure, speech can be obscure. But it can be obscure only because the clarity of some of its parts impinges, or seems to impinge, on the clarity of others.

Speech, then, presents to the understanding of the listener what the speaker himself understands. It presents to the listener nothing but combinations of νοητά. In doing that, however, speech "bespeaks" all the things and all the properties of things that abound around us, all the special circumstances and situations in which we find ourselves. The question arises: Do the νοητά presented to us in speech stem from the speaker, whoever he might be, or do they stem from the things and circumstances spoken of? Does not any human speech translate the language of the things themselves?

Let me turn for a moment to the way things and events around us have been referred to in later times. In Galileo's words: "The *book* of Nature is written in mathematical characters." Descartes said: "The science contained in the great *book* of the world . . . ." Harvey said: "The *book* of Nature lies open before us and can be easily consulted." The phrase "book of Nature" is a metaphor used long before the seventeenth century, but why was this particular metaphor ever chosen? Is it not because Nature is understood as something that can be read like a book, provided we know how to read it? What have we been doing but reading and decoding the book of Nature? But does not that indeed imply a language that is nature's own? Francis Bacon was of the opinion that Nature is subtly secretive, full of riddles, Sphinx-like. But secrets can be revealed, riddles can be solved in words. We persist, as one can read every day, in solving the "riddles of nature." In ancient times, the language of all that existed around us was taken much more directly (I was about to say "in a much more literal sense") as a spoken language, a language not written, yet visible, and if not visible, one to be guessed at. Human speech seems indeed to translate that visible or invisible language of things into the audible language of words. And just as the sound of human speech can be traced down to its ultimate components to which the letters of the alphabet correspond, things around us can be decomposed into their first rudiments — the "elements"— the original letters of the language of things, as it were. Our speech, even our unguarded colloquial way of speaking, may reveal to the attentive listener the hidden articulations of the language of things. Aristotle, no less than Plato, was constantly following up casually spoken words.

No doubt, speech can deliberately deceive us, distort and falsify the truth of things. The fireworks of the Sophists, for example — and there are always Sophists around — make things and relations of things assume a most unexpected, dazzling, and puzzling aspect: things suddenly appear not to be what they are. But who is doing the lying, if it be lying, the Sophists or the things themselves? A *critique* of speech, a critical inquisition into speaking and arguing has to be undertaken — as it was undertaken by Parmenides, by Prodicus, by Plato, by Aristotle. The result of this critique can be stated as follows: to speak does not always mean to make things appear in their true light. For Aristotle, only one kind of speech, ὁ λόγος ἀποφαντικός, the declaratory and revealing speech[3] translates or interprets the language of things. To be able to use this kind of speech requires a *discipline*, the discipline of the λόγος. Everywhere in Aristotle's work, one senses, to the annoyance of some and to the delight of others, the effectiveness of that discipline, the effectiveness of what we call the "logic" of Aristotle.

It is this emphasis on the λόγος, the λόγος ἀποφαντικός, that made Aristotle a great teacher through the centuries. But in this respect he is as much a pupil as a teacher. We have a significant passage in Plato's work that indicates that rather clearly. I mean the passage in the *Phaedo* where Plato makes Socrates meet Cebes' crucial objection concerning the deathlessness of the soul.[4] Here, Socrates, after silently looking back into himself for quite a while, reaches — in speaking — far back into his own youth. He wanted very much, he reports, to find out, with regard to any single thing or occurrence, what was responsible for its coming into being, its passing away, its being the way it was. But he could not find any satisfactory answers. Nor could he learn them from anybody else, not even from the great Anaxagoras. He had to abandon the way in which questions like his were dealt with in the various versions of the "inquiry into nature" or the "story of nature" (περὶ φύσεως ἱστορία). He decided to embark upon a different journey, his second journey, his "next best try" (δεύτερος πλοῦς ἐπὶ τὴν τῆς αἰτίας ζήτησιν). This is the presentation he makes of his new endeavor.

By looking directly at whatever presents itself in our familiar world, at things and their properties, at human affairs and actions, we run the risk of being blinded, as do people who observe the sun during an eclipse if they do not look at its image on some water surface. That may well have happened to those investigators of nature. To avoid being "blinded," Socrates thought he had to "take refuge in spoken words" (εἰς τοὺς λόγους καταφυγόντα), in exchanging questions and answers with

---

3. *On Interpretation* 5. 17 a 8; 4. 17 a 2; 6. 17 a 25; *Posterior Analytics* A 2. 72 a 11.
4. *Phaedo* 96 ff.

himself and with others and in *them* search for the truth of things.

What Socrates implies is that the reasons for things being as they are, and the truth about those things, are to be found in the spoken — or, for that matter, silent — words and the νοητά they embody. That is not to say, Socrates warns, that the example of the sun, which can only be looked at through its image, is applicable here; if one compares a man who investigates things in words with one who investigates them directly, the former can hardly be said to be dealing more with images than the latter. On the contrary, we surmise, it is the former, and not the latter, who sees things as *mere* images or copies of originals, namely of the νοητά revealed to us in speech, in spite of the widespread opinion that "mere" words and their meanings at best mirror and usually do nothing but distort what we call "reality." "Reality" is an anglicized, queer Latin term, the more adequate, if barbaric, English translation of which is "thinghood."

It is safe to say, I think, that in one respect at least, Aristotelian philosophy consists in the execution of that Socratic program. It is in speech, in searching for and finding adequate words, that the λόγος of things, the λόγος of nature (φύσις) becomes audible and capable of being understood. That is what constitutes the characteristic mode of Aristotelian language I referred to earlier. It is an unfortunate, if perhaps not surprising, historical accident that Aristotle's vocabulary acquired immeasurable weight and a fetish-like character in its Latin rendering perpetuated in almost all modern tongues. It is perhaps no exaggeration to state that something like three-quarters of all existing scientific and philosophic terminology is either determined by Aristotle's latinized vocabulary or can be traced back to it. Quite a few times in the past a revulsion against that gibberish set in. We witness some of it today. But the impact of Aristotelian terms endures: our common daily language bears witness to that.

On the other hand, Aristotle's execution of the Socratic program entails at least five interrelated modifications of some of the crucial Socratic-Platonic postulates. In trying to speak about this other aspect of Aristotelian philosophy, I shall have to consider some of the other terms in the above table.

In the *Phaedo*, Socrates decided, as he said, to take refuge in
spoken words in order to find that which is responsible for any
single thing or occurrence coming into being, passing away, being the way it is. The phrase "to be responsible for . . ." describes
the αἰτία character of the νοητά presented to our understanding in speech. Aristotle firmly holds to this view. The νοητά are
the εἴδη, the species, the invisible looks, on which the existence
of things depends. They provide us with true answers to the questions: *Why* do things come into being, why do they pass away,
why are they as they are? But the way of their having that respon-
siblity is, according to Aristotle, not made sufficiently clear by
Plato and those who follow Plato. In what sense has a νοητόν,
an εἶδος, being? What does it mean to assert that a νοητόν,
an εἶδος, "is"? The Socratic way of questioning persists. But
Aristotle's answer brings the *first* decisive modification of the
Socratic-Platonic view. What Aristotle has to say about his controversy concerning the objects of mathematical sciences is also
applicable to his controversy concerning the εἴδη: "The dispute
will not deny that they *are* but will be about the *manner* of their
being" (οὐ περὶ τοῦ εἶναι, ἀλλὰ περὶ τοῦ τρόπου).[5] The phrase
"manner of being" will be gradually clarified, I hope, as I
proceed.

The manner of being of an εἶδος is that it is altogether "at
work" (the Greek neuter adjective is ἐνεργόν), that is, *at work
right now*. Its being can, therefore, be characterized as ἐνέργεια.[6]
It is not certain whether Aristotle coined this term. But whether
he did or not, it belongs to him as intimately as our skin belongs
to our body. The being-at-work of an εἶδος makes it responsible for the work done. *How* it is done, what that responsiblitiy
entails, is a complex matter. For the work of the εἶδος is not
done by the εἶδος the way our hands, for example, do their work
(although Aristotle, on one occasion, compares the functioning
of the soul to that of a hand[7]). I shall return to that point. What
is most noteworthy about "being-at-work" is that there has to
be something else, namely, that which is being worked on. This
other something has to be *capable* of being worked on, that is

---

5. *Metaphysics* M 1. 1076 a 36.
6. *Metaphysics* Θ 8. 1050 a 21–23. Cf. *On the Soul* B 4. 416 b 3.
7. *On the Soul* Γ 8. 432 a 1.

to say, its character must be that of a suitable material, as wood or timber is suitable material for the work a carpenter has to perform. The characteristic name of that suitable material is ὕλη (actually derived from the Greek word for "wood"). Its manner of being consists in nothing but in its *ability* to play that role. Its manner of being is δύναμις. Nothing, I repeat, nothing *is* ὕλη except in relation to work it is subjected to, that is, in relation to an ἐνέργεια. Wood *is* wood. Bricks *are* bricks. Iron *is* iron. Wood can be called a material only with regard to some operation to be *performed* on it, an operation that would *transform* it, say, into a table.

Where do we get an inkling of the work involving εἶδος and ὕλη and their respective manners of being? The Aristotelian answer is: in the conspicuous phenomenon of generation, of γένεσις, of "coming to be." I mean the phenomenon, ever present before our eyes, of production and reproduction of generation and regeneration. Men generate men, cats generate cats, birds generate birds, fishes generate fishes. There are always young ones playing about, and this quite independently of any possible evolution stretched out over an exceedingly long period of time. Flowers and grass appear in the spring, disappear in the winter, only to reappear the next spring; trees bud, then blossom and grow fruit, and fruit produces seeds, and seeds grow again into plants. Every morning the sun rises, every year spring is born anew; and even moisture condenses into clouds which in turn produce water again. That is what the word γένεσις implies: it means both *coming to be* and *becoming*; the things which are generated are all things *to come*.

The old myths tell this story over and over again. In fact, genesis is the very soul of any myth. To understand the world, the story of its genesis has to be told. To understand the gods, the story of their genesis has to be told. Cosmogony and theogony are the primary subjects of any myth. In order to understand properly any event in human life or the character of a people or a city, the event and the character always have to be related, it seems, to their mythical origins. To tell the myth of something means to tell how this something came to be. An enterprise of this kind does not make much sense unless one relates everything ultimately to beginnings which make any genesis possible. These are precisely the mythical origins. The mythical origins contain, of necessity, these two elements: the male and the female. And however distant the sobriety of Aristotle is from the exuberance of those ancient tales, still the same aspect of the world as a chain or as cycles of generation dominates his thought.

One great and prime example of generation is the generation of living beings — of animals. Aristotle does not assume that all generation requires the separate existence of the male and the female; he knows that in some cases it is very difficult to attribute the role of the male or of the female to any part of the generating process. But on the whole, the male and the female are distinct. This, then, is how Aristotle describes the process of generation in those cases in which he thinks that the male animal emits semen.

"*Neither* the male *nor* the female emits semen *into the male*, but they both deposit together what they have to contribute *in the female*, because *in* the female there is the material (ὕλη) out of which that which is being fashioned is made." (Aristotle uses the word δημιουργούμενον, which means that which is worked on by an artisan, a craftsman, a δημιουργός.)

> . . . Hence, of necessity, it is in the *female* that parturition takes place. For the carpenter is close by his wood and the potter close by his clay, and, in general, the working on the material and the last motion which acts upon it is close by the material; for instance, housebuilding takes place at the houses which are being built. These instances may help us to understand how the male makes its contribution to generation; for not every male emits semen, and in the case of those which do, this semen is not a part of the embryo as it develops. In the same way, nothing passes from the carpenter into the pieces of wood which are his material, and there is no part of the art of carpentry present in the object which is being fashioned; it is the visible shape and the look (ἡ μορφὴ καὶ τὸ εἶδος) which pass from the carpenter and which come to be *in* the material by means of the movement that the carpenter executes. It is his *soul*, wherein is the look (τὸ εἶδος), and his *knowledge* which move his hands

or some other part of his body in a particular way (different ways for different products and always the same way for any one product); his hands move his tools, and his tools move the material (ὕλη). *In a similar way*, Nature, acting in the male of semen-emitting animals, uses this semen as a tool, as something that, by virtue of *being at work* (ἐνεργείᾳ) has movement; just as when objects are being produced by any art, the tools are in movement because the movement which belongs to the art is, in a way, in them.[8]

The embryology implied in this passage, as well as throughout Aristotle's work, is faulty. We know much more about the mechanism of fertilization than he could have possibly known. (We should not forget, though, how incomplete our own knowledge is.) But there are elements in this description which are quite independent of any embryology. Let me first restate what I have just quoted in a more technical way. The material factor of generation is represented by what the female contributes to the embryo. It is the ὕλη. The motion which works on that material is the motion of the semen that is emitted by the male animal, whose semen corresponds to the carpenter's tools. But what, in generation, corresponds to the table that the carpenter, as we say, has in mind, and furthermore, to the purpose that determines the looks of the table? It is Nature, φύσις, on which the motions of the male animal and of its semen ultimately depend. It is φύσις which provokes in the living being the urge to generate: ἔρως, desire, overpowers the living being. And that is how life (ζωή) is perpetuated for ever.

This process shows the double aspect of what we call Nature: φύσις (which term is derived from the verb φύω, meaning beget, engender, generate) must be understood as εἶδος *and* as ὕλη.[9] It shares in both, in ἐνέργεια *and* δύναμις. But it is of utmost importance to Aristotle — and to us who are trying to understand Aristotle's thought — that ἐνέργεια (and, therefore, any εἶδος) outweighs its correlated δύναμις (and, therefore, any ὕλη)

---

8. *Generation of Animals* A 22. 730 a 34–730 b 23.
9. *Physics* B 1. 193 a 28–31.

in significance, in rank, in manner of being. Aristotle devotes an entire book (Book Θ of the *Metaphysics*) *to showing the "priority" of* ἐνέργεια over δύναμις. The famous cliché question — What comes first, the chicken or the egg? — is no puzzle to Aristotle. The chicken — I should say more precisely, the rooster — very definitely comes first. "Coming first" means to be "first" not so much in time as in weight, in dignity, in efficacy, in the ladder and order of being. We shall see in a moment what ultimate consequences Aristotle derives from this priority.

Aristotle's emphasis on generation carries with it the *second* decisive modification of the Socratic-Platonic view. The εἶδος is perpetually "at work," is perpetually ἐνεργείᾳ without ever undergoing any change. It is efficacious *in* the ever-changing bodies of living beings, as it is effective in the motions of celestial bodies and also — but only analogously so — in the customs and institutions of men. No need, therefore, to assign to the εἴδη a "separate" existence, no need to characterize their manner of being as one of "separation" (χωρισμός). Their purity and eternity are not affected by all the changes for which they are responsible. There is no need to duplicate the world. The things around us *are*, each one of those things has "being," has οὐσία, is an οὐσία. But each thing derives its being, its οὐσία, from the ἐνέργεια of its εἶδος. Each thing has being only inasmuch as it is the manifestation of the ἐνέργεια of its εἶδος. I *am* because I am "*man*." The cat that belongs to Mrs. Brown *is* because it is "*cat*." The tiger that, this year, April 1, ate a man in India, *is* because he is "*tiger*." Much more important than the ὕλη, out of which I and the cat and the tiger are built, is, in each case, the εἶδος that determines the growth of our bodies, that holds the body together as a unit, that makes us act the way we do. The priority of ἐνέργεια over δύναμις manifests itself conspicuously in the preponderance of what is "at work" over what is being worked on, in the preponderance, which, in the ways of Nature, the εἶδος has over the ὕλη. And let us not forget that it is the very εἶδος presented to our understanding in speech — τὸ εἶδος τὸ κατὰ τὸν λόγον.[10]

---

10. *Physics* B 1. 193 a 31.

If the world need not thus be duplicated, there is indeed another duplication, an unavoidable one, which — ultimately, perhaps — threatens the integrity of Aristotle's philosophizing: the bifurcation of the direction in which the εἶδος "works." For it is most remarkable that the role of the εἶδος in the process of generation is repeated in the process of understanding. The same εἶδος which presides over the generation, the growth, and the sustenance of living beings makes us *witness* this generation, growth, and sustenance. We men — and apparently in varying degrees all living beings — are able to *perceive* what is around us. We have the capacity, the ability, the faculty, the power, the δύναμις, of receiving information (as we say in typical Aristotelian fashion) about so much that surrounds us. Leaving aside our cousins, the animals, we men see and hear and smell and taste and perceive by touch and, furthermore, understand and know quite a few things. What makes us perceive and understand are ultimately the εἴδη. Each of us as a perceiving and understanding being is said to have a soul (ψυχή), the function, the proper work, the ἔργον of which is not only to sustain our life but also to enable us to sense and to understand beyond what is necessary for our living. The ability to sense, that is, the ability to be affected bodily by bodies around us, is called the power of αἰσθάνεσθαι (or τὸ αἰσθητικόν); the ability to be affected by the νοητά is called the power of νοεῖν (or ὁ νοῦς). With respect to what we perceive and understand, with respect to the αἰσθητά and νοητά, these powers have a manner of being similar to the manner of being that the material, the ὕλη, of a thing has with respect to the εἶδος, the species, the invisible looks of that thing.[11]

Let me try to describe these powers, avoiding all latter-day philosophical jargon. Consider and reflect upon the phenomena of sensing and understanding with which we are all familiar. Put aside the picture of something, as we say, "in" us that we call "mind"— a sort of closed container or box. What characterizes us inasmuch as we are able to perceive and to understand is our being *awake*. The state of wakefulness (ἐγρήγορσις) has its degrees, as we all know. We can be drowsy

---

11. *On the Soul* Γ 4. 429 a 17–18, 27–29.

and half-asleep. We can be inattentive to what goes on around us. But as long as we are not fully asleep we are *awake*, and we know that we are. (The fact that we might dream that we are awake does not refute that knowledge but confirms it. How else could we distinguish wakefulness from dream even in sleep?) This state and manner of being is a state in which we are not closed up but *open*. Wakefulness is openness — the very openness of a huge open door.[12] It is not a state of activity, but rather a state of preparedness, of alertness. This state or manner of being is commonly called in Greek νοῦς or νοεῖν. It is a manner of being which corresponds to the manner of being of any material, any ὕλη, and, like the latter, it is only conceivable in relation to what transforms it into a finished product. This transformation and information is brought about by *what* we sense and by *what* we understand. The transformation and information being completed, we are *one* with what we perceive, understand, know. It is not we, in our state of wakefulness, who actively grasp something that is prepared to be grasped. On the contrary, we, in our state of preparedness, are being grasped, molded, formed by what is at work, by the ἐνέργεια of the εἴδη, sometimes, nay, mostly, through the intermediary of our sensing power. In our sensing we are not one with the natural thing perceived, but with what works on our sensing power, with what Aristotle calls, quite consistently, the εἶδος αἰσθητόν.[13] The relation of the εἴδη αἰσθητά to the εἴδη νοητά is comparable to the relation of the sounds *heard* in speech to what we *understand* in speech. The εἴδη αἰσθητά constitute, one might say, the very language of things that affects our waking souls. The process of understanding, the process of gaining an insight, is, in Aristotle's eyes, also a process of begetting and generating. The δύναμις of any "natural" material, any ὕλη φυσική, is here replaced by the soul's capability of being awake and of receiving. This capability includes both the capability of sensing (αἰσθάνεσθαι) and the capability of being informed by the

---

12. Cf. *Generation of Animals* B 3. 736 b 28: λείπεται δὴ τὸν νοῦν μόνον θύραθεν ἐπεισιέναι καὶ θεῖον εἶναι μόνον · οὐθὲν γὰρ αὐτοῦ τῇ ἐνεργείᾳ κοινωνεῖ σωματικὴ ἐνέργεια. "What remains, then, is that the νοῦς alone enters in, additionally, from outside the door, and that it alone is divine, for the being-at-work of the body has nothing to do with the being-at-work of the νοῦς.

13. *On the Soul* Γ 8. 432 a 3–5.

νοητά. We are commonly not aware of this capability as such, since it cannot subsist all by itself, cannot subsist without being worked on. The closest we can come to observing it is to look into the eyes of very small children.

This Aristotelian understanding of the process of understanding in our souls brings a *third* decisive departure from the Socratic-Platonic view. Since sensing, not unlike speech, makes us the material worked on by the εἴδη, it is important to revert to the πρῶτος πλοῦς, the first journey that Socrates, in the *Phaedo*, claims to have given up. There are two ways in which one is mastered by the εἴδη νοητά. One is the way of the λόγος, the way of speaking and understanding, the way of bringing together in our understanding the νοητά presented to us in speech, the way of the *syllogismos*. The second is the way in which our teachers bring us face to face with the things to be understood. This latter way is called ἐπαγωγή. The term "induction" is an exact translation of the Greek word but has come to mean something quite different. The efficacy of an ἐπαγωγή rests on our being affected, through the observable sensible features of a thing, by its εἶδος. Ἐπαγωγή does not necessarily require many and varied experiences or observations. One case might be sufficient. But a mere glance at the titles of all the Aristotelian (and pseudo-Aristotelian) writings shows how intent Aristotle must have been on engaging in protracted observations, on listing all kinds of observable phenomena, and on collecting information from all possible sources.

This activity, however, is altogether auxiliary. It serves the great and awe-inspiring goal of giving a nearly complete account of the world as a *whole*. This may be reckoned as the *fourth* radical departure from the Socratic-Platonic view. For Plato, it seems, did not believe it possible to reach that goal, although the philosophical enterprise he was engaged in, in its extravagance and divine immoderation, indeed demands that our efforts to reach it never cease. Aristotle undertook to satisfy that demand once and for all. Only a few after him made such an attempt.

The term "world" or κόσμος, in Greek as well as in English, does not mean — and never meant — simply the sum total of all

existing things. It means rather the peculiar way in which diverse
parts are suitably arranged to form *one whole,* or a "universe."
An account of the wholeness of *all* that *is* implies of necessity
an account of the intrinsic order (τάξις) which makes the whole
a whole. An account of this kind is what is called, though not
by Aristotle, a cosmo-logy.

It seems that Aristotle's philosophizing culminates in, and
rests on, a cosmology. Some of its features are quite familiar.
Within the huge sphere of the world (ridiculously small in
modern terms) there is a tiny sphere — the sublunar sphere —
encompassing the earth. This is not to say that the earth is
located at the midpoint of the world sphere, as if a mathematical
point could determine any location within the world without
regard to the body involved. It is rather the globe and the bulk
of the earth that determine where the middle region of the
cosmos is. Beyond the sublunar domain a number of concen-
tric, contiguous, rigid, and translucent spheres reach up to the
limit of the world, to the sphere of the so-called fixed stars.
Beyond that limit there is nothing — not even nothing , not even
"void." The world is, strictly speaking, nowhere.

The cosmic spheres are in perpetual regular motion around
diverse axes and at different rates of speed. Some of them carry
the planets, including the sun and the moon. The combined motions of these spheres are responsible for the appearance of all
the irregular motions of the celestial bodies that we observe from
the earth. This "saving of the phenomena," as the traditional
phrase has it, is the task of a mathematical discipline "most akin
to philosophy," namely the science of the visible, yet eternal,
bodies, the science of ἀστρολογία, the science of the fixed and
wandering stars.[14] Aristotle follows here in the footsteps of
Eudoxus and Calippus, trying to improve their hypotheses
without presuming to have the last word as far as the number,
the sequence, and the motions of all these spheres are concerned.[15] Their combination and coordination, which remain
to be decided on by mathematical astronomers, can be
represented — visibly and tangibly — by a man-made model. The
Lyceum seems to have possessed one.

---

14. *Metaphysics* Λ 8. 1073 b 4–5.
15. *Metaphysics* Λ 8. 1073 b 10–17; 1074 a 14–17.

Yet what, in Aristotle's cosmology, is more important than the proper encasement and number of the spheres is its intimate link with the highest discipline Aristotle propounds and to which he occasionally assigns the name "First Philosophy" (πρώτη φιλοσοφία). This is the discipline which considers, not particular and definite bodies of any kind that "are" or might be, but which considers Being *as such* (ὄν ἁπλῶς or ὄν ᾗ ὄν). "Indeed," says Aristotle, "*what* is being (τὸ ὄν)?—that is, *what* is beingness (οὐσία)?—that is the question of ancient times and the question now and the question always, and always the puzzle one faces." "And so," he continues, "it is incumbent upon us, too, to consider—above all and first of all and uniquely, as it were—*what* Being, taken in that sense, is."[16]

It might not be inappropriate to assign to this most fundamental discipline a name coined in the eighteenth century—onto-logy. It deals with what is ultimately responsible for the coming into being, the persisting, as well as the passing away of any single thing. It is within its province, therefore, to deal with what is ultimately responsible for the being and the intrinsic order of the world as a whole. That is to say, this highest discipline has to account for the highest, the divine, and can, accordingly, be characterized by Aristotle as the ἐπιστήμη or φιλοσοφία θεολογική, the knowledge or wisdom which consists in the comprehension of divinity.[17]

Thus Aristotle's cosmological and ontological (or theological) considerations converge at the level that marks the beginning of the bifurcation I mentioned earlier. It is the level of the εἴδη. Their manner of being, as we have seen, is characterized by ἐνέργεια, by "being-at-work." It is indeed ἐνέργεια that, for Aristotle, answers the eternal question concerning Being *as such*. Whenever we say that something is or exists we imply—without being always aware of this impliction—that it owes its being or existence to ἐνέργεια. It is tempting to substitute for that Greek word the modern term "energy." This substitution would not necessarily falsify the statement I just made but would make it somewhat misleading. For "energy" has either a strict meaning adequately rendered only by a variety of mathematical

---

16. *Metaphysics* Z 1. 1028 b 2–4, 6–7.
17. *Metaphysics* K 7. 1064 a 28–1064 b 6; E 1. 1026 a 8–22.

expressions — the physical dimensions of which will always be: (unit of mass) × (unit of distance)² × (unit of time)⁻² — or a vague meaning associated with something like vigor, aggressiveness, vitality. We observe, though, that even for us today, both meanings of "energy," the strict one and the vague one, are tied to the notion or picture of *work* done or to be done. Traditionally the translations of ἐνέργεια are mostly derivatives of the Latin verb *ago*, to wit, "act," "action," "activity," "actuality." Note how curious it is that we say: "Actually, Mr. Jones does not live in Washington," or "Actually, the earth is a planet." We may substitute for the word "actually" phrases like "in fact," "in effect," "in truth," "indeed." Such phrases are equivalent to stating: considering that which truly *is*, this or that is so or is not so. It is still an Aristotelian way of speaking, although the ontological assertion that beingness means "being-at-work" or being "active" remains hidden behind the screen of our colloquial use of weighty words.

Aristotle merges cosmology into ontology by distinguishing two aspects of the phenomenon of νοεῖν, more precisely, by reaching beyond the meaning commonly attributed to "what is called νοῦς" (ὁ καλούμενος νοῦς).[18] Νοεῖν, as I tried to say earlier, is the state of wakefulness, a state of preparedness and alertness, which, in relation to *what* we perceive, understand, or know, plays the role of the material to be worked on. In that sense, νοεῖν is "passive," is the state of being mastered by something (. . . τὸ νοεῖν πάσχειν τί ἐστιν), namely by the impact of various εἴδη.[19] Νοῦς in this sense is somehow the mere capability of becoming what is understood (δυνάμει πώς ἐστι τὰ νοητὰ ὁ νοῦς) and nothing on its own.[20] Νοῦς becomes *what it truly is* when it is *one* with what is understood, *one* with the νοητά, that is to say, when the εἴδη νοητά have done their work. Only then can the νοῦς be said to be wakefulness "at work," to be ἐνεργείᾳ νοῦς, only then is the νοῦς "at its own end," is it ἐντελεχείᾳ νοῦς. But Aristotle's thought, anticipated to a degree by Anaxagoras and by Plato, goes one crucial step further: the very being of this accomplished νοῦς is nothing but

---

18. *On the Soul* Γ 9. 432 b 26; 4. 429 a 22.
19. *On the Soul* Γ 4. 429 b 25; 429 a 14.
20. *On the Soul* Γ 4. 429 b 30–31.

ἐνέργεια, and conversely, being-at-work *is* νοῦς — impartible (ἀμερής), indivisible (ἀδιαίρετος), impassive (ἀπαθής), unchangeable (ἀναλλοίωτος), undying (ἀθάνατος), eternal (ἀΐδιος). It is eternally "at work," and it itself, as being-at-work, is its own eternal life (ζωή) and its own eternal delight (ἡδονή). It is deity (ὁ θεός).[21] The entire heaven (ὁ οὐρανός) and Nature (ἡ φύσις) hang upon (ἤρτηται) this kind of "capital beginning" (ἀρχή).[22]

Let us try to understand the full meaning of this solemn statement, which echoes Anaxagoras' famous proposition about the νοῦς "ordering everything and being responsible for everything" (διακοσμῶν τε καὶ πάντων αἴτιος).[23] We have seen that the εἴδη νοητά are responsible for the being of everything and for all the changes that occur in the world. Now, the priority of being-at-work over the manner of being manifested in the capability of being worked on, the priority of ἐνέργεια over δύναμις, on which Aristotle insists so much, demands that a νοητόν be not only something understand*able* (δυνάμει νοητόν) but also something under*stood* "in fact" (νοητὸν ἐνεργείᾳ), so that it may be efficacious, may indeed be an αἰτία. The νοητά can play their generating role only when they are one with the νοῦς "at work," one with the productive state of wakefulness, one with the νοῦς ποιητικός, as Aristotle's ancient commentators name it (relying on Aristotle's own conjoining of τὸ αἴτιον and τὸ ποιητικόν).[24] This identity of the νοῦς and the νοητόν, of the νοοῦν and the νοούμενον, as well as of the accomplished state of knowing (ἡ κατ' ἐνέργειαν ἐπιστήμη) and the known object (τὸ ἐπιστητόν or τὸ πρᾶγμα), characterizes a state of wakefulness which is not "empty" openness but complete "fullness." This state prevails only where all that *can* be *has been* realized, where there is no place for mere "possibility," "capability," "ability," δύναμις — in other words, where no material to be still worked on is in any way involved.[25] The divine

21. *Metaphysics* Λ 7. 1072 b 26–1073 a 13; *On the Soul* Γ 5. 430 a 18, 23.
22. *Metaphysics* Λ 7. 1072 b 13–14.
23. Plato *Phaedo* 97 c2; Diels-Kranz,[7] 59 b 12 (from Simplicius); Aristotle *On the Soul* Γ 4. 429 a 19.
24. *On the Soul* Γ 5. 430 a 12; 6. 430 b 5–6.
25. *Metaphysics* Λ 7. 1072 b 21; 9. 1075 a 3–4; *On the Soul* Γ 4. 430 a 3–5; 5. 430 a 19–20; 7. 431 a 1–2; 431 b 17.

νοῦς — that is to say, the sum total of all εἴδη as comprehended by that νοῦς — is totally immaterial (ἄνευ ὕλης), or, since as ἐνέργεια it requires some material to be worked on, it can be said to be itself material for itself (νοήσεως νόησις).[26] It is thus totally "separated" from everything else in the world and consequently outside of time, uncontaminated (ἀμιγής), pure (καθαρός).[27] Strangely enough, in this understanding of the "separated" νοῦς— with all the εἴδη it "contains"— Aristotle seems to revert to the position of his teacher.

First Philosophy or ontology is not confined to the consideration of νοῦς as ἐνέργεια. It has to take into account not only the manner of being labeled δύναμις, but also other manners of being, and, furthermore, the different ways in which something can be said to be responsible for something else.

As far as this latter theme is concerned, Aristotle does not deviate from the Socratic-Platonic path. There are different meanings attached to the question "Why?" and, correspondingly, there are different ways of answering that question. Why is this lectern *such as it is?* We might answer: because of the wood, the particular *material* out of which it is made. We might also say: because the particular carpenter, the *maker*, made it this way. We might also say: because of the *shape or look* the maker had in mind. We might finally say: because of the *purpose* this thing is supposed to serve. However important and even indispensable the first three answers might be, it is not difficult to agree that the choice of the material (ἡ ὕλη), the shape or looks (τὸ εἶδος) of the thing, and the performance of the maker who initiated the transformation of the material into this lectern all depend on the purpose, the end for the sake of which the lectern has been made. It is that purpose which is decisively responsible for the lectern being as it is. Its purpose, its end (τὸ τέλος), is its true "beginning" (ἀρχή). All those questions and answers are perhaps not possible with respect to every single thing or occurrence, but it is one of the most important tenets

---

26. *On the Soul* Γ 4. 430 a 3; *Metaphysics* Λ 9. 1074 b 34.
27. *On the Soul* Γ 4. 429 b 5; 5. 430 a 17–18, 23; 4. 429 a 18; *Metaphysics* A 8. 989 b 15–16.

There is a characteristic aspect of anything we call a purpose or a goal or an end, namely that it is an object of desire. The τέλος — in the making of a thing, in the contrivance of some device, in the establishment of an institution, in the action of a man — is responsible for all the changes it brings about, and yet it itself remains unchangeably, immovably, what it is. It does not manifest its efficacy the way an instrument does. It *attracts* but does not get involved in the concatenation of changes which it originates. Such is the efficacy of an εἶδος, wherever Nature rules — the generating efficacy that the εἶδος owes to its manner of being, which is being at work. An εἶδος is "at work" *as something striven for*, as an object of desire, of ὄρεξις.[28] And that is also true for the divine νοῦς as the "container" of all the εἴδη of the world. The whirling spheres of the world, including the last one, the one of the fixed stars, strive to become what the best of all, the νοῦς, beyond all time, is: this desire of theirs holds them forever in their never-ending circular motions. Thus, for Aristotle, the eternity of the world in time is an inescapable consequence of the timeless ontological character of ἐνέργεια that the εἴδη and the νοῦς possess.

As to the problem of manners of being other than that of ἐνέργεια, a *fifth* departure from the Platonic view marks Aristotle's thinking. For Plato, it seems beingness is an εδος of the highest rank, an εἶδος embracing the entire family of εἴδη within it; it is a "genus." Everything that *is*, inasmuch as it *is*, falls under it, as it were. Whenever we face "being" we face *one and the same* kind of being. For Aristotle, however, it is necessary to distinguish between "being" in the strict and primary sense of ἐνέργεια and other manners or degrees of being *related* to the former "proportionally," κατ' ἀναλογίαν.[29] It is precisely the difference in the *kinds of relation* to the primary aspect of being, that of ἐνέργεια, which justifies our speaking of "manners of being." As Aristotle says: ". . . Being is spoken of in various senses,

---

28. *Metaphysics* Λ 7. 1072 a 26–27; 1072 b 3.
29. *Metaphysics* Δ 6. 1016 b 31–1017 a 3.

but in every case *with some reference to* one capital beginning"
(. . . τὸ ὂν λέγεται πολλαχῶς μέν, ἀλλ᾽ ἅπαν πρὸς μίαν
ἀρχήν).[30] This holds not only for the manner of being which
characterizes δύναμις, but also for the various attributes of
things, such as their motion, their color and warmth, their
number and size, their health, beneficence, and well-being. The
τάξις, the hierarchy of the spheres with their specific ἐνέργειαι,
is conceived as following an "analogical" pattern, too.

Where, then, is the place of *man* in this order of things?

It is not too difficult to assess Aristotle's answer to this question. Man is said, on the one hand, to rank highest among the
perfect, that is, viviparous, animals. Nature is said to have produced everything for his sake. Among all the animals, man is
the only one with an erect posture, "for his nature and his being are divine." And yet, on the other hand, he is *not* the most
important, not the best being in the world, which becomes
perfectly clear when we consider the celestial bodies which compose the cosmos.[31]

This somewhat ambiguous position of man is rooted in the
insufficiency of man's wakefulness, in the "incompleteness" and
"passivity" of his νοῦς. Man is open to everything about him.
Whenever this openness is filled with the εἴδη of the world, he
shares in the godlike manner of being, in the ἐνέργεια of the
divine νοῦς. But this sharing is an intermittent one; ever so often
man is overcome by fatigue, his wakefulness yields to sleep. He
has to lie down. His divinity is but a passing shadow — as is his
very life.

Still, he has to make the best of it. Since he is not a solitary
being, but has to live with others of his kind, he establishes
families, rears children, acquires arts, learns and teaches, forms
tribes, founds states, and sets up institutions, rituals, customs,
and laws. In doing that, he has to have φρόνησις, has to exercise sound judgment in the conduct of his affairs. Aristotle provides the justification and the guiding rules for all these specific

---

30. *Metaphysics* Γ 2. 1003 b 5–6; Z 4. 1030 b 2–3.
31. *Generation of Animals* B 4. 737 b 26–27; *Politics* A 8. 1256 b 15–22; *Physics* B 2.
    194 a 34–35; *Parts of Animals* Δ 10. 686 a 27–28; *Nicomachean Ethics* Z 1141 a
    20–22; 1141 a 33–1141 b 2.

human activities in his teaching and writing on matters of the household, on ethics and politics, on rhetoric and poetry. All these subject matters fall within the jurisdiction of the λόγος, which is no attribute of divinity. Only to a few is given the happiness of a philosophical life, the immoderate though intermittent sharing in the timeless ἐνέργεια of the νοῦς.

Let me, by way of conclusion, report the preposterous, yet deeply significant, story told in ancient times about Aristotle's sleeping habits.[32] When he went to bed, so the story goes, he used to hold in his hand a sphere of bronze — the sphere representing the whole world, I presume — while on the floor, close to the bed, beneath his extended hand, lay a pan. As soon as Aristotle would fall asleep, the sphere would slip out of his hand, fall on that pan, and the ensuing noise would awaken him. This procedure was apparently repeated over and over again. Aristotle could hardly have survived such an ordeal for any length of time. But no story could more aptly relate his claim to immortality.

---

32. Diogenes Laertius V. 1. 16.

12 ■ Leibniz, an Introduction

L eibniz was born in 1646, four years before Descartes' death. He died in 1716, eight years before Kant's birth. His is the age of Louis XIV, of Oliver Cromwell and of William and Mary, the age of the wig and of instrumental polyphony. Among his illustrious contemporaries — and he knew quite a few of them personally — are Boyle, Huygens, Newton, Hobbes, Pascal, Spinoza, Locke, Malebranche, the great theologians Arnauld and Bossuet, the mathematicians Fermat, Roberval, Wallis, Barrow, Jacob and Johann Bernoulli, the zoologists Malpighi, Leeuwenhoek, Swammerdam, Ludwig von Ham, and further-more Milton, Corneille, Racine, Molière, Swift, Bayle and Vico. It is not easy to put an appropriate label on Leibniz in this array of famous men and their respective muses. Leibniz composed, with few exceptions, only short summarizing or polemical essays, articles, memoranda, but his correspondence was immense. He is as much a mathematician as he is a physicist, a philosopher, a theologian, an historian, a jurist and even a diplomat, not to forget his official position of librarian.

Lecture first delivered at St. John's College, Annapolis, April 26, 1963.

But this much can be said with some safety: to talk about Leibniz means to face squarely what is otherwise known as the "Quarrel of the Ancients and the Moderns." Leibniz's scientific and philosophical activities amount to an attempt to compose this quarrel by a compromise — a titanic compromise, to be sure — and all I can do is to show in what this compromise consists. Let us not forget, by the way, that just as there were plenty of "ancients" among the "moderns," so there were quite a few "moderns" among the "ancients." And let me also note, in anticipation of what I have to show later on, that Leibniz remains altogether "modern," that indeed in studying him one can discover the very roots of our own views which we are inclined to take for granted, that is to say, the very roots of our pre-judgements, of our prejudices.

Let us hear Leibniz himself. In a letter[1] towards the end of his life (1714) he says: "When I left the School of Trivial Arts [it is called High School today] I turned to the modern thinkers, and I remember taking a lonely walk in a little wood near Leipzig, by the name of Valley of the Roses, at the age of fifteen, to deliberate whether I should keep the Substantial Forms [he means the Aristotelian εἴδη or "forms" as taught by the Schoolmen]. The mechanistic doctrine prevailed and led me to the study of Mathematics. True, I embarked upon the study of highest Mathematics only after my conversation with Mr. Huygens in Paris. But searching for the ultimate foundations of the mechanistic view and even of the laws of motion, I was much surprised to discover that it was impossible to find them in Mathematics and that one had to go back to Metaphysics." As to the Formalists and Mechanists, he says a little later on: "I flatter myself to have discovered the Harmony between their different realms and to have understood that *both* sides are right, provided they do not impinge upon each other; that everything in natural phenomena occurs simultaneously in a mechanical and in a metaphysical way, but that the source of the mechanics is to be found in metaphysics. It was not easy to discover this mystery because there are few people who care to join these two kinds of studies."

---

1. Letter to Nicolas Rémond.

What does Leibniz mean by "Metaphysics," "ancient" metaphysics, that is, and what by the "modern" "mechanistic view"?

Let us consider "Metaphysics" first. Τὰ μετὰ τὰ φυσικά is the common title given to a series of books in the collection of Aristotelian writings that have come down to us. The text itself never uses this phrase. It means literally "those things which come *after* the consideration of things natural." By an almost legitimate misinterpretation the title came to mean a discipline which transcends the realm of natural changes and occurrences, which reaches *beyond* our direct experience. For Aristotle himself and the tradition which follows him the subject of this discipline has a twofold aspect: under consideration is first of all not any particular being or kind of being as, for example, man, horse, oak, gold, but rather what is *meant* whenever any of these things is said to *be* or to *exist*, what is meant by Being *itself*, by being *as* being; and secondly, after this prior question has been settled, *what* it is that can be said truthfully and strictly to *be* or to *exist*. In speaking of *metaphysical* considerations Leibniz follows this tradition and also stays within the bounds of the traditional terminology, especially in that he clings to the unfortunate rendering of "being," in Greek οὐσία, by "substance." Thus, for Leibniz, Metaphysics deals with the following questions: 1) What characterizes "substance"? 2) What can be said to be *a substance*? and 3) What is that of which "substance" *cannot* be predicated? We shall see, however, that, in answering these questions, Leibniz deviates from the tradition in a significant way.

What now does Leibniz mean by the "mechanistic view"?

He means primarily the opinions of Descartes concerning motion, and also those of Gassendi who revived the "atomistic" doctrines of Democritus, Epicurus, and Lucretius, concerning the composition of the universe. He means especially the view that all events and situations in the visible world around us can be reduced to mutual impacts of bodies, involving merely the following factors: the bulk (and shape) of the bodies themselves, their velocities, and the time and space in which their motions occur. According to Descartes[2] the fundamental and primary rule which governs all mutual impacts — and which follows

---

2. *Principles of Philosophy*, II, 36.

directly from the immutability of God — is the preservation of the "quantity of motion" in the entire universe, which, in more modern mathematical terms, amounts to saying that the sum total of the products of all m's and all v's in the world is the same for any given moment of time. Three secondary rules or *natural laws* determine, according to Descartes,[3] all particular changes in the universe: 1) anything simple and indivisible remains by itself in the state it is in and changes its status only from external causes; 2) any part of matter — that is, any part of what Descartes calls the "extended being"— whenever in motion moves by itself in a straight line;[4] 3) if a body A collides with another body B which has a *stronger* tendency than the first to persevere in its rectilinear course, the body A preserves its quantity of motion but changes its direction; if a body A has a *stronger* tendency than the body B to persevere in its rectilinear course, the body A transmits to the body B as much motion as it itself loses.[5] Implicit in these laws is a notion of "force" as identified with the product mv, that is, with the "quantity of motion" or, as we call it today, with the "momentum" of the moving body, which is responsible for imparting motion to another body or for resisting the impact of another body.

All this provides the pattern for what Leibniz calls the "mechanistic view." It cannot be made explicit without mathematical formulae. Leibniz holds that this mechanical and mathematical pattern is quite appropriate for dealing with the problem of motion. But he corrects Descartes' fundamental rule of motion as well as Descartes' notion of force in a decisive way, as we shall see. In doing that he transforms mechanics into dynamics.

II

We have heard Leibniz say that he succeeded in harmonizing meta-physical and mechanical considerations. What can har-

---

3. II, 37.
4. II, 39.
5. II, 40; cf. II, 43.

monizing mean in this case? Metaphysics presents us with the problem of Being — in Leibnizian terms, with the problem of the nature of "substance." Mechanics presents us with the problem of how to understand and how to describe motion of bodies and their mutual impact in the most appropriate way. Do these two things lend themselves to being "harmonized"? Is there any "quarrel" between them? Are they not totally disparate — not so much inimical to each other as indifferent to each other? Yet Leibniz undertook to bring them together. To do that he had to *construct* something new, something that has been called — by others as well as by himself — a "system." He keeps using these phrases: a "regulated system," a "new system," "my system."

The term "system" has a curious history. The Greek word σύστημα means "things which stand together or are made to stand together so as to form a whole," means in other words "a whole compounded of several parts," and is applied to man's body, to a government, a constitution, a confederacy, to groups of men or animals, to literary compositions, is used in the practice of arithmetic, of music, and of medicine, *but is never applied to thought*. From about the year 1600 on there is a sudden and most remarkable shift: book after book appears under titles like "System of Logic," "System of Rhetoric," "System of Grammar," "System of Theology," "System of Ethics and Politics," "System of Physics," "System of Jurisprudence," "System of Astronomy," of Arithmetic, of Geography, of Medicine and even "System of Systems." But it is due mainly to Leibniz that philosophizing becomes identified with the producing of "systems of philosophy." In a letter [6] written in 1715 Leibniz takes the opportunity to remark: "If some one were to reduce Plato to a system he would render a great service to mankind and one would be able to see that I am not very far from him." This pious wish has since been fulfilled far beyond anything Leibniz could have expected.

The harmonizing of Metaphysics and Mechanics requires the construction of a *System*, that is of a whole which encompasses and unites disparate parts. But such a work of art, such a construction, requires, in turn, *pillars* on which the system may

---

6. Letter to de Montmort.

securely rest. Leibniz erects *two* pillars which fulfill this function. One consists in a new characterization of Being or
Substance. The other consists in a re-interpretation of Force. In
both cases, though in a different way, Leibniz is helped by considerations derived from Mathematics, which very fact demands
and indeed finds justification.

In the traditional view, based on Aristotle's teaching,
whenever we say that X *is*, we mean implicitly that this X is
a *"thing,"* is *"something,"* is *"one,"* is *"true,"* and is *"good."* These
six modes of predication (*ens, res, aliquid, unum, verum,
bonum*) are traditionally called the six "transcendentals," applicable interchangeably to anything to which we attribute being. All six are of prime importance to Leibniz, but most important to him is "oneness," "unity." True being — or, as we still
say with so much ease, substantial being — must have the
character of true unity, must be a genuine unit.[7] Examples of
units are provided in Mathematics. There are arithmetical units
and geometrical units or points. But an arithmetical unit can
be fractioned *ad infinitum*: 1/2, 1/4, 1/8, 1/16, and so forth. This
divisibility seems to deprive the arithmetical unit of true unity.
Leibniz does not think that it does: he thinks the fractions
"within" an arithmetic unit are mere "possibilities," a term we
shall have to return to after a while. But because the arithmetical
unit allows itself to be interpreted as infinitely divisible, Leibniz prefers the geometrical example of a point. There is probably no one else to whom Euclid's First Definition in the
Elements, that of a point, has meant so much as it has meant
to Leibniz: "A point is that which has no parts." Leibniz is not
altogether satisfied with this definition. He prefers this one: a
point is that which has no extension.[8] Its not being extended
makes it "simple" and therefore truly one, that is, genuinely indivisible. In this respect, then, true being, "substance," must
resemble a point. Substances are not geometrical points, to be
sure, but they are "metaphysical points."

Yet Leibniz is not content with this characterization. He adds
something to it, and it is this addition which constitutes his devia-

---

7. Fourth letter to Arnauld.
8. *The Theory of Abstract Motion: Fundamental Principles* (1761).

tion from traditional metaphysics. Substantial being must have not only true unity but also *uniqueness*. Whatever truly is must be unique. Unlike geometrical points, metaphysical points must differ from each other. This *principle of uniqueness*, then, is *the first pillar of the system*. It can be stated as follows: there are *no* two true beings that can be conceived as indistinguishable from each other.[9] And this metaphysical truth may well, according to Leibniz, be verified in nature. (We shall see later, why.) There is a story about Leibniz taking a walk in a wood with ladies of the court he was attached to; the ladies pressed him to explain to them his great "principle of the identity of indistinguishables"; he suggested that they pluck leaves from the bushes and trees they were passing and try to find two identical ones; the ladies did not pass the test.

Implicit in the formulation of this principle of uniqueness is a corollary or twin principle. Being or Substance is *diversified*; Substance is by itself not singular, is not one substance (as Spinoza claims), but is plural, is *many*, and not only many but *infinitely many substances*, each one of which is one and unique. Here again a mathematical example illuminates Leibniz's thought: the metaphysical points form a *continuous series* similar to the continuum of geometrical points on a line. The twin principle, supplementing the principle of uniqueness, is the "*law of continuity*." It states that there are no "gaps" in the sequence of substances: "between" any two of them there are infinitely many others. This principle, too, can be verified in nature: all motions and changes are continuous, there is no "jumping" from one state into another. Nor is there any interruption in the chain of organic beings.

Thus Leibniz answers the first question of his Metaphysics, the question "what characterizes substance?" as follows: the fundamental characteristics of Being or Substance are Simplicity, Unity, Indivisibility, which make true being unchanging and imperishable, and furthermore, Uniqueness and Continuous Diversity.—We have to look now for his answer to the second metaphysical question: "*What* can be said to be *a substance*?"

---

9. Fifth letter to Clarke, 21-28; *Monadology* 9.

III

The foundation of his answer to this question is again to be found in Aristotle's teaching and the entire Aristotelian tradition. For Aristotle, to *be* means ultimately "to-be-at-work"— in Greek, ἐνεργεῖν. The noun ἐνέργεια is used by Aristotle almost synonymously with the noun ἐντελέχεια "being-at-one's-own-end," and Leibniz prefers the latter. These terms characterize, in Aristotle, Being itself (οὐσία) inasmuch as it is identified with νοεῖν or νοῦς, the divine source of all intellectual perceiving. In traditional terminology, Being itself is "act" or "activity," the activity of intellecting. Leibniz adheres to this teaching: Being or Substance, in its simplicity, unity, and indivisibility, is still "in act," is *active* being; the metaphysical points are, as he says, "fertile simplicities" (*des simplicités fécondes*).[10] Leibniz modifies the traditional teaching only slightly: the activity, the ἐνέργεια or ἐντελέχεια, is given the generic name "*perception*." However, this slight modification is pregnant with massive consequences. Let us first understand what Leibniz means by "perception" in contradistinction to what this term usually conveys.

When we say that we *perceive* something we mean that there is something before us which we "take in," as it were, which we see, or hear, or touch, or smell, or taste. This something is nowadays called the *object* that affects us in some way. In pre-Leibnizian or rather pre-Cartesian times this something was called the *subject* of our perception, while the term "object" was reserved to its "image" or "concept," formed, as we say "within" us. In a larger sense, to "perceive" could also mean to apprehend something entirely unrelated to an external subject. In any case, that which presents itself to us "within" us was traditionally understood as something *thrown* at us — that's what the Latin term "*objectum*" literally means. In Leibniz's way of speaking, however, what is *perceived* by us is what *we ourselves throw out* of us and put *before* us — not an *ob-jectum* but a *pro-jectum*, as it were. Now, this act of pro-jecting is, according to Leibniz, the very activity of Being as such, of Substance. And it is *this* activity that Leibniz means when he speaks of "perceiving" or of "perception."—What being, we have to ask, is capable of such

---

10. Second treatise against Boyle.

activity? It is not implausible to answer: a *soul* or something resembling a soul. This indeed is the answer Leibniz gives to his second metaphysical question, "*What* can be said to be *a* substance?" The simple and indivisible metaphysical points must be souls or, at least, resemble souls.

But does not the activity of perceiving, which implies a multiplicity of perceptions, violate the unity of the metaphysical points? Leibniz does not think so. He defines: "The transient state which encompasses and *represents* a *multiplicity within the unity* or within the simple substance is no other than what is called perception . . . ."[11] Let us note the word "represent." It is a crucial term in the Leibnizian system and in subsequent philosophies. Perception is "representation." A perception *presents* to the simple and indivisible soul a multiplicity, a diversity of what? The prefix "re-" in the term "re-presentation" suggests the answer. Perceptions re-present all the perceiving activities of all the other souls or perceiving metaphysical points. What they present *stands for* all those activities of all the other souls. But these presentations or representations do not affect the unity of their source, the unity, that is, of any of the perceiving metaphysical points.

Perception and representation are synonyms in Leibniz. And to clarify their equivalence he uses still another synonym. Souls not only "perceive" and "re-present" but also "*express*." A representation is an expression. Leibniz defines: "A thing expresses another thing (in my way of speaking) when there is a constant and regulated relation between what can be said of the one and of the other,"[12] or, in a more modern way of speaking, when there is a one-to-one correspondence between the two. Thus the diversity and infinite multiplicity of all metaphysical points find their representation or expression in any one of them.

But the activity of perceiving, representing, or expressing must also leave inviolate the uniqueness of each metaphysical point. There is an intrinsic safeguard which prevents this uniqueness from being infringed upon. The activity of perceiving proceeds in each single case *from a unique "point of view*," a phrase which Leibniz keeps repeating over and over again. This phrase

---

11. *Monadology* 14.
12. Fifth letter to Arnauld.

reveals indeed the full meaning of the term "metaphysical point."
Each "point" is strictly a "point of view"— a unique source of
viewing. And a geometrical point is but a peculiar "expression"
of a "point of view."

IV

While discussing Perception, Representation, and Expression, we have already been dealing with the third question of
Leibniz's Metaphysics, to wit: "What is that of which "substance"
cannot be predicted?" For the answer is: it is *what* the souls or
soul-like points perceive, namely the "representations" and
"expressions" which have their source in the activity of those
souls or points. We *do* understand that what is "perceived" by
a single point are *not* the activities of all the other points but
merely what *corresponds* to them, re-presents them, expresses
them and what is *spontaneously* produced "within" and by that
single, simple, indivisible, and unique metaphysical point. What
is thus produced is the entire world of living and inanimate
things which surround each of us. But what is thus produced —
this entire familiar world of ours — has no true being, is not
"substantial," is merely, as Leibniz does not tire of asserting,
phenomenal. The world as we perceive it is *projected* by each
of the metaphysical points, among which are also the human
souls. The totality of the world around us is therefore not "real,"
has not the character of an existing thing or of existing things.
It is altogether a *phenomenon,* a phenomenal world, an
appearance — which does not mean an illusion or a phantom.
The world as it appears to each of us, Leibniz keeps repeating,
is a *"well-founded"* phenomenon — well-founded because it *corresponds precisely* to all the metaphysical points and their
perceiving activities. The correspondence between the
phenomenal world and substantial being cannot, of course, be
equated, we well understand, with the correspondence which
prevails between image and original. For the phenomenal world,
which includes originals and their images, is determined by the
temporal and *spatial* cohesion of all perceptions: space is nothing
but the order by which phenomena appear to co-exist, time

nothing but the order that allows phenomena, which have no permanence but have some connection among themselves, to manifest this connection: substantial being, on the other hand, has no time and is in no space.[13]

It is the phenomenal world alone, according to Leibniz, that mechanistic philosophy or, as we should perhaps state more generally, mathematical physics tries to understand. This entirely legitimate undertaking can, however, Leibniz thinks, go one step further: it can reach a stage where the correspondence or harmony between the phenomenal world and true or "substantial" being may become mechanically manifest, and — one further step still — where the Mechanics may be seen to depend on Metaphysics. This happens when, in the science of motion, we consider the nature of Force. Descartes was mistaken, Leibniz thinks, in equating Force with the "quantity of motion," that is, with the product formed from the amount of matter in motion and its velocity (mv); this quantity is labelled by Leibniz a mere "derivative" force. Descartes was also mistaken, Leibniz thinks, in believing that (apart from its direction) the "quantity of motion" in the universe or, for that matter, in an isolated machine (even if we disregard friction) remains constant. Basing himself on Galileo's investigation of falling bodies, Leibniz shows that the proper measure of Force is the distance through which a body can lift itself upwards by the power acquired in its preceding free fall; and that consequently Force must be equated with the product of the body, i.e., its mass, and the *square* of its velocity (mv^2). He calls this Power or Force primordial, active, or "*living force*."[14] Let us hear how he describes it: "By *force* or *power* I do not mean the potentiality or mere capacity which is nothing but a possibility of future action and which, being dead, as it were, never produces any action without being prompted from the outside; I mean rather a mean between potentiality and action, something that implies an effort, an act, an entelechy, for force *by itself* goes over to action provided it is not impeded by anything." What Leibniz describes in these

13. Second treatise against Boyle.
14. Cf. *On the Emendation of First Philosophy and the Notion of Substance* (1694).

words and represents by the product mv² is called today, curiously and significantly enough, *Energy*.[15] For Leibniz himself it is the only "real" element in the phenomenon of motion; it is the one which is constantly preserved. In forming the product mv² we thus grasp symbolically the ἐνέργεια or, as Leibniz prefers to call it, the entelechy, the true activity behind the purely phenomenal. We understand thus more precisely why the phenomenal world can be called a well-founded phenomenon: the laws of Physics, the laws of Dynamics, are indeed rooted in the metaphysical realm, namely in Energy, in the activity of the simple, indivisible, "perceiving" souls or soul-like points.

This *Force*, then, is the *second pillar of Leibniz's system*. It is that because it points to something which transcends the phenomenal world and provides a link between the time-and-space-ridden domain of Mechanics and the time-and-space-less domain of Metaphysics.

Let us not forget: the temporal and spatial world is a creation of each of the infinitely many souls or soul-like points. Each of them has *within* itself a phenomenal world of its own making. How then can we have a common world in which we live, in which we act and are acted upon? This is the central problem of Leibniz's Metaphysics. Before we come to grips with it we have to consider once more and more fully what Leibniz calls "perception."

V

Not only does the perceiving of each of the souls or soul-like beings constitute a unique point of view or, better, a unique point of viewing, but the perceiving itself has infinitely many *degrees*. The law of continuity holds here, too. Perceptions can be *obscure*, which means that they hardly project anything perceivable. Leibniz's standing example is the way in which the waves of the sea affect our hearing: we can hear their roaring but we do not discern the noise each single wave produces, though it undoubtedly reaches our ears. Leibniz has a special

---

15. First treatise against Boyle; *Monadology* 18.

name for the obscure or imperceptible perceptions. He calls them "little perceptions."[16] Perceptions can be *clear*, but either confusedly or distinctly so. An example of a clear, yet *confused* perception is provided by the way in which we see a painting that either pleases or offends us, although we are not able to say what particular features make it pleasant or offensive. A *distinct* perception is one which enables us to distinguish and to enumerate the details it presents. But again a distinct perception can be either inadequate or adequate. It is *inadequate* — or "symbolic" — when the enumeration of the details remains incomplete, as for example when we imagine a figure of one thousand sides; it is *adequate* — or "intuitive" — when *all* the details are *at once* clearly, distinctly, and completely perceived. Moreover, although *any* perceiving is the very *activity* which characterizes Being, that which is perceived may have either an active or a passive character. Striking a blow, for example, is equivalent, as far as the striker is concerned, to an *active* perception; being attacked by somebody is equivalent, as far as the victim is concerned, to a *passive* one.

This classification of degrees and kinds of perception is itself an inadequate one, for it does not take into account the infinitely many intermediate stages between them. But it enables Leibniz to discriminate between three great groupings among the infinitely many perceiving points. These groupings merge into each other so as to produce borderline cases, but are still sufficiently distinguishable from each other.

Perceiving which projects entirely passive and completely confused perceptions (and should be called, according to Leibniz, *sensing* rather than perceiving) determines the domain *not* of soul, but of soul-*like* being, to which, in the phenomenal world, correspond what we call *inanimate* or *material things*. It is indeed passivity or "inertia" which, according to Leibniz, characterizes what we call "matter." Any other perceiving (which includes retention) determines the domain of soul, to which, in the phenomenal world, correspond *plants* (Leibniz is not entirely sure about that), *animals* and *men*. But perceiving can reach such a degree of distinctness and attentiveness as to turn

16. *Discourse on Metaphysics* 24; *Meditationes de cognitatione, veritate et ideis* (1684).

upon itself and become "reflexive." A perception which is thus reflexively expanded and compounded is called by Leibniz "*apperception*" (derived probably from the French "*apercevoir*" or "*s'apercevoir*"). Only the souls of men (and of angels) are capable of apperception and bear, therefore, a special name; they are called "*spirits*." To designate *all* metaphysical points by a common appellation Leibniz uses the term "monad," from the Greek μονάς, meaning unit. But the distinctions he introduces among the monads are crucial. Let us hear Leibniz himself: ". . . it is well to distinguish between *perception* which is the *inner state* of the monad and which represents the external things and *apperception* which is consciousness or the reflexive cognition of that inner state and which is not given to all souls and not even to one and the same soul all the time."[17] This reflexive cognition involves above all the perception of the perception's source, in other words, the perception of that which the pronoun "I" is meant to convey. While, on the other pole, the monads whose perceptions have an altogether passive and confused character are monads in a dead faint, as it were, or, as Leibniz also says, "completely bare monads."

VI

We can now revert to the central problem of Leibniz's Metaphysics. Given the uniqueness of each monad and the creation within each of a phenomenal world from its unique point of view, how can there be a *common* world familiar to all of us? The answer given by Leibniz is *the coping-stone of his system*. The commonness of our common phenomenal world is the result of the *Harmony* which God, the all-comprising monad, imposed upon the perceiving activities of all the infinitely many created monads at the moment of their creation. Let us understand what this means.

At this very moment, I, as a monad, have produced a series of perceptions which present to me this room with its light and its peculiar dimensions and with all of you sitting in your seats

---

17. *The Principles of Nature and Grace, Based on Reason* 4.

and listening — or attempting to listen — to me. Each one of you, as a unique monad, has at the very same moment produced a series of perceptions which present to each of you this room with all its furniture, its light and sound, with all the other people seated in rows around you and with a man standing at the lectern lecturing to you. Metaphysically speaking our monads have *no connection whatever* with each other: "monads have no windows," as Leibniz says. Each of our monads is totally isolated from all the other monads. Yet, thanks to the *pre-established harmony* among all the monads and their respective perceptions, the perceptions of each of our monads are in step, so to speak, with the perceptions of all the others. The experience which we share in common is not only purely phenomenal, though well-founded, but depends altogether on our being wound up in a matching way. The spatial and temporal character of this experience is the spatial and temporal character of each of the phenomenal worlds produced by each of the monads from its unique point of view. But all these individual phenomenal worlds match perfectly with each other. Therefore the mechanism by which the sound waves phenomenally emanate from my vocal chords and phenomenally reach your ears can be dealt with on purely physical and mathematical grounds. More generally, the pre-established harmony permits mathematical physics to be a *common* enterprise. Not only do the diversity and infinite multiplicity of all monads find their representation and expression in any one of them, but there is also complete correspondence between the monads' phenomenally common experience of the phenomenon "Nature" on the one hand and its metaphysical foundation on the other. That is why metaphysical principles, like the principle of uniqueness and the law of continuity, can be verified in nature and dealt with mathematically. His system, Leibniz remarks, makes us understand "that bodies act as if (to argue the impossible) there were no souls and that souls act as if there were no bodies and that both act as if one influenced the other."[18]

Let us look at this breath-taking spectacle in a larger perspective. I, being a monad and speaking here as a phenomenon,

18. *Monadology* 81.

represent right now within me not only what all of you in this room severally represent within yourselves at this very moment; I *also* represent within me the *entire* world of phenomena, that is to say, the perceptions of *all* the infinitely many monads of the universe. Whatever may — phenomenally — happen in the Congo, for instance, at this moment, or, for that matter, on a distant planet, has its counterpart, its corresponding perception in me. Each monad "mirrors," as Leibniz says, the entire universe. Each monad is a microcosm. But *no* monad — no created monad, that is — is *aware* of this immensity within it. Only a tiny portion of all its perceptions reach the stage of clear and distinct perceptions. The overwhelming majority of them do not reach the plateau of consciousness. As far as perceptions are concerned, we are — iceberg-like — submerged in the depths of passivity and confusion. We are *limited*. Our limits are circumscribed by what we call our bodies, which are nothing but the phenomenal expressions of monads closest to us.

What a phantasmagoric spectacle! one is inevitably led to exclaim. What a system, or rather what a systematic monstrosity! Leibniz seems quite aware of the revulsion (mingled, I think, with some admiration) which his system is bound to provoke. His reply is that his system preserves and unites the thoughts of all preceding generations about man, universe, and God; that previous philosophies show much more agreement than one is led to believe when neglecting the core of their insights, which constitutes what he calls the "perennial philosophy" (*philosophia perennis*); that the revulsion against his system stems above all from an underestimation of divine wisdom; that his doctrine of "pre-established harmony" is the best proof of God's existence, power, providence, and omniscience. He does not claim that he looks at the universe from the throne of God. He has only been admitted — and he invites us to follow him — to the audience-chamber of God. We might say, using phenomenal terms metaphorically too, that he, Leibniz, is seated on a little stool at God's feet. But we cannot help adding: Is this the proper seat for the philosopher?

God, according to Leibniz and according to the tradition as well, is not limited in his vision. In Leibnizian terms, the perceptions of the primordial and all-comprehensive monad are not encumbered by any passivity and confusion. God sees everything at once, adequately and intuitively. The cohesion of his perceptions is neither temporal nor spatial. He sees in one sweep all the monads *from the outside*, as it were, including the entire sequence of their inward perceptions. He sees, for example, that the monad named Julius Caesar includes his crossing the Rubicon or that the monad named John Smith includes his visiting his aunt on September 8, 1672. This means, in philosophical language, that anything predicable of a subject is contained in that subject, although we human beings, as limited monads, are in general unable to extract the predicates from the subject, are unable to deduce them *a priori*. Everything in this world is thus eternally known to God and appears therefore predestined. The grave problem of all Christian theology, how to reconcile human freedom with divine predestination, remains a problem for Leibniz, too.

But Leibniz has a great deal to say about the way this predestination is arrived at.

One has to distinguish sharply, says Leibniz, between what is *certain* and what is *necessary*. Necessary — that is, absolutely necessary — is that, the denial of which is *self-contradictory*. Certain is that which actually occurs, although its not occurring would *not* involve any self-contradiction. Accordingly, there are two kinds of truth: the *eternal verities*, as for example those of Mathematics, and the *verities of fact* which are not necessary but contingent. The first ones, the eternal verities, are governed by the *principle of contradiction*, and their source is ultimately God's reason. The second ones, the contingent verities, are governed by the *principle of sufficient or determining reason*, and their source is ultimately God's will. The first ones delimit what is merely *possible*, the second ones determine what actually *is*, what actually *exists*, that is to say, all the monads with their perceiving activities.

God, thinking all that is thinkable, in other words, everything which is not self-contradictory, seeing all *possibilities* which offer themselves to his reason, decides which of these possibilities have to be actualized, have to be made "real" in fact. In making this decision he applies the *rule of goodness* or *benevolence* so as to choose *the best among all the possible worlds*. The *best* is the sufficient and the *only* sufficient or determining reason for the existence of the world as it is: God wills the best and his power puts it into being. The best, in Leibniz's understanding, is the greatest possible diversity among the monads coupled with their uniqueness and governed by the least number of principles. Evil arises inevitably in this best of all possible worlds because of the limitations imposed on the monads by the very fact of their uniqueness and their diversity. These infinitely varied limitations make all created monads *imperfect*, deprive them of the perfection they *might* have but *cannot* have within the metaphysical continuum they belong to by the will of God. But these limitations do not deprive them of *perfectibility*: "everything, when it exerts its efficacy or power, that is to say, when it *acts*, changes into something better and expands in proportion to its action."[19] The world as a whole, therefore, tends to progress.

The world, then, under the rule of divine benevolence, is purposefully organized, is governed — metaphysically — by *final causes*. We need not, however, consider any final causation when we investigate the phenomenon Nature. Whatever *efficient causation* we discover in natural changes and motions will automatically reflect the purposeful metaphysical order of being. Thus Leibniz can say: "Souls act according to the laws of final causation by appetitions, ends and means. Bodies act according to the laws of efficient causation, in other words, according to the laws of motion. And the two realms, that of efficient causes and that of final causes, are in harmony with each other."[20]

There is a potent link between the two, willed by God and accessible to human understanding. This link is the domain of *Mathematics*. It is especially for the entities of this domain that Leibniz reserves the appelation of "ideal" beings. Of this kind are arithmetical units and numbers, geometrical points, algebraic symbols, curves, tangents, infinitesimals, derivatives, integrals. They are "ideal" entities because they do not have metaphysical dignity since they lack "substantial" being or "reality." On the other hand, they are the result of perceptions which have reached, at the very least, the level of symbolic distinctness and which can, moreover, impart symbolic distinctness to

---

19. *Discourse on Metaphysics* 15.
20. *Monadology* 79.

the confused perceptions of natural phenomena. They belong to the domain of "eternal verities." Leibniz, as we know, discovered the *differential and integral calculus* in partial collaboration and fierce competition with Newton. It is this calculus which clarifies phenomena of change and motion, both terrestrial and celestial; and, again, it is due to mathematical considerations that we realize the true nature of Force and are brought thereby, as we have seen, to the very threshold of Metaphysics. Whence this power of Mathematics, and especially of Calculus, the abacus of infinitesimals? It seems that Leibniz understood the "ideal" symbolic medium in which Mathematics operates as provided by the order of co-existence and the order of succession, by space and time. Now, this temporal and this spatial order *combined* give to the phenomenal world presented to us by our perceptions its typical phenomenal character. And at the same time, it is only in temporal and spatial terms that we can get hold of the law of continuity, the adjunct of the principle of uniqueness, which law determines the structure of the entire metaphysical domain. That is why mathematical considerations and even mathematical terminology are not only justified but also necessary both in mechanistic and in metaphysical investigations.

In his earlier years, Leibniz planned to exploit the power of Mathematics to the full. His predecessors, notably Vieta and Descartes, impressed by the ancient idea of a "universal science," had sought and found this "universal science" in Algebra, which they interpreted as the general "analytical art." Leibniz went one step further. He planned a *new* "general science," a "universal characteristic," that is to say, a general symbolic calculus which would enable men to find *all* humanly attainable truth. This is the way he speaks of this "philosophical calculus": "If there were available either some exact language (which some call Adamic) or at least a kind of truly philosophical writing by means of which notions were to be reduced to an *alphabet of human thought*, everything deducible by reason from given premises could be found through a kind of computation, in the same way in which arithmetical or geometrical problems find their solution."[21] The idea of such philosophical algebra presup-

---

21. *De scientia universali seu calculo philosophico* (c. 1684).

poses, as Leibniz explicitly states, the conviction, which he never abandoned, that all possible predicates are contained in their subject. The goal of this philosophical algebra would be the discovery of *all* eternal verities. It was not given to Leibniz to carry this plan into effect. It contains, in part, at least, the germ of what is known today as "symbolic logic."

VII

Let us look back for a moment with some detachment at what I have been trying to report about Leibniz's system, about his compromise between the "ancients" and the "moderns." Two incidental features of this system strike us as most remarkable.

The first is related to the distinction made by Leibniz between perception and apperception. It is only on the level of reflexive cognition, of consciousness, of apperception, that the problem of *error* arises. Leibniz himself says[22] that our perceptions are always true, in accordance with the pre-established harmony of things, but that our *judgements* may be faulty and deceiving, for which, Leibniz claims, God is not to be blamed. Judgements are made by "spirits" on the level of apperception, on the level of consciousness. Yet judgements still belong to the perceiving activity which characterizes the very being of monads. Judgements cannot help, therefore, having a share in the harmony of the world, cannot help representing or expressing, or corresponding to, something which is external to the spirits that make those judgements. What, then, corresponds to faulty judgements — what, among all the other monads, corresponds to our errors? Does not the pre-established harmony of the universe break down in this case? It seems, at any rate, significant that Leibniz pays but little attention to the grave problem of error, and to its implications, which his predecessors never neglected.

The second remarkable feature of Leibniz's system is a curious reversal of the traditional relation between the inner and the outer aspects of souls. The contrast between the "inner

---

22. Cf. *Discourse on Metaphysics* 14.

man" and the "outer man," the latter being conditioned by external circumstances of birth, wealth, and reputation, is a recurrent theme dwelt on in philosophical reflexion. The "inner" dimension of the soul of man, the "looking *into* oneself" instead of "about oneself"—these are among the most solemn topics of all Platonic philosophizing. Most of you will remember the end of the *Phaedrus*, where Socrates is praying to Pan and to any other divinity that may have been present: "Grant me to become *inwardly* beautiful; grant me that all my external possessions be in harmony with those *within* me." Or let me quote Montaigne speaking from the other end of the spectrum, as it were: "That command issued in ancient times by that god in Delphi was a paradox. It said: Look into yourself, recognize yourself, hold on to yourself, lead back your spirit and will which expend themselves elsewhere; you are leaking, you are spilling over; stick to yourselves, support yourselves; you are betrayed, dissipated, robbed of yourselves. Don't you see that this world keeps all its viewing inside itself and its eyes open to contemplate itself?"[23] And Montaigne continues: "That [Delphic] god was saying: Except for thyself, O man, each thing applies itself first to itself and sets limits to its works and desires according to its needs. There is none as empty and needy as thyself who encloses the universe. Thou art the examiner without knowledge, the magistrate without jurisdiction, and—all in all—the clown in the farce." —How different is the emphasis in Leibniz! The monad, the soul, the spirit is *inwardly* filled, filled with the phenomenon of the *external* world. To reflect on this phenomenon means to step outside, to occupy the stool at God's feet, to direct one's metaphysical gaze on the inwardness of the soul from without. What inversion! The "inner" and the "outer" aspects of things seem to have exchanged places. It is this subtle exchange, this inversion, this reversal which makes Leibniz a "modern" thinker bent on extending immeasurably and, by the same token, on reducing irretrievably the inner dimension of the soul.

---

23. III, Ch. 9, end (*De la verité*).

13 ■ On the Nature of Nature

The title of this lecture "on the nature of nature" immediately shows its complexity, for what is meant by the first use of the word *nature* is not quite the same as what is meant by the second use of this same word. This seems to indicate an unavoidable ambiguity in the word *nature*. Indeed, the ambiguity, or better, the ambiguities surrounding the use of this word are tremendous. This lecture is supposed not to remove these ambiguities but to bring them to the fore.—I am not entirely certain who is to blame if I do not reach you with my words, Nature or I. In all fairness, I think both. Let me state at the outset that any attempt to lecture on this subject is bound to remain severely limited and insufficient. Still, it is perhaps worthwhile to make the attempt, wherever it may lead.

I

Let me first give you some examples of the use of the word *nature* in ancient literature.

In Aeschylus' *Prometheus Bound*,[1] Prometheus reports how

---

1. Vv. 488–90.

Lecture first delivered at St. John's College, Annapolis, February 28, 1964. First published in *The Independent Journal of Philosophy*, Vol. III, 1979.

he made men skillful in auguries: "I carefully determined the flight of crooked-taloned birds, distinguishing which birds were auspicious and which sinister by nature (φύσιν)." What meaning has "by nature" here? The birds may pass on the right — the auspicious — side or on the left — the sinister — side of people. They do this *on their own*, that is to say, they do not follow people's wishes. In this context, the phrase "by nature" is meaningful only with respect to an implied and rejected alternative possibility.

In Sophocles' *Oedipus at Colonus*,[2] the old, weary and still proud Oedipus makes the following comment on his slaying of his father: "And yet by nature (φύσιν) how was I evil, I who merely retaliated against a wrong I suffered?" We have to understand: had Oedipus not *re*-acted to something coming from the outside, had he acted *on his own initiative*, he would have been evil "by nature." In this context again, the phrase "by nature" is meaningful only with respect to an alternative, this time explicitly stated.

In Aristophanes' *Birds*,[3] Epops exclaims to the hostile birds in defense of the two Athenians who have left their home in search for a better city: "Although they be enemies by nature (τὴν φύσιν), they are friends by their intent (τὸν νοῦν)." Men, habitually, are indeed inclined to be inimical to birds: men catch birds, put them in cages, maltreat them, but sometimes some thoughtful consideration makes them considerate and friendly towards birds, which is eminently the case in this comedy. The phrase "by nature," in the given context, derives its meaning from the *contrast* between the habitual enmity of men and birds and the exceptionally friendly purpose of the two Athenians.

In all these cases, then, *nature* carries a connotation: it is meant to be what it is within a larger horizon — it is what it is only in relation to something else. I shall call this relationship a *horizontal* one.

Let us see whether this relationship always prevails.

When — in common speech — we speak of things *natural* we tend, I think, to take them as belonging to a more comprehensive domain, to wit, to the domain of the *familiar*. The ground

---

2. Vv. 270–71.
3. V. 371.

we tread on, grass, flowers, trees, animals of all kinds, sunshine, winds, the stars, are familiar to us. But so are the houses we dwell in, the furniture we use, our clothes, tools of all sorts, as well as carriages, policemen, parking lots, and all the establishments and institutions which serve our welfare and our pleasure. What is significant is that we are inclined to take all these man-made surroundings as being natural also. It is clear, however, that there is a distinction between the non-man-made natural environment and the man-made environment in which we live. In a curious way we ourselves are, as it were, the watershed that divides the all-comprehensive domain of the familiar into that which belongs to nature and that which is the product of human artfulness. This division was not invented by, say, Aristotle, but is itself — as we are inclined to say — a natural division. Here again, *nature* connotes a horizontal relationship. The horizon within which events in nature are viewed — and again not only by Aristotle — is the workmanship of human artisans, who, in turn, find the model for their proceedings and for the *knowledge* thereof — the model for their τέχνη — in the workings of nature, the artist.

II

What is familiar is, on the whole, inconspicuous — so much so that we hardly pay any attention to it. We keep meeting the same things all the time. Or, if they do not remain the same, they repeat themselves in never-ending cycles. The sun sets and rises again. The moon waxes and wanes. The seasons follow each other in a well-known sequence. Plants die and grow again. So do all living things around us. And our man-made surroundings, too, remain the same or undergo but imperceptible changes. All these inconspicuous things, events, and situations are understood to be familar *and* natural.

But there are, on the other hand, unusual and conspicuous events — violent storms, earthquakes, strange apparitions in the sky, monstrous deformities among living beings. There are also innovations in our traditionally regulated lives, conspicuous changes in the way we use things and behave ourselves. We may break away from traditions which we have been following for a long time, and this breaking away gives rise to a great awareness of the "old" and the "new." Are we to understand such conspicuous events and changes — both man-made and not man-made — to be natural?

There is a perpetual and grand fight concerning this question.

Lucretius answers it in the affirmative. His book is entitled not "On Nature" (as so many Greek books were) but *De rerum natura*, which we should perhaps translate "On the Naturalness of Things." Eclipses of the sun and the moon, earthquakes, storms, thunder and lightning, are natural events due to "natural causes." Lucretius does not presume to describe these causes accurately. Most of the time he mentions several possible threads of causation.[4] But his point is that there *must* be a natural concatenation of events which leads to the surprising and seemingly extraordinary occurrence, that such an occurrence is *not* the result of a whimsical and irrational intervention on the part of gods or ghosts, that everything — the inconspicuous as well as the conspicuous — is bound by the "bond of nature" (*foedus naturae*),[5] as we have to learn from "nature's aspect and lesson" (*naturae species ratioque*).[6] This also holds, according to Lucretius, for the gradual as well as the violent changes in men's lives, customs and laws — changes that, although man-made, occur naturally and in accordance with the "bond of nature."

The alternative view is that conspicuous, not man-made as well as man-made occurrences are due to causes termed not-natural and sometimes "super-natural." The relationship implied in the use of the term *natural* is, in this context, one of *rivalry*. This rivalry is profound and momentous. It may lead — outside the Lucretian frame — to a deification of nature as, for instance, in Pliny[7] and Seneca[8] (first century A.D.), in Lorenzo Valla[9] (fifteenth century), in Spinoza[10] and in any so-called pantheistic

---

4. Cf. V, 752.
5. II, 302; V, 57, 924; VI, 906f.
6. I, 148; II, 61; III, 93; VI, 41.
7. *Natural History*, II, Intro., esp. 7 (5) 14 ff.
8. *Naturales quaestiones*, II, 45, 3.
9. *De voluptate*, I, 13.
10. See *Ethics IV*, Preface.

philosophy. Nature is identified with God or nearly so, as Lorenzo Valla says: "Nature is the same as God or almost the same."

As far as the non-man-made conspicuous events are concerned, the Lucretian view tends to prevail. It is dominant today. Yet the naturalness of natural phenomena is — quite apart from the relationship of rivalry — of an intricate kind. I shall have to deal with that in a moment.

As to the man-made conspicuous events, the struggle between the Lucretian and anti-Lucretian views goes on unremittingly. The question is whether the circumstances surrounding radical changes in customs and institutions are to be understood as natural or as not natural, whether man, as the principal agent of such transitions, is the product of natural forces or is himself transcending nature, guided either by his own reason or fulfilling a providential plan, whether reason itself is natural or above nature. In this struggle the relationship of rivalry implied in the use of the word *nature* is compounded with other relationships which we have to consider next.

III

Let us revert to the inconspicuous things, events and situations, and especially to those *not* man-made. Here, everything is characterized by mobility and actual movement, so that any stillness is but a transient phase in a continuous chain of change. But change itself is perceptible only with respect to, and from a background of, something stable and truly unchanging. *Nature* is indeed characterized — beyond its horizontal relationship and its relationship of rivalry — by a twofold aspect, that of *mobility* and that of *stability*, the latter being the background, the foundation, and the source of the former. To enlarge further upon this *inward relationship* of nature I shall have to make a digression and deal with the etymology of the word *nature*.

The English word *nature* stems directly from the Latin *natura*, and this is true of the corresponding words in most modern languages of Indo-European origin, except for the Slavonic ones. *Natura*, in turn, though *not* a participial form, which it seems to be, is cognate with the deponent verb *nascor,*

natus sum, nasci, meaning to be begotten, to spring up, to come
into being, to grow. In fact, the archaic form of *nascor* is *gnascor,*
and the root *gn* is clearly the same as in the Greek verb γίγνομαι,
to become, to come into being. We cannot avoid comparing this
Latin word *natura* with the Greek equivalent φύσις.

The root of φύσις, *φυ,* whenever it appears in Greek words
implies becoming, growing, begetting, shooting up, sprouting
and also being. But there is more to be said about this matter.

There is the perfect of the Latin verb *esse,* to be. This perfect
is *fui* and the root of this perfect is unmistakably related to the
Greek *φυ* and, as I learned from suitable reference books, to
the Sanskrit *bhû,* indicating becoming, flourishing, — and also
being. Let me point out that the English infinitive form *be* is
related to this Latin *fui* and the Greek φύω or φύομαι , and furthermore to the Lithuanian *bú-ti,* and the Russian *byt',* which
means *to be.*

The inflexions of the verb *to be,* which is highly irregular
in all languages, embody at least two roots that correspond to
the Latin roots *fu* and *es.* Both roots are associated with the
meaning *being,* but the root *fu* is also associated with the meaning *becoming.* There is controversy among scholars about the
priority of either of these two meanings, *being* and *becoming.*
I do not believe that this controversy can be settled by purely
etymological considerations. For what is involved in this controversy are ultimate questions concerning being and becoming, rest and change, eternity and time. And these questions
touch directly upon our understanding of *nature* and the *natural.*

The twofold aspect of nature, which I mentioned before and
which characterizes its inward relationship, that of mobility and
stability, is a manifestation of the relationship of *becoming* and
being in nature. Look at the wavy motion of a cornfield, at a
mighty waterfall, at the quick pace of running animals, at the
growing of the young ones, at the decaying summery splendor —
everywhere there is change, slow or rapid movement, as the case
may be, and everywhere also preservation of an identity,
reconstitution of what had passed away, unending repetition
and undying sameness. We call both nature, the ever-changing
and the never-changing. The changing and the changes are
before our eyes; the unchanging and resting are before our eyes,

too, but tend to mock us and to escape us. What it is in nature that accounts for the unchanging?

There are many answers to this question, but they fall into a limited number of patterns.

There is the ancient view that there are four basic ingredients or states in all natural things and changes, fundamental characters or letters out of which the script of nature is composed, as it were, the *elements*, somewhat inaccurately identified with fire, air, water, and earth. It is they that are always the same although they are transmuted into each other. —There are also the unchanging atoms and the unchanging void of Democritus, Epicurus, and Lucretius, which atoms and void make up what Lucretius calls *natura creatrix*,[11] "nature, the generator." In this phrase, we have to note, the apposition "*creatrix*" is feminine in gender, just as the word *nature* is. — There are finally the 92 elements of the nineteenth-century chemistry, the irreducible and stable foundations of all changeable and changing natural things. — In all these cases the same pattern prevails: the region of the *elemental* is the region of the ultimate immutable material out of which all things natural are constituted. Within the inward relationship of nature the elements represent the fixed pole with respect to which nature's mobility is on display. And there is always the trend to descend to the bottom of the elemental region so as to reach the *one* single element which may be *the* ultimate beginning of all.

The elements are supposed to be endowed with motions of their own and the concurrence of their respective random motions is supposed to account for the natural phenomena around us. But does it account sufficiently for the repetitiousness, the reconstitutive character, the sameness, the *regularity* and the order in the appearance of natural things and events? Lucretius for one thinks that it does. Classical statistical theories seem to support him to some extent. It is easier, however, to account for nature's regularity and order if a source or sources are assigned to them. Such a source is an ultimate beginning of its own. The

---

11. III, 1117.

Greeks called such a source an ἀρχή, meaning both a "beginning" and a "rule," meaning, more exactly, a commanding origin,
something which, by its *command*, *initiates* a chain of events
or a distribution of things. The Latin *principium* translates ἀρχή
perfectly well. Our English word *principle* means the same
thing, though it is often used vaguely and most of the time in
a modified sense. Whenever an ἀρχή, a *principium*, a principle, is invoked with respect to nature, the question of nature's
unchanging aspect is being answered. What is more, this answer
helps us to reduce the seemingly irregular and conspicuous
changes in nature to fundamental identities. And the answer
is still one concerning nature's inward relationship.

Answers which invoke an ἀρχή with respect to nature are
multifarious, but they belong again to one and the same pattern. Sometimes this pattern and the elemental one are combined, as seems to be the case in the teaching of Anaximander,
reputedly the first to use the term ἀρχή. Anaximander meant
the *infinite* and *indeterminate* (the ἄπειρον) to be the ἀρχή —
"undying and indestructible";[12] everything comes into being out
of it and everything reverts into it; it thus underlies, comprehends
and governs everything.— In the opinion of the old Stoics "fiery
breath" pervades the entire universe and forms everything— it
is divinity itself.— In general, however, the ἀρχή is either the
begetting power or the womb which gives birth to all things,
or both. For Aristotle nature is ἀρχή in a twofold sense: it is
(a) the begetting, unchanging and imperishable power which
works on a suitable material, and it is (b) that pliable material
which is being transformed by the begetting power into a natural
thing. For Giordano Bruno, in the sixteenth century, nature is
both and *simultaneously* the generator and the universal womb
or, as he says, the "matter" out of which everything comes "by
way of separation, birth, and effluxion." "That matter, then,"
he says,[13] "which unfolds what it has enfolded must be called
the divine and excellent progenitor, generator and mother of
natural things; or, in sum, nature in its totality."

Let me call your attention again to this notion of an ἀρχή,
or a principle, involved in the consideration of things natural.

---

12. Diels-Kranz,[7] Anaximander B, 1-3.
13. *Concerning the Cause, Principle and One*, Dial. IV.

It becomes necessary to invoke this notion because of the aspect
of stability and regularity of nature and it is used to account
for the inconspicuous as well as the conspicuous and seemingly
irregularly changing phenomena. The ἀρχή, as the immovable
starting point of all change, delimits, and accounts for all change.
It is indeed impossible to understand anything changing without
resort to something taken both as unchanging and as responsible for the observed changes. But this has a momentous consequence: the inward relationship of mobility and stability within
nature, the relationship between change and ἀρχή of change,
leads us to abandon the horizontal relationship which seemed
to characterize our understanding of nature. Nature identified,
in its aspect of stability, with something unchanging becomes
identifiable with its own unchanging character, with that which
it unchangeably *is*, outside of all relationships. The shift towards
one of the poles of the inward relationship, namely the pole of
stability, of rest, of being, away from the pole of mobility,
change, and becoming, permits a remarkable shift in our use
of the word *nature*. We speak of the nature of man, of the nature
of justice, of the nature of tyranny, of the nature of gods, of the
nature of a relationship, and so on and so forth. This way of
speaking is meant to signify in every case that which everything
by virtue of its inner unchanging constitution is; or, in other
words, that which makes everything be what it is. The etymology
of the word φύσις, with its root φυ pointing no less to being
than to becoming, appears justified. The title of this lecture
shows the shift in the meaning of *nature*: the "nature of nature"
means the "being of nature," that is, that which nature in its
own right is supposed to *be*.

  Nature thus becomes paradigmatic for our understanding
of Being. On a large scale, we identify "natural being" with Being
itself. Everything "out there" in nature we understand simply
to *be*, prior to any reflexion on the meaning of Being. Nobody
can resist the temptation to assert that the sky and the stars,
the land and the sea, the mountains and the rivers, the forests
and the marshes, the animals and the plants, *are*, overwhelmingly so, both in their unobtrusive and in their obtrusive
aspects; that everything is natural and that we ourselves are part
of nature, forever surrounded and dominated by it. — On a no
less large scale, however, this certainty may be threatened by

the hunch that it itself, this certainty, is by no means natural, that there may be, in fact, no nature at all, that everything which surrounds us may have a magical character, lacking identity and any being of its own. The bird that flies over my head may be a portent, a sign, or a demon, or my brother, or even I myself in a new guise; the men we know may be subject to miraculous changes at any moment; the world around us may be a snare and a delusion. Do not consider this an extravagant statement. It is deeply rooted in human possibilities and actualities, past and present. Nothing familiar to children is alien to man. And let us also remind ourselves that the word *nature* does not occur at all in the Bible, I mean, in the Old Testament. There is no Hebrew equivalent for the word *nature*. Nor is it ever used in the Gospels.

IV

Man is not only the watershed between the domain of nature and the domain of human artfulness and deviousness, which domains are linked in a horizontal relationship. Man is also an experienced juggler capable of establishing a relationship between the natural and the *un*-natural. I shall call this relationship a *vertical* one.

The ἀρχή, the principle, can indeed be understood as not belonging to nature but as merely *applied* to it, as *regulating* the change but not as initiating it from within. A mathematical principle seems to be an ἀρχή of this kind. In general, mathematical principles of nature are called *"laws of nature."* This expression "laws of nature," mentioned by Galileo in 1615[14] and by Bacon in 1623,[15] acquires citizenship in the Republic of Letters through Descartes' *Principles of Philosophy* (1644). It is safe to say that — except for the poet Ovid who uses this expression in one of his verses[16] to which Leibniz for one does not

---

14. Letter to Grand Duchess Christina (*Opere* V, p. 316): ". . . nature is inexorable and immutable; she never transgresses the laws imposed on her . . . ."
15. *De dignitate et augmentis scientiarum* I: "immovable and inviolable laws and decrees of Nature . . . ." (Cf. *Novum Organum* I, 5, 75; II, 2, 5, 17).
16. *Tristia* I, 8, 5: ". . . omnia naturae praepostera legibus ibunt . . . ."

fail to allude — nobody before 1600 spoke of laws of nature [17] and that practically everybody since Descartes has been doing that. Descartes, and after him Spinoza, calls the laws of nature both *laws* and *rules* of nature. Let us investigate this relationship of natural lawfulness by putting before us some specific laws of nature.

Consider Boyle's law (published in 1662) which states that the pressure exerted by a gas is reciprocally or inversely proportional to the expansion of its volume, provided the temperature remains constant, in other words, that the product of the two numbers which represent the results of the measuring of pressure and of volume respectively is always the same: $PV = k$. This law had to be corrected later by Van der Waals to read

$$\left(P + \frac{a}{V^2}\right)(V-b) = k \qquad ,$$

where *a* and *b* are two constants. Consider also the proportion obtaining according to Galileo — he announced it as early as 1604 [18] — between the distances traversed by bodies in free fall and the times required to traverse those distances: $s_1 : s_2 :: t_1^2 : t_2^2$. This proportion has to be corrected too, if the bodies fall from very great heights.

Boyle found his law, as we say, "empirically" by measuring the compression of air and the corresponding pressure exerted on a column of mercury and by tabulating the results. Galileo *assumed* an equal increment of velocity at every moment of the body's fall and verified the mathematical consequence of this hypothesis by letting smooth balls roll down on smooth inclined planes. His measurements, however ingenious, could achieve only a low degree of accuracy.

In the case of Boyle's law, if we take one of the variables P or V as a function of the other according to the equation $PV = k$, we get a neat geometrical representation of that function, namely a rectangular hyperbola. — In the case of the distance traversed in free fall, we have the formula $s = \frac{1}{2}gt^2$, which follows directly from Galileo's assumption of an equal increment

17. Montaigne, *Essais*, 1595, Book II, ch. xii, mentions 'la loy naturelle.' (Note later added by Klein.)
18. Letter to Paolo Sarpi (*Opere* X, p. 115).

g at every moment of a body's fall. —These are simple cases of mathematical lawfulness in nature, but they are paradigmatic for our understanding of "natural laws" as principles of nature. There is no need for us to conjure up differential equations or matrices of a complicated kind.

A fundamental question arises with regard to this mathematical lawfulness of nature.

Does the mathematical character of the laws come from nature itself? This is what Galileo himself, in a famous and often quoted statement, has to say about this subject: "Philosophy is written in this grand book, the universe, which stands continually open to our gaze. But the book cannot be understood unless one first learns to comprehend the language and read the letters in which it is composed. It is written in the language of mathematics, and its characters are triangles, circles, and other geometric figures without which it is humanly impossible to understand a single word of it; without these, one wanders about in a dark labyrinth."[19] According to Galileo, then, the language of nature is a mathematical one; to understand nature means to read nature's mathematical message.

But must we not, in Galileo's opinion, already have learned and know mathematics in order to be able to read this message transmitted by nature? Is not mathematics by itself *un*-natural? Does not mathematics belong to a region beyond and above nature, at the limit or at the apex or vertex of nature, as it were? Mathematics is accessible to reason without any reference to natural things and events. Galileo would have agreed to that proposition. He would have insisted, however, that bodies, in their materiality, have geometrical shapes, that natural things and events have by themselves mathematical features, that mathematics, therefore, cannot be characterized as un-natural. It seems hard to deny, however, that mathematical truths have a purity and precision not present in things natural. Mathematical principles are indeed *applicable* to natural distributions and events but it is doubtful whether their *source* could be found in nature.

---

19. *Il saggiatore*, 1623 (*Opere* VI, p. 232).

Where else, then, should it be found? Let us note that Newton's title of his *Principia* does not say "mathematical principles of nature," but rather "mathematical principles of the *knowledge* of nature" (*Philosophiae naturalis principia mathematica*). Are, then, the mathematical principles applicable to nature principles which govern our human understanding? But, if so, *how* do they govern our understanding? Do they determine the operations of our reason, the *process of reasoning* itself, or do they constitute an autonomous region of symbols pointing to *ideal entities* through which our reason finds its path gropingly? Furthermore, *what* makes these mathematical principles applicable to natural things and events? Is it the inner constitution of nature, the nature of nature, nature's very being, as Boyle and Galileo apparently and many with them think? Or does reason impose its strictures on whatever it meets, as Kant proclaims? Or does a divine architect choose among all possible mathematical principles some definite ones and does he then let nature conform to these, as many in the seventeenth century held?

Whatever the answer — our actual understanding of nature is stretched upwards toward a mathematical goal which our measurements tend to approximate and to support, while at the vertex the symbolic mathematical formalism retains its strange and *un*-natural independence. It is this submission of nature to mathematically formulated principles which I have called nature's *vertical relationship*. It is summarized in Leonardo da Vinci's note: "Nothing in nature happens without reason; comprehend the reason and you will not be in need of an experiment."[20] However much the men of the seventeenth century extolled the "experimental method," they were closer to the spirit of Leonardo's statement than they might have thought. Let me also observe that the submission of nature to mathematical principles makes natural phenomena independent of moral judgments. Events in nature are understood to be neither good nor bad; they obey mathematical necessity and are neutral with respect to the sphere of morality.

---

20. *Codex Atlanticus* 147v.

V

Yet, the phrase "laws of nature" is striking. Leibniz uses it constantly. Newton speaks both of "laws of motion" and of "laws of nature." Laws imply legislation. Do laws of nature imply legislation, too? It is significant, I think, that for Lucretius the "bond of nature" does not imply any legislation at all. For many, especially French writers of the eighteenth century, who speak without any hesitation of laws of nature, this way of speaking does not relate to any legislation either. They follow in Lucretius' path. But for the writers of the seventeenth century who are responsible for the phrase "laws of nature" a special kind of legislation was definitely presupposed. Laws of nature or of motion were understood to be the result of divine legislation, the subject of which was not man but nature. The law-giving to nature differed from what is commonly called legislation, i.e., from giving laws to men, by the inviolable character of the laws: laws of nature are unbreakable, they determine the *necessary* nexus of natural events. But that is precisely the paradoxical character of the phrase "laws of nature." It is in the nature of all human *and* divine laws that, although they are meant to be obeyed, they can be, and actually are, broken or ignored. Laws of nature, on the contrary, defy insubordination. For the present century there exists a minimal probability that predictable events may not occur. This minimal probability of non-occurrence even defines mathematically, one might say today, the lawfulness of a law of nature as such. But in the seventeenth century the *complete inviolability* of a mathematical law of nature is of paramount importance. Why then is a law of nature, a mathematical principle, called a *"law"* at all?

Let me press this point. In antiquity the classical opposition is not only between what is brought about "by nature" (φύσει) and what is produced by human art (τέχνη) but also — and still within the frame of the horizontal relationship — that between φύσις and νόμος, between nature on the one hand and convention, custom, and law, on the other. Φύσις and νόμος oppose each other, and the great question is, Which way should we human beings go — the way of φύσις or the way of νόμος? When, in Plato's *Gorgias*, Callicles champions the νόμος τῆς φύσεως, the "law of nature,"[21] this phrase is meant to be a deliberate challenge and a paradox. To divest this phrase of its paradoxical character it is necessary to invest nature with qualities taken from the domain of the νόμος, from the domain, that is, ruled by moral considerations, ordered according to what is right and wrong, just and unjust, proper and improper. In Plato's *Timaeus* the attempt is made to endow nature with these qualities. This is accomplished by letting ψυχή ("soul") pervade the entire φύσις, while the "soul" itself is stretched out according to a strict melody, a strict νόμος, rooted in suitably chosen numerical ratios — a melody or a νόμος which, in its *mathematical* character, represents the *moral* order of things. Thus the distinction of Good and Evil becomes crucial in our relation to nature — an everpresent possibility for our understanding of what surrounds us. Not only the thinking of Cynics, of Aristotelians, and of Stoics bears witness to that. Whenever, in the conduct of our lives, the claim is raised that the course of nature should be followed, that we should live according to nature, a moral dimension is introduced into our understanding of nature — a *moral relationship*. In a curious way, however, the vertical and the moral relationships enter into a league with each other, not only in the *Timaeus*, but also throughout the seventeenth century.

Listen to the remote, broken, and tremulous echoing of Timaeus' words in John Locke's *Essay Concerning Human Understanding*:[22] "I doubt not but it will be easily granted that the knowledge we have of *mathematical* truths, is not only certain but real knowledge, and not the bare empty vision of vain, insignificant chimeras of the brain; and yet, if we will consider, we shall find that it is only of *our own ideas* . . . . And hence it follows that *moral* knowledge is as capable of real certainty as *mathematics*. For certainty being but the perception of the agreement or disagreement of our ideas, and demonstration nothing but the perception of such agreement by the intervention of other ideas or mediums, our moral ideas as well as mathematical being archetypes themselves, and so adequate and

---

21. Cf. 483 e.
22. Bk. 4, IV, 6,7.

complete ideas, all the agreement or disagreement which we shall find in them will produce real knowledge, as well as in mathematical figures." According to Locke, it is precisely the function of *reason* to discover inwardly those ideas within us and to find the connection between them.[23] Now, in Locke's *Second Essay on Civil Government*, reason is defined as the *law of nature* "which obliges everyone."[24] We infer that the "law of nature" is *within us* and dominates the moral order of which we have certain knowledge. The moral order is thus seen as the "natural moral law." Locke only repeats what has been said by many others before him. The natural moral law is the very foundation of the *ius naturale*, the natural code of law propounded, to cite but one great example, by Hugo Grotius in his book "Concerning the Law of War and Peace" (*De iure belli et pacis*, 1625). There he says: "Natural law is unchangeable, so much so that it could not be changed even by God . . . . Just as God cannot bring it about that two times two not be four, he cannot bring it about that something which is evil according to its inner nature not be evil."

"Law of nature" is indeed a traditional phrase. It is not conceived on the level of the mathematical "laws of nature." The distinction between the two kinds of "law" is not simply the grammatical distinction between a singular and a plural. Men as diverse as Melanchthon, Hobbes, and Spinoza use, in fact, the plural for the first kind also. The distinction is that the "law of nature" indicates the moral relationship of nature, while the mathematical "laws of nature" bear upon nature's vertical relationship. Yet, as I mentioned before and as the example of Locke shows, both kinds of "law" enter into a league with each other. To mathematical principles and to moral rules a common ground is assigned. This common ground is human reason. And the profound, though circular, reason why mathematical principles of nature are called *laws* at all is that they are conceived in the image of moral rules within us, which oblige everyone, while these moral rules, in turn, are interpreted — in the seventeenth century at least — as reflecting the inviolable mathematical principles of nature.

23. Bk. 4, XVII, 2.
24. II, 6.

Traditionally, the moral relationship of nature is not tied to the mathematical aspect of nature but to reason understood as "natural reason" (*ratio naturalis*) or "natural light" (*lumen naturale*). This reason is natural because it is *inborn*, and that means first of all that reason is taken to be given to us "by nature." I quote from Francis Bacon, who summarizes the traditional view as follows: "It is true, though, that, as the saying goes, men have by the light and the law of nature (*ex lumine et lege naturae*) some notions of virtue and vice, of justice and injury, of Good and Evil; this is most true."[25] Although the larger part of the "moral law" (*lex moralis*) is not accessible directly to that natural light but has to be acquired otherwise, there is, according to the tradition as Bacon presents it, an inborn "instinct" in us, a "law of conscience," a certain spark and, as it were, a vestige of a pristine and original purity of reason which enables us to get hold of the moral law. But that this reason is understood to be natural or inborn means secondly that we can understand nature as providing a home for reason, as incorporating reason within itself.

This leads us back to the question, raised earlier in this lecture, whether conspicuous changes in man-made surroundings, in customs and institutions, are natural or not natural, whether man, in bringing about such changes, is a natural agent or not. From the point of view of the moral relationship of nature which conjoins nature and reason it is possible to claim that radical changes accomplished by man and stemming from his rational insight into the rightness of the undertaking are indeed natural, since they are based on moral certainty. Man, prompted by moral considerations, is thus to be considered a *natural* agent. And the question posed by Hamilton, in the *Federalist Papers* No. 1—"whether societies of men are really capable or not of establishing good government from reflection and choice, or whether they are forever destined to depend for their political constitutions on accident or force"— this question is to be answered — prior to any action — by the affirmation that societies of men are *naturally* capable of instituting a moral and beneficent political order as well as chang-

---

25. *De dignitate et augmentis scientiarum*, 1623, IX.

ing an existing one into a better one. Violent changes stemming
from men's passions, on the other hand, are to be rejected as
not natural.

VI

Immediately, an objection passionately raises its head. Are
not men's passions the effective forces that determine to a very
large extent men's lives and fortunes? Do not passions prompt
men to change their private and public ways? Is not indeed passion rather than reason indicative of what is natural? This objection stems from an understanding of nature which responds
primarily to what, in nature, is untamed, violent, devouring,
and passionate. The relationship involved in such a view of
nature I shall call the *passionate relationship*.

Fierce desires, love, hate, burning ambition, pride, vanity,
compassion, deep-seated fear, and the human weaknesses in the
wake of such passions, seem to lord it over man's nature. How
often do we not use this excuse for our weakness: we are human,
aren't we? Do we not mean thereby that our natures are
dominated by passion? And, in a larger perspective, are we not
impressed by the fiery eruptions of volcanos, by the darkness
of jungles, the treacherous sunlit peacefulness of prairies and
the threatening depth of the sea where, everywhere, the passionate struggle for self-preservation at the expense of everything
else living goes on incessantly? Unbending passions are displayed
in the fighting among factions, parties and wilful men wherever
political power is at stake. Over-reaching itself, nature sweeps
away the remonstrances of reason, the feeble attempts to control exuberance, luxury, and profligacy. Disease and health
become indistinguishable, the one being no less natural than
the other. The passionate relationship reduces every natural state
of affairs to a pathological one.

The conflict between the moral and the passionate relationships of nature is profound. The passionate relationship tends
to eliminate not only the distinction between health and disease
but also that between Good and Evil. In this respect it is —
strangely enough — akin to the vertical relationship, inasmuch
as the latter may — and actually does — separate itself totally from

all moral connotations and treat natural phenomena as lying beneath or, if you please, beyond, Good and Evil. The clash between reason and the passions is reflected in our divergent and yet co-existent interpretations of what is natural. We are bound to nature but the nature of the bond is always in question. It is especially in question when political doctrines postulate a "state of nature" as the basis for the civil state.

VII

The bond takes on a peculiar aspect in a relationship which I have not touched upon so far and which I shall call the *relationship of detached nearness*. Nature may manifest itself as a landscape or as an enchanting display of color and fragrance. The majesty of mountain crests, the gentleness of meadows, the face and figure of human beings, the vigor or the languor of all living things around us, the solitude of the desert, the infinity of the ocean — all this and much more than this may overwhelm our senses, elate us or fill us with melancholy, yet leave us at a distance, secluded in detachment. We may be struck with awe at the sublime spectacle of nature's irresistible power and unimaginable magnitude. The impact of the sublime may shake our detachment and transform it into the feeling of our minuteness and insignificance. At this point nature's moral relationship begins to impinge upon the relationship of detached nearness.

Let me stop enumerating all the possible relationships nature has to itself and we have to nature, and let me try to summarize what I have been saying. I have distinguished seven relationships, the horizontal one, the one of rivalry, the inward one, the vertical one, the moral one, the passionate one, and the one of detached nearness. It looks as if I have been trying to catch nature in a net of relationships. But you will realize, no doubt, that it is I who am caught in the net nature cleverly weaves around all of us. Nature is, in human understanding, multidimensional. The ambiguities of the term *nature* express nature's all-pervasive presence in all human *understanding*. It seems as if what our understanding is intent on reaching is always clad in the garb of nature.

Let me confirm — and complicate — what I just said by calling an entirely different aspect of "nature" to your attention. There are some birds, especially some water-birds (as all have probably heard), that engage in fantastic, highly complex, yet well-coordinated and rhythmic dances while wooing their mates. We are inclined to say that the birds thus perform a "ritual"— using a word that describes certain actions and habits of men. What is striking about our "rituals' is that they acquire the character of a "second nature," as it were, and display as many relational dimensions as "nature" does, each one showing some analogy to the corresponding "natural" one.

As far as the horizontal relationship is concerned, almost every artful human activity tends to reproduce itself, to repeat itself, to make the artful product as familiar, in its constant re-appearing, as a natural thing, be it an object put to immediate use, be it a tool, a machine, be it a device or an institution. The art of *making* involves a ritual, a *routine*, to which we submit readily to achieve our purposes.

Within the relationship of rivalry, namely of that between the natural and the not-natural or super-natural, the latter is approached in words, in songs, in sacrifices, in ceremonial offerings, in ways of behavior which all follow a strict ritual prescribed to the last detail and to which, again, we submit "naturally."

The inward relationship of nature finds its ritualistic complement not so much in human actions as in human language, which is ever-new, conjoining and disjoining the elements of speech in ever-changing variations, while those elements themselves, welcome food for dictionaries, constitute the stable basis on which the flow of language expands. But language tends unavoidably to condense, to become sedentary, to wear itself out, to ritualize itself in idioms, figures of speech, clichés and empty phrases.

There is also a ritualistic complement to the vertical relationship of nature expressing itself in our social demeanor, in the symbolic ritual of polite formulae and manners which become more numerous and more intricate the higher the rungs on the ladder of human society.

The moral relationship of nature translates itself directly into our own moral attitudes and actions towards others, into *habitual* morality, which Aristotle emphasizes and which, he says, "resembles nature."[26] (This is actually the source of the phrase "second nature.") This habitual morality may even lose itself into an empty moralism, into a ritualistic insistence on ways of behavior beyond the pale of reason.

Corresponding to the passionate relationship is the passion of addiction, which is many-headed, ranging from drug-addiction and compulsive reflexes to fanaticism of every kind. The ritualism in all these cases is the addiction itself.

Finally, the relationship of detached nearness finds its complement on the wings of that peculiar human urge to make images and to love image-making for its own sake. The artifices employed in this undertaking — a source of unending delight, heart-ache, and exhilaration — tend to become ritualistic not only as to fashions, styles, procedures, and mannerisms but also as to their self-interpretation, their self-sufficiency, and their self-mirroring. The purest expression of the ritual in this region of artful activities is the self-perpetuating pattern of the ornament.

Thus nature has its counterpart in the multidimensionality of human rituals. Beneath the garbs of nature and of ritual lie hidden, we may well suspect, the features of nakedness. Caution then, is needed whenever we invoke nature, talk about nature, deal with nature. The nakedness of things might wreck our schemes.

---

26. Cf. Aristotle, *Eth. Nic.* VII, 11, 1152 a 29 ff.

14 ■ On Dante's Mount of Purgation

To talk *well* about anything Dante wrote requires a vast amount of knowledge which I do not possess. I propose, therefore, to give you a homespun account of the middle cantos of the *Purgatorio*, of cantos X to XXVII. My aim, modest and ambitious at the same time, is to show how these cantos are built. I shall stick to the text as closely as I can in the short time at my disposal. I shall have to leave out a great many things. I shall make some use of the commentaries I have read. Everything else I am going to say may have been said by commentators whom I have not read. You will forgive me.

It is not unimportant to mention first certain general characteristics of the mount of purgation. Let me remind you that Dante puts this mount in the southern hemisphere, exactly opposite Jerusalem. When Satan fell headlong from heaven into the center of the terrestrial globe a lump of earth bearing the garden of Eden surged upwards. As a result of this surge the mount appears placed between Satan's feet and the rays of heavenly grace. This situation determines the intrinsic *duality* of everything pertaining to the mount.

Paper presented at the Dante Symposium at Wellesley College, October, 1964.
First published in the *Cesare Barbieri Courier*, Vol. VII, No. 2 (Trinity College, Hartford, Conn., 1965).

In Hell reigns eternally the darkness of night, in the celestial paradise eternally the brightness of daylight. In purgatory there is both day *and* night. On every circle of the mount there is always both the bit of the remembered sin *and* the whip fitting the punishment, that is to say, on every circle both the sin to be punished *and* the corresponding acts of virtue are conjured up in visible or audible evocations. — I shall have to mention more examples of this duality as I proceed.

There is another characteristic feature of the purgatory which — for want of a better word — I shall call *inversion*. I mean by this term the change of something into its opposite. Here are instances of this inversion. 1) Since the mount is located in the southern hemisphere the rays of the sun strike from a direction opposite to that in the northern hemisphere. 2) In contrast to our common experience, the higher one climbs up the mount the lighter the ascent — and the easier it is to converse. 3) As a pine tree in our world "grows gradually less from bough to bough upwards" so do the trees on the circle of gluttony downwards. (This is said only of the first tree the travellers meet, but I assume that the other trees grow in the same way.) 4) While here on earth an earthquake is a calamity, the shaking of the mount whenever one of the souls is freed from its penitence is a blessing. — All these inversions, however, are mere "figures," reflections, or — in Dante's understanding of the word —"allegories" of the fundamental inversion proper to the purgatory. It is the character of penitence itself. The bitterness of the suffering which the souls undergo is sweetness to them; their pain is solace; they enjoy immeasurably the "sweet wormwood" of their torments. And it may be added that the *progress*, the going forward of the penitent sinner, is precisely his *returning*, his going back to the state he was in before his sinning. It is through this character of penitence that the duality I mentioned before acquires its deepest significance.

A question has to be raised at this point which concerns the *Comedy* as a whole and the *Purgatory* in particular. I hesitate to raise it. What is the role of Dante, the live and shadow-casting traveller, in the kingdoms of those who have left this life? This question is inseparable from this other one: What is the underlying theme and what is the purpose of the *Comedy*? Now, Dante, in his letter to Can Grande, says explicitly, as you all must know, that the underlying theme of the *Comedy*, in its literal sense, is "the state of souls after death," while taken allegorically it is "man as by good or ill desserts, in the exercise of the freedom of his choice, he becomes liable to rewarding or punishing justice." The *purpose* of the *Comedy*, Dante says in that same letter, "is to remove those living *in this life* from the state of misery and lead them to the state of felicity." This statement can be paraphrased as follows: Dante's poem, which describes his journey through Hell, Purgatory, and Heaven, is meant to *reform* men so as to enable them to achieve happiness both here on earth and thereafter. It prescribes the ways and means to achieve this happiness by biblical and pagan examples to be shunned or to be emulated. It passes judgement on the dead and the living. It is prophetic. It mediates between men as they are and the will of God. It is not possible to exaggerate the boldness of this undertaking. It relies explicitly on the help of Virgil, the dispenser of human wisdom, on that of Beatrice, the bearer of beatitude, and on that of Bernard of Clairvaux, the ultimate intercessor between Dante and the glory of God. The one who is thus wondrously helped is Dante, the poet. Dante's own visionary involvement shapes the very *content* of what he sees. He is not a passive or "objective" spectator. *What he observes is attuned to him; how* he observes derives from *his* powers; not only do his experiences affect him directly and personally — without his presence in the kingdoms of the dead those domains would not be as they are. Let me give an example.

Emerging on the terrace of the first circle of the mount of purgation (after climbing through a cleft rock which bestows upon the "needle's eye" of the gospels the features of the "wandering" or "clashing" rocks in Homer's *Odyssey* and the *Argonautica* of Apollonius of Rhodes)[1] this is what Dante sees and describes: a high and completely upright bank of pure white marble on which examples of profound humility are vividly represented in sculptures done in relief. Dante can hardly detach his eyes from them. Now, it is important to note that the penitent souls circling this terrace are bent down, corbel-like, under heavy stony burdens and are therefore totally unable to see these engrav-

---

1. *Purg.* X, 7-9, 16. Matthew XIX, 24-26; Mark X, 25; Luke XVIII, 25. *Odyssey* XII, 59 ff. Apollonius of Rhodes II, 317 ff., 549 ff. (Cf. Euripides, *Medea*, 2).

ings. What they can and do see are only examples of wrecked pride put in relief on the pavement. It is true, any one of them, purged and freed from the burden of penitence, may resume his upright posture on his way to the terrestrial paradise and thus get sight of the engravings on the wall. But then these souls have already transcended at least this stage of purgation. It is thus Dante alone — if we disregard Virgil's shade — who sees those reliefs. They are there, on the mount, for Dante's — and our — sake, not for the sake of the penitent souls. Dante's presence on the mount is an *essential* part of the panorama of purgation. There is a dual reaction to penitence, that of the penitent souls and that of Dante himself.

This is *one* way of saying that Dante, the pilgrim, is not engaged in penitence while on the mount. Let us understand this more precisely. When he arrives at the gate of purgatory and faces the Guardian Angel, who seems to represent the priest confessor, Dante — upon Virgil's prodding — flings himself at his feet, craves for mercy that the gate may be opened to him and smites his breast thrice. The letter "P" is scratched seven times on his forehead and the gate is opened with the help of two keys which the angel holds from Peter. According to the tradition of the church based on Matthew XVI, 19 these two keys are the ability to discern the sin and the power of condemning and of absolving.[2] Do we witness Dante's confession and absolution in this scene? No doubt, he is contrite, but he does not actually confess nor does he receive absolution. Without Lucia's heavenly intervention he could not have entered the Purgatory. All he is told by the angel is this: "Do thou wash these wounds when thou art within," the wounds being the seven P's on his forehead which it is hard not to interpret as standing for seven *peccata*, the seven deadly sins or capital vices.[3] This washing, which is the washing of sinful habits, occurs on every one of the seven circles of the mount — not by penitence but by acts of virtue. In every case a "particular virtue" *(virtus specialis)* is involved for, as Thomas says,[4] "to any specific natural inclination is ad-

---

2. Cf. Thomas, *Contr. Gent.* 4, LXXII.
3. Cf. Thomas, *Summa* 1 2ae, LXXXIV, 4 c.
4. *Ibid.* 2 2ae, CLIII, 2 c.

joined some particular virtue." And while, according to Thomas,[5] penitence expels every sin in being "operative," that is, in actual fact and once and for all (*effective*), any particular virtue expels the habit of the opposite vice only formally (*formaliter*), that is, by way of re-formation, by way of substituting one form for another, as white may substitute for black. This difference is reducible — in Aristotelian language — to the difference between the second and the first entelechy, as, for example, to that between the actual contemplation of the truth and the quiet possession of knowledge, or as to that between waking and sleep.[6] The "formal" washing is accomplished by Dante on every circle, and in each case an angel confirms this by removing one of the P's. But no penitence is involved in this washing. For one thing, there is not enough time for penitence on Dante's journey. Dante, the pilgrim, knows that he will have to come back to the mount of purgation after his death and does not fail to mention this time and again. He "justifies" himself, but not completely so. Let us accompany him and witness his washings.

On the first circle, on which Pride (*superbia* or *inanis gloria*) is purged, Dante spontaneously and humbly bends himself down to share the posture of the penitent souls. What the soul of Oderisi tells him a short while later fills his heart with humility and lowers his swollen pride. "Even in step, like oxen, which go in the yoke," he "went beside that burdened soul," and later on, erect again, his thoughts "remained bowed down and shrunken." This is how Dante's virtue counterbalances his vice. A great deal of pride remains in him, even on the mount. And he seems well aware of that.

On the second circle the aim is the purgation of Envy (*invidia*). Envy, in the context of the cantos which deal with this sin, has a dual meaning. It is both the sadness that one feels at the fortune of others and the joy that one experiences at the misfortune of others. The eyelids of the penitent souls are pierced and sewed up by means of an iron wire so that they cannot see (that is how Dante understands the Latin verb *invidere*). When Dante discovers the condition they are in, he says, full of com-

---

5. *Ibid.* 3, LXXXV, 2, ad 3.
6. *De anima* II, 1, 412a 21 ff.

passion for their present misfortune: "I seemed to do them wrong as I went my way seeing others, not being seen." This is how Dante's virtue of compassion prevails.

On the third circle Wrath (*Ira*) is the sin aimed at. In speaking to the soul of Marco, the Lombard, Dante manifests his anger with the world in these words: "The world is indeed so wholly bereft of every virtue, even as thy words sound to me, and heavy and covered with sin." But he adds: "I pray that thou point the cause out to me so that I may see it, and that I may show it to others." To ask for the cause of that which provokes anger means to pierce the smoky cloud with which anger envelops one's soul, means to cease being wrathful. This is the way in which Dante manifests the virtue of his meekness.

I should like to add that Marco proceeds to indicate the cause, the ultimate cause of the world's ills, which is the lack of leadership, the absence of the pacifying imperatorial rule. This rule has to supplement the spiritual power of the Church: *two* suns are needed to make the road of the world *and* the road of God visible. It is not insignificant that this doctrine of *dual* leadership is enunciated for the first time in the *Comedy* on the mount of purgation.

When Virgil and Dante arrive at the cornice of the fourth circle, where Sloth (in Latin: *acedia*) is punished and repented of, it is night. Virgil discourses on Love and unveils to Dante, in the middle canto of the *Purgatorio*, which is also the middle canto of the entire *Comedy*, the central doctrine of the poem, the doctrine of Love, as well as the relations which the various circles of the mount bear to Love's aberrations. Rivalling the ceaseless motion of the penitent souls on this circle, a motion that does not stop even at night, Dante's thinking, Dante's intellectual movement, is raised to its highest pitch. Encouraged by Virgil, Dante, burning to understand, decides to ask his guide to clarify the nature of Love to him. It is this passionate questioning and intense thinking which reveals Dante's virtue, Dante's zeal.

On the fifth circle, that of Avarice and of Prodigality, Dante kneels before the prostrate soul of Pope Adrian V. He explains his gesture to the pope in these words: "Because of your dignity, my conscience smote me for standing." It is in this unselfish tribute to a good which is not of an earthly kind that Dante manifests his virtue,— in this case, the particular virtue of liberality.

On the sixth circle reign hunger and thirst, the dual punishment for Gluttony (*gula*). Far from succumbing to the temptations of food and drink, Dante discourses with some of the penitent souls about a nourishment of a different kind (which I shall have to deal with in a moment) and, together with Virgil and Statius, resolutely passes by the tree raised from the one "eaten of by Eve." This is the way he shows his virtue of temperance.

Lastly, on the seventh circle, the circle of Lust (*luxuria*), Dante with utter reluctance, fearful of death, finally consents to enter the fire. He does this only after Virgil mentions Beatrice, and while Dante traverses the wall of fire Virgil keeps discoursing of her and her eyes. "When I was within," says Dante, within the fire, that is, "I would have flung me into molten glass to cool me, so immeasurable there was the burning." This awesome purification is, I presume, the seventh washing which takes the seventh P away. The virtue manifested here by Dante is Love, as ardent as any, yet freed from the flames of sensuality.

These, then, are the various ways in which particular acts of virtue on Dante's part "formally" expel his sinful habits on the mount of purgation.

We have not dealt as yet with the pattern or patterns according to which the journey on the mount is built. Dante's involvement and the limits of his involvement will become more apparent in them.

Let us remind ourselves first of all that Dante's rhyming scheme in the *Comedy* is the chain-linked tercet, conceived, no doubt, as a reflex of the trinity. The characteristic feature of this device is that the *middle* line of each tercet is the *first* line of a sequence of three rhymed lines and that the *first* line of each tercet is the *middle* line of such a sequence:

xAx ABA ByB.

Rhyming schemes may have a life of their own. But in the *Comedy*, and especially in the *Purgatorio*, they seem to adumbrate the way in which the themes of the poem are linked together or echo each other. Dante's precision is immense. Let me pursue this in the series of cantos under consideration.

Simultaneously, let us take notice of the fact that the sin purged on each of the circles is tied to a dominant medium and that the nature of the tie is different in the lower half and the upper half of the mount.

First circle. The sin is Pride. According to Ecclesiasticus X, 15 (in the Vulgate), this sin is the "beginning" of all sin.[7] It is, according to the tradition, the first sin of Adam, the first of Man.[8] There is an intimate relation between Pride and the organs of sight. Thomas[9] mentions Gregory the Great who said: "Pride, while extending itself outwardly to the body, is mostly indicated by the eyes," the eyes where, as Dante says in a later canto, "the soul is fixed most."[10] And Thomas also quotes Psalm 131,1: "Lord, my heart is not haughty, nor mine eyes lofty." Moreover we have to consider this: the object of sight, the visible object, is potentially visible to all. Glory, the object of pride, also tends to manifest itself visibly, publicly. Monuments, visible far away, reflect it. That which is so visibly displayed in pride claims uniqueness. This claim puts a burden on the proud. The proud wants to excel, wants his uniqueness to be seen by all. There is a clear discrepancy between his claim to uniqueness and his desire to share the commonness of a visible object. The meaning of "being seen" becomes questionable. Pride thus, indirectly, perverts the faculty of seeing. Accordingly, what is *first* presented to Dante's eyes on the mount are scenes of humility. But the important thing is precisely that the theme of pride and humility is here taken up in the medium of *sight*. The power of the soul which dominates the first circle is *seeing*. It is an exalted seeing with which nothing on earth can be compared. The engravings on the steep bank represent above all speech. It is speech made visible, as Dante himself says. They also represent what here on earth can only be apprehended by smell — the exhalation of incense. And let us not forget — it is Dante's own seeing which is thus affected.

---

7. Cf. *Summa* 1 2ae, LXXXIV, 2.
8. Cf. *ibid.* 2 2ae, CLXIII, 1.
9. *Ibid.* 2 2ae, CLXI, 2, o. 1.
10. XXI, 111.

The middle scene on the circle of pride — corresponding to the middle line of a tercet — is the scene of the "contracted" and burdened penitent souls. Oderisi's soul repudiates worldly fame, the "inane glory of human powers."[11] The perspicacity of the penitent souls has grown, but their sight is narrowed. Thus the link is forged that binds the theme of this circle to that of the following, the one of *invidia*, of clumsy seeing.

The third and last part of the story of pride's purgation echoes the first: engravings on the pavement present examples of wrecked pride. Dante views them with eyes turned downward.

Second circle. The sin is Envy. There is an intimate relation between Envy and the voices one hears. Envy is not jealousy. Jealousy sees its object directly. Envy relies on what is *said* of others, on the good or bad luck of those others as reported by word of mouth. Envy listens to voices. Its object is the audible. What is audible is potentially audible to all. Envy, however, — primarily in the sense of the joy one experiences at the misfortune of others — this envy, closing its eyes, as it were, listens to hearsay, to gossip. Gossip whispers. What is being said is not supposed to be heard by all. Envy, thus, indirectly, perverts the faculty of hearing. Accordingly, what is *first* presented to Dante's ears on this circle are voices which speak of compassion. Again, the important thing here is that the theme of Envy (in its dual meaning) and of compassion is taken up in the medium of *hearing*. The voices Dante hears are loud and persistent. The power of the soul which dominates the second circle is *hearing*. And it is Dante, first of all, who is engaged in listening.

The middle scene of the circle of Envy is provided by the penitent souls and their speaking. It is the soul of Guido del Duca who, taking up Dante's statement about his origin, launches into a diatribe about the cities on the Arno and inveighs violently against Romagna. He is full of wrath, though of legitimate wrath. Thus the link is forged that binds this circle to the theme of the next one, which is the theme of wrath.

The third and last part is tied to the first by way of contrast: new voices present examples of envy.

Third circle. The sin is Wrath. Wrath beclouds our souls,

---

11. XI, 100, 91.

engulfs us in billows of smoke, as it were. The angrier we are the more fuel is supplied by our imagination, which makes us see things at their worst. Our anger thus feeds on itself. Whatever we imagine is by the very nature of the faculty of imagination "unreal," untruthful, is an "error," as Dante himself says. Most of the time we imagine what is not there. But wrath may also be legitimate, as Guido del Duca's outburst on the preceding circle shows. We may occasionally imagine what is true. We may, as we say, "remember." We may truly recreate events of the past. It is indeed *imagination*, in its dual aspect, that dominates the third circle. Accordingly, the first sights that present themselves to Dante on this circle he owes to an exalted state of imagining, to an ecstatic vision of his own. Examples of meekness are thus supplied to him, truly representing events of the past. This happens so that his heart may be opened to "the waters of peace, which are poured from the eternal fount," in Virgil's words.[12]

The conversation with Marco Lombardo, who remains invisible amidst the smoke, the "bitter and foul air," which envelops the penitent souls on this circle, is the content of the middle scene. Dante's inquiring into the ultimate cause of the ills of the world not only testifies to his virtue, as we have seen, but also opens the way to a reasoned discourse on the part of Marco, which discourse touches upon most weighty matters and appeals to Dante's understanding. Thus the link is forged which binds this circle to the theme of the following one, where understanding is dominant.

In the last scene Dante finds himself once again alone with his "lofty fantasy," which this time offers him true examples of punished scorn and wrath.

Fourth circle. The sin is Sloth, physical, moral, emotional, and intellectual inertia, a capital vice which, according to Thomas[13] (and to Gregory the Great) has six daughters: malice, rancor, pusillanimity, despair, moral torpor, dissolute mind. The pattern of the three lower circles is broken on this fourth. It is Virgil who speaks, solemnly and authoritatively, about Love and Freewill. Dante's comprehension ripens. *Understanding* is the dominant medium throughout. The flow of Virgil's philosophical

---

12. XV, 131–32.
13. *Summa* 2 2ae, XXXV, 4.

discourse and of the corresponding intellectual movement in Dante is interrupted — the latter only for a short while — by the appearance of the penitent souls who, in running ceaselessly ahead, conjure up in words examples of active zeal. Their running again links, this time by way of inversion, the happenings on the circle of sloth to the punishment inflicted on the next circle. — But from now on, throughout the upper half of the mount, we face a pattern differing sharply from that on the lower half.

Fifth circle. The sin is Avarice and also Prodigality. According to the tradition, which Thomas[14] upholds, avarice (*avaritia* or *cupiditas*) as "an inclination of a corrupt nature towards corruptible goods which are pursued in an inordinate way" is the "root" of all sin, as pride, on the first circle, is its "beginning." Accordingly, "no more bitter penalty has the mount" than that for avarice. It consists in lying on the ground motionless and prostrate, with one's face downwards on the dusty earth. This is the spectacle Dante — and we through him — encounters from the very beginning on this circle, a spectacle of total immobility in contrast to that of never ceasing motion on the preceding circle. What is stressed here is the nearness of sin and penalty alike to — *Earth*.[15] What is dominant on this circle is the first of the traditional "elements," earth, and — to anticipate what is going to follow — the sway of the elemental will persist through the entire upper half of the mount.

The penitent souls themselves recite and present examples of liberality and of avarice. But, in addition — and this is the middle scene on this circle — an extraordinary event happens here, and we should note that it is *this* circle which is chosen by Dante for this event to happen. The entire mount shakes, signaling the release of a soul from the straits of its punishment. It is a moment of highest bliss. It is said in Matthew 27, 51-52 that at the moment of Jesus' death "the earth did quake, and the rocks (were) rent; and the graves were opened; and many bodies of the saints which slept arose." The shaking of the mount imitates this moment. Twice before, in Hell, Dante could continue his journey only because the earthquake which coincided

---

14. *Ibid.* 1 2ae, LXXXIV, 1.
15. XIX, 52, 72, 119, 120, XX, 143.

with Jesus' death had made rocks fall down and thus created negotiable passages. Divine grace proves efficient even in Hell. Here, in Purgatory, the shaking of the earth is a direct manifestation of the resurrecting power of Christ. Within the concatenation of the events on the mount this middle event rhymes with the theme of the following circle, as we shall see in a short while.

It is the soul of the poet Statius which is released at this juncture. As we learn later, Statius' main sins consisted in his hiding his conversion to Christianity and in his being prodigal. Statius joins Virgil and Dante, and from then on the three poets remain together until they reach the terrestrial paradise. Their conversation, which continues on the stairway leading to the sixth circle, fills the last part of the story of perverted liberality. Thus, the trinity of Poetry makes its appearance on the circle of avarice and prodigality dominated by the element "earth." We have to ask: What is the significance of this fact?

Within the household of nature the elements, especially earth and water, constitute — according to Aristotle[16] and the tradition that follows him — the foundations of the nourishment on which all living beings, including humans, thrive. (We shall have to consider this point more fully when dealing with the theme of the next circle.) A common metaphor attributes a desire for "earthly" goods to the human soul, a desire that can reach extravagant proportions in the "accursed hunger for gold."[17] This is what avarice in its naked manifestation is. Such hunger misinterprets the nature of the proper *human* nourishment, of what is genuinely "gold" to the human soul. Its proper nourishment, the genuine gold, is provided by — Poetry, by poetry's flavor, grace and elevation, to use Dante's words in *De vulgari eloquentia*.[18] Statius is a great and grave example of this fact. He was nourished by Virgil's *Aeneid* and the *Fourth Eclogue*. The former led him to his own poetry as well as to his belated liberality, the latter to Christianity. The poetic potency of the human soul shows itself in the art both of producing poetry *and* of absorbing it.

We gather that the relation of Statius to Virgil repeats itself

---

16. *De gen. animal.* III, 11 762b 12-13.
17. *Auri sacra fames* — Virgil, *Aeneid* III, 57. Cf. *Purg.* XXII, 40-41.
18. 2, VI.

in the relation of Dante to Virgil. But there is more to be said on this occasion. Any great work at some point justifies, explicitly or implicitly, its own existence. It seems that Dante's enterprise, of which the *Comedy* is the fruit, receives its justification and vindication on this circle of the mount. The nourishment Poetry provides is the seed out of which grows faith. The things seen in poetic vision may seem "unreal," as we say so glibly, may lack "thinghood," to use an English, if somewhat barbarous, word. The exploits on the Trojan battlefields, for example, or Aeneas' expedition into the underworld, or prophetic utterances clad in symbols and figures, do not seem credible from the point of view of our common experience. Yet poetic experience has its own validity and credibility, deplored by some, exalted by others. Dante appears to imply that the power of poetry is akin to the power of revelation. Does not genuine poetry prepare us — in Dante's view — for the "conviction about things unseen"? Does it not point to that which can be held only in faith?

We have to note, furthermore, that, while on the lower half of the mount the mention of the power of the soul *initiated* the development of the theme proper to each circle and involved Dante immediately and predominantly, here, on the first circle of the upper half of the mount, it *terminates* that development and involves Dante only indirectly. A structural inversion has taken place.

Sixth circle. The sin is Gluttony. Virgil and Statius converse about poetry and, in doing so, give Dante "understanding in poesy." They come upon a tree standing in the middle of the road "with fruit wholesome and pleasant to smell." The tree owes this bounty to clear water which falls from the high rock and spreads itself over the leaves. Thus the second element, *water*, is introduced on this circle. It dominates its climate. Water — again according to Aristotle[19] — is the *main* elemental ingredient of all food. A mysterious voice from within the foliage orders the virtue of abstinence and cites examples of it. It contradicts the serpent of the Bible. To prescribe abstinence means to combat gluttony. Gluttony, however, is but the extravagant outgrowth of our natural craving for nourishment. Nourishment

---

19. *De gen. animal.* IV, 2, 767a 29-33.

sustains life. Our craving for nourishment, our hunger and thirst, indicate our craving for life. Our desire of an immediate, as we say, physical satisfaction of hunger and thirst, which can be supplied by elemental nourishment, is but a symbol of our craving for everlasting life. Behind our desire of food and drink lies our deeper cravings for immortality both of soul and of body. The penitent souls who suffer immeasurably from hunger and thirst so as to be reduced in their appearance to the mere skeletal outline of their frames are well aware of the full significance of their terrible want. Forese Donati's soul expresses this as follows: "From the eternal counsel virtue descends into the water, and into the tree . . ., whereby I thus do waste away."[20] Elemental water is but a vehicle for the divine nourishment which makes our souls strive gluttonously after eternal life. In their longing for food and drink and in their joyful suffering the penitent souls imitate the passion of Jesus Christ, which passion was meant to make eternal life an achievable aim. But the thirst for immortality is understood as an original and innate power of the human soul.

Let us not forget that the shaking of the mount, the middle scene on the preceding circle, had set the theme we were just discussing. The middle scene of the circle we are now on is divided into two parts, which both again anticipate — though in a different way — the theme of the next circle. There are two speakers: Forese Donati and Bonagiunta of Lucca. Forese, continuing his conversation with Dante, castigates the licentiousness of the women of Florence, which rhymes with the sin of the lustful, the one to be purged on the last circle. Bonagiunta recognizes in Dante the champion of the "new sweet style" in poetry, which style — as far as Dante is concerned — could not have been maintained without the love of Beatrice. And Beatrice is indeed the link between Dante's poetic preoccupation and the aim of the last purgation on the mount, the overcoming of carnality by the love of the highest.

The third scene of the circle rhymes directly with the first: the three poets meet another tree laden with fruit, towards which the penitent souls lift up their hands crying and begging. But

---

20. XXIII, 61-63.

they depart "as though undeceived." A voice from the tree proclaims examples of punished gluttony.

So far, on the fifth and sixth circles, the dominant media
were Earth and Water. The dominant medium of the seventh
circle is Fire. The quaternity of elements would be complete
but for the missing *Air*. But Air is not missing. It is precisely
on the stairway which connects the sixth with the seventh circle that Dante asks a question which he could have asked, with
appropriate modification, anywhere else on the mount, and that
he receives an answer which, without any change, could have
been given to him at any other point of the purgatory. The question is: "How can one grow lean there where the need of food
is not felt?" The more comprehensive question implied in this
specific one is: How can the souls suffer the pain they suffer
while lacking all bodily organs of sense, since they have left their
bodies altogether behind them? Statius explains to Dante that
the disembodied souls retain and even increase their ability to
understand, to remember, and to will, but that in addition they
acquire, through their formative virtue, bodies made up of air.
That is why their "semblances" are called "shades." And that
is how they form "the organs of every sense even to sight." Statius'
explanation could be supported by a reference to Thomas'
description[21] of the bodily appearance of angels: just as in the
formation of clouds a condensation of air takes place, which
makes the air appear shaped and colored, so "angels assume
bodies out of air, condensing this air with divine help as much
as it is necessary for the formation of the body they have to
assume." We have to understand: the aerial bodies Statius talks
about replace the bodies left behind, but this substitution lasts
only as long as the purgation lasts. The emphasis given to the
body in Dante's question and Statius' answer is directly tied to
the theme of the sixth circle, the theme of immortality: the *resur-
rected* body is destined to re-join the soul.

At any rate, the quaternity of the elements is indeed complete on the upper half of the mount. These elements of the sublunar sphere are not primordial. As we learn from the seventh
canto of *Paradiso*, they were not created by God directly, but
were formed secondarily, so to speak, by powers already

21. *Summa* 1, LI, 1, ad 3.

created.[22] The tradition of centuries tied these elements to the four humors of the human body, which humors were thought to be responsible for the temperaments, the moral characters, the virtues and especially the vices of men. No wonder, then, that the elements are present on the mount of purgation. They keep playing here their dual role in pointing both to vices and to virtues. As to the nourishment they provide, the organic growth they ordinarily support, these are taken here as indices or carriers of a higher kind of nourishment and growth.

Seventh circle. The sin is carnal Lust. The very first experience the three poets have when they reach the terrace of this circle is that of fire, which flashes forth from the bank, while the cornice breathes a blast upward, which bends the flames back and keeps them away from it. The *fire* is all-dominant. The poets have to walk one by one close by the precipice. The penitent souls go through the flames chanting and crying out examples of chastity as well as of lust. There are two groups among these souls, walking in opposite directions. They represent the duality of illicit and of unnatural love. It is through flames that the flames of all this love are purified.

The middle scene on this circle consists in the conversations Dante has with the poets Guido Guinizelli and Arnaut Daniel. The first one Dante considers as his father in poetry, the second is pointed out to him by Guido as "a better craftsman of the mother tongue." More important perhaps than what is said in these conversations is the fact that here again two poets are brought to the fore. In addition to Dante, Statius and Virgil, three poets (if we do not include Forese in the count) make themselves heard on the last three circles. Thus, there are altogether six poets on the upper half of the mount, while none appear on the lower half, except Virgil and Dante. Poetry is predominant in the upper region. Let us remind ourselves that, in Dante's own words taken from *De vulgari eloquentia*,[23] true poetry must rest on these three pillars: alertness of mind (*strenuitas ingenii*), steadfastness in the practice of the art (*assiduitas artis*) and familiarity with the sciences (*habitus scientiarum*). Only poetry thus endowed and equipped can serve as

---

22. *Par.* VII, 124 ff.
23. 2, IV.

nourishment to the human soul. To continue quoting from *De vulgari eloquentia:* "Let therefore those who, innocent of art and science, and trusting to genius alone, rush forward upon the highest subjects, which must be sung in the highest style, be confounded in their folly and let them refrain from such presumption." The mention of the "new sweet style" on the sixth circle brings in a new dimension, brings in Love, Love that reveals itself in dictating to the poet within the poet's soul. The mention of the new style in poetry foreshadows what is going to happen on the last circle.

Now, in the third and last scene of the last circle the freeing of love from the shackles of carnality occurs. Poetry prepared for it. The burning fire accomplishes it. This fire is as much elemental as it is spiritual in its nature. It frees Dante for the love of God, for the love of Love, which is the true character of the human will. And it does this only through the beneficence and munificence of Beatrice's name.

The structural inversion of the fifth circle repeats itself on the seventh. The power of the human soul to love God is the terminal point of the movement on the last circle. The next station is the terrestrial paradise.

Let me put together what I have been trying to report so far. In showing the working of penitence on the mount Dante has described the faculties of the human soul which are necessary for its salvation. There are seven of them: the power of seeing, the power of hearing, the power of imagining, the power of understanding, the poetic potency, the thirst for immortality, the love of God. Whatever Dante may owe to Aristotle, to Virgil, to Ovid, to Augustine, to Thomas, to Allain of Lille, to Brunetto Latini and to many others, this description is his own. The sequence of those faculties has an ascending order. The smaller the radius of the circles, and correspondingly the greater their curvature, the greater also the intensity of the soul's commitment. At the beginning of the fourth canto of the *Purgatorio* Dante criticizes a doctrine according to which the soul is divided into separate compartments, each with a specific and unchanging function. According to Dante the *whole* soul may be totally concentrated in any one of its faculties. Dante himself, in his pilgrimage on the mount, bears testimony to the truth of this view. He is engaged alternately in seeing, in hearing, in ecstatic visions, and in understanding. He is wholeheartedly a partner in the poetic companionship of Statius and Virgil, he shares in the thirst for immortality exhibited by the penitent souls, and he is finally overcome — both Virgil and Beatrice serving as mediators — by the love of God. On these last three stages of the soul's expansion the soul is not alone, does not face its object in isolation, but rather, directed by "the love of the highest sphere," possesses the good so much the more the more there are souls who claim this good as their own. That is the reason why, on the last three circles, Dante does not initiate the movement. The "initiation," on these circles, is left to the elements of this world, which elements, in turn, merely "image" the truly elemental ingredients of the nourishment of the human soul, to wit: poetry — which is of things not seen; thirst for immortality — for immortality not yet vouch-safed; love of Love — that has not yet reached its fulfilment. These three potencies *prefigure* Faith, Hope, and Charity, the virtues traditionally called "theological." Even before being admitted to the Purgatory, Dante saw these virtues in the sky as three bright stars.[24]

The ascending order of the soul's saving faculties implies that the highest of them, the ability to love God, ultimately determines the very being of each of them. Seeing and hearing acquire a new dignity in ecstatic imagination; imagining together with seeing and hearing is elevated in understanding; understanding, in turn, rises to a new height in poetic vision; such visions reach into the region of eternal peace that the thirst for immortality is after; and this thirst is felt most deeply in the love of God, the love of Love. The interlocking of the themes and events on the seven circles of the mount reflects the nesting of the soul's faculties of salvation inside one another. All-encompassing is the love of God. Virgil, from his vantage point of human wisdom, speaks — in the seventeenth canto — of God as "Prime Being" and identifies the love of God with the "love of good" or the love of "primal goods." This love has paradigmatic character. Whatever inclination, whatever willing the human heart is

---

24. VIII, 85-93.

capable of, is derived from this highest power: "Love must be the seed of every virtue in you, and of every act that merits punishment," says Virgil to Dante.[25] This love, then, also reigns over the power of seeing, the power of hearing, the power of imagining, and, above all, the power of understanding, in which the first three merge and culminate. The power of understanding gives wisdom. But without Love this wisdom, this human wisdom, could not take shape and substance, could not become—"Philosophy." Philosophy, we read in the *Convivio*,[26] "has Wisdom for its material subject and Love for its form, and the habit of Contemplation (*l'uso di speculazione*) for the union of the two." However intense the thinking and understanding on the fourth circle of the mount is, this thinking and understanding, as manifestations of the intellect, are not ripe to become contemplative—if Love is not present. Indeed, Dante "rambles" in his thoughts after listening to Virgil (he says: *d'uno in altro vaneggiai*). The very content of Virgil's discoursing about Love is aimed at linking the faculties exhibited on the lower half of the mount with the one appearing on the last circle. Contemplation, genuine beholding, true "philosophy," are only possible when love unites with understanding, when the willing of the good unites with the intellection of the true.

This kind of contemplation becomes actual in Beatrice, manifests itself in the Saturnian sphere of Heaven, and is fully realized perhaps only in Bernard at the very end of Dante's journey. On the mount, Dante is given merely a glimpse of it, in a prophetic dream he has at the threshold of the summit. It is the third such dream he is permitted to have on the mount in the early hours of the morning. The three prophetic dreams, at the beginning, the middle, and the end of Purgatory, mark decisive caesuras in Dante's journey and clearly set the boundaries to the upper and the lower halves of the mount, thus underscoring its intrinsic duality. The first prophetic dream occurs before Dante reaches the gate of Purgatory and coincides with Lucia's transporting him to this gate. The second takes place before his experiences on the upper half of the mount and anticipates the sins punished there in the figure of a stuttering,

25. XVII, 103-105.
26. 3, XIV.

cross-eyed woman, the Siren, out of whose belly issues stench. Now, in the third prophetic dream, he sees Leah gathering flowers, Leah whom, as she says, *action* satisfies. And it is Leah who speaks of her sister Rachel, whom Dante does not actually see and who, according to Leah, never stirs from her mirror. Rachel is looking into her own fair eyes and is satisfied by this beholding, this *contemplation*.

This is the way the climb up the mount of purgation ends. An active life without blemish and, above all, a contemplative life beckon to Dante — and to us, his readers. Virgil releases Dante "free, upright, and whole" in his will. Crown and mitre are bestowed on Dante by Virgil. From this moment on, Dante, the pilgrim, is not subject to any temporal lordship nor dependent on the guidance of the church. But this is another theme, the pursuit of which would exceed by far the task I have set myself.

15 ■ On Liberal Education

From the very beginning, if it is possible to speak of a beginning in this case, liberal education meant the education of free men. From the very beginning one detects an ambiguity in the meaning of "free men." In ancient times free men are contrasted with slaves and, moreover, with men who, though not slaves, are engaged in menial labor and have to do that to cope with the necessities of life. To bring up children to the level of free men means to bring them up for the enjoyment and duties of a life which, secure in its subsistence, is attuned to the pleasures of bodily, sensual and intellectual exercises and to the challenges of military and political activity. Such life tends, however, to move along traditional lines, be it in games, in polite conversation or in the turmoil of public affairs. Its freedom is endangered by the dominance of accepted opinions, the "idols of the market-place," in Baconian terminology. However "free" the free man may be, he has thus still to free himself from the shackles of conventional views which pass for the truth of things. He has to cultivate pursuits in which the truth of things is truly made an attainable goal. These pursuits constitute the arts of

Lecture delivered March 25, 1965, at the Colloquium held at St. Mary's College, California. First published in *The Bulletin of the Association of American Colleges*, Vol. 52, No. 2 (1966).

freedom, the "liberal arts." Liberal education, then, consists in the acquisition of the liberal arts. And again from the very beginning there are genuine difficulties in the understanding and the practice of these arts. These difficulties relate (1) to their content and (2) to their preservation through generations of men. Let me first speak of the difficulties which relate to their content.

The quaternity of the original liberal arts — Arithmetic, Geometry, Music, Astronomy — is characterized by the immensely fascinating fact that their content can be *understood* and therefore *learned* and therefore *known*. The Greek word that embodies these three meanings is *mathēma*, the learnable. Thus the traditional liberal arts are originally "mathematical," that is, understandable, learnable, and knowable. Cassiodorus calls therefore such a liberal mathematical art quite suitably an *ars doctrinalis*. We should not forget that antiquity had, unofficially, as it were, a fifth liberal preoccupation — the inquiry into nature *(hē peri phuseōs historia)*, natural history, as it was called later. There was something to be "learned" here, too.

And we know that Grammar, Rhetoric and Logic were added to the list, the emphasis shifting gradually from the quaternity of the mathematical arts to these trivial supplements. Why this shift? The answer is: The ultimate foundations of the original four or, if you please, five liberal arts remained doubtful, becoming the concern of a deeper investigation, the subject matter of philosophical reflection. The pursuit of truth in these arts, through which the freedom of man was meant to find its integrity, seemed to become truncated and encroached upon by definitions and hypotheses which lacked certainty and persuasiveness and put limits to our understanding. This could not be said of the trivial arts. It can be said, however, that integral knowledge was not achievable in any of the seven arts. That is why it is proper that they preserved the name of "arts" *(technai)* in contradistinction to "knowledges" *(scientiae, epistēmai)*. Philosophical wisdom was meant to supply what they were lacking. And, whatever else may be said about liberal education, we are justified in setting down as a first rule that liberal education requires — for the learner as well as for the teacher — the practice of philosophical reflection and the awareness of its guiding role.

Let me turn to the difficulties inherent in the preservation of the liberal arts through generations of men. Words used in common speech do not always preserve their commonly accepted meaning. This commonly accepted meaning itself ranges, more often than not, over a series of connected shadings and connotations. In the perspective of a detached inquiry the meaning of a word usually loses its "natural" ambiguity, becomes more fixed, gains a definite significance determined by the scope of the attempted and sustained investigation, which investigation may lead to the establishment of a science, an art, a *technē*. The inquirer then turns, of necessity, into an "expert" who is able to pass his knowledge on to others, who is able, in other words, to become a teacher. It is thus that words do indeed become "technical" and transcend the habitual and familiar. Special terms, moreover, may be coined to satisfy more fully the understanding gained in the investigation. And yet, the "technical" use of words tends, in turn, to become accepted and to win a familiarity of its own. The passing on of sciences, arts, and skills, especially of intellectual ones, cannot quite avoid the danger of blurring the original understanding on which those disciplines are based. The terms which embody that understanding, the indispensable terms of the art, of the *technē* in question, the "technical" terms, acquire gradually a life of their own, severed from the original insights. In the process of perpetuating the art those insights tend to approach the status of sediments, that is, of something understood derivately and in a matter-of-course fashion. The technical terms begin to form a technical jargon spreading a thick veil over the primordial sources. Again, whatever else may be said about liberal education, we are justified in setting down as a second rule that liberal education has to counteract this process of sedimentation and to find the proper ways of doing this.

The background of what I have been saying so far is classical liberal education. But in the last four hundred years the background of the educational scene has changed tremendously. The pertinence of the two rules I mentioned has increased accordingly. Let us take a glimpse at this change.

Music has almost ceased to be a liberal art. Arithmetic, geometry, astronomy, and natural history have merged and

expanded into a towering, multi-storied edifice called
mathematical physics to which are attached a number of an-
cillary disciplines, the mightiest among them named biology.
Analytic mathematics has formed an entirely new New Atlantis. The arts of grammar and rhetoric have transformed
themselves into the preoccupation with diverse languages, and
especially with the classical ones, which preoccupation is called
philology, and embrace quite disparate subjects as, for example,
classical philosophical texts, poetic works, literature in general,
and the modern novel in particular. The art of logic has become,
on the one hand, an adjunct of mathematics and has usurped,
on the other hand, the place of the uppermost level of all
knowledge. Philosophy is taught as a special discipline by professors of philosophy and is, more often than not, identified with
mathematical logic. I omit mentioning a plethora of other
sciences cultivated in our universities. All these disciplines are
supposed to be classifiable into two vast domains, that of science
proper and that of the humanities. The subject matter of liberal
education is thought to belong almost exclusively to the latter
domain, the domain of humanities, which includes — we ought
to note — history and all kinds of historical disciplines.

The multiversity of our universities is likely to increase in
the future rather than to decrease. Will a genuine liberal education be able to remain a desirable goal? Will the idea of a "free
man" persist? This will depend, I submit, on whether the two
rules I have referred to will be observed in the process of learning. It is safe to say that in any *good* course of study — whatever
the subject matter — these two rules find, to a greater or lesser
degree, their application: the learner is made to reflect on the
assumptions underlying the way the subject matter is presented
to him and the technical notions governing the presentation are
shown to arise from fundamental insights freed from their status
of sedimentation. I would not venture to state how often or how
rarely this actually occurs. A little later I shall have to come
back to this question again. What is to be aimed at, at any rate,
is the setting up of a program of study in which those two rules
can be consciously and persistently applied at all times.

Let me talk, then, about such a program. It has first of all
to select the material which would compel the learner to reflect

and to get rid of the sediments in his thinking so as to enable him to reach the level of intellectual clarity. This material is available in the great documents of human seeing, hearing, imagining, and understanding, that is to say, in the Old Testament, in the works of Homer, Aeschylus, Sophocles, Euripides, Plato, Aristotle, in the New Testament, in Augustine, Thomas Aquinas, Dante, Francis Bacon, Shakespeare, Galileo, Descartes, Newton, Locke, Hume, Rousseau, Kant, Hegel, Darwin, the great novelists of the nineteenth century, Nietzsche, Freud, Whitehead and many others. The task is to read these works, which contain our intellectual heritage — which, in turn, is permeated by vagueness and sedimentation — in such a way as to re-awaken the insights in which they are rooted and to reflect on these insights and their ultimate assumptions. This task is tremendous; at best, only a beginning can be made.

Those works present human speech, bereft of its spontaneity, but composed artfully and purposefully. To understand the content, the art, and the purpose of this speaking, help is required. The signifying function of words and the ramifications of this function are at stake. It is necessary, therefore, secondly, to arrange for a concentrated study of the interconnection of words, of their inflections and concatenations, of the grammatical rules in which they are bound and of the flexibility they still may preserve. This study should bypass the familiarity of the mother tongue and its sedimented use. Two foreign languages, preferably an ancient one and a modern one, should be chosen, the scrutiny of which may provide the learner with an understanding of what grammar entails. And it is in translating that the learner should be able to recognize the similar, yet different structure of his mother tongue. Translation, moreover, should acquaint him with the various rhetorical devices language uses to articulate thought by means of combinations and stratifications of sentences, by means of figures of speech, metaphors and idiomatic expressions. To understand the embodiment of thought in speech — this is the aim of such a study of language.

What characterizes words is the union of their sound with their functioning as signs. This union can be broken: both sound and sign may become autonomous. The naked signs, turned later on into symbols, constitute the skeletal language of mathematics;

similarly, the naked sounds become the tonal language of music. Liberal education cannot dispense with the task of focusing its attention on both.

It is necessary, therefore, thirdly, to study mathematics, always bearing in mind that this studying has to be reflective and cannot be satisfied with a sedimented understanding of mathematical relationships. How to begin here is an open question. But it is not questionable that, whatever the beginning, the mathematical considerations have to be tied to the inquiry into nature, be it to the observation of celestial phenomena or to the investigation of events and conditions on this our earth. Everything around us, as we know, all motion and change, hangs on number, weight, and measure. After a while, the shores of the new New Atlantis of pure mathematics may be within our reach.

And fourthly, music too, the region of sounds, either tied to words or received in their purity, should be opened to our understanding though vying with our pleasure. I cannot omit mentioning in this connection the mysterious link between musical sounds and sequences of numerical ratios. Music's formalism in pitch, rhythm and meter, seems to be an ultimate formal reflection of the rhetoric inherent in human speech.

I have been speaking of modern pure mathematics as a new New Atlantis, using a Baconian phrase. Now, Bacon's *New Atlantis*, as we know, pictures this island not as a mathematical one, comparable to Swift's Laputa, but as treasuring a vast laboratory in which man "interprets" Nature in extracting her secrets from her and subduing her to his will. Thus Bacon, though neglecting the tie between mathematics and the inquiry into nature, anticipated the work of the centuries that followed him. We have indeed transformed our habitat from a place of nurture into a place of experimentation. Our relation to Nature is quite Baconian. Can liberal education ignore this tremendous change? Has not the Baconian enterprise added a new dimension of freedom to man's life — the freedom to control the ways of Nature and to put them to our use? Yes, it has done that, but it has also brought us face to face with forces which we seem unable to control. Liberal education has, therefore, fifthly, to apply itself to experimentation, not to increase the storehouse of our powers, not to reach any new and unexpected results, but to gain insight into the condition of possibility of such undertakings so as to understand how they come about and what caution they demand. The ways of the inquiry into nature proper to physics and to biology have to be scrutinized and marvelled at.

This program of liberal learning I have been trying to sketch is the program of St. John's College. Needless to say, we do not live up to our own goals. But I am not here to speak of our faults and defects. What I have to speak about, briefly and in a most elementary way, is what both learning and teaching mean and do not mean. Learning and teaching are mysterious processes. To understand them fully would mean to discover the secret of our lives. For we are, perhaps above anything else, learning and teaching animals. I hope we all agree that teaching does not consist in telling and insisting, nor learning in listening and repeating. The image of the learner's soul is not an empty pitcher into which the teacher pours the fluid of knowledge. This picture of teaching and learning, by the way, however wrong, is ineradicable.

There are perhaps two ways of describing teaching and learning in an appropriate manner. The one is that of begetting and conceiving. The word of the teacher acts as the form which in-forms the material of the learner's soul, in-forms the capability this soul has, and trans-forms it into a knowing soul. This is, on the whole, the Aristotelian view. The process of learning and teaching is a generative one, and a great deal depends not only on the activity and effectiveness of the teacher's word but also on the receptivity and potentiality of the learner's soul. The other way of describing teaching and learning is that of eliciting answers and gaining insight from within. Through questioning and arguing the teacher compels the learner to pull out of himself, as it were, something slumbering in him at all times. This is, on the whole, the Socratic and Platonic view. Here again a great deal depends on the quality of the teacher's questions and on the quality of the learner's soul. But just as questioning has its place in the Aristotelian scheme, begetting is an important element in Socrates' practice. Learning from books, by images, through associations, and whatever other ways of learning may be mentioned, falls easily into the patterns of those two fundamental views. I doubt whether modern psychologies of learning have added anything to them.

It is perhaps not unimportant to note that the role of the teacher who engages in questioning cannot simply be identified with the role of the "midwife" that the teacher has occasionally to assume. This "midwife" image, mentioned in only *one* of the Platonic dialogues, in the *Theaetetus* and nowhere else, is a tricky one. The midwife, the *maia*, delivers women of children that have been fathered, and the teacher is a "midwife" only when he delivers the learner's soul of opinions, mostly wrong ones, "fathered" by others. Truth, according to Plato, has no father.

At any rate, a program of liberal education implies teaching both as begetting and eliciting, in fact, more the latter than the former. The great vehicle of learning is discussion in which begetting, questioning, refuting, and again questioning take place. This is not to say that all drudgery, all routine work is eliminated. The learning process requires that too. But it is not the pivot on which failure or success depends. How to gauge whether learning has actually occurred is extremely difficult. For what has been formed in the learner's soul or what insights have been re-awakened in him depends on factors often totally unknown to the teacher. Both learner and teacher are members of a learning community. Inasmuch as this learning community is an institutionalized one, it is bound to fall short of its goal. All the institution can do is to set the *conditions* for learning. This in itself is an immense task. Learning under these conditions does not consist in "mastering" a body of knowledge. The conditions merely provide the horizon in which fruitful learning can take place. The conditions determine the existence of a "school."

[Editor's Note: The concluding portion of this lecture is almost identical with Sections IV and V of the lecture "The Idea of Liberal Education" above.]

16 ■ The Myth of Virgil's *Aeneid*

It is impossible to read the *Aeneid* without being constantly reminded of the *Iliad* and the *Odyssey*. Nor can one read the *Aeneid* without becoming aware that the poem intends to glorify Rome and Rome's imperial and pacifying power under Caesar Octavian Augustus. All of you, I think, and also all Virgil commentators agree on these points. Let me quote two ancient ones.

Servius, fourth century A.D., has this to say: "This is Virgil's purpose: to imitate Homer and to praise Augustus in the light of his ancestors" *(Intentio Vergilii haec est, Homerum imitari et Augustum laudare a parentibus).*

Macrobius, fifth century, explains: Virgil

> held his eyes intently upon Homer in order to emulate not only Homer's greatness but also the simplicity and power of his diction and its quiet majesty. Hence the multifarious magnificence of the various personages among his heroes; hence the intervention of the gods; hence the weight of mythical details; hence the natural way of expressing passions; hence the tracing back of

Lecture first delivered at St. John's College, Annapolis, February 25, 1966. First published in *Interpretation*, Vol. 2, Issue 1 (1971).

the origin of monuments; hence the elevation of his
metaphors; hence the ringing sound of his rolling dic-
tion; hence the climactic splendor of single incidents.

This "sweet imitation," says Macrobius, leads Virgil to the point
of even imitating Homer's vices.

We have to note that these ancient commentators attribute
to Virgil a double purpose: not only is it his intention to praise
Augustus, his imitation of Homer is, according to them, also
an end in itself.

Let me give you a series of examples of what these commentators call Virgil's imitation of Homer. I shall quote, in an
English version, lines from the *Iliad* and the *Odyssey* and corresponding lines, again in an English version, from the *Aeneid*.

Odyss. XII, 403: "But when we left that island and no other
land appeared, but only sky and sea, then verily the son of
Kronos set a black cloud above the hollow ship, and the sea grew
dark beneath it." *Aen.* III, 192: "After our ships gained the deep,
and now no longer any land is seen, but sky on all sides and
on all sides sea, then a murky rain-cloud loomed overhead,
bringing night and tempest, while the wave shuddered dark-
ling." This is repeated in *Aen.* V, 8. (Note that Virgil does not
mention Zeus, the son of Kronos.)

Iliad VIII, 16: "Tartaros . . . as far beneath Hades as heaven
is high above the earth." *Aen.* VI, 578: "While Tartarus' self gapes
with abrupt descent and stretches twice as far, down through
the shades, as the heavenward gazing eye looks up to Olympus
and the firmament." (Note the change from a one to one ratio
to a two to one ratio.)

Iliad VI, 305: Theano, wife of Antenor, priestess of Athene
in Troy, prays: "Lady Athene, that dost guard our city, fairest
among goddesses, break now the spear of Diomedes, and grant
furthermore that himself may fall headlong before the Scaean
gates." *Aen.* XI, 483: The Latin matrons implore Minerva: "O
mighty in arms, mistress in war, Tritonian maid, break with
thine hand the spear of the Phrygian pirate [that is, of Aeneas],
hurl him prone to earth and stretch him prostrate beneath our
lofty gates."

Iliad I, 234: Achilles swears, in *enmity* towards Agamemnon: "verily by this staff, that shall no more put forth leaves

or shoots since at the first it left its stump among the mountains, neither shall it again grow great . . ." *Aen.* XII, 206: Latinus swears, in *friendship* towards Aeneas: "even as this scepter shall never again be dressed in light foliage and put forth branch and shade, since once in the forest it was hewn from the nether stem . . ."

Iliad XVI, 249: "So spake he [Achilles] in prayer, and Zeus, the counsellor, heard him, and a part the Father granted him, and a part denied." *Aen.* XI, 794: "Phoebus heard [the prayer of Arruns about Camilla], and in thought vouchsafed that part of his vow should prosper; the other part he scattered to the flying breezes."

Iliad IV, 122: "And he [Pandarus] drew the bow, clutching at once the notched arrow and the string of ox's sinew: the string he brought to his breast and to the bow the iron arrow-head. But when he had drawn the great bow into a round, the bow twanged and the string sang aloud, and the keen arrow lept" (namely towards Menelaus who is *not* killed). *Aen.* XI, 858: The nymph Opis, sent by Diana, "drew the fleet arrow from the golden quiver, stretched the bow with grim intent, and drew it afar, till the curving ends met each with other, and at length, with levelled hands, she touched the pointed steel with her left, her breast with her right and with the bow-string.' (She aims at Arruns, who *is* killed.)

Odyss. XI, 206: "Thrice I [Odysseus] sprang towards her [his mother], and my heart bade me clasp her, and thrice she flitted from my arms like a shadow or a dream, and pain grew ever sharper at my heart." *Aen.* VI, 699: "Thrice, where he [Aeneas] stood, he assayed to throw his arms round his neck [his father's neck]: thrice the phantom fled through the hands that clutched in vain, light as the winds and fleet as the pinions of sleep." But we can also read in the second book of the *Aeneid*, verse 792: "Thrice, then I [Aeneas] strove to throw my arms round her neck [the neck of Aeneas' wife's shadow]: thrice the form, that I clasped in vain, fled through my hands, light as the winds and fleet as the pinions of sleep."

Odyss. XIX, 562: "For two are the gates of shadowy dreams, and one is fashioned of horn and one of ivory. Those dreams that pass through the gate of sawn ivory deceive men, bringing words that find no fulfilment. But those that come forth through the gate of polished horn bring true issues to pass, when any mortal sees them." (Penelope is saying these words.) *Aen.* VI, 892: "There are two gates of Sleep: of horn, fame tells, the one, through which the spirits of truth find an easy passage; the other, wrought smooth-gleaming with sheen of ivory, but false the dreams that the nether powers speed therefrom to the heaven above." (Virgil, the author, is saying this.)

These examples can be multiplied many, many times. There would be no point for me to continue quoting. But let us take notice of the fact that there is almost always some weighty difference embedded in the otherwise completely analogous phrasing and imagery.

However, the similarity between the *Iliad* and the *Odyssey* on the one hand and the *Aenead* on the other goes far beyond phrasing and imagery. Let me give you another series of examples of what is called Virgil's imitation of Homer.

When Odysseus arrives in Ithaca, Pallas Athene fills the countryside with mist so that Odysseus cannot recognize it. When Aeneas arrives in Carthage, Venus conveys him in a cloud so that nobody can see him. Before meeting with Penelope Odysseus is beautified by Pallas Athene. Before meeting Dido Aeneas is beautified by Venus. A young man, Elpenor, falls from the roof of Circe's house; Odysseus sees his shade in Hades and buries the corpse when he returns to the light of day. The pilot of Aeneas' fleet, Palinurus, falls from his ship and is subsequently killed by a barbarous tribe; his shade is seen by Aeneas in the nether world and his corpse buried later on. Diomedes and Odysseus, two seasoned warriors, engage in a spying mission at night, kill a quantity of Trojans and bring their enterprise to a successful and glorious end. Nisus and Euryalus, two young men, try to break through the enemy lines at night, kill a quantity of Latins and die gloriously but unsuccesfully at the end. The shade of Ajax keeps a contemptuous silence when facing Odysseus in Hades. So does the shade of Dido when confronted by Aeneas in the nether world. In point of fact, innumerable episodes in the *Aenead* have their analogues in the *Iliad* or the *Odyssey*. There are exceptions, as, for instance, the diverse prophecies addressed to Aeneas, the transformation of the Trojan ships into mermaids in Book IX and the role of the warrior maid

Camilla. Camilla has her analogue, however in Penthesilea who, although not to be found in Homer, appears in many classical Greek texts and is mentioned by Virgil himself (I, 491; also XI, 662). There is parallelism between Menelaus, Paris and Helen on the one hand, and Turnus, Aeneas and Lavinia on the other, whatever the difference between these personages and their relationships. There is parallelism between Achilles and Patroklos on the one hand, and Aeneas and Pallas on the other, again whatever the difference between these pairs. To the catalogue of ships in the second book of the *Iliad* corresponds the catalogue of the Latin armies in the seventh book of the *Aeneid*. To the funeral games in honor of Patroklos correspond the games in honor of Anchises. Three times does Achilles circle the city of Priam in hot pursuit of Hector, while Aeneas covers five circles on the plain around the city of Latinus in hot pursuit of Turnus. To the shield of Archilles fashioned by Hephaistos upon the insistence of Achilles' mother corresponds the shield of Aeneas fashioned by Vulcan upon the insistence of Aeneas' mother. But the difference here is great: on Achilles' shield are moulded Heaven and Earth, Peace and War, Marriage and Litigation, Work and Leisure, and all the bounties of the earth; on Aeneas' shield are shown the glorious deeds of the Romans culminating in Octavian's victory at Actium.

What is the significance of this persistent and detailed, yet unfaithful "imitation"? In other poems, written before the *Aeneid*, especially in the *Bucolics*, Virgil also imitated his Greek predecessors, especially Theocritus. But this imitation involved only the general pattern, the general mood and style of the poems and hardly any of their details. The tradition tells us that Virgil, in his younger years, conceived the plan to write an epic poem devoted to the glory of Rome but that he gave up that plan because he found the task too difficult. In his later years he took it up again, prodded by Augustus, perhaps, and worked on the *Aeneid* for eleven years — until his death. It is in this period that what is called his imitation of Homer flourished supremely. The question we face is just this: Why was it necessary for Virgil to imitate Homer to the extent he did? The ancient commentators I quoted in the beginning were late commentators. Their opinion that one of the purposes of the poem was the imitation of Homer and their implied opinion that such an undertaking was in itself praiseworthy were not shared by Virgil's contemporaries, we are told. His contemporaries reproached him for borrowing too much from Homer. Virgil is reported to have answered them, proudly and enigmatically, that it was easier to steal from Neptune his trident and from Hercules his club than to steal a verse from Homer. What did he mean by that?

Let us go back to the unquestionable purpose of the *Aeneid*. It is the praise of Augustus and the projection of an exalted version of the Roman world. What is the background of this praise and this projection? The answer is: a century of civil disorders and wars, beginning in 133 B.C., after the end of the Punic and Spanish wars, and a passionate and wide-spread desire for peace. Peace is finally restored by Octavian in the year 31. Let me quote from a modern critic, Edward Kennard Rand: "To Virgil's contemporaries, hardly any religious or political event could have had a more spectacular importance than the closing of Janus' temple [which act signified peace] twice in the reign of Augustus, once after the victory of Actium [over Anthony] and once in the year 25 . . . . Only once before in all Roman history had this happy event occurred, namely, at the completion of the First Punic War."

This peace is based on Roman rule under Caesar Augustus. And the origin of this Roman rule is the great subject of Virgil's epic endeavor.

But how to attack so vast a subject? Let us understand Virgil's predicament. We, today, have an easy way of dealing with such a subject. To praise deeds or events, we call them "historical." We say: an historical meeting or an historical battle took place on such and such a day. In saying this we mean to pay tribute to the importance of that meeting or that battle. The adjective "historical" is used as a superlative which confers to an event a transcendent rank and the laurel of undying glory. But to Virgil — and not to him alone — the medium of praise is not History but Myth. For only the glowing light of myth is able to illuminate the intrinsic unintelligibility of human deeds and sufferings. To write an epic poem on the grandeur of Rome means, therefore, to construct a myth. To use a Greek word familiar to Virgil, it means to μυθοποιεῖν.

Most myths are anonymous. They are there, filling, mirror-like, the horizon of human lives with splendid or dark or sometimes terrifying figures that bring to pass wondrous and awesome events. But there are also myths attached to names, to names of "mythmakers," as, for example, to Homer, to Hesiod, to Plato. Can one compete with these mythmakers? Can one invent "new" myths? In fact, did those mythmakers I have just mentioned invent theirs? Did they not merely imitate or modify or transpose myths in existence long before them, just as the Greek tragedians did? How, then, shall Virgil go about it? Virgil has before him a plethora of legends related to various sites and monuments in Rome and Italy. The legend of Aeneas himself, of Aeneas the Trojan, the source of Roman stock, is well known in Roman lands. Can these legends lend themselves to form the nucleus of the myth Virgil is after? Must not other myths be taken into consideration? Virgil himself seems to have cherished the myth of the succession of the ages of mankind. Let us consider this myth briefly.

Hesiod tells it in his *Works and Days*. Five generations of men have so far succeeded each other: first the golden one, in Kronos' time, when men lived as if they were gods, abundantly, without hard work or pain, without suffering from old age; then the gods created the second generation, of silver, far worse than the first, short-lived, troublesome, lacking piety; then came the age of bronze, when men were terrible and strong, destroying each other; then Zeus created the fourth generation of hero-men, who are also called half-gods; they besieged seven-gated Thebes and fought before Troy for the sake of lovely-haired Helen; those who did not perish in carnage and war were settled by Zeus in the islands of the blessed, at the extreme end of the world, with Kronos, freed from bondage, as their king; finally came the age of iron, in which we live now, in which the sense of right and wrong has been almost entirely lost, in which force reigns and vengeance and weariness; but Zeus will destroy this generation of mortals also. This story of the ages of men can also be found in the *Book of Daniel*, supposedly written some hundred years before Virgil and in all probability unknown to him, but still symptomatic for the myth's universality and influence. In the second chapter of this book Daniel interprets a dream King Nebuchadnezzar had had. According to this interpretation the kingdom of Nebuchadnezzar is the kingdom of gold, of power and strength and glory; it will be succeeded by another, presumably of silver, which in turn will be followed by a kingdom of brass; then will come a fourth kingdom, that or iron and clay, in which kingdom men "shall not cleave to one another, even as iron is not mixed with clay"; at last the God of heaven will set up a kingdom which will stand forever. So much, then, for the myth of the ages of mankind.

But Virgil also knew the oriental and Greek doctrines of the Great Year. The Great Year is the time it takes for all stars and planets to return to the same position, with respect to us, that they once occupied. This time constitutes an age, an αἰών. Once this age reaches its completion, a palingenesis occurs and a new αἰών begins, identical with the preceding one. This doctrine was also preserved in the collection of oracles of the Cumaean Sibyl, which oracles constitute the books of Sibylline songs widely diffused among the people. The cycle of cosmic life, the αἰών, was divided into ten great months. The end of each of these months and the transition into a new one was supposed to be announced by a celestial sign. The sun grew pale after the murder of Julius Caesar, and it is reported that the apparition of a comet during the funeral honors rendered to the victim was interpreted by a soothsayer to indicate the end of the ninth cosmic month and the beginning of the tenth. Some amalgamation between the doctrine of cosmic cycles and the myth of the four or five ages of mankind must have occurred in the course of time. Each cycle repeats the succession of ages, from the golden to the iron one. We witness this in Virgil's fourth Eclogue in the *Bucolics*, which, I hope, most of you have read. Let me quote a few lines from it: "Now is come the last age of the song of Cumae; the great line of the centuries begins anew. Now the Virgin too returns, the reign of Saturn returns; now a new generation descends from heaven on high." The Virgin is Astraea or Justice, the last of the immortals to leave the earth. The eclogue is addressed and dedicated to Asinius Pollio, a patron of Virgil, who was elected consul in the year 41 and played a decisive role in the reconciliation between the two mighty leaders, Marc Antony and Octavian, at Brundisium in the year 40. But the emphasis in the eclogue is on a child "in whom the iron brood shall

first cease and a golden race spring up throughout the world."
The new age shall begin in the consulship of Pollio and the
mighty months will then commence their march. The babe shall
have the gift of divine life and rule over a world pacified through
his father's virtues. His cradle shall pour forth flowers for his
delight. Goats will come to the milking unbidden and the ox
lie down with the lion. "On wild brambles shall hang the pur-
ple grape, and the stubborn oak shall distil dewy honey." The
serpent will be no more, and the false poison-plant perish. Any
lingering traces of human crime shall gradually disappear. In
the beginning these traces will still be visible — in sailings across
the seas, in the building of walls around towns, in the cleaving
of the earth with furrows. Another Argo shall be manned to
seek the golden fleece, "and again shall a great Achilles be sent
to Troy." But when the child will have become a man,

> the trader shall quit the sea, . . . every land shall bear
> all fruits . . . . The earth shall not feel the harrow,
> nor the vine the pruning hook; the sturdy ploughman,
> too, shall now loose his oxen from the yoke. Wools shall
> no more learn to counterfeit varied hues, but of
> himself the ram in the meadows shall change his
> fleece, now to sweetly blushing purple, now to saf-
> fron yellow; of its own will shall scarlet clothe the
> grazing lambs.

This prophetic poem is written in a dark and oracular vein, imitating, perhaps, the Sibylline songs. The identity of the child
has remained a controversial subject among scholars. The
preponderant opinion tends to recognize in the child a son of
Asinius Pollio. Christian interpreters considered the fourth
Eclogue as a prophecy of the Messiah, saw in the child Jesus,
the Christ, and in Virgil a pagan Isaiah. Not by chance does
Virgil play the role of Dante's guide and mentor in Hell and
Purgatory. It is conceivable that the Sibylline oracles, re-
assembled after the genuine ones had burned with the Capitol
in the year 83, might have contained some Jewish oracles reflecting the spirit and the substance of Isaiah's prophecy and that
Virgil might have experienced their spell. What seems in-
dubitable is that the fourth Eclogue expresses the overwhelm-

ing longing for a New Beginning, a new age of Peace. The mythical idea of the completion of a cosmic cycle and of a return to the happy days of Kronos, the days of Saturn, seems ever-present to Virgil's mind.

We thus perceive the factors which determine the composition of the *Aeneid* devoted to the glories of Rome and to the bounties of Peace under the aegis of Caesar Augustus. The legend of the Trojan hero Aeneas, the ancestor of Roman power, would become part and parcel of the myth of rebirth which tells of the return of the days of Saturn, of the golden age, after completion of a cosmic cycle and the beginning of a new αἰών.

Aeneas will land on Saturnian soil, in Latium. King Latinus, who rules "over lands and towns in the calm of a long peace" and himself descends from Saturn, will tell Aeneas, an offspring of Jupiter: "Be not unaware that the Latins are Saturn's race, righteous not by bond or laws, but self-controlled of their own free will and by the custom of their ancient god." Evander, the "good man," king of the Arcadians, who is going to ally himself with Aeneas at precisely the spot where Rome shall stand, will recount to Aeneas the origins of the Saturnian rule:

> In these woodlands the native Fauns and Nymphs once dwelt, and a race of men sprung from the trunks of trees and hardy oak, who had no rule or art of life, and knew not how to yoke the ox or to lay up stores, or to husband their gains; but tree branches nurtured them and the huntsman's savage fare. First from heavenly Olympus came Saturn, fleeing from the weapons of Jove and exiled from his lost realm. He gathered together the unruly race, scattered over mountain heights, and gave them laws, and chose that the land be called Latium, since in these borders he had found a safe hiding-place [from the Latin verb *latere*]. Under his reign were the golden ages men tell of: in such perfect peace he ruled the nations; till little by little then crept in a race of worse sort and duller hue, the frenzy of war, and the passion for gain.

And before the final triumph of Aeneas, Juno, Aeneas' implacable enemy, will yield to destiny, but will request this from

Jove: "Command not the native Latins to change their ancient name, nor to become Trojans and be called Teucrians, or to change their tongue and alter their attire: let Latinum be, let Alban kings endure through ages, let be a Roman stock, strong in Italian valour: fallen is Troy, and fallen let her be, together with her name." Jove will grant Juno's wish, and Rome's future will be secure. Under Caesar Augustus the reign of peace will begin anew.

But is all this sufficient to account for the composition of the great Roman epic poem? Is *this* the myth of the *Aeneid?* Have we not overlooked a crucial point in the very conception of the poem, to wit, that the epic poem itself, while embodying a myth, cannot help reflecting the age it belongs to? But are not the great cosmic cycles, the αἰῶνες, identical? Do not in each of them the Argo, and Troy, and Caesar reappear? It is with respect to this point that a Platonic myth becomes of utmost importance to Virgil. It can be found in Plato's dialogue *The Statesman.*

The interlocutors in this dialogue are the Stranger from Elea and a young man, a namesake of Socrates. The Stranger tells a myth:

> During a certain epoch god himself goes with the universe as guide in its revolving course, but at another epoch, when the cycles have at length reached the measure of the allotted time, he lets it go, and of its own accord it turns backwards in the opposite direction, since it is a living being and is endowed with intelligence by him who fashioned it in the beginning.

Thus, we read further, "the universe is guided at one time by an extrinsic divine cause, acquiring the power of living again and receiving renewed immortality from the divine artisan, and at another time it is left to itself and then moves by its own motion . . . ." Young Socrates asks: "But was the life in the region of Kronos . . . in that previous period of revolution or in ours?" The Stranger answers:

> No, the life about which you ask, when all the fruits of the earth sprang up of their own accord for men,

did not belong at all to the present period of revolution, but this also belonged to the previous one. For them, in the beginning, god ruled and supervised the whole revolution, and so again, in the same way, all the parts of the universe were divided by regions among gods who ruled them, and, moreover, the animals were distributed by species and flocks among inferior deities as divine shepherds, each of whom was in all respects the independent guardian of the creatures under his own care, so that no creature was wild, nor did they eat one another, and there was no war among them, nor any strife whatsoever.

The Stranger goes on to describe how god himself was the shepherd of man in that age:

And under his care there were no states, nor did men possess wives or children; for they all came to life again out of the earth, with no recollection of their former lives. So there were no states or families, but they had fruits in plenty from the trees and other plants, which the earth furnished them of its own accord, without help from agriculture. And they lived for the most part in the open air, without clothing or bedding; for the climate was tempered for their comfort, and the abundant grass that grew up out of the earth furnished them soft couches. That, Socrates, was the life of men in the reign of Kronos; but the life of the present age, which is said to be the age of Zeus, you know by your own experience.

The Stranger summarizes his tale in the following way:

Now as long as the world was nurturing the animals within itself under the guidance of the Pilot, it produced little evil and great good; but in becoming separated from him it always got on most excellently during the time immediately after it was let go, but

as time went on and it grew forgetful, the ancient condition of disorder prevailed more and more and
towards the end of the time reached its height, and
the universe, mingling but little good with much of
the opposite sort, was in danger of destruction for itself
and those within it. Therefore at that moment the god,
who made the order of the universe, perceived that
it was in dire trouble, and fearing that it might
founder in the tempest of confusion and sink in the
boundless sea of diversity, he took again his place as
its helmsman, reversed whatever had become unsound
and unsettled in the previous period when the world
was left to itself, set the world in order, restored it and
made it immortal and ageless.

This is the myth of the Stranger in Plato's *Statesman*, of
which I have read to you only a small part. It changes the old
myth of the cosmic cycles, which repeat themselves and remain
identical, in a significant way. Diagrammatically this can be
shown as follows:

Old pattern:

Platonic pattern:

The identity of the cycles in the Platonic pattern is, as it were,
intermittent. And the reversal of the direction can be best seen
at the beginnings of two consecutive cycles. What is important
for us to see is this: to be able to accomplish his work, Virgil
has to adopt this Platonic myth and to disregard its highly comical and self-refuting context. This adoption determines the composition of the *Aeneid* and, by implication, Virgil's true relation to Homer. The age of Homer is the age of Zeus, an age

characterized by calamitous expeditions, disastrous wars, anar-
chical diversity. Its beginning is reflected in the *Iliad* and the
Odyssey, its climax reached in the Punic wars. The content of
the Homeric poems has to be understood as a derived one. What
underlies this content is the reversal of the preceding age of
Kronos. Virgil's epic of Rome will have to reverse this reversal.
It cannot avoid reproducing the main features and the single
episodes of the Greek work, but it will reverse their order, shift
the emphasis in them, exchange the nature and the role of the
leading personages; for the age of Jove is but a mirror-image
of the age of Saturn. Does that mean that Virgil is bound to
imitate Homer? No, on the contrary, it is Homer who cannot
help imitating Virgil or, if you please, cannot help imitating the
epic poet of the preceding Saturnian age, who is identical with
Virgil. That is why there has to be so much unfaithful
resemblance between the *Aeneid* and Homer's work. Virgil's own
relation to the epic poem of the preceding age constitutes, it
seems to me, Virgil's myth of the *Aeneid*. This is what he must
have meant when he declared that it was easier to steal the club
of Hercules and the trident of Neptune than to steal a verse from
Homer. A poet of the god-led Saturnian age is incapable of steal-
ing verses from a Jovian poet, however excellent this Jovian poet
may be.

It might be objected that the Platonic myth, as a Greek myth,
adopted by Virgil, is itself a product of the Jovian age. I venture to think that Virgil considered words of sages, words of
philosophers, as not subjugated to the dominion of the age in
which these words were uttered, just as Tartarus and Elysium
are outside the sway of the ages. It may be worthwhile to report
to you what an unknown hand has inscribed into a manuscript
of Donatus' *Life of Virgil* (Donatus himself wrote in the fourth
century A.D.): ". . . although he [Virgil] seems to have put the
opinions of diverse philosophers into his writings with most
serious intent, he himself was a devotee of the Academy; for he
preferred Plato's views to all the others."

Let me sketch briefly the way the reversal of the Jovian order
is accomplished in Virgil's poem. First of all, the *Odyssey*
precedes the *Iliad* here, as every commentator since Servius has
remarked. But, as we shall see in a moment, the first six books,
which correspond to the *Odyssey*, still belong to the old Homeric

age. When Aeneas and his men arrive in Carthage, they face a bas-relief on the temple of Juno which depicts the Trojan war and all the events described in the *Iliad*. Their past is before them. But this past also casts a shadow on Aeneas' sojourn in Carthage. Aeneas falls in love with Dido, whose role in the *Aeneid* corresponds to that of Calypso in the *Odyssey*, suitably reversed. Aeneas' passion for this woman shows his lingering affinity to the Jovian age, to which Carthage itself, Rome's eternal foe, belongs. A violent separation from Dido becomes necessary, a separation consummated only Elysium, when the golden bough, the gift to Proserpine, is planted by Aeneas on the threshold of the land of joy, the abode of the blest in the nether world. There, in Elysium, Aeneas sees the shade of his *father*, while Odysseus, in Hades, meets the shade of his *mother*. There Aeneas is shown by Anchises the *future* of Rome, while Odysseus, in Hades, is told of the past and the present, except for the prophecy of the seer Teiresias. When Aeneas is leaving Elysium, a decisive event occurs, challenging our imagination. I quoted earlier the passage in the 19th book of the *Odyssey* and the corresponding passage at the end of the 6th book of the *Aenead* about the two gates of sleep, one of horn through which true dreams pass and one of ivory through which false visions and shades issue forth. Anchises dismisses the Sibyl and Aeneas by *the ivory gate (portaque emittit eburna)*. How shall we understand these words? Is Aeneas, the pious Aeneas, led on by divine power, a false dream? Is the grandeur of Rome, Aeneas' treasure and burden, a melancholy illusion? Or do not these words, uttered at the very center of the poem, rather symbolize a cosmic reversal in the structure of the universe, marking the transition from the age of Jove to the reign of Saturn? In Greek, the words for "horn" and for "ivory" are attuned to the meaning of "fulfilment" and of "deception." Not so in Latin. Aeneas emerges from the nether world a changed man. A rebirth has taken place. *His* passing through the gate of ivory transmutes *its* function. From now on the poem changes its character, too. As the poet himself says: "Greater is the order of things that opens before me; greater is the task I essay."

The task is greater indeed. The poem has to describe the beginning of the golden age. This beginning is marred by the inherited features of the preceding one, the iron one. Violence and fury will display themselves. Under Turnus' leadership, Amata's predilections and Juno's help, the Latins and their allies will oppose the Trojans, aided by the Arcadians and Etruscans. A new Trojan war will rage in a reversed order. This time it will end with the victory of Aeneas, the new Hector, over Turnus, the new Achilles. After this victory there will be reconciliation between the Trojans and the Latins according to the terms agreed on by Jove and Juno. There will be reconciliation between Jove and Saturn, too. From then on Rome will begin its tumultuous ascent, until she reaches the height of Augustan peace.

The tradition has it that Virgil, when he had finished (or almost finished) writing the *Aenead*, wanted to burn all he had written. Augustus himself is said to have prevented this from happening. We may surmise that Virgil knew this much about his myth: its truth depended on the actual destiny of Rome. And, prophet that he was, he foresaw the future *pax romana*, the future Roman peace, more often than not immersed in a sea of corruption, of monstrous crimes and dismal anarchy. We should be grateful to Augustus, though. For even if the gate of ivory may have preserved its Homeric character, the nobility of Virgil's attempt and the boldness of his mythical vision make us bow our heads and raise our minds.

17 ■ A Note on Plato's *Parmenides*

Alexander of Aphrodisias, in his commentary on Aristotle's *Metaphysics* I, 6, 987 b 33, reports: "Aristotle, in his writings 'concerning the Good' (περὶ τἀγαθοῦ), says that Plato posited . . . as Beginnings (ἀρχαί) both of number and of all beings the One and the Dyad." This Dyad, according to what Alexander reports a little later (on *Met.* I, 9, 990 b 17), is the "indeterminate dyad": ἀρχαί εἰσι τό τε ἕν καὶ ἡ ἀόριστος δυάς. The "indeterminate dyad" is explicitly mentioned by Aristotle in a number of passages: *Metaphysics* XIII, 7, 1081 a 15, b 21, 32, 1082 a 13, b 30; 9, 1085 b 7; XIV, 2, 1088 b 28, 1089 a 35; 3, 1091 a 5. It has a "doubling power," a power of "making two" (δυοποιός — 1082 a 15, 1083 b 36), and is also described as "the Great and the Small" (τὸ μέγα καὶ τὸ μικρόν — cf. *Met* I, 6, 987 b 20; 7, 988 a 26; III, 3, 998 b 10; *Phys.* I, 4, 187 a 17; 9, 192 a 7, 11). In *Metaphysics* I, 6, 987 b 25 Aristotle says that it was peculiar to Plato to substitute for the single "unlimited" or "indeterminate" (τὸ ἄπειρον) a dyad and to make the "unlimited" consist of "the Great and the Small" (cf. *Phys.* III, 4, 203 a 15). The *Philebus* (especially 24 a–25 a) seems to confirm this.

First published in *Orbis Scriptus, Dimitrij Tschizewskij* zum 70. Geburtstag (München: Wilhelm Fink, 1966).

The "indeterminate dyad" is never explictly mentioned in Platonic dialogues. It is possible to interpret the ἀρχή "Otherness," dealt with in the *Sophist*, as representing this dyad since θἄτερον is by itself undetermined and intrinsically double: it is always a ἕτερον ἑτέρου (see, for instance, *Parmenides* 146 c 5–6; cf. 139 c 3–5, e 3). "Other" is always relative to something "other": τὸ δέ γ'ἕτερον ἀεὶ πρὸς ἕτερον— *Sophist* 255 d 1; cf. d 6–7. Still, the phrase ἀόριστος δυάς cannot be found in any of the Platonic dialogues.

To search for an *explicit* mention of the "indeterminate dyad" in the Platonic dialogues means, however, to neglect their dramatic and mimetic character. Let us consider the *Parmenides*.

The dialogue is narrated by Cephalus of Clazomenae, but this narration merely repeats what Cephalus had heard Antiphon recite, and Antiphon's recitation, in turn, repeats what Antiphon had heard Pythodorus narrate. Now, according to Pythodorus, Parmenides and Zeno had come to Athens and had lodged with him. To Pythodorus' house came Socrates, at that time a very young man (127 c 4–5), and with him certain other (presumably also young) men, a good many (. . .καὶ ἄλλους τινὰς μετ' αὐτοῦ [Σωκράτους] πολλούς — 127 c 2), who wanted to hear the writings of Zeno. Zeno complied with their wishes *in the absence of Parmenides*. Towards the end of the lecture, Parmenides joined them and also Pythodorus himself, as well as a young man named Aristotle, who later on was to become one of the Thirty Tyrants. Present at the conversation which followed Zeno's lecture were thus five persons, Parmenides, Zeno, Pythodorus, Socrates, Aristotle, and "many" others. To our surprise, however, Socrates mentions a little later (129 d 1), in a most casual way, that the gathering comprised altogether — *seven* people. The "many" others turn out to be just *two*. Nothing is said about them — they remain completely "undetermined," except perhaps for their age.

Can we neglect this circumstance which is carefully brought to our attention? We are reminded by Zeno (136 d 6–8) that it would be inappropriate for the old Parmenides to discourse on a weighty subject before many (πολλῶν ἐναντίον), and that it would be undignified to ask him to do so if the audience were more numerous. A little later on (137 a 7) Parmenides himself, referring to Zeno's statement, expresses his readiness to engage in a dialectical investigation "since, in addition, we are among ourselves" (ἐπειδὴ καί . . . αὐτοί ἐσμεν). It seems impossible to disregard these hints. Rather we have to see what they may allude to in the context of the dialogue.

Zeno's lecture (composed in his youth) was meant to show that the consequences which flow from *the assumption of multiplicity* in this world are even more absurd and ridiculous than the consequences which flow from the derided Parmenidean assumption that "the One is" (128 d). The thesis of multiplicity, in Zeno's presentation, seems to imply the absence of unity, just as Parmenides' assumption divorces the One entirely from any multiplicity. It is noteworthy that, in the dialogue, Parmenides himself unfolds before his listeners — young Aristotle acting as his dialectical partner — the contradictions involved *both in the assumption and in the rejection of the "One"* as the one and only ἀρχή. There is an imbalance between Zeno's thesis and Parmenides' performance: the denial of multiplicity is not subjected to any scrutiny. What is lacking is a discussion of the consequences which flow from an explicit *rejection of the "many"* (cf. 136 a).

Instead we are led by Parmenides and Aristotle to the threshold of the insight that the root of the contradictions concerning the "One" taken by itself is precisely the non-admittance of *another* ἀρχή responsible for the "Many" and correlated with the "One." The dialectic of the "One" cannot avoid bringing this other ἀρχή, the "Other," into play. But its role within the framework of the dialogue is, as it were, illegitimate. Still, its power is there, conspicuously, though silently, present. The two undetermined men in the audience represent it. They embody the elusive "indeterminate dyad" itself. This is their mimetically ironic role.

It is rather curious that the emendation οὐ πολλούς for πολλούς in 127 c 2 should have been proposed by some (cf. F. M. Cornford, *Plato and Parmenides*, London 1950, p. 65).

18 ■ On Precision

I am afraid this will be a tedious and annoying lecture. I
do not know how you will stand it. I propose to reflect
on the meaning and the various implications of precision. Why
should I do that? Well, however untidy, vague, and undisciplined
we may be, something like precision rules over our lives, rules
in fact over the Western world as a whole. And by the West I
mean a great many parts, although not *all* parts, of our globe.
I said something *like* precision is a ruling power in our lives.
For the very word "precision" is ambiguous. To begin with, it
is not identical with "clarity." Something that is clear need not
be precise, and something that is precise need not be clear.
Moreover we should note that the English word "precision" does
not retain the connotations of its Latin root. I shall have to come
back to this point later on. On the other hand there is close kinship between "precision," "accuracy," "correctness," and "exactitude," but these words are not synonyms, although very often
they appear to be and are used interchangeably. (Modern
statistical theories do, by the way, make a distinction between
exactitude and precision.) At the risk of treading in the footsteps
of Prodicus, the man most concerned with the right use of words,

Lecture first delivered at St. John's College in Annapolis, February 23, 1968. First
published in *The College*, Vol. XXIII, No. 3 (October, 1971).

the man whom Socrates calls his "teacher"— a deceptively ironic appellation, which is as much funny as it is serious — I shall try right away to distinguish the meanings of these four words. Many examples will be needed for this purpose.

A tailor has to be very careful about the length and the width of a suit at different points of the body of the man for whom the suit is made. The tailor has to be *accurate* in his measuring, cutting, and sewing. So has a carpenter in making a table or a door. Accuracy is required to fit a part of a machine into or onto another part or other parts of that machine so that it can do its work properly. If I am asked by a stranger how to get from the place where we meet to a certain building in town, I have to be careful in describing the way he has to take, as for instance: three blocks ahead, then turn to your right, continue for two blocks and then turn to your left; then you will see the building you are looking for. In saying this, I must be confident that the description I give is *accurate* enough. *In all these cases, accuracy connotes carefulness in the work one is doing or in the words one is uttering.* Let us turn to correctness. I might ask someone to answer a question. After the question is given, I say: This is correct. I mean the answer is a right one. I might advise a friend to behave in a certain way when he faces Mr. X and Mr. Y or some peculiar circumstances. If he does, he behaves *correctly*, that is, in the right way. I might instruct someone how to pronounce certain words in a foreign language. If he learns how to do that, he will pronounce those words in the right way, that is, *correctly*. Children are supposed to learn (and sometimes do not learn) how to conduct themselves *correctly*, that is, according to accepted standards and modes of life. *In every case correctness implies rightness in speaking, behaving, reacting.* What about exactitude? We say: The collection comprises exactly 1163 paintings; or, This lump of metal fits *exactly* into this hole; or, I feel *exactly* as you do about this event; or, the distinction you just mentioned coincides with that which exists between justice and mercy. *Exactitude seems to point to the perfect matching of something with something* in terms of number or of size or of some other quantity or even of some yardstick that cannot be quantified. It is in this vein that we speak of various mathematical disciplines as of *exact* sciences, allowing for approximation procedures which do not detract from their exactitude.

Thus carefulness, rightness, and perfect matching characterize accuracy, correctness, and exactitude. Do they not also circumscribe the meaning of precision? They do, and let me repeat forcefully: *They do;* and that is the reason why these words are so often used interchangeably. But precision seems to have broader connotations. Let us again consider some examples.

In a novel by Henry James, we find the following description. I quote, leaving out a great deal:

> He [Christopher Newman] had a very well-formed head, with a shapely, symmetrical balance of the frontal and the occipital development, and a good deal of straight, rather dry brown hair. His complexion was brown, and his nose had a bold, well-marked arch. His eye was of a clear, cold gray, and save for a rather abundant mustache he was clean-shaved. He had the flat jaw and sinewy neck which are frequent in the American type . . . . The cut of this gentleman's mustache, with the two premature wrinkles in the cheek above it, and the fashion of his garments, in which an exposed shirt-front and a cerulean cravat played perhaps an obtrusive part, completed the conditions of his identity.

Henry James is praised for the "extreme precision of his style," but we might remain dissatisfied by this description of Christopher Newman. Are the "conditions of his identity," to use Henry James' own words, sufficiently delineated? Can this be done at all?

Let us turn to another example. In an old zoology textbook a precise description of the *leech* is given, which again I shall not quote in full:

> The leech is an elongated flattened worm, from three to five inches in length, and provided with a muscular sucker at each end. The body is marked externally by

> a series of transverse constrictions dividing it into rings
> of annuli, and is capable of considerable elongation
> and contraction . . . . The shape varies greatly with
> the degree of elongation or contraction. The body is
> broadest a little way behind the middle of its length,
> and is oval in transverse section, the dorsal surface
> being more convex than the ventral . . . . The an-
> terior sucker is oval, with the longer axis longitudi-
> nal . . . . The posterior sucker is circular and larger
> than the anterior one . . . .

The picture of the leech emerges distinctly, and we would appreciate its precision even more if I had quoted the text in its
entirety. We note, it is *meant* to be precise in the first place.

The last example is taken from *Gulliver's Travels*. Most of
you will remember that the Lilliputian king orders a search of
Gulliver's belongings and persuades Gulliver to submit to the
search. Two officers are appointed for the task. Gulliver lifts
them gently up and puts them into his pockets, although some
of them he chooses not to divulge. The officers examine
everything they find and write a formal and precise report about
their findings. Most of the objects in Gulliver's pockets are unfamiliar to the two Lilliputians, and especially his watch,
which — parenthetically — is odd, considering the Lilliputians'
indisputable mathematical and mechanical competence and in-
ventiveness. This is what they write:

> Out of the right fob hung a great silver chain, with
> a wonderful kind of engine at the bottom. We directed
> him to draw out whatever was fastened to that chain;
> which appeared to be a globe, half silver, and half
> of some transparent metal; for on the transparent side
> we saw certain strange figures circularly drawn, and
> thought we could touch them till we found our fingers
> stopped by that lucid substance. He put his engine to
> our ears, which made an incessant noise like that of
> a watermill and we conjecture it is either some
> unknown animal or the god that he worships . . . .

The description of Christopher Newman is that of an imaginary being. The description of the leech applies to any leech and is a description of a living creature. The description of Gulliver's watch might also apply to any watch, although the investigators do not know what it is, what purpose it serves. All these descriptions are as precise as they could be. What is to be learned from them about precision?

In every case the description intends to show *what* the object described *looks like*, be that object familiar or unfamiliar to us. Depending on the degree of its precision, the description will enable us to recognize the object in question more or less readily. In the case of Christopher Newman, we are somewhat doubtful. But we should certainly be able to identify with the help of the description a leech as a leech. And being familiar with old-fashioned watches, we recognize in the "wonderful kind of engine" described by the Lilliputians—a watch. Note that in every case the description appeals to features assumed to be *known*: to a "well-formed head," a "mustache," a person "of American type"; to a "worm," "elongation" and "contraction," an "oval" and "circular" shape; to a "globe," "transparency," the noise of a watermill. The description brings up a realm of known things and appearances to which the object described is supposed to *belong*. This is all-important: without such a known realm to which the object described can be allocated, precision is not possible at all. The closer this allocation, the better described the object becomes. This is how all legal documents tend to be precise, so much so that precision in the domain of jurisprudence is the prototype of all precision everywhere else. The relation between persons, or bodies of men, or estates, must indeed be stated in terms that make it possible to apply the stated relation *precisely* to any particular case; or, conversely, actions of men, together with the circumstances surrounding these actions, must be described in a way which permits us to refer to these actions as *precisely* falling or not falling under certain statutes or laws. To point out *where* something can be located, to *what sort of thing or stuff* something *belongs*, is indeed the primary task of a *precise* description, the primary concern of precision itself. And—to repeat—this allocation is accomplished by describing *what* the thing or event in question *looks like*.

I just said: what something looks like. But should I not rather
have said: *what it is?* You sense immediately that the phrases
"what something looks like" and "what something is" *can* be,
but *need not* be, identical. And you know, or at least you ought
to know, that this phrase "*what* is it?" (τί ἐστι) is *the* Socratic
question, which — in all its seeming simplicity — revolutionized
human thinking and human behavior. To answer this question
requires indeed — precision. Both the closeness and the disparity
of what things *look like* and of *what* they *are* have been forever
incorporated in the Greek word εἶδος (or ἰδέα) and in its literal
Latin translation *species* (in English parlance: species). These
words do indeed signify both the *looks* and the *what* of a thing.
The use and abuse of these words have moulded human thought
in various ways for more than two thousand years. Whether the
looks and the *what* of a thing can be identified or must be
separated depends on what the thing in question is allocated
to, to what sort of group or family or tribe or genus of things
this particular thing *belongs*. Examples: an oak looks like a tree
and *is* a tree; a marine polyp (a coral) looks like a tree, but is
not a tree. And let us not forget: while we were trying to grasp
the meaning of precision, we had to use examples of precision,
and these examples showed us either something that was *like*
what we were seeking or *the very thing itself*. Let us also keep
in mind that the group or family or genus to which the thing
sought is allocated, to which it is supposed to belong or actually
belongs, is something familiar, something if not known, at least
quasi-known to us.

There is hardly any doubt that young and old in Plato's
Academy exercised their powers to answer the Socratic question,
what this or that thing *is*, with precision. (And may I say, this
entailed *more* than I had occasion to mention so far.) Not only
do Platonic dialogues bear witness to such exercises in
precision — and do that as much seriously as playfully, ironically,
and even critically — but there are stories which report both
gleeful and malicious attacks on this Academic preoccupation.
There is a passage in Plato's dialogue, the *Statesman*,[1] in which
Man is described — playfully, to be sure — as a "featherless biped."

---

1. 266e.

And there is the story[2] that a Socratic extremist, Diogenes the Cynic, threw a plucked rooster into the Academy, saying: "There you have the Platonic man," whereupon the Academy is supposed to have added to "featherless biped" the expression "with flat nails." It is possible that the passage in the *Statesman*, far from being the source of Diogenes' joke, is — among other things — an echo of it. Athenaeus the Grammarian (about 200 A.D.) quotes[3] a fragment of Epicrates, a contemporary of Plato, of Plato's nephew, Speusippos, who succeeded Plato as head of the Academy, and of Aristotle. In this fragment Epicrates, who must have been an eyewitness of many things in and about Athens and presumably an avid collector of all the gossip swirling around him, gently parodies the pursuit of precision in the Academy. I shall quote it in full. It is — understandably enough — a dialogue. I shall call the two speakers Q and A. Mentioned in this dialogue are not only Plato and Speusippos, but also Menedemus, another follower of Plato. Here it is:

> Q. What are Plato, Speusippos and Menedemus doing? With what are they busying themselves now? What are they speculating about? What proposition are these people tracking down? Tell me this discreetly, if you have reached the point of understanding anything about it, tell me, by the Earth . . . .
>
> A. Oh, but I know how to speak about these things in all clarity. For, at the Panathenaean festival, I saw a herd of striplings . . . in the school of the Academy and heard them say things ineffable, out of all order. They produced definitions about nature, distinguishing the ways of life of animals, and the natures of trees, and the genera of vegetables; and, among the latter, they scrutinized the — *pumpkin*, searching to what genus *it* belongs.
>
> Q. And how in the world did they define it and to what genus did they say this plant belongs? Reveal it, if you know.

2. Diog. Laert. VI, 40.
3. II, 59 D–F.

A. First all of them were speechless, then they looked at it attentively and, bent forward, meditated for quite a while. Suddenly, while the lads were still bent and searching, one of them said: The pumpkin is a round *vegetable*, another said: a round *grass*, and another again: a round *tree*. Hearing this, a doctor from Sicilian lands farted, intimating that they were talking nonsense.

Q. They must have been terribly angry, weren't they? Did they not shout that this was an insult? For to do that in public is unbecoming!

A. The lads didn't blink an eye. Plato, who was present and exceedingly mild, did not stir a bit, and enjoined them to define the pumpkin again and anew and to state to what genus it belongs . . . . And they went on dividing.

Some of the comical effects of this parody do not come through in an English translation. For the words "define," "distinguish," "divide," as well as "genus" do not retain in this translation the flavor of the *unusual* mixed with their accepted colloquial meaning. And yet the pomposity of these technically inflated terms is not the least important element of the parody. These terms are the fruit of the pursuit of precision. Accustomed as we are to them, we understand — and misunderstand — them easily. There is, however, one word in the last sentence of Epicrates' fragment ("and they went on dividing") which certainly attracts our attention. It is the word "divide." It is pretty clear, by the way, that many exchanges between Q and A, which have preceded the last sentence, were not recorded by Athenaeus. What does that word "divide" mean?

Let us assume that agreement is reached about the family, the genus, of the pumpkin or of anything else. The family is familiar to us (as in Epicrates' parody "vegetable," "grass," "tree" are familiar to the young men), but is at best only a quasi-known. Does not, therefore, for the sake of precision, a new question necessarily arise: *What* is *this* genus, that is, to what family does *this* genus belong, what is the genus of *this* genus? This new genus, this new family, will have to be larger than the first. And then again the question will have to be repeated for this new genus, and then again for the next one, and so on, and so on. Is there an end to this questioning in the pursuit of precision? If there is, will not the final genus be the all-comprehensive one? Will it still be a "genus" then? And shall we be able to comprehend it? It will have to be something that does not lack anything, that is self-sufficient, complete,— perfect. Will it be accessible to us at all? And this question means: Is it within our powers to be really precise? Let me say haltingly and unprecisely that this is the point around which the intellectual effort of Plato and of those who follow him always gravitates.

Let us consider anew what I have been saying. In order to grasp what something is, we have to allocate it to a family of things quasi-known to us, and then to allocate this family of things, this genus, to another larger family, also quasi-known to us, and to keep on ascending. Only when and if the last step has been made, can we say that we have found out what the unknown thing, that X which started us off on this journey, *is*, can we say that we *know what it is*. It is this last step that illuminates — sun-like — not only all the intermediary genera, but the very thing, the *what* of which we wanted to know.

This entire procedure so far can be likened to an *analysis* in mathematics. A mathematical analysis handles the unknown as if it were known by relating it to known, or as we say, *given*, quantities, that is, by setting up an equation, and then, by reversing itself, finds out what the unknown is. I say "by reversing itself," because the final computation is not analytic, but, as the tradition calls it, synthetic. A Euclidean proof is synthetic: it descends *from given* magnitudes, through *given* magnitudes, to the unknown magnitude and thus makes it known. This is what is called a de-monstration, an ἀπόδειξις, a *showing* by starting *from* something that is *known*. The *finding*, the *discovery of a de-monstration* is accomplished analytically: we have to *ascend* from the *unknown, taken as known*, to the *actually known*. The proof, then, the synthetic de-monstration, is the reversal of the analysis.

What we have been dealing with so far in the pursuit of precision was the ascent from the unknown, allocated to the quasi-known, up to the highest point which we have to assume as actually known. This assumption is fraught with uncertainty, and yet precision hinges on it. This much, however, can be said: if we reverse the *direction* of our pursuit and descend from the highest point to the unknown of which we want to know *what* it is, we shall "define" it. "Definition" in the Socratic-Platonic scheme amounts indeed to "de-monstration" in the strict sense of the word.

How can this descent be accomplished? The simple succession downwards of the genera that could lead to Epicrates' stately and ridiculous pumpkin for instance may not be immediately and directly available. What we have to do is to "*divide*" every family, every genus, *suitably* into parts, into sub-genera (or sub-species, if you please), then choose *that* family part in which the pumpkin itself is finally reached. It is to this procedure that the word "divide" in Epicrates' fragment alludes.[4] Had we more of Epicrates' test, we could perhaps witness Q's astonishment and A's joking explanations of such "divisions." As matters stand, we have to rely on Plato's dialogues. There we find prescriptions for how to go about dividing a genus. In the *Phaedrus*, it is said[5] that we should do the cutting "where the natural joints are" and not try to break any part after the manner of a bad carver. But where are the natural joints? In the *Statesman*,[6] we are enjoined to cut every genus "through the middle," for in that way one is more likely to find the species, the "ideas," inherent in the genus that is being cut. This prescription seems to favor the halving of the genus so as to get *two* sub-genera, *two* species, and it is not immediately clear why this should be the most desirable, the most advantageous, the most precise dividing. Nor is it clear how we can start dividing the all-comprehensive genus, if there be one.

In the examples of division given in Plato's *Sophist* and *Statesman*, the cutting does not begin that high. The first division in the *Sophist* begins with the family of human arts, the genus "art," and "defines," that is, de-monstrates "angling" as follows (I quote the summary of the division)[7]:

---

4. Cf. Aristophanes, *Clouds*, 742.
5. 265e.
6. 262b.
7. 221b–c.

Of Art as a whole half was acquisitive, and of the acquisitive, half was coercive, and of the coercive, half
was hunting, and of hunting half was animal hunting, and of animal hunting half was water-hunting,
and of water-hunting the lower part was fishing, and
of fishing half was striking, and of striking half was
barb-hunting, and of this the part in which the blow
is pulled from below upwards [at an angle] has a name
in the very likeness of the art and is called *angling*,
which is at this moment the object of our search.

It is assumed in this definition, this de-monstration, that the
starting point, the genus "art" is *known*. Each cut divides the
genus in question into two parts. The summary lists only the
right-hand parts, as it were, and ignores of course the left-hand
ones and their possible sub-divisions. The procedure thus delimits
what is to be found out, and this is precisely the meaning of
the word "definition," so unbelievably familiar to us, namely —
delimitation. In the dialogue, this division serves a deeply serious
purpose, but we would be singularly blind if we overlooked its
playfulness. There is still another awfully important aspect to
it which becomes clearer in the first division of the *Statesman*.
Here the starting point is the family of knowledges, the genus
"knowledge," and that which is being defined, delimited, is
"statesmanship." Again "knowledge," the starting point, is taken
as a genus *known*. This genus is first divided into two parts:
one, detached from all manual work, all handicraft; the other,
manifesting itself in any art, as for example in carpentry. The
first one, the purely cognitive one, the one detached from all
handicraft, is then again subdivided, and now I quote the summary of the delimitation which is given after the two main
speakers in the dialogue had gone to great lengths to reach their
goal.[8]

The purely cognitive knowledge had, to begin with,
a part that gives commands; and a portion of this was
called — from [its] resemblance [to the way of those

---

8. 267a–c.

who sell what they *themselves* produce] — the part that
gives its *own* commands; and again the *art of rearing living beings* was detached, which is by no means
the smallest part of the art which gives its own commands; and a species of rearing living beings was *herd-
tending,* and a part of this again the *herding of walking animals*; and from the herding of walking animals
the art of rearing *those without horns* was cut off; and
of this in turn the part called the science of herding
animals *that mate only with their own kind* will have
to be intertwined in no less than in a threefold way,
if one wants to draw together into *one name* the very
thing we seek; the only further cut, executed on the
flock of *bipeds,* leads to the *science of herding human
beings,* and this is what we were looking for, namely
what is called both *statesmanship* and *kingship.*

What this delimitation then finally amounts to is the statement
that statesmanship is the "science of herding human beings,"
which in Greek is only one word (ἀνθρωπονομική).

It turns out, as we see, that the way of reaching this result
is far from precise. We do actually see that, in delimitations,
precision may *overreach* itself. The explicit delimitation, to
which the summary I just quoted refers, makes this even clearer.
On the other hand, the *subsequent* discussion of the delimitation of statesmanship reveals that it not only overreached itself,
but also neglected to separate statesmanship from other arts and
activities which compete with it in the herding and nurturing
of human beings. The delimitation proves to be not only
excessive, but also *deficient.*

The lesson Aristotle (and perhaps other people in the
Academy) drew from these blemishes of divisional definition was
to limit it to the closest family, the nearest genus, and to add
to it the unique feature which, within this genus, characterizes
the thing sought. This remained the classical way of defining
for centuries to come, of defining by the nearest genus and the
specific difference (*per genus proximum et differentiam spec-
ificam*). Aristotle cut the delimitation short, and the etymology

of the Latin word *praecisio* reflects this shortcut.[9] We should not forget that in crucial cases Aristotle does not stick to this pattern at all. And Plato himself has his own way of coping with the task of delimitation.

Let me try to pursue Plato's own path or rather paths. Let us note, first of all, that both in the *Sophist* and in the *Statesman* the delimitation procedure is taken to be unaffected by the dignity or meanness of the genera it happens to descend on. The art of generalship and the art of louse-catching are equally well suited to belong to the genus "hunting";[10] kingship and swineherdship are on par[11] as sub-genera of the genus "art of herding animals that mate only with their own kind." The delimitation procedure "pays no more heed to the noble than to the ignoble, and no less honor to the small than to the great."[12] It does not prefer the king Odysseus to the swineherd Eumaeus. It is in this "neutrality" that the possibility of excess or deficiency in the procedure of delimitation appears to be rooted. Now, in pointing to this possibility of both excess and deficiency, Plato makes us understand that all artful activity has to be governed by the concern for the standard of *due measure*, the standard of the *right mean*. This concern is actually kept alive by a power that man — and perhaps only man — possesses, namely the power of making *comparisons*. It is in comparing — and only in comparing — that we may find different degrees of size, or of weight, or of beauty, or of worth. It is comparing that lets us see something as "*better*" or "*worse*" than something else, that makes us discern the noble from the ignoble, the impeccable from the faulty. To live up to the standard of *due measure* we have to refine our comparing power: we have to learn from "examples." To cope with the danger of excess or deficiency in the delimitation procedure we have to turn to an "example."[13] This is what happens in the dialogue the *Statesman*. But before this happens the very meaning of "example" is subjected to a close

---

9. *Prae* + *caedo* = *praecido*.
10. *Soph.* 227b.
11. *Statesman* 266c.
12. *Ibid.*, 266d.
13. *Exemplum* (from *eximo*): something chosen out of an assemblage of similar things.

scrutiny. Example, as the Greek word παράδειγμα implies, is something *shown alongside of* the thing we want to grasp. To use an example is to be engaged not in ἀποδεικνύναι, in "showing down from . . . ," but in παραδεικνύναι, in "showing alongside of . . . ." This kind of showing can elucidate the thing we are after *only* if there is some *resemblance* between this thing and the example used. To avoid excess or deficiency in the delimitation procedure, this procedure must, then, be supplemented by the use of examples, based on resemblances. It is thus that the ambiguity of the word εἶδος finds its ultimate justification: both the *what* and the *looks* of the thing in question become apparent. And it is thus that out of "delimitations" *and* "examples"— or, as we could say, though perhaps less precisely, out of definitions *and* comparisons — the web of learning can be woven. To rely on examples alone, that is, on nothing but resemblances (as Speusippos seems to have been inclined to do) is dangerous: a marine polyp resembles an oak and could be used as an "example," but not much would be gained by this. And let us not forget: in the dialogue the *Statesman* the Stranger asserts that there are *no* examples for the most important cases, that is, on the highest level of intellectual scrutiny.[14]

What examples have to provide, according to Plato, are safeguards against the dangers of excess and deficiency inherent in the pursuit of precision. They have to lead us to what must be the ultimate guiding light in the effort of delimitation. This light is *that which is precise in itself*, as it is said in the *Statesman* pointedly and yet obscurely.[15] It would follow that the pursuit of precision which is required to answer the Socratic question has the "precise itself" (αὐτὸ τἀκριβές) as its beginning and its end. Isn't this mockery! some of you may be tempted to exclaim. What is this "precise itself"? Let me try to answer this question. There are quite a few hints in Plato's dialogues and also explicit statements on Aristotle's part, when he refers to Plato's intimate views, which allow me to do that. The "precise itself" is *oneness* itself, is *the* One, not one thing or one unit among many things or many units which, when gathered together, form a number of things or a number of units, but that which makes

---

14. 285d–286a.
15. 284d.

any one thing or any unit *one*, which puts on any one thing the stamp of its sameness, without which neither a world, nor thinking, nor speaking, nor learning, nor precision would be possible at all. It is, by the same token, that which I hesitatingly called a short while ago the all-comprehensive final stage to be reached when, facing a thing, we try to answer the Socratic question "What is it?" Being all-comprehensive, it is self-sufficient, perfect. Plato calls it the Good itself. The "precise itself" is the "good itself" beckoning to the cognizing soul. The pursuit of precision leads to *the* Good.

Still, the uncertainty remains: *can* it be reached? We tend to assume that it can *not*. More than that: that it *ought* not to be reached. When I say "we tend to assume," I do not mean that, traveling the path I have just indicated, we may arrive at this melancholy conclusion. I do mean that to insist on precision, to persist in being precise, shows, often enough, lack of good manners, is offensive and ruins social intercourse. Does not this insistence lead to *quibbling*, a word derived from the formalistic precision in legal documents? Does not a pronounced and rigidly maintained tidiness in our living quarters stifle the spirit of a party? Let us hear Plato himself. In the *Gorgias*[16] he makes Socrates report the opinions of some well-bred and sophisticated young men to the effect that one should not be eager to be minutely precise in the pursuit of wisdom. In the *Theaetetus*[17] Socrates says: "The avoidance of strict precision is in general a sign of good breeding; indeed, the opposite is hardly worthy of a gentleman"; but Socrates adds: "Sometimes though it is necessary." Wherein lies the necessity? The Platonic answer to this question runs against the most cherished and most deeply seated habit of our thinking, not only in our age, but at all times. We are inclined to think that things just are as they are; to attribute goodness or badness to their factual existence is to make "value judgments," as we say cheerfully and with conviction. Such attribution is rooted, we think, in our prejudices, in our being conditioned by the prevailing circumstances, in our "culture," as we say no less glibly, perhaps in our gregariousness, perhaps in divine commandments. The Platonic answer is that

16. 487c.
17. 184c.

the very *being* of things depends on Goodness, and that this alone
makes the pursuit of precision *possible* and *necessary*.

But enough of Plato and his kin. Why bring up this old, old
wisdom, this alleged wisdom? some of you might have been
thinking all along. Did I not say in the beginning that the world
in which *we* live is full of something like precision? Are not our
lives regulated to an immense extent by schedules which depend
on the ever-abiding motion of the hand of a clock? Do not the
marching of drum majorettes and the twirling of their batons
seem to some ridiculously and to some pleasantly precise? Is not
the step of soldiers — in peace time at least — impressively precise?
But more than that: some of our joys and deep satisfactions depend on precision. It is my guess that a piece of music is the
more excellent the more precisely it is constructed. The lasting
impact of a poem is tied to its precision. I do not refer to meter
and rhyme. In a poem that deserves this name, no word or, to
be very cautious, almost no word, both in meaning and sound,
can be replaced by another word; the sequence of words and
lines is unalterable; any one line wins its significance only from
the context of the whole. And something analogous holds for
great works of prose. Do we not know that everything in good
writing depends on how precisely the words we use are chosen?
Flaubert, we have heard, spent sometimes *one week* to complete *one page*. He is one of those who is overwhelmed by the
insight that what matters is to know not only *what* to say, but
also *how* to say it. In all of these cases, we see, or in almost all
of them, precision evokes praise. *This* precision does not imply
all-comprehensiveness. It implies either *regularity* or the *exclu-
sion of alternatives*.

But what about our knowledge of the world? What is striking, first of all, is that we use mostly another word for this
knowledge, the word "science." "Science" is derived directly from
the Latin *scientia*, which can only be translated by "knowledge."
Yet, in common usage, we *distinguish* knowledge and science.
Sometimes we say, redundantly, it seems: scientific knowledge.
Occasionally we identify knowledge and science, as I have done
in naming a sub-genus in the delimitation of "statemanship."
There is the verb "to know," a cognate of the noun "knowledge,"
but there is no English verb corresponding to the noun "science."

Is all this a matter of chance, or does it have a good reason? It has, and this reason is not beyond our reach, although we are not always aware of it. Let me state it in the simplest way. The centerpiece of science, mathematical physics, this colossal edifice which has been built in the last four hundred years, has — on the whole — abandoned the Socratic question "*What is* it?" in favor of the question "*How does* it *happen?*" And the answers that it gives are *indispensably* mathematical. The image of edifice is not quite appropriate. Science is like a very large city with many suburbs and parks, wide avenues and many smaller streets, with huge traffic in them, not too well regulated, and a massive downtown section consisting of quite a few blocks which are constantly renovated. This downtown section corresponds to mathematical physics. We all live in this city or in its suburbs and, although we might not be close enough to the downtown area, we all get our sustenance from it. It shapes our way of thinking and our way of living. The countryside around the city, on the other hand, corresponds to the vast complex of "social sciences" and to the domain called the "humanities"— a strange word, as if the life in the city itself were not a human life. Now, the downtown area, mathematical physics, thrives on *exactitude*, that very exactitude I talked about at the beginning of this lecture. It is bent on *matching* the consequences derived mathematically from hypotheses with observations dictated by these hypotheses. The endeavor to accomplish such a matching is called an *experiment*. The mathematical derivation by means of differential equations or other equating devices is exact. Only slightly less exact or, as we usually say, precise or accurate are the experimental measurements made to verify the mathematical results and thereby the hypotheses. These measurements, in turn, depend on the efficacy, precision, or exactness of the instruments used. Precision and exactitude are indistinguishable in this context. We speak of instruments of precision to indicate that the results obtained by using them in observations are as exact as possible, that is, yield, on the average, numbers irreplaceable by others. Whatever mathematical operations and experimental observations might be performed, they have nothing to do with anything that could be called goodness or badness, the dignity or baseness of the events considered.

Science is totally neutral with regard to worth or worthlessness. It is proud of this neutrality. We are reminded of the provisional neutrality of the Academic delimitation procedure. The scientific neutrality, however, is not provisional, but *final*. It is only its exactitude itself, the perfect matching of mathematically obtained results with the observable data, that science considers praiseworthy. This matching provides the answers to the question "How does it happen?" It is the light that shines over the city I have just described. It is the peculiar — and intrinsically *incomprehensible —*"morality" of science. This has ever been so since Galileo established that in a motion which proceeds with a uniformly accelerated velocity, the distances traversed are as the squares of the times in which these distances are traversed. The Socratic question "What is it?" lurks, as it were, behind the bright light of exactitude. But mathematical physics does not presume to answer this question. It is not its business to say *what*, for example, gravitation, or electromagnetism, or energy *is*, except by establishing in a symbolic-mathematical formula the relations that bind these entities (if it is at all permissible to use this word) to observable and mathematically describable magnitudes. To try to state *what* something is *otherwise* we consider a vain *"metaphysical"* endeavor, to use a post-Aristotelian term. We are still in need of "definitions" in our quest of knowledge, but their character is very different. A definition is now either a readily acceptable description of the meaning of a term, to which we are asked to subscribe, or a statement used as an irreducible element in a subsequent mathematical exposition. However important the role of such definitions may be, it is subsidiary. A modern book on precise thinking need not mention the term "definition" at all.[18]

The truly amazing intellectual effort that underlies our science cannot be disregarded for a single moment. It is one of the greatest achievements of man. It is the very foundation of the city in which we live, the city of science, the source of genetics, of electronic computers, of nuclear fission and fusion — the source of technocracy. It is our duty, I think, to acknowledge

---

18. E.g., Quine, *Methods of Logic.*

this fundamental fact and to try to understand its meaning. The more so, since in the countryside surrounding our city, in the region of the humanities and social sciences, and in the region of politics as well, the light of exactitude or, if you like, of precision tends to dim. Let me give you two random examples of the dimness of this light, and I readily confess to being unfair by quoting out of context. Example *one* from a book on "personality":

> Personality may be defined as that which tells what a man will do when placed in a given situation. This statement can be formulated: $R = f(S,P)$, which says that R, the nature and magnitude of a person's behavioral response, i.e. what he says, thinks, or does, is some function of the S, the stimulus situation in which he is placed, and of P, the nature of his personality. For the moment, we do not attempt to say precisely what f, the function, is. That is something to be found by research.

Example *two* from a book on sociology:

> Falling in love is a universal psycho-dynamic potential in the human being. Most human beings in all societies are capable of it. It is not . . . [as another scholar says] a psychological abnormality about as common as epilepsy . . . . Far from being uncommon, . . . love relationships are a basis of the final choice of mate among a large minority of the societies of the earth. If all this is so . . . how is the love relationship handled? As can be seen, this problem is derived from the problem discussed earlier, the relation of structural variables to the functions of socialization and social control.

That's what I meant by the dimming of the light of exactitude in the countryside around our city of science.

Beyond this, exactitude, the rule of the clock, of schedules, of tidiness, of squareness in our world today begins to produce waves of revulsion. You probably know this better than I do. But the remedy for this disease of exactitude is not rebellion, or vagueness, or wildness, or love of flowers. It is the pursuit of precision in our speaking and thinking and acting. It is the concern about the "precise itself."

19 ■ About Plato's *Philebus*

To speak about a Platonic dialogue, *about* a Platonic dialogue, means to do violence to it. A sense of guilt will, therefore, be a continuous source of pain within me while I am speaking. But I cannot resist the temptation to shed some light — some moonlight, as it were — on the *Philebus*. I hope you will forgive me — I cannot — for sounding extremely pedantic, for speaking much longer than I should, and for making it sometimes very difficult for you to follow.

Let me state five basic points on which my talk about the *Philebus* will rest.

First: a Platonic dialogue is *not* a treatise or the text of a lecture; it is not comparable in this respect to a work of Aristotle or, for that matter, to any of Plotinus' *Enneads* as edited by Porphyry. A Platonic dialogue is usually a drama, a mime, in which what *happens* cannot be separated from what is said and argued about.

Secondly: however serious the purpose and the content of a Platonic dialogue, its seriousness is permeated by playfulness; indeed, as we can read in the sixth letter attributed to Plato,

Lecture first delivered at St. John's College, Annapolis, May 20, 1971. First published in *Interpretation*, Vol. 2, issue 3 (Spring, 1972).

seriousness and play are *sisters*. The comical aspect of a Platonic dialogue can never be completely disregarded.

Thirdly: no Platonic dialogue can be said to represent what might be called and has been called *the* "Platonic doctrine." The dialogue may well hint, though never "with perfect clarity,"[1] at genuine and ultimate thoughts of Plato, the thinker. The *Sophist*, for example, does that most certainly. But an unimpeachable source provides us with more direct information about Plato's thinking than he himself ever put down in writing. This source is Aristotle, who spent twenty years at that place of leisure, the Academy, and heard what Plato himself *said*. I assume that we have to pay attention to Aristotle's reports, *never forgetting* that Aristotle has his *own* way of describing other people's thoughts, a peculiar terminology rooted in his *own* thinking and not in the thinking of those other people about whom he reports.

Fourthly: in the last two centuries scholars, not all, but most of them, have tried to understand the Platonic dialogues as belonging to different stages of a "development" in Plato's own thinking. Now, it is of course possible that Plato, in his long life, changed his views on many and perhaps even on most important points. But to follow a Platonic dialogue means to take it as it *is* as one whole, in which the interlocutors play a definite and unique role and in which what is *said* and what is *happening* does not depend on anything that is said and is happening in any other dialogue. Before we could understand any "development" in Plato's thinking, it is incumbent on us to understand each dialogue in its *own* terms. This understanding is not helped by assigning a dialogue to a certain period in Plato's life. Yet, in the case of the *Philebus*, it will not be unimportant to take notice of the time this dialogue was written — not in order to track some "developmental" deviation in Plato's thinking, but merely to establish whether certain statements in the dialogue may refer to somebody's conspicuous behavior within the Academy in Plato's later days. And, happily enough, there is general agreement that the *Philebus* is a *late* dialogue, although some of the reasons for this dating might be questionable.

Fifthly: every word in a Platonic dialogue counts, and for somebody in the dialogue to remain silent may count even more.

---

1. *Soph.* 254 c.

That's why talking *about* a dialogue must necessarily remain insufficient.

And now let us approach the *Philebus*. The conversation takes place in Athens; we do not learn exactly where; it may be at a gymnastic school or at a wrestling school. What we read is a *part* of a *very long* conversation which begins some time in the afternoon. There are three interlocutors: Socrates, Protarchus, Philebus; many young men, half a dozen or a dozen perhaps, are listening. Socrates is, well, Socrates — a man devoted to inquiries and discussions and a friend and lover of youth. Protarchus is the son of a well-known Athenian, Callias. Philebus is not known at all. He is one of the few personages in the Platonic dialogues, like Callicles, Diotima, Timaeus, invented by Plato; if they do not remain nameless, like the Stranger from Elea and the Stranger from Athens, their names are appropriately coined. The name of Philebus indicates that he is a "lover of youth"— as Socrates is. Philebus seems to be young, but slightly older than Protarchus and all the listening young men around them.[2]

The title of the dialogue as it has been handed down to us is *Philebus*. This title is never mentioned in the writings of Plato's contemporaries. Aristotle refers to what is *said* in the dialogue at least eight times, mentioning Plato once. There seems to be no reason, however, to doubt that the title "Philebus" is genuine. Moreover, there is one good reason which speaks forcefully for its authenticity. The dialogue contains 2,369 lines (I did not count them, but somebody did). Of these 2,369 lines only 23 are spoken by Philebus (those I counted). He raises his voice altogether only 14 times. Under these circumstances, who else but *Plato* could have chosen the name of *Philebus* for the title of the dialogue? There will be more to say about this matter later on.

The main question raised in the dialogue is: *What is the best human life?* And this question has to cope primarily with the all-pervasive feeling of *pleasure*, common to all living beings —

---

2. 16 b.

haunting, filling, mocking us. All of us — without exception — want to be pleased in thousands and thousands of different ways: we seek to lie down or to sit comfortably; we like hearing things that flatter us; we enjoy good company, witty words, good drink and food; we delight in traveling, in going to the theatre or to the movies, in looking at beautiful things; we love caresses, precious gifts, wild emotions; we *loose* ourselves with rapture in exerting power, in sexual satisfaction, in ecstasies, and so on, and so on. A list of pleasures like the one I have just given is not to be found in the dialogue, but an infinite number of possible pleasures is implied in the arguments we are facing. It is Philebus who looks at Pleasure as the highest good, who sees in Pleasure not only the best of human possessions, but the goal after which *all living beings* strive. Pleasure (ἡδονή) is the goddess he worships. And quite a few of us, I think, follow him.

Socrates does not. He contends that there is something better and more desirable than pleasure, to wit, *thoughtfulness in deciding how to act* (τὸ φρονεῖν), *the apprehending of what is intelligible only* (τὸ νοεῖν), *the power of memory* (τὸ μεμνῆσθαι) and that which is akin to these, *right opinion* (δόξα ὀρθή) and *true calculations* (ἀληθεῖς λογισμοί); but Socrates carefully adds that these powers are better and more desirable than pleasure for those beings who are able to share in these powers; only to beings who have this ability will these powers be profitable, now and in the future.

This juxtaposition of both contentions, of that of Philebus and of that of Socrates, is made by Socrates very shortly after we begin reading. It is introduced by Socrates with the following words: "See, *then*, Protarchus, what the assertion is which you are *now* to accept from Philebus, and what our assertion is against which you are to argue, if you do not agree with it. Shall we give a summary of each of them?"[3] These words are the very first words of the dialogue. But what strikes us immediately is that they cannot be understood as indicating the beginning of a conversation; they just continue what was said before; if they were the beginning of a conversation, the vocative

---

3. 11 a.

Πρώταρχε would be preceded by ὦ (ὦ Πρώταρχε, not simply
Πρώταρχε); and the words "then" (δή) and "now" (νυνί) would
not be used. Listen again: "See, *then* Protarchus, what the assertion is which you are *now* to accept from Philebus . . . ." The
dialogue has no true beginning. Nor does it have a true ending.
This is the last sentence we read, spoken by Protarchus: "There
is still a little left, Socrates; you will certainly not give up before
we do, and I shall remind you of what remains." We do not yet
understand why the dialogue has no beginning and no ending.
But we see (and this is important), when we begin reading, that
Protarchus has to take over the thesis upheld by Philebus. More
about that later.

Enjoyment and thoughtfulness are the two banners that Protarchus and Socrates are respectively waving. The life of pleasure
and the life of thoughtfulness face each other. But it becomes
clear immediately that Socrates is considering some other life
superior to both of them.[4] He will keep reverting to this third
life. It will finally be described in the last pages of the dialogue.

What follows the juxtaposition of the two views, that of
Philebus and Protarchus on the one hand and that of Socrates
on the other, is Socrates' insistence that pleasure has many different aspects: "For, when you just simply hear her named, she
is *one thing*, but surely she takes on all sorts of shapes which
are, in a way, *unlike* each other."[5] Socrates gives two simple,
though significant, examples: the pleasures of a licentious man
are very different from those of a self-restrained man, who enjoys his very self-restraint; the pleasures of a fool are very different from those of a thoughtful man, who enjoys his very
thoughtfulness. No, says Protarchus, the *sources* of pleasure may
be different, may have an opposite character, but "how can
pleasure help being of all things most like pleasure, that is, like
itself."[6] Yes, says Socrates, color and figure are what they are,
but colors and figures can be very, very different and even, in
the case of colors, most opposed to each other, like black and
white. Protarchus does not see how this could make him change

---

4. 11 d.
5. 12 c.
6. 12 d/e

his mind. Socrates tries for the *third* time, this time incisively, anticipating what will be said later in the dialogue. No argument, he says, disputes that pleasant things are pleasant. But Protarchus' contention, which upholds Philebus' conviction, implies that all pleasant things are *good*. That's what is wrong. Pleasant things are for the most part *bad* and only some are good. But you, Protarchus, says Socrates, call *all* of them *good*, although you might be forced by the argument to agree that they are otherwise different. Protarchus tacitly admits that pleasures may be very different from each other, and even *opposed* to each other, but sticks to his main point that pleasures, inasmuch as they are *pleasures*, are always good.

At this point Socrates goes back to his own contention, namely, that *thoughtfulness* (φρόνησις) and *the apprehension of the intelligible* (νοῦς) are good. He adds to these — for the first time — *knowledge* (ἐπιστήμη) and predicts that many kinds of knowledge will come to the fore, some among them unlike each other. Should it turn out that some are even opposed to each other, could he, Socrates, then cling to the point that all knowledge is alike and — not unlike Protarchus —"save himself" in an absurdity?

Protarchus is pleased that both, his assertion and that of Socrates, receive the same treatment and is now willing to grant that there are many *different* pleasures just as there are many *different* knowledges (we have to note that he does not mention *opposite* pleasures and knowledges).

Socrates is satisfied with Protarchus' concession about the manyness within knowledge and within pleasure and speaks as follows: "With no concealment, then, Protarchus, of the differentiation within my good and within yours, but facing it squarely, let us be bold and see if perchance, on examination, it will tell us whether we should say that the good is pleasure or thoughtfulness or some other *third* thing."[7] It is the second time that Socrates reverts to the possibility that something third may be the best of human possessions. He proceeds by strengthening this statement by an assertion which has a wide, wide range.

---

7. 14 b

This is one of the transitions in which the dialogue abounds. (Parenthetical remark: in the second century A.D. Galen wrote a treatise entitled "On the transitions in the *Philebus*," which is unfortunately not extant.) Let me say a few words about the transition we are now facing.

Up to this point the talk was about things most familiar to all of us, about pleasure and about thoughtfulness and about knowledge, this last word taken in its colloquial and vague sense. The talk was concerned about our lives in this our world. What Socrates is undertaking now is to lift the conversation to a level of all-embracing universality, disregarding pleasure and knowledge altogether. He will come back to them after a short while and then launch out to an even higher level. Why does he do that? The answer is: to find the *ultimate sources* of what is so close to us and usually unquestioned by us. The dialogue seeks to link the most common to the most uncommon and fundamental. To find the link will require a great deal of vigor on Socrates' part.

The manyness within pleasure and within knowledge leads Socrates to remind Protarchus of the "astounding" assertions that *"many are one"* and that *"one is many."*[8] There is nothing particularly surprising and difficult about these assertions if they refer to visible and tangible things, which come into being and perish. A man, for example, is *one*, but he is also *many*, because he has many members and parts. But when we consider intelligibles, the εἴδη of things, the "invisible looks," which can be encountered only in speech (ἐν λόγῳ), and each one of which is one and unique, the "one and many" problem becomes extremely perplexing (Socrates mentions four of the intelligibles: the *One Man*, the *One Ox*, the *One Beauty*, the *One Good*). That's where the trouble sets in. Any young man, says Socrates, challenging those present, any young man, once he has tasted the flavor of that perplexity and thinks he has found a treasure of wisdom, does not spare anyone, neither himself, nor his parents, nor any human being, who can hear him, and joyfully sets every possible argument in motion, confounding everybody. Protarchus feels hit. "Do you not see, Socrates," he says, "how

---

8. 14 c.

many we are and that we are all young men? Are you not afraid that we shall join with Philebus and attack you, if you revile us?"[9] But Socrates' challenge works. Protarchus wants Socrates to find a better road than was used up to now and to lead them on.

Socrates retorts that there *is* a better road, which he always loved, which is easy to point out, but very difficult to follow. Whatever human art has discovered had been brought to light through it. Socrates' description of this better road marks a new transition in the dialogue.

Socrates calls this road a "gift of gods to men," which we owe to some Prometheus together with some gleaming fire (let me remind you: Prometheus *stole* the fire he gave to men). The ancients, who were better than we and lived nearer the gods, says Socrates with deadpan seriousness, have handed down to us the tradition that all the things which are ever said to exist are sprung from *One* and *Many* and have, inherent in their nature, *Limit* (πέρας) and *Infinitude* (ἀπειρία). We shall come back to this point in a little while. What Socrates emphasizes now is that we must, in every case, look for *one* εἶδος (he uses the word ἰδέα here) and next for *two*, if there be two, and if not, for *three* or some other *number*; and we must treat each of these εἴδη in the same way, that is, subdivide each of them, "until we can see that the original one is not just one and many and infinite, but also *how many* it is."[10] Then we may bid farewell to infinity, bid farewell to the ἰδέα of infinity.

Protarchus wants Socrates to clarify what he has said. No wonder! Socrates provides this clarification by pointing to the letters of the alphabet. The sound which we emit through our mouth can be called one, yet it is infinite in diversity. A god or a godlike man, as an Egyptian story tells, observed, however, that there are distinct vowel sounds, semi-vowel sounds and consonants — in Greek 7 vowels, 3 semi-vowels or sonants (λ, ρ, σ), and 14 consonants, more exactly 10, if we include the rough breathing sound h and exclude the 5 double consonants. This means that between the *oneness* and the *infinitude* of sound there

---

9. 16 a.
10. 16 d.

are *definite numbers* of sounds. One has to know *all* of them
to possess the *art* of reading and writing. Socrates *emphasizes*
the *numbers* of sounds and letters. But this example of the
alphabet and the example of the numbers of musical intervals,
which Socrates also gives, are meant to let Protarchus and
Philebus and us understand that there are *numbers* in the realm
of the εἴδη. Later in the dialogue[11] Socrates will clearly
distinguish between numbers of unequal units, that is, numbers
of sensible things, and pure mathematical numbers of units, that
is, of units which do not differ at all from each other. But we
learn from Aristotle[12] that Plato also spoke of *eidetic numbers*,
of numbers of units which are themselves nothing but εἴδη. To
try to find them means to embark upon that better, but difficult road.

Protarchus and Philebus do not understand what is going
on. Philebus especially does not see what the theme of *numbers*,
which Socrates has injected into the discussion, has to do with
the alternative of pleasure and thoughtfulness, which was in
question. Socrates reminds him that they were wondering how
each of them, pleasure as well as thoughtfulness, was one and
many, and whether "each of them possessed a number before
becoming infinite,"[13] that is to say, whether there were εἴδη of
pleasure as well as of thoughtfulness, which then are dispersed
among beings that continually come into being and perish and
that live their lives in pleasure and thought.

Protarchus is perturbed. He understands what Socrates is
after. He cannot find an answer to the question. He wants
Philebus to answer it. And he formulates the question as follows:
"I think Socrates is asking us whether there are or are not εἴδη
of pleasure, how many there are and of what sort they are, and
the same of thoughtfulness."[14] Philebus does not utter a word.
But Socrates remarks: "What you say is most true, son of
Callias."[15] He underscores the importance of this fact by addressing Protarchus ceremonially as son of Callias.

---

11. 56 d–e.
12. See esp. *Met.* XIV, 3, 1090 b 32ff.
13. 18 e.
14. 19 b.
15. *Ibid.*

Protarchus is intent on bringing the discussion about pleasure and thoughtfulness to a satisfactory end. We learn from what he says that Socrates *promised* that he would stay on and not go home before this end was reached. This promise must have been given, we have to assume, during the discussion which preceded what we read in the dialogue, and we should not forget that. Protarchus demands that Socrates stop perplexing him and the other young men and decide *either* to divide pleasure and knowledge into their εἴδη himself *or* to let that go, if there be some other way to solve the matters at issue among them. Socrates is willing to do the latter, and this marks a new transition in the dialogue.

Socrates claims playfully that some god has just reminded him of some talk about pleasure and thoughtfulness, which he heard when he was dreaming or perhaps when he was awake. What he heard was that neither pleasure nor thoughtfulness was the good, but some *third* thing, different from both and better than both. We remember, of course, that Socrates himself had intimated this twice. He does it now for the *third* time. If this could be clearly shown now, says Socrates, pleasure would not be the victor and it would no longer be necessary to divide pleasure into its εἴδη. And Socrates adds that, while the discussion proceeds, this will become still clearer.

What follows leads to three insights: (1) it is the lot of the Good and only of the Good to be self-sufficient; (2) if we take the life of pleasure and the thoughtful life separately, so that the life of pleasure is totally divested of any thought, any knowledge, any opinion, any memory, and the thoughtful life, on the other hand, totally untouched by any pleasure, both lives — in this bare form — cannot be conceived as self-sufficient, as desirable, and as good; (3) only a life made up of a *mixture* of pleasure and thoughtfulness and sharing in both will be the kind of life everybody would choose. Let me remark that Socrates and also Protarchus list under the powers associated with thoughtfulness the power of apprehending the intelligibles, νοῦς, which in common parlance may simply mean *good sense*. This term will now play a central role for quite a while. Socrates concludes: it has been sufficiently shown that Philebus' goddess, Pleasure, cannot be considered identical with the good. Thereupon Philebus raises his voice: "Nor is your νοῦς the good,

Socrates; it will be open to the same objections."[16] Let us hear
Socrates' reaction: "*My* νοῦς perhaps, Philebus; but not so the
true νοῦς, which is also *divine*; that one, I guess, is different.
I do not as yet claim for the νοῦς the prize of victory over the
combined life, but we must look and see what is to be done about
the *second prize*."[17] Socrates goes on, still speaking to Philebus:
"Each of us might perhaps put forward a claim, one that νοῦς
is *responsible* for this combined life, is its *cause*, the other that
pleasure is: and thus neither of these two would be the good,
but one or the other of them might be regarded as the *cause*
[of the combined life]."[18] Then, turning to Protarchus, Socrates
claims he might keep up his fight against Philebus in an even
stronger way and might contend "that in this mixed life it is
νοῦς that is more akin and more similar than pleasure to that,
whatever it may be, which makes that life both desirable and
good." As to pleasure, he adds, "it is farther behind than the
third place, if *my* νοῦς is at all to be trusted at present."[19]

The emphasis in this passage is clearly on the terms νοῦς
and "cause" (αἴτιον). What remains unclear is the sense in which
the term "cause" is to be taken and the rank to be attributed
ultimately to the νοῦς. And let us not for a moment forget
Socrates' own νοῦς.

Socrates suggests that it might be better to leave pleasure
and not to *pain* her by testing her in the most precise way and
thus proving her in the wrong. Protarchus disagrees. Socrates
asks whether Protarchus disagrees because he, Socrates, spoke
of *paining* pleasure. It is the *second* time that pain is mentioned
in the dialogue. It is done jokingly. Pain was mentioned for the
first time when Socrates dealt with the thoughtful life, totally
untouched by pleasure. The way he put it then was this: "Would
anyone be willing to live possessing thoughtfulness and νοῦς and
knowledge and perfect memory of all things, but having no
share, great or small, in pleasure, or in *pain*, for that matter,
but being utterly unaffected by everything of that sort?"[20] The
question, which is supposed to be negated, when put in this form

---

16. 22 c.
17. 22 c–d.
18. 22 d.
19. 22 e.
20. 21 d/e.

actually involves a difficulty: one would perhaps be willing to accept a thoughtful pleasureless life, which does not involve us in any pain. The *third* time pain will be mentioned is going to show pain as a close companion of pleasure and as a real evil. Protarchus says he is not shocked by Socrates' phrase "paining pleasure," but rather by Socrates' apparent attempt to stop talking about pleasure altogether and because Socrates does not seem to understand "that not one of us will let you go yet until you have brought the argument about these matters to an end."[21] This is the second time Socrates is warned about leaving too early.

Whew, Socrates exclaims, and predicts that a long and difficult discussion lies ahead of them. To fight the battle of the νοῦς for the second prize requires new weapons in *addition* to those already used. A new beginning has to be made, and this will mean a new transition in the dialogue.

Let us be on our guard in making this beginning, says Socrates, and we should indeed pay attention to these words. Socrates suggests that everything that now exists in the world be distributed in a twofold, or rather in a threefold way. The results of this distribution are very different from each other. They are called by Socrates, indiscriminately and imprecisely, εἴδη or γένη, which I shall translate by the word "tribes." The first two have been mentioned before as a kind of Promethean gift: the "*limitless*" (τὸ ἄπειρον) and the "*limit*" (τὸ πέρας). The third is the *mixture* of these two into one. This is not to be taken literally, as we shall see in a moment: let us be on our guard. And now Socrates adds: "But I cut a considerably ridiculous figure, I think, when I attempt a separation into tribes and an enumeration."[22] Protarchus wonders why. Socrates: "It seems to me, a fourth tribe is needed besides."[23] It turns out that Socrates means the *cause* of the commixture of those first two. And Protarchus, who is eager to supply even a fifth, namely the power of separation, is told in affable words that this fifth is not needed now, but that if it be needed later, he should excuse Socrates

---

21. 23 b.
22. 23 d.
23. *Ibid.*

for going after it. The mentioning of Protarchus' proposal and
the way of handling it cast a doubt on the necessity of the fourth
tribe, the *cause*. There might be something strange and even
ridiculous indeed about that. We should be on our guard.

Let us consider one of the first two tribes, namely τὸ ἄπειρον.
The following English translations are all adequate: the limitless,
the endless, the boundless, the unlimited, the infinite, the innumerable, the indefinite, the indeterminate. And we must not
forget the homonym ἄπειρος, meaning the inexperienced one,
upon which word Plato does not fail to pun. [24]

As to the second tribe, τὸ πέρας, the "limit," it becomes
almost immediately apparent that, although Socrates keeps using this term, he also substitutes for it the phrase "that which
has limit," τὸ πέρας ἔχον, that is to say, the "limited." Protarchus and the other young men as well as we are somewhat confused. Socrates proposes to investigate how each of them, the
"limitless" and the "limited," are both "one and many"; for he
contends that each one of them is split up and scattered into
many. He starts with the "*limitless*," warning Protarchus again:
"What I ask you to consider is difficult and debatable." [25]

Here are special cases of this tribe, parts of its manyness:
"hotter and colder," "quicker and slower," "greater and smaller,"
"exceedingly and slightly," "excessive and lacking." [26] In each there
is "the more *as well as* the less" (τὸ μᾶλλόν τε καὶ ἧττον). Each
of them is constantly *advancing* and *never stationary* — in sharp
contrast to what is determined by a fixed number, by just "that
much": if such a number advances, it ceases to exist. What cap-
tures our attention is the expression τὸ μᾶλλόν τε καὶ ἧττον.
This expression is meant to gather together the tribe of the
"limitless" and to put upon it the seal of a single nature. [27] It
is used six times in the passage we are now considering and once
more much later on. *Once* the particle τε is omitted. This omission focuses our attention on the use of this particle in all the
other cases. The verbs related to this expression are all in the
dual. And Socrates summarizes pointedly: "By this argument

---

24. 17 e.
25. 24 a.
26. "Lacking" is not mentioned. It is lacking in deed.
27. 25 a.

the hotter and its *opposite* become together limitless."[28] The "limitless" is a pair. The expression "the more as well as the less," as the seal of a single nature, seals a *duality*. And this duality remains completely *indeterminate*. The "limitless" is an *indeterminate pair*.

But what about the "limit," on the one hand, and the "limited," that "which has limit," on the other? Let us take the "limited" first. It is, as Socrates quite clearly states,[29] contrary to "the more as well as the less"; it is the *equal*, and *equality*, the *double*, and any number in firm *relation* to another number or a measure in firm *relation* to another measure, that is, everything which "puts an end to the variability between the opposites and makes them proportionable and harmonious by the introduction of number."[30]

We understand that what Socrates means by this tribe of the "limited" is what we read in the Fifth Book of Euclid's *Elements*. This book is in all probability either a perhaps somewhat condensed copy of an original work of Eudoxus or imitates this work. Who is *Eudoxus*? He was born in Cnidus, on the shores of Asia Minor, came to Athens and stayed at Plato's Academy for a while. He was an astronomer, a mathematician, and a geographer; he firmly established the doctrine of ratios and proportions, including those of numerically incommensurable magnitudes; he tried to "*mix*" the εἴδη, as understood by Plato, with all the sensible things; and — what is most important to us — he declared *pleasure* to be the *supreme good*. But pleasure was not his goddess, as she is for Philebus. Eudoxus, as Aristotle reports, "seemed to be a man of exceptional temperance, and hence he was thought to uphold this view not because he was a lover of pleasure, but because it seemed to him that it was so in truth."[31] Socrates, as we see in the dialogue, disagrees.

The tribe of the "limited" then consists of *ratios*. The tribe of the scattered "limitless," of the ἄπειρον, in its infinite manyness

---

28. 24 d.
29. 25 a/b.
30. 25 d/e.
31. Arist. *Met.* XII, 8 1073 b 17ff.; Proclus, *In Eucl. Comm.* (Teubner) pp. 67, 2ff.; Arist. *Met.* I, 9, 991 a 14ff.; *Nic. Eth.* X, 2, 1172 b 9ff.

found its unity in the seal of "the more and its opposite,"[32] that is, in "the more as well as the less." The tribe of the "limited," the manyness of determinate ratios, has not yet found its unity. This unity was only postulated, was only, as Socrates says, "referred to." There was indeed a direct "reference" to the "limit" itself (εἰς τὸ πέρας).[33] And Socrates concludes: "The limit did not concontain a multitude nor did we feel a difficulty that it might not be *one* by nature."[34]

It is at this point that we might turn to Aristotle's reports about Plato's unwritten words to confirm what we found in the dialogue and to win greater clarity.

In the Sixth Chapter of the First Book of the *Metaphysics*[35] Aristotle says of Plato: "It is *peculiar* to him [i.e., Plato] to posit a duality instead of the single Limitless, and to make the Limitless consist of 'the Great and the Small.' " In the Third Book of the *Physics*, where Aristotle discusses the ἄπειρον at great length, we read in the Fourth Chapter[36] again: "For Plato there are two Infinites, 'the Great and the Small.' " We see thus confirmed what we read in the *Philebus*, except that Aristotle, in his own way, uses the words "great" and "small" without their comparative forms.[37] He keeps using these words, in speaking about Plato, at many other places. But, what is more important, in Books XIII and XIV of the *Metaphysics* Aristotle mentions several times two "elements," as he puts it, out of which, according to Plato, "numbers" are derived. We have to understand that Aristotle has in mind "eidetic numbers," assemblages of εἴδη. These two sources are the "indeterminate dyad" (ἡ ἀόριστος δυάς) and the "one" (τὸ ἕν). We recognize the indeterminate pair of the *Philebus* in the "indeterminate dyad," the duality of the Limitless, "the more as well as the less." But we see now that what was named the "Limit" in the *Philebus* can also be named the "One." What Aristotle calls the "elements" can be called the *ultimate sources* of everything, that which has

---

32. 26 d.
33. 25 b.
34. 26 d.
35. 987 b 26–28.
36. 203 a 15.
37. Cf. 37 c end.

the *first* rank both as *beginnings* and as *ruling powers*. That is what is meant by ἀρχή, in common parlance as well as in most thoughtful speech. We should not assume, I think, that Plato had a definitely fixed name for each of these ἀρχαί. The terms *the Good, the One, the Precise itself, the Same, the Limit*, and perhaps *the Whole* are all suited to one of the ἀρχαί, depending on the context in which they are used. As to the names of the second ἀρχή, the "indeterminate dyad," "the more as well as the less," and the *Other* (which also implies a duality[38]) seem all of them no less suitable. In the *Philebus* Socrates, in putting a seal on the tribe of the ἄπειρον, makes its intrinsic character perfectly clear. But the character of the πέρας, the "limit," remains obscured.

Now let us take up the third tribe, the "mixture" of the "Limitless" and of the "Limit." What does "mixing" here mean? It means that the two ἀρχαί, the "Limitless," the "indeterminate dyad," and the "Limit," the "One," exert their power on each other. What happens then may be described as follows. The "indeterminate dyad" duplicates the "One," that is to say, produces two entities, two εἴδη, duplicates each of these εἴδη — we may also say "divides" each of these εἴδη — and keeps on duplicating — we have to assume up to a certain point. In Aristotle's reports the "indeterminate dyad" is explicitly characterized as a "doubling power" (δυοποιός).[39] It is the ultimate source of definite manyness, of "numbers," in the realm of the εἴδη as well as in our world. In the earlier passage, when Socrates first introduced the Promethean gift of "infinitude" and of "limit" and urged that in every case a definite number of εἴδη had to be found (the alphabet helping him to clarify this point), there was hardly a discernible hint that the "Limitless" with its doubling power is responsible for the *multiplicity of the* εἴδη. You will remember that in this context the "limitless," the infinite, was ultimately dismissed. Not so in the world in which we live. What happens here is this: the "Limit," the "One," transforms the "indeterminate dyad" into a *determinate* one, that is to say, transforms the two constantly and indeterminately changing terms of the dyad into two stationary and determinate ones and

---

38. Cf. *Soph.* 255 d and 256 e–257 a.
39. *Met.* XIII, 7, 1082 a 15, and 8, 1083 b 36.

keeps doing this, produces, in other words, a multitude of *ratios*. That's why Socrates can call the manyness of ratios "the offspring of the limit."[40]

We understand now what confused Protarchus and us when Socrates substituted "that which has limit," the "limited," for the "limit" itself. The "limited," the assemblage of ratios, is already a part of the mixture, of the third tribe. But it represents a mixture, or rather mixtures, of a special kind, mathematical partnerships that can give to parts of the world we live in a certain rightness, remove the excess and indefiniteness, and produce balance and right measure.[41] Such mathematical partnerships engender, for example, *health*, establish the entire *genuine* art of *music*, bring about the *temperate seasons* and all the bounties of our world, beauty and strength of the body, and all the beauties of the soul. And Socrates, addressing Philebus directly and speaking about that proper partnership (ὀρθὴ κοινωνία)[42] of mathematical ratios, has this to say: "For this goddess, my beautiful Philebus, beholding the wanton violence and universal wickedness which prevailed, since there was no limit of pleasures or of excess in them, established law and order [νόμος καὶ τάξις] in which there is *limit*. You say she exhausted us; I say, on the contrary, she kept us safe."[43] Socrates addresses Philebus, but we cannot help thinking of Eudoxus. Philebus remains completely silent. Socrates turns to Protarchus: "How does this appear to you, Protarchus?" And Protarchus answers: "It is very much how I feel, Socrates."[44]

Let us conclude: the common power of the two ἀρχαί determines the mixture. Sometimes the community of this power is lacking.

Socrates turns now to the fourth tribe, the *cause*. You will remember that Socrates seemed somewhat reluctant to add this fourth to the first three. And indeed, is there any need for it? The common power of the "Limitless" and the "Limit" appeared as the *cause* of the mixture and of what is engendered in this mixture. Listen now to Socrates' words: "Should I sound a *false*

---

40. 25 d.
41. 26 a.
42. 25 e.
43. 26 b–c.
44. 26 c.

note if I called the fourth the *cause* of the mixture and generation?"[45] And listen to what Socrates one moment earlier says
with regard to *all* the first *three* tribes: "That which fabricates
all these, the cause, we call the fourth, as it has been sufficiently
shown to be distinct from the others."[46] That has not been shown
at all! How can ultimate sources, ἀρχαί, be caused by something
else? If that were so, the first two tribes, the "Limitless" and
the "Limit," would not be what they are.

The exploration of this fourth tribe, the "cause," is left *pend-
ing,* and Socrates makes a new transition, which helps him to
turn backwards.

What was the purpose, he asks, of coming to the point they
have reached? They were trying to find out whether the second
prize belonged to pleasure or to thoughtfulness (φρόνησις). They
had posited, Socrates reminds Protarchus and us, that the *mixed
life* was the victor. We can see now, he continues, to which tribe
it belongs, namely, to the third tribe, formed by the mixture
of all that is "limitless" and all that is "bound by the limit."[47]
And now Socrates asks Philebus to which of the three tribes his
life of *unmixed pleasure* belongs. The *full* question is this: Have
pleasure *and pain* a limit or are they among the things which
admit "the more as well as the less"? Philebus' answer is: "Yes,
among those which admit the more; for pleasure would not be
all the good, if it were not limitless in multitude and in the
'more.' "[48] Socrates dryly replies: "Nor would *pain,* Philebus, be
all the evil."[49] This is how pain is introduced in the discussion
for the *third* time, and this time *decisively.* For Socrates adds
he would grant Philebus that both, pleasure *and* pain, are in
the tribe of the Limitless. We note Philebus meant only pleasure,
not pain. Socrates' addition is decisive.

Pleasure and pain are a limitless pair. One of the consequences of this finding is that there are no εἴδη of pleasure, in
the strict sense of this word. We remember that Socrates had
intimated that the discussion would show in a clearer way why

---

45. 27 b/c.
46. 27 b.
47. 27 d.
48. 27 e.
49. 28 a.

it would not be necessary to divide pleasure into its εἴδη. Socrates will use this term later on in discussing pleasure, but it will not have to be taken in its strict sense.

The next question Socrates asks Protarchus and Philebus is: to what tribe thoughtfulness, knowledge, and νοῦς shall be assigned without impiety. Socrates explains: "For I think that our risk is not a small one in finding or not finding the right answer to what is being asked now."[50] Philebus: "You exalt your own god, Socrates, you do."[51] Socrates: "And you your goddess, my friend. But the question calls for an answer, all the same."[52] Protarchus intervenes and urges Philebus to answer. Whereupon Philebus says: *"Did you not, Protarchus, choose to reply in my place?"*[53] This is the *last* time Philebus raises his voice. Let us look back for a moment.

At the beginning of our reading we learn that Protarchus will defend Philebus' thesis of pleasure, because Philebus himself, as Protarchus says, "has grown tired" (the Greek word is ἀπείρηκε, a pun on the word ἄπειρον). A little later Philebus has an opportunity to *regret* that he spoke up again and calls upon his own goddess to witness that he *does* regret. When the "one and many" question comes up, Protarchus remarks: "It is perhaps best for the inquirer not to disturb Philebus in his sweet repose."[54] And now he will be silent all the time, even when pleasure, his goddess, is thoroughly discussed. What is he doing all this time? Just listening?

Protarchus has some difficulty in answering Socrates' last question, namely, to what tribe knowledge and νοῦς should be assigned, and asks Socrates to answer this question himself. Socrates is willing. He declares: "What you enjoin me to do *is not difficult*,"[55] and he repeats: "It is easy." Let us be on our guard. All wise men agree, and thereby really exalt *themselves*, says Socrates, that νοῦς is king of heaven and earth. Socrates adds: "Perhaps they are right."[56]

---

50. *Ibid.*
51. 28 b.
52. *Ibid.*
53. *Ibid.*
54. 15 c [tacit reference to the proverb: μὴ κινεῖν κακὸν εὖ κείμενον].
55. 28 c.
56. *Ibid.*

What follows is indeed an easy, but not too convincing "cosmological" account, which ends with the statement that νοῦς belongs to that of the four tribes which was called "*the cause of all*."[57] Notice, please, again, "*of all*." And Socrates adds: "Now, you have at last your answer." Protarchus: "Yes, and a very sufficient one; and yet you answered without my noticing it."[58] Socrates: "Yes, Protarchus, for sometimes *playing* provides rest from *serious* pursuit."[59] We understand: the "cosmological" account, which makes the νοῦς the *cause* of all the other tribes, was a *playful* account. We are not sure whether this νοῦς is the "divine νοῦς" mentioned before. And let us not forget that, within the confines of human life, the best νοῦς could obtain was the *second prize*.

Socrates concludes this entire discussion of the four tribes by pointing to νοῦς and to pleasure. He does not mention anything pertaining to "limit" and to the "mixture." Let us remember, he says, "that νοῦς was akin to cause and belonged roughly speaking [σχεδόν] to this tribe and that pleasure was itself limitless and belonged to the tribe which, in and by itself, *has* not and *never will have* either beginning or middle or end."[60] We must add that this holds also for pain. As we have seen, the dialogue, too, has neither a beginning nor an end, and for that matter, no middle. The graph of a Platonic dialogue usually— not always—looks like this:

But the graph of the *Philebus* looks like this:

57. 30 e.
58. *Ibid.*
59. *Ibid.*
60. *Ibid.*

The dialogue itself, taken as a drama, in which we, the readers or listeners, are involved, seems to resemble pleasure and pain. If it does that, it must be pleasurable and painful. We will have to wait and see. . . . But we need not wait to register the most important result of the preceding discussion. All the pleasures and pains, small or great, which pervade our lives, reflect in their duality an ultimate source, one of the ἀρχαί, namely the "indeterminate dyad." It is thus that some of our most familiar and common experiences are tied to one of the highest points human reflection can reach.

Socrates now abandons this high level and turns to a much lower one. A new transition is made. Only about a third of the dialogue has been considered so far. I shall be able to proceed much faster from now on.

The next task is to see, says Socrates, *where* each of them, that is, νοῦς and pleasure, can be found and by means of what affection both come into being, *whenever they come into being.*[61] Note, please, that the νοῦς mentioned here is said to come into being and cannot, therefore, be understood as the eternal divine νοῦς. Socrates takes pleasure first, and immediately adds that it is impossible to examine pleasure sufficiently apart from pain.

Socrates' contention is that pain and pleasure emerge in the combined tribe, the one, we remember, where the "limitless" and the "limit" join together and form a mathematical partnership conducive to balance and right measure. When this balance is broken in us, living beings, "a disruption of nature and a generation of pain also take place at the same time."[62] "If, on the other hand, balance is being restored and is returning to its own nature, pleasure is generated."[63] The *process* of destruction is *pain,* and the *process* of restoration is *pleasure.* When we are being *emptied,* we are becoming *hungry* and pained; when we are filling up again through eating, we are pleased. And the same can be said of *thirst.* It is shown later that it is *not* the body that hungers or thirsts or has any such affection, that the body cannot, therefore, be pained or pleased.

---

61. 31 b.
62. 31 d.
63. *Ibid.*

Pleasure and pain belong to the *soul*, and to the soul only. But sometimes, or rather often enough, as in the case of hunger and thirst, the *body* is involved. Whenever this is the case, we face one kind of pleasure and pain.

Another kind of pleasure and pain does not involve the body at all. It arises within the soul itself as the sweet and cheering *hope* of pleasant things to come and as the fearful and woeful *expectation* of painful things to come. Both the pleasant and the painful expectations originate within the soul in memory. Socrates proceeds to give a circumstantial description of this origin by passing from perception to memory, to forgetfulness, to recollection, and finally to desire. But he ends this passage by reverting to pleasure and pain that involve the body. He points to a man who is empty and suffers pain, but who, because of his memory, hopes to be filled again and enjoys this hope. "At such a time, then, a man, or any other living being, has both pain and joy at once."[64] If, however, an empty man is without hope of being filled, a twofold feeling of pain arises in him. The stress is on the duality of pleasure and pain. The possibility of a twofold pain and—although this is not mentioned—of a twofold pleasure emphasizes the duality even more. Let us not forget its ultimate source.

Looked at in this passage is also a life in which there is no feeling of pleasure or pain at all, but only thoughtfulness and νοῦς. Such a life had been considered much earlier in the dialogue and had been rejected as totally undesirable, lacking self-sufficiency and, therefore, goodness. Now Socrates calls it "the *most divine* life." Protarchus chimes in: "Certainly it is not likely that gods feel either joy or its opposite."[65] And Socrates agrees: "No, it is very unlikely; for either is unseemly for them." Socrates adds that they may consider this point later on, if it would help the argument; they might give νοῦς credit for it in contending for the second prize. We shall be watching.

A new transition takes place. What follows can be subdivided into three parts, and the title that can be given to all of them is "On *false* pleasures." This is what happens in *part one:* Protarchus is unwilling to agree that pleasures and pains could be

---

64. 36 b.
65. 33 b.

false; he accepts the possibility of false opinions, but rejects the possibility of false fears, false expectations, and false pleasures; a lengthy discussion follows which culminates in the assertion that a "just, pious and good man," a "friend of the gods," has "true pleasures," while an "unjust and thoroughly bad man" can only have "false pleasures," which imitate the "true pleasures" to the point of ridicule; and the same can be said of pains.[66]

This, now, is what happens in *part two:* we are reminded that pleasure and pain are a limitless pair tied to "the more as well as the less"; anyone who feels pleasure in any way always really feels pleasure; but these pleasures may be felt as present pleasures and also as pleasures *to be felt* in the future; the latter ones may be *false* because they may not come into being as expected, not as great and intense as expected; and when, in our feelings, we are trying to compare pleasures with pleasures, or pains with pains, or pleasures with pains, we may reach entirely *false* results, because of the limitless and indeterminate character of both, pleasure and pain.

The *third part* of this passage does not concern false pleasures directly, but rather pleasures falsely understood or falsely judged. The theme of pleasure and pain is a common topic in Plato's own time, widely discussed by outstanding men. One of the opinions about pleasure, rejected by Socrates, is that freedom from pain is identified with pleasure. For some men this opinion amounts to the firm denial of the existence of pleasures altogether. For them that which Philebus and his friends call pleasures are merely escapes from pain. These men are men "of harsh judgments."[67] Socrates does not mention any names, but it is highly probable that *Antisthenes* is one of these men. Antisthenes is reputed to have said: "Should I ever meet Aphrodite, I would strangle her with my own hands."

I have condensed this passage of the dialogue to the utmost. But you understand that it challenges the conviction of Philebus radically. Let us look at him again. He has not said a word. Is he really listening? We know, he had grown tired. Has not his sweet repose mentioned by Protarchus a long time ago transformed itself into sound sleep? And *sleep*, sound, dreamless sleep,

---

66. 39 e–40 c.
67. 44 c–d.

we should observe, excludes any feeling of pleasure and pain, brings about, in other words, a condition of the "most divine life," yet a condition not compatible with Philebus' own aspirations. Yes, there he lies, the beautiful Philebus, with closed eyes and closed ears, while Socrates continues the inquiry, imposed upon him by Philebus, Protarchus, and the other young men. In sharp contrast to Philebus' fatigue and somnolence are Socrates' vigor and straightforwardness.[68]

A subtle transition is brought to pass inasmuch as Socrates takes those men "of harsh judgments" with whom he disagrees as allies. He is going to describe more accurately what pleasure means to these men, who oppose it or deny its existence. We have already seen that pain and joy can be felt at the same time. The point is now emphasized: pain and pleasure do not only constitute an indeterminate pair, but they also *mix* with each other. This is again shown by Socrates in a tripartite way. *Some* mixtures of pleasure and pain are those in which both pleasure and pain involve the body, as, for example, *itching* and *scratching*, which Protarchus tends to consider a "mixed evil."[69] *Some* mixtures are those in which the body and the soul contribute the opposite elements, "each adding pain or pleasure to the other's pleasure and pain,"[70] as, for example—we have heard that before—a man suffers from thirst, is pained by his bodily emptiness, but rejoices in his hope to be filled, a hope entertained only by his soul. The *third* kind of mixture is the most important; it is the one in which the soul and only the soul is involved. Socrates gives as examples of pains belonging to this third kind: anger, fear, longing, mourning, love, jealousy, envy—and he asks: "Shall we not find them full of ineffable pleasures?"[71] He then refers—*in one sentence only*—to anger and to mournings and longings in order to show the mixture of pain and of pleasure to them. Protarchus fully agrees. Socrates' next question is: "And you remember, too, how people, at *tragedies, enjoy* the spectacle and at the same time *weep*?"[72]

---

68. See, for example, 34 d 4–8 and 38 b 3–4.
69. 46 a.
70. 47 c.
71. 47 e.
72. 48 a.

"Yes, certainly," says Protarchus. Whereupon Socrates asks: "And the condition of our souls at *comedies* — do you know that there, too, there is a mixture of pain and pleasure?"[73] Protarchus' answer is: "I do not quite understand." Socrates confirms that it is *not easy* to understand such a condition under such circumstances, and Protarchus, on his part, confirms that it is not easy for him. It is not easy for us either.

This is the short beginning of the discussion about the third kind of mixture of pleasure and pain, which involves only the soul. And now, surprisingly, Socrates launches into a *lengthy* explanation of what happens to spectators at comedies. It takes no less than four pages, and ends with Socrates' contention that pain is mixed with pleasure — not only for spectators in the theater, where tragedies and comedies are performed — but also "in all the tragedy and comedy of life."[74] Today, we are prone to call any horrible or simply sad event a "tragedy" and a funny one a "comedy." But that was not done in ancient times. The expression "tragedy and comedy of life" in the dialogue is highly unusual and even paradoxical. It is almost unique; a somewhat similar phrase referring to tragedy, *not* to comedy, can be found only in Plato's *Laws*.[75] Why is this expression used in the *Philebus?* Let us hear what Socrates says.

He takes up *envy* first. Envy is a pain of the soul, but we also see an envious man rejoicing in the evils that befall those close to him. Thus envy is both pain and pleasure. Socrates then takes up the *ridiculous*. The ridiculous is in the main the consequence of a disposition in the human soul which contradicts the famous inscription at Delphi. A ridiculous man is a man who does not know himself. This folly of not knowing oneself can have three aspects: (1) the conceit of being *richer* than one is; (2) the conceit of being more *beautiful* than one is; (3) the conceit of being more *virtuous* than one is, especially *wiser* than one is (δοξοσοφία). This third kind of conceit is the most numerous. Now, we tend to laugh at men thus conceited. But two cases must be distinguished here. Those who are laughed

---

73. *Ibid.*
74. 50 b.
75. 817 b.

at may be strong and able to revenge themselves, and are then powerful, terrible, and hateful; for folly in the powerful is hateful and base. Or they are weak and unable to revenge themselves, and then they are truly ridiculous. When we laugh at the follies of such men, who may be our friends, we feel pleasure. But to feel pleasure at the follies of our friends is what envy brings about, since it is *envy* that makes us rejoice in the evils that befall these our friends, and envy is painful. Therefore, when we laugh at what is ridiculous in our friends, we mix pleasure and pain.

It is not quite clear how all this explains what happens at comedies, although Protarchus appears to be satisfied. Socrates adds that all that was said by him so far concerned only envy, mourning, and anger (he omits *longing*, which was also mentioned by him in that one sentence he uttered before passing on to tragedies and comedies). And now, Socrates declares, he need not go further and Protarchus ought to accept the assertion that there are plenty of mixtures of pain and of pleasure. But now something extraordinary happens that sheds more light on the theme of comedy.

You will remember that the young men, who surround Socrates, extracted from him the promise not to go home before bringing the discussion about pleasure and thoughtfulness to a satisfactory end. And you will also remember that Protarchus, later on, reminded Socrates of this promise and assured him that not one of the young men would let him go before the end of the discussion was reached. Listen to what Socrates says now: "Tell me then: will you let me off, *or will you let midnight come?* I think only a few words are needed to induce you to let me off."[76] How strange! Why on earth does Socrates utter these words? Is this the Socrates who is known for his never abating eagerness to discuss things? Has he grown tired like Philebus? Or is it that *envy* has entered not only the λόγος but also the stage, the "comedy of life" presented in the dialogue? Incredible as it might seem, Socrates appears to be *envious* seeing Philebus asleep, "divinely" asleep, without pleasure and pain.[77] Does that not mean that Socrates is *pained* by this envy and yet also *pleased* by the ridiculous aspect of Philebus' sleep, which

76. 50 d.
77. Cf. *Apology* 40 c–e.

manifests the latter's "conceit of wisdom," the δοξοσοφία of friend Philebus? But what about *us*, who read or hear the words of the dialogue and are the spectators of this "comedy of life"? Well, we are puzzled and *pleased* by realizing that *Socrates* of all people is envious at this moment, and we are also *pained* by witnessing what happens to him. We might refuse to accept that this is what is going on at this moment, but this refusal would only mean that we *expect* to be pained and pleased, *if* we accepted it.

Yes, the dialogue is pleasurable and painful in deed (ἔργῳ), in addition to dealing with pleasure and pain in speech (λόγῳ). And is there any need to mention the pain and the pleasure one feels in reading, or listening to, the dialogue in all its deliberately complex and inordinate convolution? We understand now, I think, why the title of the dialogue is *Philebus*.

Socrates proceeds, of course. He takes up now — and this is a new transition — the *pure* pleasures, that is, pleasures *unmixed* with pain. Socrates lists five kinds of such pleasures, *four* of them conveyed to us by our senses, *one* involving that which cannot be sensed. The first four kinds of pure pleasure have their source in beautiful figures, in beautiful colors, in clear sounds, and in many odors. The beautiful *figures* are *not* beautiful living beings or paintings, but —"says the argument"[78]— a straight line drawn with the help of a ruler, a circular line drawn with the help of a compass, plane figures drawn with the help of these same tools, and solid figures constructed with the help of suitable instruments.[79] The beautiful *colors* are pure colors, in which there is no trace of any other color. Clear *sounds* are those that send forth a single pure tone. The pleasures these figures, colors, and sounds generate are pure pleasures, unmixed with pain. As to the pleasures of smell, they are, as Socrates playfully says, "less divine." The last kind of pure pleasure — and this is deeply serious — is that which has its source in the known or the knowable, accessible to human beings without hunger for learning and without pangs of such hunger.[80] What Socrates means is *contemplation* (θεωρία), which is *not* preceded by ἔρως, the

---

78. 51 c.
79. 53 a–b.
80. 52 a.

desire to know, as we feel it in the pursuit of knowledge. This pleasure of contemplation is felt by exceedingly few.

The transition now made leads to a passage that again has three parts, of which again the third is the most important. The first part extends in some way the realm of pure pleasures by the statement that what characterizes such pleasures is *due measure*. The second part makes us understand that the pure pleasures are, because of their purity, also *true* pleasures. In the third — the longest — part Socrates refutes "certain ingenious people"[81] while accepting one of their premises. These "ingenious people" are reduced a little later to *one* man, and there is hardly any doubt that this man is *Aristippus*. His premise, which Socrates accepts, is that pleasure consists in a process of generation and has *no stable being*. What is rejected by Socrates is that such a process in itself is a good. To refute this assertion, Socrates proposes to consider the relation that the process of *coming* into being (γένεσις) has to *being* (οὐσία). The question is: Which one of the two is for the sake of the other? Protarchus rephrases the question as follows: Do ships exist for the sake of shipbuilding or is shipbuilding for the sake of ships? Protarchus knows the answer to this question, of course, but Socrates gives the answer in an all-comprising form: "Every instance of *generation* is for the sake of some *being* or other, and *all* generation is *always* for the sake of being."[82] Now, the being for the sake of which the process of generation takes place is "of the order of the good," while the process of generation itself is *not* of that order. Therefore, says Socrates, we must be grateful to him who pointed out that there is only a *generation*, but no *being* of pleasure. He makes a laughingstock of all those who find their highest end in pleasure and know that pleasure is nothing but a process of generation. For their highest end is not of the order of the good. Protarchus concludes: "It is a great absurdity, as it appears, Socrates, to tell us that pleasure is a good."[83]

There is a new transition, in which courage, self-restraint and νοῦς are mentioned and which begins to move the dialogue upward. The task is now to consider νοῦς and *knowledge*

---

81. 53 c.
82. 54 c.
83. 55 a.

carefully and to find out what is by nature *purest* in them. We
expect that *their* truest parts will be joined with the truest parts
of *pleasure* in the desired mixed life.

Two kinds of knowledge are distinguished. One is necessary
to *produce* things, the other serves *education and nurture.* The
productive knowledge, the "know-how" of the producing arts,
is taken up first, and here again a division is to be made. Some
of those parts are acquired by practice and toil, aided by guess-
ing, and lack precision. They do not use sufficiently the arts of
counting, measuring, and weighing. This holds, Socrates says,
for music, as it is commonly practiced, for medicine, agriculture,
piloting, and generalship. But in the arts of building, shipbuilding, and housebuilding, for example, there is much more
precision, because measuring and the use of ingenious instruments play a much greater role in them. It is at this point
that Socrates divides the arts of counting and of measuring (not,
however, that of weighing) into two kinds. Some counting refers
to visible and tangible units, which are all unequal; but there
is also counting of units that do not differ at all from each other.
This kind of counting is the basis of the true art of numbering,
of true "arithmetic." The art of measuring may also refer either
to visible and tangible things or to entities that cannot be sensed.
To measure, and to deal with, the latter entities means to be
engaged in "geometry," not for the purpose of production and
trade, but for the purpose of knowing. And this holds also for
the careful study of ratios and proportions. These true arts of
numbering and measuring serve education and nurture. We see
that there is a kind of knowledge *purer* than another, as one
pleasure is *purer* than another. This purity of knowledge brings
about much greater clarity and precision and much more truth.

But there is, beyond that pure mathematical knowledge, the
power of *dialectic.* It deals with Being, True Being, with that
which always *immutably* is. Protarchus remembers at this point
the claim of Gorgias that the art of persuasion, the rhetorical
art, surpasses all other arts. Socrates replies that he was not
thinking of the art that surpasses all others by being the
"greatest," the "best," and the "most useful" to men; he was thinking of the art or the knowledge which is most concerned about
clearness, precision, and *the most true,* however little and of
little use it might be. Socrates asks Protarchus to look neither

at the usefulness nor at the reputation of the various sciences, but to consider whether there is a power in our souls which is *in love with Truth* and does everything for the sake of Truth. Would this power possess thoughtfulness (φρόνησις) and νοῦς in the greatest purity? Protarchus concedes that this must be so.

To be in love with Truth does not mean to possess it or to comtemplate it. It means to pursue it, to try to find it, indefatigably, unremittingly; to pursue it means to submit to the power of discourse, a power that is able to discover in the spoken or silent *words* that which makes speaking and thinking ultimately possible, namely the unchangeable and, thereby, *true* beings. But, as Socrates points out, the many existing arts and the men engaged in them do not submit to the power of discourse, but are satisfied with their opinions. If a man sees fit to investigate nature, he spends his life in studying this world of ours — that is to say, tries to find out how it came into being, how it is acted upon and how it acts itself. By doing that, that man toils to discover transient productions of the present, the future and the past, *not* what unchangeably *always* is. And Socrates asks: "How can we gain anything *stable* about things which have *no stability* whatsoever?"[84] The argument compels us thus to see that the stable, pure, and true, can only be found in what is eternally the same without change or mixture or, Socrates surprisingly adds, "in what is most akin to it."[85] He may mean the moving, but never changing celestial bodies.

This passage which deals with the *purest* knowledge ends with the repeated reference to νοῦς and φρόνησις, which have to be honored most. This reference is the *last* transition in the dialogue to the *last* passage of the dialogue.

This last passage is about *the most desirable life*, in which thoughtfulness and pleasure are mixed. Socrates undertakes now to make this mixture with the help of Protarchus. We expected and still expect that the *pure* pleasures and the *purest* knowledge will be joined in this mixture.

Before the mixing begins, Socrates reminds Protarchus and us of what had been said before. Philebus had claimed that

---

84. 59 b.
85. 59 c.

pleasure was the true goal of every living being and that these
two words, "good" and "pleasant," mean the same thing. Socrates, on the other hand, claimed that "good" and "pleasant"
mean different things and that the share of thoughtfulness in
the good is greater than pleasure's. They had agreed, Socrates
continues, that any living being, in whom the good is present
always, altogether, and in all ways, has no further need of
anything, but is perfectly self-sufficient; but that neither a life
of pleasure unmixed with thoughtfulness nor a thoughtful life
unmixed with pleasure was a desirable life.

Directly related to the task of making the mixture is the task
of winning a clear understanding of the *good* in the well-mixed
life, *or at least an outline of it*,[86] so as to be better able to find
out *to what* in the well-mixed life the second prize should be
assigned. We remember that Socrates had raised the question
before. At that time the possible recipients of the second prize
were νοῦς and pleasure. Note that in this last passage of the
dialogue νοῦς has not been mentioned so far.

This is now what Socrates says jovially and playfully just
before he begins to make the mixture: "Let us make the mixture, Protarchus, with a proper prayer to the gods, Dionysus or
Hephaestus, or whoever he be who presides over the mixing."[87]
Dionysus leads on revellers and presides over orgies; he stands
here for pleasure. Hephaestus is known for his thoughtful and
sober craftsmanship. Socrates continues: "We are like wine
pourers, and beside us are fountains — that of pleasure may be
likened to a fount of *honey*, and the sober, wineless fount of
thoughtfulness to one of pure, health-giving *water* — of which
we must do our best to mix as well as possible."[88]

The first question is: Should Socrates and Protarchus mix
all pleasure with *all* thoughtfulness? Socrates observes that this
would not be safe. It would be better to mix first that pleasure
which was *more truly* pleasure with that knowledge which was
most true and *most precise*. Protarchus agrees. But Socrates is
not satisfied. Let us assume, he says, a man who is thoughtful

---

86. 61 a.
87. 61 b/c.
88. 61 c.

about justice itself, that is, about the εἶδος of justice, and is guided in his reasoning about everything that *truly* is by his apprehension of the intelligible, by his νοεῖν (it is the first time that νοῦς is mentioned in this last passage of the dialogue). If this man is fully cognizant of the mathematical circle and the all-embracing celestial sphere, but is ignorant of our *human* sphere and *human* circles, will this man have *sufficient* knowledge? No, says Protarchus, it would be ridiculous for a man to be concerned only with divine knowledge. "Do you mean," Socrates asks, "that the unstable and impure art of the untrue rule and circle is to be put with the other arts into the mixture?"[89] Yes, says Protarchus, that is necessary, if any man is ever to find his way home. Socrates and Protarchus go further. They put *music*, which they said a while ago was full of guesswork and lacked purity, and *all* the deficient kinds of knowledge mingling with the pure into the mixture.

Then Socrates turns to the pleasures. Here again the pure and true pleasures are not the only ones to be put into the mixture. For the first and only time in the dialogue Socrates mentions "necessary pleasures,"[90] by which he means pleasures connected with the satisfaction of vital needs, and adds them to the pure ones. And the further question arises: Is it not advantageous and harmless to let *all* pleasures be a part of the mixture, just as it was harmless and advantageous to let *all* the arts and *all* knowledge be such a part? Whereupon Socrates says: "There is no use in asking us, Protarchus; we must ask the pleasures themselves and the different kinds of thoughtfulness about one another."[91] That's what Socrates does. He asks first the pleasures: "Would you choose to dwell with the whole of thoughtfulness or with none at all?"[92] And Socrates lets them answer that for any tribe to be solitary and unalloyed is neither possible nor profitable: "We think the best to live with is the knowledge of all other things and, so far as is possible, the perfect knowledge of ourselves"[93] Let us not forget, it is Socrates whom

---

89. 62 b.
90. 62 e.
91. 63 a/b.
92. 63 b.
93. 63 b/c.

we hear speaking. It is highly doubtful whether the pleasures can speak—and can have any knowledge of themselves. And now Socrates turns to thoughtfulness and νοῦς. (It is the second time that νοῦς is mentioned in this last passage of the dialogue.) Socrates asks them whether they want the greatest and most intense pleasures to dwell with them in addition to the true and pure pleasures. And Socrates replies *for them*—that is, for thoughtfulness and νοῦς—that the true and pure pleasures are almost their own, and also those which are united to *health* and *self-restraint* and all those which are handmaids of *virtue*; they should be added to the mixture; as to the pleasures which madden the souls of men, which are the companions of folly and of all the other vices, it would be senseless to mix them with the νοῦς.

This is the third time that νοῦς is mentioned in the passage, while thoughtfulness (φρόνησις), which was also addressed by Socrates, is left out. When Socrates has finished replying in the name of both νοῦς and φρόνησις, he says to Protarchus: "Shall we not say that this reply which the νοῦς has now made for itself and memory and right opinion is thoughtful and sensible?"[94] And Protarchus says: "Very much so." Which νοῦς is this νοῦς? Is it the "divine νοῦς" that Socrates contrasted with his own in his reply to Philebus a long time ago? No, it is *Socrates* who was speaking guided by *his own* νοῦς. It is *not* the νοῦς that the "easy" cosmological account found to be "the cause of all" and that the sages, in exalting themselves, declare to be "king of heaven and earth." It is *not* the fourth tribe of the Promethean gift, which Socrates introduced, fearing to appear ridiculous by doing that. Socrates' *own* νοῦς is responsible for the kind of mixture he makes to produce the life which combines thoughtfulness and pleasure, is the cause of *this life*. It is neither the cause of the commixture of the "limitless" and of the "limit," nor the cause of these first two tribes of the Promethean gift.

What does the original introduction of the νοῦς as the "cause of all" and the subsequent somewhat veiled rejection of this νοῦς mean? I think it means a subtle mocking of Plato's great pupil Aristotle. Aristotle's thoughts must certainly have been familiar

---

94. 64 a.

to Plato in his late years. A passage in an ancient manuscript,[95] that informs us about Aristotle's life, hints at lively controversies between Plato and Aristotle. Plato appears to have nicknamed Aristotle ὁ νοῦς, and to have once said, when Aristotle was not present at a meeting: "The νοῦς is absent; dullness reigns in the lecture room." We do know that the investigation of the different meanings of *cause* (αἰτία) and of the *divine* νοῦς plays a decisive role in Aristotle's works. What the dialogue intimates is that νοῦς is above all a *human* possession, and that Socrates is the embodiment of this νοῦς.

Socrates completes the mixture by pointing to the necessity that *truth* must be a part of it, and then asks what is the most precious in it and the *chief cause* for this mixed life to be most lovable. The answer is: *due measure* and *proportion*, which bring about beauty and excellence. Nobody is ignorant of this. We should more properly, however, consider these three, *beauty, truth, due measure,* as the components of the goodness of the mixture. We see, first: νοῦς is more akin to truth than pleasure; secondly: nothing could be found more immoderate than pleasure and nothing is more in harmony with due measure than νοῦς and knowledge; and thirdly: νοῦς has a greater share in beauty than pleasure.

And now, finally, Socrates gives a list of the best human possessions in their proper order. *First* something like Measure, Due Measure, Propriety, and like everything which must be considered of the same order. *Secondly* comes what is well proportioned, beautiful, has been completed and is sufficient, and all that belongs to that very family. Socrates continues: "As to the *third* — this is my prophecy — if you insist on νοῦς and φρόνησις, you will not wander far from the truth."[96] Is νοῦς relegated to the third place? No, it is elevated to the proper rank, if you consider the role the *triad* played in the entire dialogue. *Fourthly* come the different kinds of knowledge, the arts, the true opinions; and *fifthly* the painless pure pleasures of the soul, some of which accompany *knowledge* and some of which — as we have

95. Codex Marcianus. See Paul Friedländer's "Akademische Randglossen" in *Die Gegenwart der Griechen im Neueren Denken,* Festschrift für Hans-Georg Gadamer, 1960, p. 317.
96. 66 b.

seen — accompany *perceptions* (observe that knowledge was not mentioned before among the pure pleasures, presumably because the *pursuit* of knowledge involves the *desire* to know, involves ἔρως, in which pain and pleasure are mixed). There is no sixth place, says Socrates, quoting Orpheus. He reminds us that neither νοῦς nor pleasure is the good itself, since both are devoid of self-sufficiency. But within the mixed life, which is the victor, νοῦς *has* now been given the second prize, while pleasure — as Socrates' own νοῦς had predicted a long time ago — is further behind than the third place. Note that this holds even for pure pleasure and that the satisfaction of vital needs is not mentioned at all. Pleasure is fifth. We should be aware that, according to the tradition, the people called "Pythagoreans" associated the goddess Aphrodite with the number *five*.

The list given by Socrates is strangely imprecise and inordinate. It is indeed only an *outline* of the good in the most desirable life. The ἄπειρον, the "limitless," the "indeterminate," reigns, though not supremely, in the dialogue.

I shall not keep you until midnight. Good night! But there will be a discussion.

20 ■ Plato's *Ion*

This lecture is, as you know, about Plato's dialogue entitled
Ion. My main purpose is to show how, I think, a Platonic
dialogue ought to be read. The lecture will have two parts. The
first will present to you what *happens* in the dialogue; in the
second part I shall try to describe the wider frame into which
what happens in the dialogue fits.

Socrates meets Ion in Athens. We are inclined to think that
Socrates is known to us, to some extent at least, but we might
be mistaken. As to Ion, his home is Ephesus, an Ionian city on
the shores of Asia Minor. He is well known as a rhapsode. He
tells Socrates that he has just arrived from Epidaurus, where
he attended—as a rhapsode—the festival in honor of Asclepius,
the healing god. What is a rhapsode? A rhapsode (literally: a
stitcher of verses) is a man who, at appropriate occasions, recites
or, better, declaims poetry majestically and touchingly. Socrates
wonders whether the Epidaurians honor the healing god with
a contest of rhapsodes also, and Ion confirms this, adding that
everything else that belongs to the art over which the Muses
preside is involved. We suspect that Socrates wonders what relation the declaiming of poetry has to healing. Socrates—and

Lecture first delivered at St. John's College, Annapolis, October 1, 1971. First published
in the *Claremont Journal of Public Affairs*, Vol. 2, No. 1 (1973).

we — learn that Ion won the first prize in that rhapsodic contest, and Socrates urges him to achieve the same result in Athens
at the Panathenaean festival celebrated in honor of Athena, the
goddess not only of war, but also — among other things — of
health. Ion confidently expects this to happen.

Socrates begins his challenge. He says: "I have been often,
yes, jealous of you rhapsodes, Ion, because of your art" (530b).
The English word "art," which I have just used, translates the
Greek word *technē*. It was implied in Ion's use of the word
mousikē, the art over which the Muses preside. Today, we mean
by "art" something highly admired and respected, attributed
to "creativity" or to "genius" or, at least, to talent, but also
something that is taught to children in school. A similar ambiguity characterizes the word *technē*, as we shall see in a moment, but what is much more emphasized in it than in the
English word "art" is knowledge, the skill, the "know-how," involved in any making, producing, and behaving that men engage
in. In continuing his speech Socrates uses the word *technē* for
the second time, right away. He exposes the sources of his
jealousy: the *technē* of the rhapsode, Socrates says, teaches him
how to adorn his body so that he should look as beautiful as
possible, and it also imposes upon the rhapsode the necessity
of passing all his time with the works of many good poets and
especially with those of Homer, the best and divinest poet of
all of them, so that he would know Homer's thought full well
and not only his words. For, as Socrates suggests, there couldn't
be a good rhapsode, if he did not *understand* what the poet says;
the rhapsode should be an expounder of the poet's thought to
those who listen to him; and it is impossible to be a good expounder, if one does not know *what* the poet says. It is all this
that makes Socrates jealous.

Ion agrees with Socrates. This matter of expounding, says
Ion, is certainly the most laborious part of his art; and he thinks
that he can speak about Homer better and provide more and
better *thoughts* about Homer than anybody else.

"Good news, Ion!" exclaims Socrates (530d). He understands
Ion's words to mean that Ion will not grudge him an exhibition
of this power. And Ion stresses that it is indeed worth-while hearing how well he has adorned Homer, so much so, that he deserves
to be crowned with a golden crown by the lovers of Homer. In

mentioning his "adorning" of Homer, Ion uses the very word Socrates used with reference to the rhapsode's body.

It turns out that Socrates is not yet ready to listen to Ion's exhibition. Instead he begins to question Ion, and this questioning leads to most comical and, at the same time, most serious results.

The first question is whether Ion is so marvelously skillful about Homer *only* or also about other poets. Ion's reply is: about Homer only, and that is sufficient. Ion agrees that there are things about which Homer and Hesiod, for example, both say the same; in such cases, Ion asserts, he would of course expound equally well both Homer's and Hesiod's words. But what happens, Socrates inquires, if the two poets do not agree, as, for example, about the "art of divination"? Who then would expound better what the two poets say, Ion or one of the good seers? Ion's answer is: one of the seers.

We have to note that the first and *only* example chosen by Socrates to illustrate possible disagreement among the two poets, namely the "art of divination," that is, the *technē* called *mantikē*, shows clearly the ambiguity of the word *technē*. Does the seer, the *mantis*, possess any knowledge about his seeing, prophesying, divining? Is the "know-how" of divination at his disposal? Would he be a *seer* if it were?

The next point of Socrates is that *Homer* and *all the other poets* spoke about *the same things*, about war, about the mutual intercourse of men, about the gods in their intercourse with each other and with men, about the heavens and Hades, about the origin of gods and heroes. Socrates does not say whether the poets *agreed* or *disagreed* in speaking about these things. It is Ion who makes the point that the other poets did not treat these things the way Homer did. He asserts that they did it in a far worse way. We remember that Socrates, too, called Homer the best and divinest of all the poets. But now Socrates turns to Ion's ability to distinguish between *good* and *bad* ways of speaking about something. If the talk is about numbers, who will be able to distinguish between the good and the bad speakers? The answer is, Ion has to agree, a man who possess the *art of numbering*, the "arithmetical art," the *technē arithmētikē*, that is to say, the "know-how" of counting and of handling numbers. And if the talk is about wholesome food, the man who will be able to distinguish between the good and the bad speakers is a *doctor*, that is, a man who possesses the *art of healing* (the *technē iatrikē*). In summing up, Socrates can now state that, whenever many people talk about the same thing, one and the same man will know who speaks well and who speaks badly. We have to surmise that Socrates means that this man possesses the appropriate knowledge, the appropriate *technē*. And Socrates concludes that, since Homer and the other poets speak about the same things and Ion knows who among all of these poets speaks well and who speaks in a worse way, he must be marvelously skillful and knowledgeable about *all* these poets, that is, we understand, must have the suitable *technē* which in this case ought to be called the rhapsodic art (538b). Socrates, we remember, had spoken of this *technē* at the beginning of the conversation.

Ion cannot help accepting Socrates' conclusion and is thereby led to wonder *why* he "simply" (*atechnōs*, pun on *átechnos*) drops into a doze when he hears somebody discuss poets other than Homer and wakes up and pays close attention and has plenty to say himself *only* when Homer is mentioned. Socrates claims to know the answer. "This is not difficult to guess," he says (532c); and he states explicitly that Ion is clearly unable to speak on Homer *with art and knowledge* (*technēi kai epistēmēi*), for if he were able to do it with art, that is knowingly, he would be able to speak about *all* the *other* poets as well. We have indeed to suppose, Socrates says, that the *whole* in question here is the *art of poetry* (*poiētikē*), and to speak about it knowingly means to *know* it *as a whole*, that is, to know what *all* the poets said and meant. Socrates asks Ion whether this is so.

All that Ion has to say in answer to this rather puzzling question is "Yes" (532c). Socrates is not certain whether Ion understands his point, to wit, that whatever the art, the *technē*, may be, once it is given *as a whole*, the way to look at its parts is always the same. Socrates will expound this, therefore, at some length by giving quite a few examples. But before doing that he asks Ion: "Are you in need of hearing from me what I mean?" And Ion replies that he certainly is: "for I enjoy listening to you sages." Whereupon Socrates remarks: "Surely it is you rhapsodes and actors, and the men whose poems you chant, who are sage; whereas I speak nothing but the plain truth, as a simple layman might" (532d). And he adds that what he means is indeed a trivial commonplace, not arrived at by rules of art, but within reach of everyone.

Here are the examples. There is the whole *art of painting*. It is impossible to find a man capable of declaring which paintings of *one* painter are good or bad and totally incapable of judging the works of any other painter. The same holds of the *art of sculpture*, of *flute-playing*, of *harp-playing*, of *singing to the harp*, and of the *art of rhapsody*. With these examples Socrates changes his point somewhat: the skillful and knowledgeable speaker is able to distinguish not only between the good and the bad artists but also between the good and the bad *works* of any one of those artists. Could there be a man, for instance, who would be able to talk with understanding about a number of rhapsodes, but would be unable to say what Ion of Ephesus does *well* and what he does *badly*?

Ion is compelled to accept Socrates' point; but this makes the experience he has of himself completely incomprehensible to him: he excels all men in speaking on Homer, everybody is in agreement about that (let us not forget: he just won the first prize in Epidaurus), but he cannot speak well on the other poets. How come! It is up to Socrates, Ion says, to see what that means.

Socrates retorts that he *does* see what it means and launches into a lengthy speech. *What* he says and the *way* he says it make this speech the central *event* in the drama which the dialogue presents. Socrates first repeats what he had said before about Ion's ability to speak well on Homer and Homer only: this ability is not due to a *technē*, to any knowledge that Ion possesses. But Socrates now supplies a positive addition to that statement: this ability of Ion stems from a "divine power"; and Socrates provides a vivid image of this power and of its work. It is like the power in the "magnetic" stone, so called, namely "magnetic," by Euripides, the *poet*. This power not only makes the stone attract iron rings but also infuses itself into those rings so that they can attract other rings and thus form sometimes a long chain of iron rings suspended one from another; the power in all of them stems from that one "magnetic" stone. The "magnetic" power helps us to understand the power of the Muses which makes some men spellbound and spreads through them to other men so as to hold them all in a chain. It is thus that all *good poets* indite all their beautiful epic or lyrical poems not because they are guided by a *technē*, by some knowledge, but because they are spellbound and possessed by a Muse, just as the Corybantian worshippers and the bacchants are frantic and possessed and *not* in their senses. The poets tell us, they do, that (I quote—534b) "they bring us songs from honeyed fountains, culling them out of the gardens and dells of the Muses—like the bees, and winging the air as these do. And what they tell is true." I keep quoting: "For a poet is a light and winged and sacred thing, and is unable ever to indite, to be a poet, until he is spellbound and out of his senses, and his wits are no longer in him." Socrates sums up: Poets compose and utter so many and so beautiful things about the deeds of men—as Ion does about Homer—not by art (by *technē*) but by a "divine allotment" (*theiāi moirāi*) (534c): it is thus that each poet is able to compose well only that kind of poetry to which the *Muse* has stirred him, but is not good at any other kind of verse. Indeed, if the poets knew *by rules of art* how to speak well on *one* thing, they would know how to speak on *all*. At this point Socrates' speech grows in intensity and straightforwardness. I quote: "That is why the *god* takes away the wits of these men and uses them as his ministers, just as he does with soothsayers and godly seers, in order that we who hear them may know that it is *not they* who utter these priceless words, when they are out of their wits, but that it is the god himself who speaks and addresses us through them" (534c-d). And to confirm this, Socrates finally cites the case of a most mediocre poet, who had never composed a single poem that deserved any mention at all and then produced a hymn which is in everyone's mouth, a song that is—as this man says himself—"simply" "something found by the Muses" (534d). The god apparently intended him to be a sign that beautiful poems are not human or the work of men, but divine and the work of gods, and that the poets are merely the expounders of the gods, according as each is possessed by one of them. And Socrates asks: "Or do you not think that I speak the truth, Ion?" (535a).

"By Zeus," Ion exclaims, "I do." And he explains: "You do touch my soul with your words, Socrates, and it does seem to me that the good poets expound to us what comes from the gods."

Whereupon Socrates adds — with Ion's approval — that the rhapsodes expound the poets' words and are thus expounders of expounders.

Let us reflect on what has happened. We do remember that, just a while ago, Socrates called himself a "simple layman" who utters nothing but the plain truth. We might have smiled hearing this, thinking of Socrates' dissembling ways. Yet we *do* assume that Socrates speaks the truth. But is his long speech a truthful speech? How can he *know* that beautiful poems are the work of gods? How can he *know* that this claim of the poets is a true claim? It is certainly not something that could be characterized as plain truth. Is not his speech, which reaches poetic heights and touches not only Ion's soul, but also *our* souls, dictated by a Muse? Or rather, isn't Socrates playing the Muse himself? Indeed, and this is the point, he is.

Let us have a closer look at Socrates' speech. Ion's rhapsodic art is mentioned at the beginning of the speech, once more briefly in the middle of the speech, and is then taken up again only at the final exchange of questions and answers between Socrates and Ion. Socrates puts at the top of the ladder the divine power, the Muse or the god; one rung below — the poet, the *good* poet; two rungs below — the rhapsode; three rungs below — the audience, the people who listen to the rhapsode, all of them spellbound. The bulk of the speech deals with the *poets*, the *good poets*. But these poets are grouped together with the soothsayers and seers (the *manteis*), whose non-existent *technē* was mentioned earlier as the one Homer and Hesiod allegedly disagreed about. In composing their poems, the speech asserts, the poets are out of their senses, and so are the rhapsodes when they declaim those poems. And this is what Ion, spellbound and possessed by the Muse, that is, by Socrates, wholeheartedly accepts. It is hardly possible not to be amused by the double change which has occurred in the dialogue, by that of the Muse into the "simple-minded" Socrates and by that of Socrates into the "magnetic" Muse.

Socrates now proceeds to check whether what he described in his speech, and was agreed to by Ion, actually occurs when Ion declaims Homer's verses. Is Ion, Socrates asks, in his senses or is he carried out of himself when he declaims verses which move his audience; does not his soul, possessed by a god, find herself among the very things he describes? And Ion reports how his eyes are filled with tears when he relates a tale of woe, and how his hair stands on end and his heart throbs when he speaks of horrors. Ion agrees that at such moments he is *out* of his senses; as Socrates puts it, Ion *weeps* although not robbed of his precious attire and his golden crowns and he is *panic-stricken* in the presence of more than twenty thousand *friendly* people, none of whom is stripping or injuring him. Does Ion know, Socrates then inquires, that the rhapsodes makes the spectators in their audience feel the very same way? He knows it very well, Ion replies. Let me quote: "For I have to pay the *closest attention* to them; since, if I set *them* crying, *I* shall laugh myself because of the money I take, but if *they* laugh, *I* myself shall cry because of the money I lose" (535e). We see: the spell has been broken; Ion now asserts that he is *not* out of his senses when he declaims and weeps and acts as if panic-stricken; neither the Socratean Muse nor any other Muse possesses him. The contrast between Ion's previous assertion and the words he now uses is as great as it is comical. That does not mean that Ion has changed; it means that Ion has now revealed what kind of man he as rhapsode truly is. Socrates' questioning and the Muse Socrates was playing have brought this about. The point we have reached lies at the very middle of the dialogue.

Socrates can now abandon the guise of the Muse. We see him indeed repeat what he had said before in his lengthy speech, but what he says now is much shorter and not "poetic" at all. He describes the chain reaching from the god or the Muse down to the audience, but he now adds to the rings mentioned before other rings attached *obliquely* to the chain; they represent choral dancers and masters and under-masters of the dance. It is indeed not straight-forwardness but *obliquity* that characterizes the new speech. Socrates puns on the term "is possessed" (*katechetai*) and equates it, in view of the image of the rings, with the term "is held" (*echetai*) (536b). Most of the rhapsodes are possessed and held by Homer, as Ion is. But the main point is again that Ion says what he says not by art or knowledge (*ou technēi oud' epistēmēi*) but by "divine allotment and possession" (*theiāi moirāi kai katokōchēi*) (536c).

Ion is not moved now by Socrates' speech. On the contrary, he does not believe that Socrates could convince him that he, Ion, is possessed and mad when he praises Homer. Hearing him speak about Homer, Socrates would not believe that himself. But Socrates again postpones listening to Ion's exhibition. He begins questioning Ion again.

Can Ion speak well about things in Homer of which Ion happens not to have any knowledge? About the art of chariot-driving, for example? It is the charioteer and nobody else who will know best whether Homer is right or not when he speaks about this art, and Ion has to agree. Ion cannot but assent again to Socrates' statement that the ability to know about *one definite kind of work* has been assigned to *each* of the arts (and Socrates inserts in a rather strange and deliberately strange way: assigned "by the god") (537c). What we know by the art of piloting we cannot know by the art of healing, what we know by the art of healing we cannot know by the art of carpentry, and so on. Socrates himself begins quoting from the *Iliad* and the *Odyssey*. He does it four times, three times inaccurately and only once accurately. Ion has to agree that it is not for the rhapsode to discern whether Homer speaks correctly or not, but for the doctor in the first case, for the fisherman in the second case, for the seer in the third and fourth cases. (We should not forget, by the way, that the seer's "art" is not a *technē* at all.) Socrates then invites Ion to pick out passages from Homer, the rightness or wrongness of which the rhapsode *alone* should be able to discern. Ion claims — what else could he do? — that this holds of *all* passages. Socrates reminds him of the passages they just went through and which the rhapsode was incompetent to judge. Ion cannot help excluding these passages and the arts they imply. Pressed by Socrates to tell what arts the rhapsode will be competent to judge, Ion assigns to the rhapsode the vast knowledge of things which it is fitting for a *man* to say, and of those which it is fitting for a *woman* to say, and again of those for a *slave*, and of those for a *freeman*, and of those for him who has to *obey*, and of those for him who is *in command*. But it turns out, as Ion has to admit, that the *pilot* will know better than the rhapsode what the captain of a storm-tossed vessel should say, and that the *doctor* will know better than the rhapsode what he who takes care of a sick man ought to say. If a slave is a *cowherd*, it is *not* the rhapsode who will know better what to say about cattle tending. And if a woman is a *spinning-woman*, it is *not* the rhapsode who will know better what to say about the working of wool. But what about a man who is a *general exhorting his men*? What *such* a man should say, Ion *immediately* declares, the rhapsode *will* know. And when Socrates asks him whether he is knowledgeable about generalship as a *general* or as a *rhapsode*, we hear Ion state that he does not perceive any difference here. He explicitly says that the rhapsodic art and the art of generalship are *one* art, not two. It follows that anyone who is a good rhapsode is also a good general, but Ion cannot admit, thus contradicting himself, that anyone who is a good general is also a good rhapsode. He probably assumes — and rightly so — that some generals are not good at exhorting their men. Since Ion considers himself the best rhapsode in Greece, he is also, in his own eyes, the best general in Greece, and Ion adds that he learned to be that from Homer. For a short while the highly amusing question is debated why the Athenians have not chosen Ion to be their general. Socrates then reproaches Ion for not telling in what his knowledge of Homer consists and for finally escaping in the guise of a general so as to avoid displaying his wisdom concerning Homer. If Ion is an artist, that is, a man who *knows*, and deceives Socrates by not telling him *what* he knows, he is wicked. If Ion is *not* an artist but speaks fully and finely about Homer by divine allotment, possessed by Homer, and without any knowledge, he is not doing anything wrong. Here then is the choice: to be *dishonest* or to be *divine*. Ion (I quote): "The difference is great, Socrates; for it is far nobler to be called divine" (542a). And Socrates closes the dialogue by assigning this nobler title to Ion: he is to be known as a *divine* and not an artful, that is *knowing*, praiser of Homer.

You realize, I am sure, the utterly comic character of the dialogue and the disparagement of what in this dialogue Socrates calls the *theia moira*, the "divine allotment." But you also realize that the mocking of the rhapsode is meant to cast doubt, above all, on the *poets*, whose works the rhapsodes declaim. And this is a serious and difficult matter, to which I shall devote the second part of this lecture.

In Plato's *Phaedrus* we hear Socrates describe the greatest blessings as derived from these four kinds of madness: the prophetic, the cathartic, the poetic, and the erotic (244a ff). In this connection the expression "divine allotment" is used again. The third kind of madness, *the poetic*, comes about when one is possessed by the Muses. I quote: "He who without the madness of the Muses comes to the doors of poetry, confident that he will be a good poet by art (*ek technēs*), meets with no success, and the poetry of the sane man vanishes into nothingness before that of the madmen" (245a). Does that mean that the Socrates of the *Phaedrus* is serious about "divine allotment"? The answer to this question depends on our understanding of "madness" (mania, in Greek: *mania*) as this word is used in the *Phaedrus*. It is first mentioned in the description of the first kind of madness, *the prophetic one*. The men of old who invented names, we read in the text, thought that madness was neither shameful nor disgraceful. I quote: "Otherwise they would not have connected the very word '*mania*' with the noblest of arts, that which foretells the future, by calling it the *manic art* (*manikē*). No, they gave this name thinking that 'mania,' when it comes by divine allotment, is a noble thing, but nowadays people call it the *mantic art* (*mantikē*), tastelessly inserting a *T* into the word, 'mantic' instead of 'manic' " (244c). Socrates is dissembling: the so-called mantic art is, to begin with, not an art, not a *technē*, and it is not the alleged insertion of the letter T into the word "manic" which is to be condemned; it is the soothsayers, the seers themselves, who — on the whole, I repeat, on the whole — are contemptible and ridiculous, as Plato often enough implies or even explicitly states in his dialogues. The "divine allotment" dispensed to these seers is an empty fraud. But there are exceptions, and Socrates is one of them. He *does* prophesy sometimes. Right here, in the *Phaedrus*, about to begin his recantation, his palinode about divine madness to defend the *lover*, he says: "I am, yes, a seer (a *mantis*), not a very good one, but — as poor writers might say — it is just sufficient for what I need" (242c). Socrates is again dissembling, of course: his prophetic power is clairvoyance; it can be attributed to "divine allotment," but it is *not* madness. In that same palinode of the *Phaedrus*, Socrates, summarizing what he said before about the erotic kind of madness, describes the lover as one who, when he sees the beautiful here, on earth, remembers the *true* beauty, feels his wings growing and would like to fly away, but cannot; like a bird he gazes upward and neglects the things below; and thus, Socrates says, this fourth kind of madness is *imputed* to the lover (249d-e: *aitian echei hos manikos diakeimenos*). That is to say: the state a true lover is in *looks* like madness because we are usually insufficiently aware of what loving means. Can this be said also of the state a good poet is in? You remember what Socrates says in the *Ion:* the ability to know about *one definite* kind of *work* has been assigned to each of the arts, and I mentioned that Socrates explicitly and rather strangely inserts that this assignment is made "by the god." Why does Socrates insert these words? The answer is: he inserts them to hint at the wide range of meanings in the expression "divine allotment." This expression might be used farcically as in the case of the rhapsode Ion; it might be applied with seriousness to the knowledge inherent in any *technē* and with even deeper seriousness, although ambiguously, to the work of *erōs*, of love. The question we face is: *In what sense is it applied to a work of poetry?* In what sense is a good poet "mad"? Let me be bold, very bold, and try to answer that question by speaking about Homer's *Iliad*, thus running the risk of becoming a rhapsodic expounder.

Disregarding the more or less superficial division into books and even allowing for all kinds of tampering with, and dislocations of, the original song, there is no denying that the decisive events are crowded into the last third of the *Iliad*. In the first half events of great significance certainly do occur: the quarrel between Agamemnon and Achilles which leads Achilles' withdrawing from the fight; the death and the wounding of many warriors; the Diomedean terror; the wounding of two gods; the encounter of Diomedes and Glaucus; the peaceful scenes in Troy; the unsuccessful embassy to Achilles; inconclusive duels among men and wonderfully treacherous actions on the part of the gods. All these events contribute in varying degrees to the unfolding of the plot. (For there *is* a plot in the *Iliad*.) In the main, however, the battle is swaying back and forth all the time until finally the Trojans reach the ships of the Achaeans. During all that time Achilles sits in his tent, sulking, and only occasionally watching the fight. The pivotal event, the death of Patroclus, which changes, which reverses everything, occurs very late in the poem. It is as if the poem took an exceedingly long breath to reach that point and afterwards rushed with breathtaking speed to its end. This is the more remarkable since the entire period of time the poem encompasses is one of 49 days and Patroclus' death occurs on the 26th day, that is, very nearly in the middle of that period.

There are two events — among many others — which I have not mentioned at all. Yet it is these two events that seem to be the two foci from which all light dispersed throughout the poem stems.

The first takes place when Thetis, Achilles' mother, goes up to Zeus to ask for his help on behalf of her son, reminding Zeus of the help he once received from her. She wants Zeus to turn the scales of the war, to let the Trojans have the upper hand until finally, in the hour of the Achaeans' greatest peril, Achilles, *and only Achilles*, might be able to save *them* from certain defeat, lead them to victory, and thus regain *his* honor, which he allegedly lost through Agamemnon's action. It is then said: "But Zeus, the cloud-gatherer, said nothing at all to her and sat in silence for a long while (*dēn*)" (I, 511–12). An awful silence! Thetis repeats her plea. At last, Zeus consents and nods, a sign of an irrevocable decision. Olympus shakes. Thetis departs, apparently satisfied that she has accomplished her mission. Has she?

The second event (XVIII, 165–229) occurs after Patroclus' death, while the battle for Patroclus' body rages before the ships between Hector and the Aiantes and while Thetis is on her way to get new arms for her son from Hephaestus. Hera sends Iris to Achilles to urge him to intervene in the struggle for Patroclus' body. Since Achilles has no arms at this juncture, he is asked by Iris to do nothing but to show himself to the Trojans, to frighten them by his mere appearance. Achilles, "dear to Zeus" (203), obeys and does more than what Hera through Iris asked him to do. Pallas Athene, who is nearby, does her share: she casts the tasseled aegis around his shoulders and she sets a crown in the guise of a golden cloud about his head, and from it issues a blazing flame. Thus he appears — alone, separated from the other Achaeans — in the sight of the foe, a flaming torch. But not only does he appear, he shouts, three times, a terrible shout, clearly heard — and "from afar Pallas Athene uttered her voice" (217–18). Unspeakable confusion and terror seizes the Trojans. Patroclus' body is saved.

What kind of shout is this? Is it one of triumph? Or threat? Is it an ordinary war cry, raised to a very high pitch? It is certainly not like the bellowing of the wounded Ares (V, 859, 863). The verb used to describe that shout has a range of meanings. One of them is "crying out of grief." Why does Achilles shout now, though not urged to do so by Iris? Certainly, to frighten the Trojans, to make them desist from Patroclus' body. But can this shouting fail to express the unspeakable pain that fills his heart, the pain which had just brought his mother to him from the depth of the sea? Here indeed is a terrible sight to behold: a man raised to his highest glory by Pallas Athene, wearing the aegis, crowned by flames, truly godlike — and this same man crushed by grief, miserable in his awareness of having himself brought the immensity of this grief upon himself. The apotheosis of Achilles is the seal of his doom. And it is his voice, his brazen voice, his terrible shouting, which brings terror to the foe, that expresses his misery and his doom (XVIII, 228). Pallas Athene's voice seems but a weak echo of that of Achilles or is even completely drowned out by the latter's intensity.

But are not these two events, the long silence of Zeus and the shouting of Achilles, related?

Does not Achilles' shout sonorously echo Zeus' silence? Can we not guess now why Zeus remained silent for a long while? Surely, he had to take account of the susceptibilities of his wife, as any husband would — and in his marital relations Zeus is no exception — but is it only Hera whom he was silently thinking about? Must he not have been concerned about the whimsical nature of Achilles' plight and Thetis' plea? And, on the other hand, how could he have refused to satisfy Thetis in whose debt he was? Is it not right then and there that Zeus decided, in wisdom and sadness, irrevocably too, to accede to Thetis' demand, to give honor and glory to Achilles, but to do so in a manner which neither Thetis nor Achilles expected? He decided that *Patroclus* should be *slain* and — what is more — that his beloved son, *Sarpedon*, should be slain by Patroclus to balance the loss Achilles will suffer by the loss he, Zeus, himself will suffer. There will be a moment when Zeus will hesitate about Sarpedon's death, but Hera will persuade him to let Sarpedon perish. While the tide of the battle is being reversed, Patroclus' approaching death is announced by Zeus *twice*; the steps which lead to it are carefully pointed out (VIII, 476; XV, 64-7; XI, 604, 790-804). Achilles will get what he wants, but at the price of the greatest loss — the loss of his beloved friend, of his *other self* (XVIII, 79-82). In the hour of his triumph he will be the most miserable of men. The coincidence of triumph and misery characterizes a situation as *tragic*, in the strict sense of this much abused word. Achilles grasps Zeus' intent. He says himself: "Not all the thoughts of men does Zeus fulfill" (XVIII, 328) — as Homer had said before, commenting on Achilles' prayer before the slaying of Patroclus: "One thing the father granted him, the other he denied" (XVI, 250). Zeus denied him the safe return of Patroclus while granting him glory. Achilles' suffering at the moment of his triumph is Achilles' own. It cannot be matched by anything on Olympus. It is as much the prerogative of a mortal as it is the attribute of a hero. This is one of the reasons — perhaps *the* reason — why we are deeply moved while reading, or listening to, the *Iliad*. And this means that we are, at the same time, pleased and pained beyond words.

We are asking in what sense is the good poet "mad," as Plato makes Socrates claim in the *Phaedrus*. Was Homer "mad" when he indited the *Iliad*? Does not the highly articulated sequence of events in the *Iliad* depend on the poet's familiarity with human frailty and human strength and on his masterly skill in presenting them, which skill is but an expression of the knowledge of the rules of art, of the poetic *technē*, he possesses? But should not, on the other hand, the *uniqueness* of what is presented to us be understood as something *found* or *spontaneously produced* by the poet, beyond anything he might otherwise know, and, therefore, as the result indeed of a peculiar "madness"? It is difficult to deny, I think, that both, sane sobriety and mad exuberance, mark the work of the good poet. This duality, merging into oneness, is hard to grasp. It makes Socrates speak of "divine allotment" in a serious and yet again ambiguous way. And what I said applies, of course, not only to the *Iliad*, but to all kinds of poetic works. We *do* understand that *without* the knowledge inherent in the poetic *techne*, *without serious* thought, the poetic "madness" becomes ridiculous, be the madman a rhapsode like Ion or a man who *claims*, who *wants* to be a poet, not knowing what poetry requires. Hence the neverceasing flow of *so-called* poetry and the pretentious, "rhapsodic" way of speaking about "art," prevailing at almost all times and especially today.

It might be useful to remind ourselves at this point of the way Dante, the poet, spoke about poetry. In his Latin treatise *De vulgari eloquentia* (in English: *On Vernacular Eloquence*) Dante asserts that true poetry must rest on these three pillars: alertness of mind (*strenuitas ingenii*), steadfastness in the practice of the art (*assiduitas artis*) and familiarity with the sciences (*habitus scientiarum*). Only poetry thus endowed and equipped can serve as nourishment to the human soul. And I quote: "Let therefore those who, innocent of art and knowledge, and trusting to genius alone, rush forward upon the highest subjects, which must be sung in the highest style, be confounded in their folly and let them refrain from such presumption."

There is another aspect of poetry, all-important to Plato, I have not touched on so far. The deeply serious background of the *Ion* cannot be sufficiently gauged, if we do not consider the role epic and tragic poetry plays in the education and nurture of the young. Homer's and Hesiod's verses, well-known and quoted again and again, must have had a deep impact on the *best* of the young, not only in Plato's time. Plato's concern is the nature of this impact and its relation to our understanding of what is truly noble and unmistakably true. That's why Plato lets Socrates censure the poets wittingly and harshly, especially in the second, third, and tenth book of the *Republic*. What is appropriate to the gods in their intercourse with each other and with men, what should be praised and blamed in the actions of men, how the narration of events and the reporting of speeches ought to be done — all this becomes part and parcel of the criticism of poetic lore.

No less important to Plato is the "mixture" of pleasure and pain which we experience in coping with tragic poetry. I invite you to consider what this "mixture" implies. Plato's *Philebus* might be of some help.

21 ■ Speech, Its Strength and Its Weaknesses

To undertake to speak about speech means to embark upon an endless task. Yet there are strict limits that I have to observe and to be aware of: limits of time, of redundancy, of attentiveness on your part. I shall have to focus your attention on what people mostly concerned about speech have said. These were the people whom we call οἱ φιλόσοφοι, the "lovers of wisdom" among the Greeks. But I shall also have to appeal to an understanding of what usually happens to speech, to an understanding which those people do not seem to have had. I shall be as brief as possible, and I hope you will not mind my careful—nay, my pedantic use of English and Greek words.

(Parenthetical remark: Some of what I am going to say I have said before in lectures and in print, *but not all* of it.)

Let me begin by quoting from Plato's dialogue entitled *Phaedo.* This dialogue pretends to describe what happened during the very last day of Socrates. Attentive reading shows that the content of the dialogue is mythical, but that the mythical frame allows us to become aware of what Plato understood to be Socrates' unique and overwhelming impact. At a crucial point of the dialogue (95 e ff.) Socrates, after silently looking back

Lecture first delivered at St. John's College, Annapolis, February 23, 1973. First published in *The College*, Vol. XXV, No. 2 (July, 1973).

into himself for quite a while, reaches — in speaking — far back
into his own youth. He wanted very much, he reports, to find
out, with regard to any single thing or occurrence, what was
responsible for its coming into being, its passing away, its being
the way it was; but he could not find any satisfactory answers.
Nor could he learn anything from anybody else, not even from
the great Anaxagoras. He had to abandon the way in which questions like these were dealt with in the various versions of the
"inquiry into nature" (περὶ φύσεως ἱστορία). He decided to embark upon a different journey, a "second journey," which means
he decided to take to the oars, since the wind had failed. This
is the presentation he makes of his new endeavor.

By looking directly at whatever presents itself in our familiar
world, at things and their properties, at human affairs and actions, we run the risk of being blinded, as people do when they
observe the sun during an eclipse, if they do not look at its image on some watery surface. That may well have happened to
those investigators of nature. To avoid being blinded, Socrates
thought he had to "have recourse to spoken words" (εἰς τοὺς
λόγους καταφυγεῖν) and "see in them the truth of whatever is"
(99 e).

In the dialogue entitled *Philebus*, Plato again makes Socrates
refer to men engaged in the study of nature (59 a–c): these men
want to understand how this world of ours came into being,
how it is acted upon and how it acts itself, that is to say, they
are trying to discover transient productions of the present, the
future, and the past, *not* what unchangeably *always* is. To
discover the immutable it is necessary to rely on the power of
discourse (ἡ τοῦ διαλέγεσθαι δύναμις—57 e), in exchanging
questions and answers with oneself and with others. The power
of discourse is the power inherent in human speech, this marvel,
let me say, this greatest marvel perhaps under the sun.

The Greek noun λόγος and the Greek verb λέγειν have a
vast range of meanings. They may refer to reckoning, account-
ing, measuring, relating, gathering, picking up (let us not forget
the English words "col*lect*" and "se*lect*," derived from λέγειν).
But, above all, they refer to *speaking, discoursing, arguing,
discussing, reasoning*. That's how we have to understand Aristotle's statement (*Politics* I, 2, 1253 a 10): λόγον . . . μόνον
ἄνθρωπος ἔχει τῶν ζῴων, "man alone among living beings

possesses speech," and that implies: man alone possesses the ability to *understand* the spoken word, to understand articulated speech.

We mean by speech — everybody means by it — a sequence of sounds uttered by somebody in such a way as to be understandable to others. The verb "to understand" refers primarily, though not uniquely, to speech. Hearing somebody speak, we may say; "I understand what you are saying." We may, in fact, misunderstand, but even misunderstanding involves understanding. But *what* do we understand in hearing somebody speak? Not the sounds in themselves, the audible low and high pitched noises issuing from somebody's mouth (or some machine, for that matter). We *hear* these noises, but hearing is not understanding. That is why we do not understand speech in a foreign tongue. In a manner which, itself, is hardly or not at all understandable, the sounds carry with them — or embody or represent — something else, precisely that which *makes* us understand, whenever we understand. This source and target of our understanding consists of units to which single words correspond as well as of combinations of units to which sequences of words correspond. The speaker and the hearer share — or, at least, intend to share — the understanding of those units and of those combinations of units. The speaker transposes what he means into sounding words variably intoned, and the hearer who understands reverses that process in reaching back to the intended meaning. The intended meaning is what the Greeks call τὸ νοητόν (νοητόν being a verbal adjective of νοεῖν, which means "to *receive* the intelligible"). Among the intelligible units, the νοητά, there are two kinds: some are intelligible by themselves, some *help* us to *receive* those first ones, help us to *understand* what is being said. Speech and understanding are inseparable. Λόγος means inseparably both speech and that which can be and is being understood *in* speech. It is in *man* and, to repeat, *only* through *man* that λόγος manifests itself conspicuously. Neither birds nor porpoises nor seals have λόγος, though they are able to "communicate" with each other and even with human beings.

We all remember, I think, a phrase that Homer uses so often when describing human speech, the phrase "winged words" (ἔπεα πτερόεντα). Whence this image? In most cases the phrase occurs when a personage, a god or a man, addresses another single personage, a god or a man. Occasionally it is also used when someone speaks to a group or a crowd of people. Minstrels in Homer are never said to utter or sing "winged words." Now, words are not call "winged" to indicate their soaring or lofty quality. The image seems rather to imply that words, after escaping "the fence of the teeth," as Homer puts it, are guided swiftly, and therefore surely, to their destination, the ears and the soul and the *understanding* of the addressee. It is more difficult to reach a crowd of men than a single man. Exertions of a special kind are then required.

What is speech "about?" About everything man is familiar with — the sky and the earth, the rivers and the sea, the living beings around him, on land, in water, in the air, the things he himself builds and produces, as well as the tools and appurtenances that his arts and skills require to produce those things, and furthermore, the knowledge that guides his arts and skills, not only to satisfy his most elementary needs, but also to establish customs and institutions in which his life flows from generation to generation, in happiness or misery, in friendship or enmity, in praise or blame, and to which customs and institutions he is attached beyond his most pressing wants. That is what his speech and his understanding are *mostly* about.

What we say, however circuitously or confusedly or loosely, is said in words and sentences, each of which conveys immediate meaning. The λόγος cannot help moving in the medium of the immediately understandable. But words and sentences can also be involuntarily or deliberately ambiguous. We can play on words. Plato's dialogues, for example, are replete with puns. However, ambiguities and puns are only possible because words and sentences carry with them several distinct meanings which, separately, are clearly understood. To be sure, speech can be obscure. But it can be obscure only because the clarity of some of its parts impinges, or seems to impinge, on the clarity of others.

Speech, then, presents to the understanding of the listener what the speaker himself understands. It presents to the listener nothing but combinations of νοητά, of intelligibles. In doing that, however, speech speaks about all the things and all the properties of things that abound around us, all the special circumstances and situations in which we find ourselves. The question arises: Do the νοητά, the intelligibles, presented to us in speech, have their foundation in themselves, or do they stem from the things and circumstances spoken about? Does not human speech translate the language, the γλῶσσα, of the *things* themselves?

Let me turn for a moment to the way things and events around us have been and are being referred to. In Galileo's words: "The *book* of Nature is written in mathematical characters." Descartes said: "The science contained in the great *book* of the world . . . ." Harvey said: "The *book* of Nature lies open before us and can be easily consulted." The phrase "book of Nature" is a metaphor used *long before* the seventeenth century, but why was this particular metaphor ever chosen? Is it not because Nature is understood as something that can be read like a book, provided we know how to read it? But does not that indeed imply a language that is Nature's own? Francis Bacon was of the opinion that Nature is subtly secretive, full of riddles, Sphinx-like. But secrets can be revealed, riddles can be solved in words. We persist, don't we, in solving the "riddles of nature." In *ancient* times the order of all that exists around us was taken much more directly as a language, a language not heard and not written, yet visible, and if not visible, one to be guessed at. Human speech seems indeed to translate that visible or invisible language of things into the audible language of words. And just as the sounds of human speech can be traced down to their ultimate components to which the letters of the alphabet correspond, things around us can be decomposed into their first rudiments — the "elements"— the original letters of the language of things, as it were. Our speech, even our unguarded colloquial way of speaking, may reveal to the attentive listener the hidden articulations of the language of things. Aristotle, no less than Plato, was constantly following up casually spoken words. It seems that Heraclitus, the "obscure," used the word "*logos*" in reference to the language of things. Let me quote from the fragments in question. First: "Of the *Logos*, which is as I describe it, men always prove to be uncomprehending, both *before* they have heard it and when once they *have* heard it. For although all things happen according to this *Logos*, men are like people of *no* experience, even when they experience such sayings and deeds as I explain, when I distinguish each thing according to its nature and declare how it is; but all the other men fail to notice what they do after they wake up, just as they forget what they do when asleep." Then this: "Therefore it is necessary to follow what is *common*; but although the *Logos* is *common*,the many live as though they had their *own* thoughts." Then this: "Listening not to me, but to the *Logos*, it is wise to agree that all things are one." And finally, to supplement the last fragment: "Out of all things — one, and out of one — all things." (Kirk and Raven, *The Presocratic Philosophers*, 1957, pp. 187–88, 191). The *Logos* makes us understand, if we follow Heraclitus, what the things themselves are saying, brightly and darkly, in tune and out of tune.

Speaking and understanding what is being said involves *thinking*, involves what the Greeks call διάνοια. Let us hear what Plato has to say about the relation of speaking to thinking. In the dialogue entitled *The Sophist*, in which Plato makes the Stranger from Elea converse with the young mathematician Theaetetus, the Stranger remarks (263 e): ". . . thought [διάνοια] and speech [λόγος] are the same, only that the former [that is, διάνοια], which is a *silent inner conversation* of the soul with itself, has been given the special name of thought." Thinking, as Plato understands it, is *not* tied to what the moderns mean by the "stream of consciousness." It can be imagined as a discontinuous, not always regular, stepping forward, and stepping aside, and stepping backward and forward again, what speech, too, usually does. It is necessary to note that for Plato, and for Plato *alone*, this identity of thought and speech is *not* a complete one: facing the highest, all-comprehending intelligibles, thought is not able to transpose itself into suitable words. In the seventh letter attributed to Plato we read the phrase "the weakness of spoken words" (τὸ τῶν λόγων ἀσθενές— 343 a 1), and the dialogue entitled *The Sophist* itself shows this weakness rather clearly, as we shall see in a moment. Moreover, speech and thinking can both *deceive* us, disconnect our steps, and thus distort and falsify the truth of things. The fireworks of the sophists, for example, — and there are always sophists around — make things and relations of things assume a most unexpected, dazzling, and puzzling aspect: things suddenly appear not to be what they are. But who is doing the lying, if it be lying, the sophists or the things themselves? A *critique* of speech and of thinking, a critical inquisition into speaking, thinking and arguing has to be undertaken — as it was undertaken by men as diverse as Parmenides, Prodicus, Plato, Aristotle. The result of this critique can be stated as follows: to speak does not always mean to make things appear in their true light. For Aristotle only one kind of speech, ὁ λόγος ἀποφαντικός, the declaratory and revealing speech, and the thinking which belongs to it, translate and present the language of things. To be able to use this kind of speech requires a *discipline*, the discipline of the λόγος. Everywhere in Aristotle's work, one senses, to the annoyance of some and to the delight of others, the effectiveness of that discipline, the effectiveness of what *we* call (and the author himself does *not* call) the "logic" of Aristotle. (Cf. *On Interpretation* 5, 17 a 8; 4, 17 a 2; 6, 17 a 25; *Posterior Analytics* I 2, 72 a 11.)

Given the ever-present possibility of declaratory and revealing speech, Aristotle need not, and does not, set limits to the power of the *Logos*. For Plato, however, as I have mentioned, there are limits that spoken words cannot transcend. This becomes quite clear in the dialogue entitle *Cratylus*. In it Socrates first invents fantastically funny "etymologies" of words, etymologies of proper names of heroes and gods as well as of familiar designations given to the ways men behave and think. Socrates then contrives rather playfully (422 e ff.) to describe the letters and syllables of any word as providing an "imitation," a μίμημα(423 b; 430 a,b,e; 437 a) of the very being (οὐσία) of what is supposed to be "imitated." This "imitation" is also said by Socrates — said more accurately — to be a "disclosure," a revelation," a δήλωμα (425 a,b; 433 b,d; 435 a,b) of the thing in question. Finally, the assertion is made that even "revealing" words may well be interpreted as not fostering our understanding. One has to agree, says Socrates, that things which *are* can be learned and *sought for* "much better through themselves than through names" (439 b). And that is only possible if what *truly is* is not subject to change, as Heraclitus claims, but is *immutably* what it is. Whether this is so or whether what the Heracliteans and many others say is true, is a question difficult to decide, but "no man of sense can help himself and his own soul by relying on names" (440 c). The power of the spoken word is thus a limited one, according to Plato, which makes his dialogues as troublesome and as wonderful as they appear to be.

Let me try to show you this by referring to, and quoting from, the dialogue entitled *The Sophist*. This dialogue is the central piece of a *trilogy*, namely the trilogy of the dialogues entitled *Theaetetus, The Sophist,* and *The Statesman.* The conversations and events which are presented in these mimes are supposed to take place at the very time the suit against Socrates has its beginning — as you can read at the very end of the first piece of the trilogy. We find in the second and the third dialogue, namely in *The Sophist* and in *The Statesman,* an abundance of so-called "divisions" (διαιρέσεις) which, in *The Sophist,* are supposed to be the means to establish *what* a "sophist" *is.* Opposed to the "divisions" are the "collections" (συναγωγαί), and let me quote what, in the dialogue entitled *Phaedrus,* Socrates has to say about these "divisions" and "collections" to that lovable young man, Phaedrus: "Now I myself, Phaedrus, am a lover of these divisions and collections as aids to speech and thought; and if I think any other man is able to see things that can naturally be *collected into one and divided into many,* him I follow after and walk in his footsteps as if he were a god [this is a playful and ambiguous reference to a line in the fifth book of the *Odyssey*]. And whether the name I give to those who can do this is right or wrong, god knows, but I have called them hitherto *dialecticians" (Phaedrus* 266 b-c). Now, the first five "divisions" in the dialogue entitled *The Sophist* do not reach their goal, except in one very peculiar case. The goal is to establish, as I said, *what* a "sophist" *is.* In this dialogue, a nameless Stranger from Elea performs these dialectical exercises with the help of young Theaetetus, whose looks resemble those of Socrates *(Theaetetus* 143 e). Of Theaetetus we also know, from the dialogue that bears his name as well as from other sources, that he was a powerful mathematician, especially interested in incommensurable magnitudes and multitudes. Books X and XIII of Euclid's *Elements* are based, in part at least, on his work. In the dialogue entitled *The Sophist* young Theaetetus is shown to *distinguish* and to *count* well, so well, indeed, that he helps us to understand what the Eleatic Stranger, alone, by himself, could not make us understand. Let us see.

There are five "divisions" in the beginning of the dialogue, meant to catch the "sophist." After they have been made they are counted up by the Stranger and Theaetetus in the following way: "*Stranger: First*, if I am not mistaken, he [that is, the "sophist"] was found to be a paid hunter after the young and wealthy. *Theaetetus:* Yes. *Stranger: Secondly*, a sort of merchant in articles of knowledge for the soul. *Theaetetus:* Very much so. *Stranger:* And *Thirdly*, did he not turn up as *retailer* [κάπηλος] of these same articles of knowledge? *Theaetetus:* Yes, and *fourthly*, we found he was a *seller of his own productions* [αὐτοπώλης]. *Stranger:* You remember well" (231 d). I have to interrupt this quoting to check whether Theaetetus *does* remember well. By going back, we see that the Stranger had previously summarized (224 d-e) the *third* division in these words: "And *that* part of *acquisitive art* which proceeds *by exchange* and *by sale* in *both* ways [ἀμφοτέρως] as mere *retail* trade [καπηλικόν] or as *the sale of one's own production* [αὐτοπωλικόν], so long as it belongs to the family of merchandising in knowledge, that part you will apparently always call sophistry." Theaetetus had then answered: "Necessarily so, for I have to follow the argument [the λόγος]." Theaetetus remembers well: he remembers that *retail trade* and *also the sale of one's own production* had been mentioned, but he forgot, *he forgot*, the word ἀμφοτέρως (in *both* ways), and this makes him add to the *third* description a new one, which he calls the *fourth*. *Both*, his remembering *and* his forgetting, have remarkable consequences. In the counting up of the "divisions" the *fourth* becomes the *fifth*, and the *fifth*, which is the one that reaches its goal, namely the correct description of the work performed by a quasi-sophist, namely by Socrates himself, — this *fifth* "division" becomes the *sixth*. Let us not forget: six is the first "perfect" number, and only a "perfect" number is fit to be applied to Socrates' work. But, moreover, the forgetfulness of Theaetetus compels us to pay special attention to the word which he forgot, to the word ἀμφοτέρως, or more exactly to the word ἄμφω (both) and to its cognates. We become aware that this word is used over and over again in the diaglogue. Here is just one example. Speaking of the "sophist," the Stranger remarks at one point (226 a): "Do you see the truth of the statement that this beast is many-sided and, as the saying is, not to be caught with one hand? *Theaetetus*: Then we must catch him *with both*."

The significance of this word "both" becomes fully apparent when the Stranger and Theaetetus focus their attention on "Change" (κίνησις) and "Rest" (στάσις). I shall quote again (250 a-c): "*Stranger*: You say that Change and Rest are entirely opposed to each other? *Theaetetus*: How could I say anything else? *Stranger*: And yet you say that both and each of them equally *are*. *Theaetetus*: Yes, I do. *Stranger*: And in admitting that they *are*, are you saying that both and each of them are *changing*? *Theaetetus*: No, no! *Stranger*: Then, perhaps, by saying that both *are*, you mean they are both *at rest*? *Theaetetus*: How could I? *Stranger*: Then you put before you Being [τὸ ὄν] as a *third*, as something beside these, inasmuch as you think Rest and Change are *embraced* by it; and since you comprehend and observe that these commune with Being, are you saying that they both *are*? *Theaetetus*: We truly happen to divine that Being is something *third*, when we say that Change and Rest *are*. *Stranger*: Then *Being* is *not* BOTH *Change* and *Rest* TOGETHER, but something else, *different* from them. *Theaetetus*: So it seems. *Stranger*: According to its own nature, then, being is *neither* at rest *nor* changing. *Theaetetus*: M-hm [in Greek: σχεδόν]." The last statement of the Stranger cannot be taken at face value. And Theaetetus immediately afterwards recognizes that it is totally impossible for Being to be neither at rest nor changing. The root of the difficulty, of the perplexity in which we, who listen to this conversation, find ourselves is that, in the case of Being, Change and Rest, our human speech, the λόγος, is *failing*. It is failing when it tries to speak about such greatest "looks" (μέγιστα εἴδη—245 c 2–3), that is, such all-comprehending νοητά. Being (τὸ ὄν), Change (κίνησις) and Rest (στάσις) appear to be *three* εἴδη, *three* "invisible looks," while in truth Change and Rest are "each one" (ἑκάτερον ἕν) and "both two" (ἀμφότερα δύο). *Both together* they constitute Being (τὸ ὄν). This means that, according to Plato, Being must be understood as the *eidetic* Two. The eidetic Two is not a mathematical number of two indivisible and indistinguishable monads, among infinitely many such mathematical twos. Nor is it two visible, divisible and unequal things, two houses or two dogs or two apples, for example. The eidetic Two is a unique dyad of two unique εἴδη, of two "invisible looks," namely of Change and Rest. And just as they *both together*, and only *both together*, are the εἶδος, the "look," the "invisible look" *Being*, so the Stranger from Elea and Theaetetus can only *both together* deal with the question of Being. That's why the Stranger says at one point to Theaetetus (239 c): "Let us bid farewell to you and to me." He means that neither he *alone* nor Theaetetus *alone* can accomplish the task, but that they can do it only *both together*. But this they can do "not with complete clarity" (μὴ πάσῃ σαφηνείᾳ— 254 c 6), because they are *speaking* about it.

It is thus that a weakness of speech is revealed in the dialogue entitled *The Sophist*. But this dialogue also shows why there *can* be *falsehood* uttered in speech, why speech can state what is *not* true. There is, however, a wide spectrum of the *un-true*, ranging from falsehood to likelihood. This is the background of the dialogue entitled *Timaeus*, and I would like to quote a passage from this dialogue to make you experience the playful and saddening ambiguity of this passage. It deals with the *human mouth*. It claims that it was fashioned "for ends both necessary and most good," "as an *entrance* with a view to what is *necessary* and as an *outlet* with a view to what is *most good*." I keep quoting (75 d-e): "For all that *enters in* and supplies food to the body is *necessary;* while the stream of speech which *flows out* and ministers to thoughtfulness is of all streams the most beautiful and most good." Can we forget how much evil, how much falsehood, how much trifling, how much nonsense also flows out? No, we cannot, But this must be added: in all those cases I just mentioned speech does not minister to thoughtfulness, to φρόνησις.

Let me now turn to a character of speech to which the ancients apparently did pay only scant attention. A most remarkable similarity obtains between *words*, spoken words of live speech, and *money* — money, that is, available in coins and bills. Both are precious, both circulate freely, coins and bills from hand to hand, words from mouth to mouth. The imprints on coins and bills are gradually erased, effaced, rubbed off, just as the meanings of words seem to become fuzzy, blurred and empty with the passage of time. There is even counterfeiting in language as there is in money. Human speech can and does deteriorate to an extent which renders it obnoxious, makes it unable to reach anyone, deprives it totally of wings.

It was Edmund Husserl who, in modern times pointed to this inevitable deterioration of human speech. According to him the signifying power of a word has, by its very nature, the tendency to lose its revealing character. The more we become accustomed to words, the less we perceive their original and precise significance: a kind of superficial and vague understanding is the necessary result of the increasing familarity with spoken — and written — words. Yet that original significance is still there, in every word, somehow "forgotten," but still at the bottom of our speaking and our understanding, however vague the meaning conveyed by our speech might be. The original "evidence" has faded away, but has not dissappeared completely. It need not be "awakened" even, it underlies our mutual understanding in a *"sedimented"* form. "Sedimentation is always somehow forgetfulness" ("Die Frage nach dem Ursprung der Geometrie als intentional-historisches Problem," first published by Eugen Fink in *Revue internationale de philosophie*, I, 2, 1939, p. 212). And this kind of forgetfulness accompanies, of necessity, according to Husserl, the development and growth of any science. (The text about the "origin of geometry" appears also — in a slightly changed form — as the 3rd Appendix to Walter Biemel's edition of the *Crisis of European Sciences and Transcendental Phenomenology — Husserliana*, Vol. VI, 1962 — and as the 6th Appendix to David Carr's translation of the *Crisis* — Northwestern University Press, 1970. The sentence "sedimentation is always somehow forgetfulness" is omitted in Biemel's and Carr's versions. I assume, however, that this sentence is based on Husserl's own words, uttered in conversation with Fink.)

To be sure, the original evidence can be "reactivated," and indeed is reactivated at definite times. This interlacement of the original significance and of its "sedimentation" constitutes, we read in Husserl's late work, the true character of "history" (*Ibid.*, p. 220). From that point of view there is only *one* legitimate form of history: the history of human thought. History, in this understanding, cannot be separated from Philosophy. Husserl's own philosophy, as it develops in its latest phase (1935–1937), is a most remarkable attempt to restore the integrity of knowledge, of ἐπιστήμη, threatened by the all-prevading tendency of "sedimentation." It has remained an attempt. But it may help us, in any event, to understand the character of speech, the character of the spoken word. It may help us to be cautious in our speaking and listening.

When we hear — or read — words intended to convey opinions about things, about *what* they are and *how* they are, it is amazing to observe their almost total dependence on the Latin rendering of crucial Greek, and especially Aristotelian, terms used in searching or revealing speech or, as we say, in "philosophical" discourse. The adoption of this Latin rendering by modern western languages usually involves a radical change and certainly a "sedimentation" of the very meaning of the terms in question. We hear a great deal about pollution today — the pollution of air, water, and land, which burdens our lives. But we hear rarely about the pollution of our language, which burdens our understanding. Our daily language, not to mention the "elevated" language of inquiry and exposition, is permeated and polluted by distorted terms in pseudo-Latin or even pseudo-Greek guise. Don't we use words like the following ones all the time: "actual," "dynamic," "potentialities," "matter," "substance," "theory," "information," "energy," "category," "logical," "formal," "abstract"? How strange and how discouraging! Do we know what we mean by these words? I could extend this list quite a bit, but I should like to add only these six terms: "ideal," "essence," "concept," "reality," "individual," and — *horribile dictu* — "mind."

This tendency of "sedimentation" of human speech finds, it is true, its counterpart in the tendency to reactivate its original significance. Beyond that, it may happen that human speech reaches levels previously not experienced at all: they may increase its vigor, lift its signifying power to new heights, elevate it truly. Responsible for this are mostly — and rarely enough, to be sure — *written* words. New words or new combinations of words can be "coined," as we so aptly and significantly say. At decisive points in his dialogues Plato resorts to this kind of coining; in the dialogue entitled *The Republic*, for example, but most notably in the dialogue entitled *The Statesman*. (We are aware, of course, that Plato's dialogues, although presenting lively spoken words, are the result of uniquely careful editing and *writing*.) Story-writers engage — sometimes — in this kind of inventive writing, as Joyce and Faulkner did. The most important cases of newly articulated written speech, however, are found in declaratory works which intend to convey knowledge, derived from questioning that is profound and deeply serious. Such works are those of Aristotle, of Hegel who raises Aristotle to new levels, and of Heidegger who opposes Aristotle radically. Their peculiar way of speaking sheds new light on things, on their roots, their relations, their very being. We have to note: none of these authors has written works that are easily translatable — and this cannot be otherwise.

Let me be fair to people of the Latin tongue and, by way of conclusion, quote Virgil, the poet. In a letter to a friend Virgil says that he gives birth to verses in the manner of bears and according to their custom (*parere se versus modo atque ritu ursino*), that is to say, that he produces his verses the way the mother bear handles her newly born cubs: assiduously and persistently she licks them into their proper shape. Such assiduous work, performed on the written word and undertaken to assure the right articulation of a composed whole, can and does restore and preserve the integrity of human speech. It is thus that the written word repays its eternal debt to the spoken word.

22 ■ Plato's *Phaedo*

There is — as most of you probably know — what we call (in words derived from Latin and Greek) a legend or a myth or (in plain English) a tale according to which certain fabulous events occurred on the island of Crete and in Athens and between these two in the very ancient past. There are different versions of that complex story, but I shall limit myself to the following points.

First: Minos, the king of Crete, has a wife, Pasiphaë, and many children. Pasiphaë falls in love with a wonderful white bull. The famous craftsman Daedalus helps her in a most ingenious way to satisfy her desires. She gives birth to the Minotaur, a monster with a bull's head and a human body. The Minotaur's abode, constructed by Daedalus, is the Labyrinth, a large building consisting of numerous halls connected by intricate and tortuous passages.

Secondly: one of the sons of Minos, Androgeus, visits Athens. The king of Athens, Aegeus, fearing that Androgeus might persuade his father Minos to support a revolt in Athens, arranges an ambush that leads to the death of Androgeus. Many things happen after that. Finally Minos imposes a tribute on Athens:

Lecture first delivered at St. John's College, Annapolis, May 3, 1974. First published in *The College*, Vol. XXVI, No. 4 (January, 1975).

every ninth year the Athenians have to send seven young men
and seven young women to Crete as a prey for the Minotaur.

Thirdly: when this tribute is due for the third time, the *son*
of the Athenian king, *Theseus*, decides that *he* will go to Crete
with those fourteen and will kill the Minotaur. He takes with
him, as we can read in Plutarch's *Lives* (Theseus XXIII, 2), not
seven, but nine young men, two of them having fresh and girlish
faces, but possessed of an eager and manly spirit. These two
have to dress and walk as if they were women. As soon as Theseus
and the fourteen arrive in Crete, one of the daughters of Minos,
Ariadne, falls in love with Theseus. She gives Theseus a ball of
thread which has to be tied with its loose end to the door of
the Labyrinth and which rolls along with the walking Theseus
until he reaches the Minotaur. Theseus, after killing the
Minotaur, finds his way back through the tortuous Labyrinth
by rolling up the thread again. Then Theseus and the fourteen
go back to Athens. Theseus takes Ariadne with him, but leaves
her on an island before reaching Athens.

Why do I tell you all this? Because the very beginning of
Plato's dialogue entitled *Phaedo* refers to these fabulous events.
The dialogue consists of a conversation held in Phlius, a city
in the Peloponnese, between Echecrates, a citizen of Phlius, and
Phaedo, who is not an Athenian either. Echecrates wants to know
what Socrates said before he died and how he died. Echecrates
has heard that a long time elapsed between the conviction of
Socrates and his execution. He does not know why this was so,
and Phaedo tells him why. The Athenians, he recounts, had
made a vow to Apollo — so it is said — that they would send a
mission every year to Apollo's temple in Delos, if Theseus and
(58 a 11) "those twice seven" whom he took with him were saved.
That's what the Athenians have done ever since. And (58 b 5–c
1) "it is their law that, after the mission begins, the city must
be pure and no one may be publicly executed until the ship has
gone to Delos and back; and sometimes, when contrary winds
detain it, this takes a long time." The ship had left on the day
before the trial of Socrates (58 a and c). "That's why Socrates
passed a long time in prison between his trial and his death"
(58 c 4–5). Answering Echecrates' questions, Phaedo tells him
which of Socrates' friends were with him on his last day. Watch,
please, how Phaedo does that in the dialogue circumspectly and

precisely (59 b–c). He says: "Of natives [that is, of native Athenians] there was this Apollodorus [Phaedo had mentioned him just before] and Cristobulus and his father Crito and also Hermogenes and Epigenes and Aeschines and Antisthenes [these are seven], and Ctesippus of the deme of Paeania *was there too*, and Menexenus and some other natives [two more names are thus conspicuously added and some people that remain unnamed]." And Phaedo continues: "But Plato, I think, was ill." "Were any non-Athenians there?" asks Echecrates. And Phaedo replies: "Yes, Simmias of Thebes as well as Cebes and Phaedonides and from Megara Euclides and Terpsion" (that is to say, five). To make sure that we realize the importance of all this naming, Plato, who was not there, makes Echecrates ask whether Aristippus and Cleombrotus were present. No, says Phaedo, they were not. Echecrates: "Was anyone else there?" Phaedo: "I think these were about all." It is thus established that fourteen people, whose names are given, namely nine Athenians and five non-Athenians, were present plus some unnamed Athenian men. Can we remain unaware of the fact that these correspond to the nine young men, the five young women and the crew that Theseus took with him on his voyage to Crete? The two young men who are conspicuously added in Phaedo's report to the seven first named, namely Ctesippus and Menexenus, have indeed an eager and manly spirit, as we can see when reading Plato's dialogue entitled *Lysis*. But what about Phaedo, the non-Athenian, who supposedly was also present at the last day of Socrates? Well, let us hear what Phaedo says himself about his relation to Socrates. At one point, he says (89 b), Socrates "stroked my head and gathered the hair on the back of my neck into his hand — he had a habit of playing with my hair on occasion . . . ." And a little later on (89 c) he compares the relation between himself and Socrates with the relation between Iolaus and Heracles. Iolaus is the nephew, the charioteer, and the beloved comrade of Heracles. And let us not forget: the thread of Phaedo's narrative in the dialogue goes through a labyrinth of questions and arguments. Can we fail to see that Phaedo corresponds to Ariadne of the ancient tale? Can we remain unaware of the fact that the dialogue does not give a so-called "historical" account of Socrates' death, but gives a mythical presentation of that crucial event, which however is truer than the tale about Theseus and the Minotaur, accepted as true by the average Athenian? In the dialogue the new and *true* Theseus is *Socrates* and the old and *true* Minotaur is the monster called *Fear of Death*. But while the Minotaur was, according to Euripides (Plutarch's *Lives*, Theseus XV, 2), "a commingled look and a monstrous babe," in which "two different natures, bull and man, were joined," in Fear of Death an awesome pain of the soul, namely fear, is joined to death, which is but a hobgoblin or a bugbear, as Cebes later in the dialogue (77 e) intimates. Let us not forget for a moment that the dialogue is a δρᾶμα presenting a Platonic myth. Athenaeus, a writer of the second century A.D., who to-day would be called a "literary critic," composed a lengthy work named "The Sophists at Dinner," the content of which is mostly inimical gossip. But it is worth noting that Athenaeus makes Phaedo state (XI, 505 e) that he never said or heard what he is supposed to have said or heard in the dialogue named after him. Indeed, what is happening in the dialogue is *invented* by Plato. It is thus that Plato makes us see Socrates' struggle with the Fear of Death. How does he do that? Let us watch.

I

When Socrates' friends enter the room in the prison, where Socrates had been staying all the time, they find him just released from his fetters and his wife Xanthippe sitting with one of their little sons beside him. Xanthippe is crying and Socrates asks Crito to let somebody take her home. Socrates sits up on his couch, bends his leg and rubs it with his hand. The Greek word which I translated with the word "bend" is συγκάμπτειν. It can be used to describe the bent position of a foetus in the womb. Since Socrates' rubbing of his leg gives him some *pleasure*, he contrasts this pleasure with the *pain* that the fetters had produced and goes on — calmly and playfully — to imagine how Aesop could have composed a fable about pleasure and pain fastened together by their heads so that they could never be completely separated. Phaedo had mentioned before that he had been overcome by a strange mixture of pain and pleasure at the thought of Socrates' impending death and the anticipation of the thoughtful and exciting discussion that was bound to occur in the prison, as it had occurred on previous days. Socrates' mentioning of Aesop reminds Cebes of what Socrates had been doing in his prison days, namely putting Aesop's fables into verse and composing a song to Apollo. Cebes asks why Socrates, who had never done that kind of thing before, should be doing that now. The poet Evenus had asked Cebes this question a few days previously. Socrates answers that he kept having dreams in his former life in which he was always told the same thing: "engage in the Muses' art and work at it" (μουσικὴν ποίει καὶ ἐργάζου). He had been interpreting this saying as encouraging him to do what he always had been doing, namely philosophizing, since he understood philosophy to be the greatest art of the Muses. Now, however, while the festival of Apollo delayed his execution, he considered the possibility that the dream might have meant what is usually understood to be the Muses' art (μουσική) and he decided not to disobey the dream, but to compose verses. And Phaedo makes Socrates say that *not* being a poet, that is, a man who invents myths, he turned to the fables of Aesop and put the first ones he came upon into verse. Can we forget the many myths that Plato makes Socrates invent in his dialogues? Socrates concludes his answer by begging Cebes to bid Evenus farewell and to tell him that he should follow Socrates as quickly as he can. Simmias intervenes and claims that Evenus certainly would not take Socrates' advice. Whereupon Socrates: "Is not Evenus a philosopher?" "I think so," says Simmias. Then Evenus will be willing to do so, says Socrates, as any one would be who has a worthy share in philosophy. But Socrates adds something to this statement, and while doing so puts his feet down on the ground. What he adds is this: "Perhaps he [that is, Evenus] will not take his own life, for they say that is not permitted." The ensuing conversation is about this addition. How can Socrates claim that philosophers desire to die, while asserting at the same time that it is not permitted to take one's own life? This assertion refers to what Philolaus — and also other people — have been saying. It is necessary at this point to note that the background of the *entire* dialogue is "Pythagorean" and "orphic." A Pythagorean brotherhood is known to have resided in Phlius, where Phaedo talks to Echecrates. Philolaus is the founder of a similar brotherhood in Thebes, to which Cebes and Simmias apparently belonged. The assertion that it is not permitted to take one's own life is — as Socrates intimates (62 b) — a part of an esoteric doctrine of the Pythagoreans, according to which men live in a kind of enclosure, namely the body, and ought not to set themselves free and run away. And in the light of this doctrine Phaedo makes Socrates claim that men are one of the chattels of the gods, who are their guardians, and that the gods would be angry if a man escaped by killing himself. This claim of Socrates forces Cebes and Simmias to wonder why Socrates is so much willing to leave them and the gods by wishing to die. This wonder amounts to an accusation, and Socrates declares that he has to *defend* himself as if he were in a court of law. What follows can, therefore, be called Socrates' "Defense," an ἀπολογία indeed, unlike his alleged "defense" in the dialogue called in a dissembling way "Apology."

Before beginning his defense, Phaedo narrates, Socrates has to listen to Crito, the point being that the man who will administer the poison has asked Crito to warn Socrates to talk as little as possible, lest the effects of the poison be diminished so that it would have to be administered again and again. Socrates does not pay any attention to this warning and proceeds to his lengthy defense.

It consists in claiming that a lover of wisdom, a "philosopher," in pursuing philosophy practices nothing but dying and being dead (64 a). Simmias can't help laughing — though reluctantly — because he thinks of the many in Thebes who would also say what Socrates just said and would add to it that the philosophers do indeed deserve nothing but death. They would be right, says Socrates, although they would not understand their own saying. What the philosopher wants above all is to let the soul alone, itself by itself, consider that which truly is, without being troubled by the body, the bodily sensing, the bodily desires and fears, the bodily pleasures and pains. What truly *is* cannot be seen or heard or sensed in any way. Now, since death is the separation of the soul from the body, as Phaedo makes Socrates say (64 c, 66 e–67 a), the philosophers must obviously desire death, that is, the complete purification of the soul. And Phaedo makes Socrates refer to orphic sayings according to which the thyrsus-bearers are many, but the initiated and purified are few, and only these few will dwell "over there" with the gods. This is the gist of Socrates' "defense."

II

Quite naturally the question arises whether the soul, when it leaves the body, still exists. Does it not perish altogether? That is the question Cebes immediately raises, and this is the way Socrates answers it, according to Phaedo's narrative.

There is an ancient argument, an "orphic" one, we have to understand, that we go there from here and come back here again and thus are born from the dead (70 c). If this is so, our soul must exist there. And Socrates proceeds, according to Phaedo, to show in a detailed way how that argument might be true. He invites Cebes to consider that in this visible world of ours everything, if there is something *opposite* to it, inevitably comes into being *from* this opposite. He cites examples: the greater becomes greater after having been smaller and vice versa, the weaker is generated from the stronger and vice versa, the slower from the quicker, the worse from the better, the more just from the more unjust, being cooler from being hotter, being awake from being asleep, and so on, and so on. The opposite of living is being dead. It follows that all living things, and that means also all living people, are generated from the dead. Then, Socrates concludes, our souls *do* exist in Hades, and there is such a thing as "coming to life again" (ἀναβιώσκεσθαι — 71 e–72 a). If that were not so, all things would be swallowed up in death.

III

We may have some doubts about the soundness of this orphic argument, as Cebes apparently has; for he reminds Socrates of another way to show the pre-existence of our souls. As Socrates so often says (we have to assume not only in Platonic dialogues), learning is nothing else but recollection (ἀνάμνησις), and that implies that the soul must already have existed somewhere before it came into being in human bodies, so that in this way also the soul appears to be deathless. Simmias wants to learn — that is, to recollect — more about this argument, and Socrates goes on showing — again in a most detailed way — the different cases of recollecting which we experience, up to the case of recollecting *equality itself* (74 a ff.). What is important about this case is that we can never see, never sense "equality itself." We perceive through our senses equal things, stones or pieces of wood, for example. We realize, however, that the quality of two visibly equal things is a deficient one: these things may appear to one man equal and to another unequal. To be able to recognize this deficiency means that we must have previously known perfect equality. And it is this previous, but forgotten knowledge that we *recollect* when, in perceiving visibly equal things, we realize that their equality is merely an approximation, a copy, an "image" of perfect equality, of "the equal itself." We must have acquired that knowledge of perfect equality, Socrates submits (75 c), before we were born. And that applies not only to equality, but to any intelligible entity on which we put the seal of "its being what it is" (αὐτὸ ὅ ἐστι). Thus there is the same necessity for our soul to exist before our birth and for all intelligibles, all νοητά, to have being. We have to note that the necessity of asserting the soul's pre-existence is understood here, in the dialogue, to *depend* on the presupposed being of the intelligibles, the νοητά, the ἔιδη, the "invisible looks."

Simmias and Cebes now agree that the soul must have existed before our birth. But what has not been proved, they both assert, is that the soul also exists *after* we are dead. Socrates claims that that proof had already been given, referring to the previous orphic argument that every living being is born from the dead. Must not the soul exist after we die, since it must be born again? But Socrates also agrees that the discussion has to proceed. There is some jesting about the possibility that the soul might be blown away by a high wind after we die, and Cebes says that there is perhaps a child within us who has such a fear. This is the moment when he mentions the need to pursuade that child "not to fear death as if it were a hobgoblin." What is required for that child, says Socrates playfully and truthfully, are daily incantations until that fear is charmed away (77 e). And the struggle with Fear of Death continues.

IV

The emphasis is now on the distinction between what is compounded and what is uncompounded. The compounded is liable to be decomposed, which cannot be said of the uncompounded. That which is uniquely "itself by itself," like "Equality itself," "Beauty itself," "Being itself," "Man himself," "Horse itself," is compounded and always the same, while there are things like men, horses, cloaks, that are constantly changing. What is mentioned first, the εἴδη, the "looks," are only reachable in thought, are *invisible*, while what is mentioned later is perceived by our senses, is *visible*. And Socrates asks Cebes forcefully (79 a): "Are you willing then to posit two kinds of beings, one visible, the other invisible [ἀϊδές]?" Cebes is willing. He is willing to admit that the visible is constantly changing and that the invisible is always the same. It is clear to him that the body belongs to the visible and the soul to the invisible. He has to agree that when the soul makes use of the body for any inquiry, that is, makes use of the senses, it is dragged to the things which never remain the same, but when the soul inquires alone by itself, it departs into the realm of the pure, the everlasting, the deathless and the changeless (79 d). And Cebes also agrees that, when a man dies, the soul, the invisible (ἀϊδές), goes to a place which is, like itself, noble and pure and invisible, goes to the true Hades ("Αιδης), to the good and wise god. And Socrates concludes that the soul departs in purity, if it never associated itself with the body in life but gathered itself into itself alone, that is to say, philosophized in the right way and willingly practiced dying. If it did that, it will be happy in Hades and henceforward live there, as the initiated say, truly with the gods. Socrates continues in this Pythagorean-orphic vein, describing what happens to the soul of a man devoted to bodily desires and pleasures after this man dies. His soul is dragged back to the visible world, through fear of the ἀϊδές and of "Αιδης, flits about monuments and tombs, passes into the body of an ass or a wolf or a hawk or a kite. The souls of better men, who by habit and practice, without philosophy and true understanding, have lived moderately and justly, pass into the bodies of bees or wasps or ants or of men again. It is only true philosophizing that attempts to free the soul from the prison of the body, from the bondage to pleasure and pain. Only a soul nurtured in this way is not going to fear that it will be destroyed at its departure from the body and vanish into nothingness (80 d–84 b). The soul is entirely indissoluble, "or nearly so" (80 b 10: ἢ ἐγγύς τι τούτου).

V

There is a long silence after Socrates' speech. But finally Socrates addresses Cebes and Simmias, who had talked to each other, and asks them whether they had any doubts about what had been said. Simmias confirms that they are doubtful, have questions to ask, but hesitate to trouble Socrates in his last hours. Socrates laughs gently, Phaedo narrates, compares himself to the swans that sing most and best when they feel that they are about to die, and urges Simmias and Cebes to speak up and to ask whatever questions they have. Simmias and Cebes comply.

The question of Simmias is this: Is not what Socrates had said about the body and the soul comparable to what could be said about the well attuned strings of a lyre and the concord of sounds produced by those strings? If the lyre is destroyed, could it be claimed that the concord will still exist?

The question of Cebes is this: Granted that the soul survives when a man dies and even wears out many bodies, might it not *finally* perish altogether in one of its deaths?

These questions, as narrated by Phaedo, are asked in a most serious and circumstantial way. Not only are all the people, who are said to surround Socrates, deeply troubled, but this is also true of Echecrates, Phaedo's interlocutor. It is not unimportant to note what Phaedo has to say at this point. What astonished him most, he says, was "first the pleasant, kind and respectful manner in which he [Socrates] accepted the arguments of the young men; secondly, his quick sense of the effect their words had upon us; and finally, how well he cured us . . . ." (89 a) This is the moment when Socrates' habit of playing with Phaedo's hair is mentioned by Phaedo. Socrates is doing that right now, while telling Phaedo to cut his beautiful hair — not the next day, but this very day, as Socrates will also do, if his argument dies and cannot be brought to life again. This is the moment when

Iolaus' relation to Heracles is compared to that of Phaedo to Socrates. But this is also the moment when Socrates launches into a lengthy discussion about the danger of becoming misologists, haters of argument, and of believing that there is no soundness in arguments at all (89 c–91 c). Let us note that this discussion is at the very middle of Phaedo's narrative. We have to infer that nothing is more important to Socrates than to keep arguing about a difficult question, never to despair, never to give up the hope of reaching a final and sound conclusion. And after finishing the discussion about misology Socrates takes up the question raised by both Simmias and Cebes.

VI

The doubts and fears of Simmias that the soul may perish first, being a kind of concord, are dealt with by Socrates first. (Let me remark parenthetically that the word "concord" translates the Greek word ἁρμονία, which it is wrong to translate by the English word "harmony.") Socrates makes sure that Simmias accepts, as Cebes does too, the argument according to which learning is recollection and that, therefore, he also agrees that the soul must have existed somewhere before it was imprisoned in the body. But a concord of sounds cannot exist before the lyre and its strings come into being. The concord of sounds is the last to come into being. There is no consonance then between the recollection argument and the argument that the soul might be something like a concord of sounds. Simmias is ready to yield. But Socrates goes on demolishing the concord thesis by reasons which are quite independent of the recollection argument. He shows that concords of sounds can be more or less concordant, while souls cannot be more or less souls. On the other hand, a soul may possess sense and virtue and be good, while another soul may be foolish and wicked. Those who claim that the soul is comparable to a concord of sounds will have to claim that the virtue of a soul is another concord and the wickedness of a soul is a discord of a concord. Or, to say it better, if the soul is a concord, it cannot be discordant, cannot be wicked at all. And finally Socrates points to our experience that the soul, if it is thoughtful, rules over its desires and passions and fears,

which it could not do if it were like a concord, since that which
is concordant depends on its concordant parts and does not rule
over them. Does not Homer say of Odysseus (*Odyssey* XX, 17
f.): "He smote his breast, and thus rebuked his heart: endure,
my heart; a worse thing even than this didst thou once endure"?
Phaedo makes Socrates say judiciously and probably smilingly
that Homer could not have said that, if he had thought of the
soul as a concord. This is how the concord theme of Simmias,
the Theban, is brought to an end. And Socrates proceeds to meet
the doubt of the other Theban, Cebes. Before doing that he appeals, solemnly and playfully, to the graces of the Theban goddess Harmonia, who is the daughter of Ares and Aphrodite, as
well as to the graces of Cadmus, who is Harmonia's husband
and who, according to the legend, killed that great serpent, out
of whose teeth armed men sprang up, clashing their weapons
together.

VII

To meet the doubt of Cebes is the most difficult task Socrates
faces. According to Phaedo, you will remember, Cebes had insisted on the possibility that the soul, after wearing out many
bodies, might *finally* perish altogether. In doing that, he had,
in fact, relied on Socrates' own saying that the soul is entirely
indissoluble "or nearly so." What can the phrase "nearly so" mean
but final dissolution! Socrates pauses for awhile, considering
something deeply by himself. And then the struggle with Fear
of Death reaches its height.

Socrates has to show *why* the soul can never die. Before doing this, he has to make clear the meaning of the word "why."
The question "why" comes up whenever we are unable to understand something in our immediate experience. We are asking
what is "responsible" for this something, what "causes" it. A
crucial distinction is made by Socrates (99 a–b): "One thing is
what is truly responsible [for something], another thing is that
without which what is responsible could not possibly become
[effectively] responsible." To be unable to make that distinction
is a sign of "profound sluggishness" in speaking and thinking.
To say, for example, the causes of Socrates' sitting in the prison

on his couch with his feet on the ground are these, that his body
is composed of bones and sinews and that the bones hang loose
in their ligaments while the sinews, by relaxing and contracting, make him bend his limbs — to say that is to fail to mention
the true causes of Socrates' sitting in the prison room, namely
that the *Athenians* decided that it was best to condemn him and
that *he* decided that it was right for him to stay and undergo
whatever penalty they would order (98 c–e). The confusion
about the meaning of "cause" (αἰτία) leads to that special wisdom
known by the name of "inquiry about nature" (περὶ φύσεως
ἱστορία — 96 a 8). In his youth, Socrates reports in Phaedo's narrative, he wanted very much to find out, with regard to any
single thing or occurrence, what was responsible for its coming
into being, its passing away, its being the way it was (96 a). But
he could not find any satisfactory answers. Nor could he learn
them from anybody else, not even from the great Anaxagoras.
The cause of this inability was precisely the confusion about
the meaning of "cause." Socrates had to embark upon a different
journey, his "next best try," which means he had to take to the
oars, since the wind had failed, and seek to find out in a better
way "why" things are as they are. He had to "take refuge in the
spoken word" (99 e 5), in exchanging questions and answers with
himself and with others and in *them* search for the truth of
things.

Socrates gives the following outline of the way he now proceeds. On each occasion he chooses as a supposition (an
ὑπόθεσις) the most reliable statement which would make us
understand what remains obscure and concealed in our immediate experience. Whatever appears to be consonant with that
statement is to be posited as genuinely true, and that applies
especially to what is being said about the "cause" of something;
whatever does not conform to the statement is to be taken as
untrue.

Cebes does not quite follow. He is not saying anything new,
Socrates explains, but rather what he has never stopped saying,
at other times as well as in the preceding discussion. And now
again he is going to revert to those much babbled-about words
and make them his starting point, his initial supposition being
that there *is* something named "itself by itself beautiful" and
also something "itself by itself good" and something "itself by

itself big" and all the rest. Consonant with this statement is a
further one of the following type: If there be anything beautiful
besides Beauty itself, it will be beautiful for no other reason than
that it *shares in*, or *partakes of*, Beauty itself. It is this kind of
cause which is responsible for things being beautiful, which
"makes" them beautiful. Statements of this type provide the
safest answer to the question: *Why* are things as they are? In
a dissembling and yet truthful way Socrates characterizes this
way of understanding why things are as they are as "simple,"
"artless," and "perhaps foolish." His answer, with all its safety,
is a simple-minded, "unlearned" one, as he later adds. Its safety
is based entirely on the reliability of the underlying statement
that the "intelligibles," the νοητά, have being. Everybody
present — and also Echecrates who listens to Phaedo's story —
agrees. And then Socrates proceeds to show *why* the soul can
never die.

The "demonstration" he offers, according to Phaedo's narrative, resembles indeed a most intricate maze. It is ultimately
based, first, on the underlying and most reliable statement that
each of the intelligibles, each of the εἴδη, is something which
has *being*; secondly, on its corollary that everything else, by "sharing in" those εἴδη, derives its *name* from them; and thirdly, on
the kindred corollary that this sharing in the various εἴδη can
be safely understood as the "cause" for everything being as it is.

Socrates takes care to remark that the two ways of proceeding
in all this, the one towards *consequences* which spring from the
safe supposition and the other towards the very *source* of the
safe supposition, the way downwards and the way upwards,
should not be mixed up. But we cannot fail to observe that in
Phaedo's narrative these two ways do get mixed up. It is noteworthy, for instance, that what remains shrouded in darkness
is whether the way to the "true Hades" is downwards or upwards.

A long series of examples of true causation is presented by
Socrates. I shall mention only a few. A man is big, and is called
big and not small, because of his sharing in Bigness or, as we
may say, because Bigness is "in" him; a body is hot, and is called
hot and not cold, because it contains Heat; a body is sick, and
is called sick and not healthy, because Sickness is "in" it; a
number of things is odd, and is called odd and not even, because
these things share in Oddness. And now Socrates adds: a hot

body may cool off and then again become hot, but the Heat "in" it can never become cold nor the Cold "in" it ever become hot. For Heat and Cold, just as Bigness and Smallness, are *by themselves* incompatible with each other.

Somebody among those present interjects full of surprise: What is being said now is opposite to what was said before about opposites, to wit, that the greater is generated from the less and the less from the greater, and that *is* simply the way opposites are generated, namely from opposites. And now it is being said that that can never happen! Socrates listens attentively and then explains: What was said before was said about visible things in this visible world of ours, but now the talk is about intelligibles, about the opposites as they are in themselves, about the εἴδη like Bigness itself, Heat itself, Sickness itself, Oddness itself. But at this point Socrates begins to complicate his simple-minded account of how causation has to be understood by another safe and "more ingenious" (105 c 2) way of answering the question why things are as they are.

VIII

A body is hot not only because of the Heat "in" it, but also because of *fire*; a body is sick not only because of Sickness "in" it, but also because of *fever*; a number of things will be an odd number of things not only because of Oddness "in" it, but also because of the *unit* which makes an odd number odd; and *soul* is going to join the rank of these new entities as a cause of life. What characterizes these new entities? First, their names are entirely different from the names of what they are causes of: fire–hot, fever–sick, unit–odd, soul–life; secondly, these entities are *not* intelligibles, are *not* εἴδη. "Fire" and "fever" have an elemental character. The mode of being of "unit" is highly debatable. And even more so is the mode of being of "soul." Up to this moment in Phaedo's narrative what characterized the soul was its thoughtfulness, its φρόνησις, its ability to deal with intelligibles, the νοητά, the εἴδη, its power to think, to learn, to recollect. Socrates proposes to Cebes twice that they determine what sort of entities these newly introduced ones are. What is said of them is this: the new entities, while not accepting *one*

of two opposites, "bring up" the *other* opposite and impose it
on what they approach. Thus Cebes, imitating Socrates' "more
ingenious" way, claims that soul, ψυχή, entering a body, will
make it a living body (ζῶν). The simple-minded account would
have been that Life (ζωή) does that. The account of Cebes
follows the pattern set by Socrates: the opposite of Life is Death
(105 d 6–9); soul (ψυχή), by itself not "opposed" to Death, "brings
up" Death's opposite, Life (105 d 10–11), brings Life to whatever
it "occupies"; and since, in analogy to Socrates' examples, "soul"
does not "accept" Life's opposite, does not "accept" Death, "soul"
cannot be touched by Death; the soul, therefore, will never "die."
The demonstration seems to have reached its end.

But Socrates immediately presents the difficulty which is
bound to come up. The entities, the "sharing" in which is responsible for certain features of the visible world (according to the
simple-minded and the new account) — as well as those sensible features themselves — carry, by virtue of their *not* "accepting" one of the opposites in question, a negative appellation,
for instance, "not even" (ἀνάρτιον), "not just" (ἄδικον),
"deathless" (ἀθάνατον). But these negatives do not tell whether
that which they signify "departs" or vanishes altogether whenever
the negated opposite approaches. This alternative is mentioned
in Phaedo's narrative repeatedly and well in advance of the final
conclusion: the *one* opposite *either* escapes, retires, withdraws,
goes away *or* perishes at the approach of the *other* opposite.
Could not the same be true of "soul"? That is Socrates' query.
As something to which the appellation "deathless" applies, it
might nevertheless share this same fate: it could be "extinguished"
and perish at the approach of Death. It would be a "living" soul
only *as long* as it exists in a body and no longer. The demonstration, with which Cebes was satisfied (105 e 9), amounts to
nothing if one considers that possibility.

It is Cebes who dismisses it. He asks: Does not the deathless
mean that which never dies? And must not that which never
dies exist forever? If the "deathless" were subject to destruction,
Cebes exclaims in an orphic vein, could there be anything else
that would escape it! Whereupon Socrates (106 d 5–7): "The
god, at least, life itself by itself [αὐτὸ τὸ τῆς ζωῆς εἶδος], and
if there be anything else 'deathless'— that these never perish
might, I think, be agreed upon by all." There is as much am-

biguity as solemnity in these words. Cebes catches the irony and chimes in (106 d 8–9): "By all men, to be sure, Zeus knows, and even more so by the gods as I, for my part, suppose." But Socrates and Cebes do agree on this: since "soul" does not "accept" Death and *if* thus the soul is indeed deathless, there could be no alternative to its being indestructible; when Death approaches man, what is mortal about him dies, while what is "deathless," retiring before Death, departs safe and unimpaired (106 e 7). "Soul, then, Cebes," Socrates concludes in Phaedo's narrative, "is more than anything deathless and indestructible, and our souls will truly be in Hades" (106 e 9–107 a 1). Let us note that what the word "soul" now means remains unstated. Nor are we told what kind of place "Hades" is.

IX

Cebes and Simmias are satisfied. But Simmias feels bound to make a reservation: considering the human weakness (ἡ ἀνθρωπίνη ἀσθένεια – 107 b 1) as against the magnitude of the subject under discussion, he for one cannot completely trust the argument. Socrates fully approves of Simmias' standard and even extends the distrust (ἀπιστία) to the very first suppositions underlying the entire argument. The inconclusiveness of the "demonstration" hinges on Cebes' imitating Socrates' "more ingenious" accounts. The assertion that sharing in "soul," in ψυχή, is responsible for Life, ζωή, in a body, that "soul" is thus "life-bringing," is rooted in the common identification of "living being" and "animate being," of ζῷον and ἔμψυχον. The emphasis in the preceding discussion lay on the kinship between soul and the intelligible. What characterized soul was φρόνησις, thoughtfulness, and all that this entails. Cebes' "imitating" answer gives ψυχή a radically different meaning, relating it not to φρόνησις, but to "living," to ζῆν. The indestructibility of this soul, as the exchange between Cebes and Socrates shows, and as Simmias confirms, is far from certain.

Does all this mean that the argument, intended to cast away Cebes's doubt and built up with so much care and circumspection, does not fulfill its task? Taken by itself, it fails indeed. But had not Socrates said (77 e 8–9), playfully and truthfully, that daily incantations are required to charm the fear of death away? Are not *all* the arguments of the dialogue a series of such incantations? But will they not, and necessarily so, remain ineffective unless supported by evidence more powerful than the evidence they are able to supply by themselves? This supporting evidence is there, in the very δρᾶμα presented by Phaedo. We witness Socrates' behavior during the long hours before he drinks the draught. For it is not only the content of the arguments, their cogency and insufficiency, that mark the struggle with Fear of Death, it is also, *and more so*, the adult sobriety, the serenity in gravity and jest, imposed by Socrates on the conversation. The final story Socrates is telling, according to Phaedo's narrative, shows perhaps more than anything else Socrates' imperturbable calm. He reverts to the kind of journey he claims to have undertaken in his youth. He describes our earth, not as we see it, but as it would appear to us if we were looking at it from above and from within. The story, a long and complex one, is told in complete tranquility and—we have to assume—with recurrent smiles. It presents not so much an "inquiry about nature" (περὶ φύσεως ἱστορία) as an "inquiry about the soul" (περὶ ψυχῆς ἱστορία). It tells what happens to the souls of men after death. Socrates does not pretend that his story is a true one, and that's why he probably keeps smiling: "It would not be fitting for a man of sense to maintain that all this is just as I have described it" (114 d 1–2). But since the soul appears to be deathless, a man of sense should take the risk to accept a tale like the one Socrates was telling. "For it is a noble risk" (114 d 6). And one should *continue* to charm oneself in this very way.

X

After finishing this story, Phaedo reports, Socrates is about to go to take a bath. Crito intervenes again. He asks what Socrates wants his friends to do about his children and about anything else, notably his burial. He has nothing to say about all that, says Socrates and, quietly laughing, he explains to his friends that it is difficult to persuade Crito that burying the body, which will remain when he, Socrates, is gone, has nothing to

do with him. He will have departed. He then goes into another
room to bathe. When he returns, his three children and the
women of his family appear. He talks with them, gives them
his advice, and then tells them to leave. The sun is setting, the
drinking of the poison is near. Phaedo reports a touching scene
between Socrates and one of the wardens of the prison. Socrates
demands that the poison be brought to him. Crito tries to persuade Socrates to wait a little longer. Socrates says that that
would be ridiculous. The poison is brought in a cup. Socrates
is told to drink and then to walk till his legs feel heavy. Socrates
asks whether he should not pour a libation to a deity. It is hard
not to sense the irony of this question. Socrates is told that there
is not enough for that in the cup. Socrates prays that his departure from here to there be a fortunate one. And he drinks the
poison coolly and calmly.

An outburst of fierce emotions and of tears and of wailing
among Socrates' friends follows. Socrates says to them: "Keep
quiet and be steadfast" (117 e 2). He lies down on his back, and
the man who administered the poison as well as Socrates' friends
watch death approaching. Uncovering his face, which had been
covered, Socrates says to Crito: "We owe a cock to Asclepius;
pay this debt and do not neglect it" (118 a 7–8). These are his
last words. To sacrifice to Asclepius, the healing god, means to
thank him for one's recovery from a disease. Socrates' last words
imply that he is recovering from the most disastrous disease, the
one that imprisons his soul in his body. He is recovering from
this disease because his soul is leaving its prison. Crito closes
Socrates' mouth and eyes. And Phaedo ends his narrative by telling Echecrates that this was the end of the best, of the most
thoughtful and most just man of his time.

What shall *we* conclude from all that we have heard? Three
things. First, in the struggle we have been witnessing, Socrates,
the true Theseus, annihilates the true Minotaur, the Fear of
Death. Secondly, it remains completely uncertain whether
Socrates' soul is now in the true Hades, the realm of the invisible looks. Thirdly, it *is* certain that *Plato*, through Phaedo's narrative, has made Socrates live forever — or, to be as cautious as
possible, has made Socrates live as long as people will be able
to read what Plato wrote.